IN AN
UNCERTAIN WORLD

TOUGH CHOICES

FROM WALL STREET

TO WASHINGTON

ROBERT E. RUBIN AND JACOB WEISBERG

 RANDOM HOUSE | NEW YORK

LIBRARY OF CONGRESS CATALOGING-IN-PUBLICATION DATA
Rubin, Robert Edward.
In an uncertain world : tough choices from Wall Street to Washington / Robert Rubin with Jacob Weisberg.
p. cm.
ISBN 0-375-50585-7
1. Rubin, Robert Edward. 2. United States. Dept. of the Treasury—Officials and employees—Biography. 3. Finance ministers—United States—Biography. 4. Fiscal policy—United States. 5. United States—Economic policy—1993–2001. I. Weisberg, Jacob. II. Title.

HJ268.R78 2003
336.73′092—dc21
[B]   2003046693

Random House website address: www.atrandom.com

Printed in the United States of America on acid-free paper

987654321

FIRST EDITION

Book design by Barbara M. Bachman

To my parents, Sylvia and Alexander, who have given me so much,

and

to my wife, Judy, my one certainty in an uncertain world

CONTENTS

P EOPLE WHO HAVE WORKED with me know that I don't believe in certainty. But one thing I thought I was sure of during my six and a half years in government was that I wouldn't write a book after I left. The idea seemed uncomfortably self-focused to me. Yet by the time I departed Washington and the Clinton administration in the summer of 1999, my feelings had begun to shift.

Both in Washington and on Wall Street, I found myself at the center of periods of great change and momentous issues and events. As I thought more about those times, I realized I had much yet to learn from what I had lived through. Writing a book seemed a way to think more systematically about that involvement and to understand it better. More important, I hoped my experiences and reflections might be of some interest and utility to others.

Today, markets are more important to the lives of more people than at any previous time in history. Government is vital to all of us. An integrated understanding of both worlds is necessary to deal with the economic and political issues we face. Having crossed over from business and the realm of markets to government, and now crossed back again, I thought I might be in a position to shed some light on these two worlds and their interaction.

The growing feeling that I had something I wanted to say coincided with an approach from a journalist named Jacob Weisberg, who proposed that we work together on a book growing in part out of an article he had written in *The New York Times Magazine.* That story had at its core a discussion of my fundamental view that nothing in life is certain and that, consequently, all decisions are about probabilities. Talking to Jacob, I became intrigued by the idea of trying to convey to others how my approach to decision making and my view of life permeate all that I do.

After considerable discussion, we decided to collaborate on a book that would draw on my personal history—twenty-six years at Goldman Sachs; six and a half in the White House and Treasury; then four at the world's largest financial institution, Citigroup—to express my views on questions of future importance to policy makers, investors, businesspeople, and all of us as citizens. As we began writing, debate continued to swirl around many of the same policy and political issues that had come to the fore during the Clinton years. For example: What are the merits of fiscal responsibility versus tax cuts as a core economic strategy for the future? Are globalization and market-based economics the right policy paths for the world economy? How can the international community best prevent or respond to the periodic financial crises that so far seem to be an inevitable feature of the advancement of developing nations? Central to all of these issues is the question of how markets behave, a matter also of interest to the average person investing in stocks.

Through narrative and reconsideration of my own experience as a decision maker, I hope to contribute to choices others will make in the future, individually and collectively. That is the primary purpose of this book. I'll share some of the views I've formed through the course of a life in these two worlds—about the psychology of markets, how government functions in relation to the economy, and how to make decisions and work effectively within vast organizations on both sides of the divide.

The second purpose is to explain my method of decision making. A probabilistic approach is far from unusual and, at some level, merely describes what most people do, or think they are doing, when they describe weighing the pros and cons of an issue. But somehow or other, the discussion in Jacob's *New York Times Magazine* piece resonated, and since then people in all kinds of circumstances have told me it affected them.

Two years after its publication, I met a money manager on a tennis court who told me he had pinned the key section of the article on his office wall. Someone else I know told me that a manager of a baseball team had also posted that part of the article in his office. (I don't know where that team finished in the standings.)

The best explanation I can offer for why this discussion drew the response it did is something Larry Summers once suggested when we were both at the Treasury Department: that while a great many people accept the concept of probabilistic decision making and even think of themselves as practitioners, very few have internalized the mind-set. For me, probabilistic thinking has long been a highly conscious process. I imagine the mind as a virtual legal pad, with the factors involved in a decision gathered, weighed, and totaled up. To describe probabilistic thinking this way does not, however, mean that it can be reduced to a mathematical formula, with the best decision jumping automatically off a legal pad. Sound decisions are based on identifying relevant variables and attaching probabilities to each of them. That's an analytic process but also involves subjective judgments. The ultimate decision then reflects all of this input, but also instinct, experience, and "feel."

This book also provides an opportunity for me to explore the thinking that underlies my approach to decision making and to life more generally. At the core of this outlook is the conviction that nothing can be proven to be certain. Modern science says this is so even in physics and chemistry, where the most familiar and fundamental precepts are based on assumptions about perception and reality that cannot be proven. That outlook runs like a thread throughout this book. It has, I suppose, been taking shape from my early college days in Professor Raphael Demos's Philosophy I course at Harvard, to arguments with classmates in the Coke lounge at Yale Law School, to some of the discussions during four years of breakfast meetings with Larry Summers and Alan Greenspan while I was at Treasury.

And once you enter the realm of probabilities, nothing is ever simple again. A truly probabilistic view of life quickly leads to the recognition that almost all significant issues are enormously complex and demand that one delve into those complexities to identify the relevant considerations and the inevitable trade-offs. Some people I've encountered in various phases of my career seem more certain about everything than I am about anything. That kind of certainty isn't just a personality trait I lack. It's an attitude that seems to me to misunderstand the very nature of reality—its complexity and ambiguity—and thereby to provide a rather poor basis for working through decisions in a way that is likely to lead to the best results.

Although the fundamental purpose of this book is to help readers think more clearly about the future, it is grounded in narrative about the past. While this isn't a history or an academic text, my recollections of issues, events, debates, and my own reactions to them may contribute something to the work of historians who study the Clinton years and other times I've lived through. Public service provided me with an unparalleled opportunity to apply my experience to issues that matter to vast numbers of people, here and around the world, and to see how our system of government operates by working at the intersection of policy, politics, and communication. Perhaps in relating my own experiences in government, and providing some sense of the great ability and commitment of so many of the political appointees and career public servants I worked with, this book will encourage young people to consider spending at least part of their careers in public service—for the good of the country and to enrich their own lives. More broadly, I would like to prompt readers to get more involved in our political system by supporting candidates, ideas, and causes they believe in.

For me, the opportunity to reflect back systematically has led to a refinement and a greater rigor in many of the views I hold. The ideas expressed here are mine, but on virtually every matter they have been strongly influenced by many others. I have been fortunate in all phases of my life—in my education, on Wall Street, and in government—to have had colleagues and friends who, through their insight, experience, intellectual power, and philosophical mind-set, contributed to my own understanding. Many of those people combine an ironic attitude toward human pretension, including their own, with a strong sense of purpose and commitment. That mixture of seriousness and irreverence, which especially marked my colleagues and my time at Treasury, is as good an attitude toward daily life as I know. You learn more by listening than by talking, and I've had the opportunity to listen to many who had much of great value to say. My hope is that the views I've developed through a lifetime of such interaction will be of use to others in dealing with the personal, professional, and policy challenges that lie ahead.

Robert E. Rubin
New York City
September 30, 2003

At various points in this book, I relate comments from private conversations or meetings with fellow members of the Clinton administration, business colleagues, and other public figures. The people have graciously granted me permission to quote or paraphrase their remarks. But of course these are my own recollections and any inaccuracies they contain remain my responsibility alone.

IN AN UNCERTAIN WORLD

CHAPTER ONE

The First Crisis of the Twenty-first Century

ON THE EVENING OF January 10, 1995, I stood on the Great Seal woven into the carpet of the Oval Office and swore to uphold the Constitution of the United States as Secretary of the Treasury. Confirmed earlier that day, I had been waiting all afternoon for the official document that would allow me to take the oath of office. Once the papers arrived from Capitol Hill, a small group of family, friends, and colleagues assembled at the White House for a hasty ceremony.

As soon as the formalities were over, I said good-bye to my wife, Judy, and our other guests and remained behind with President Bill Clinton, Treasury's top international official, Larry Summers, and a few of Clinton's senior advisers, for an emergency meeting about the financial crisis in Mexico.

I told the President that the Mexican government faced an imminent threat of default and that, in the hope of preventing it, we were recommending that he support a massive, potentially unpopular, and risky intervention: providing billions of dollars to the Mexican government to avoid a collapse in its currency and economy. Then I asked Larry to explain the situation in more detail. It took him ten minutes to spell out our essential analysis and recommendation, which we'd finished formulating in a meeting with Fed chairman Alan Greenspan hours earlier. If our government didn't step in to help, and help quickly, the immediate and long-term consequences for Mexico could be severe. But the real reason for acting was that critical American interests were at stake.

The alternatives to the massive intervention we were recommending were not promising. If Mexico defaulted on its foreign obligations, Larry and I went on to explain, the flow of capital out of Mexico would probably accelerate and the peso would collapse, likely triggering severe inflation, a deep and prolonged recession, and massive unemployment. And that would surely have a substantial impact on the United States. Mexico was our third-largest trading partner, which meant that many American companies and workers would be hurt. We presented estimates that a Mexican default could increase illegal immigration by 30 percent, a half-million additional refugees a year. The flow of illegal drugs could intensify as well.

A crisis in Mexico might also hurt us indirectly, by affecting other countries. Fears of a Mexican default were already producing wobbles in developing markets throughout the hemisphere, a phenomenon that came to be known as the "Tequila Effect." Such a chain reaction could lead investors to pull back from emerging markets around the world indiscriminately. That, in turn, could affect economic conditions in the United States—since roughly 40 percent of our exports went to developing countries. According to an estimate made by the Federal Reserve Board, a Mexican default and the consequent "contagion" that was possible could, in a worst-case scenario, reduce growth in the United States by $\frac{1}{2}$ to 1 percent a year. We weren't proposing intervention for the sake of Mexico, despite our special relationship, but to protect ourselves. That was our case for asking Congress to provide billions of dollars in loan guarantees, as part of a package to be coordinated with the International Monetary Fund (IMF).

As Treasury Secretary, I avoided using words such as "panic" and "meltdown," preferring less vivid terms such as "contagion" and "loss of confidence." I'd learned while working in the White House as director of the National Economic Council (NEC) that the words public officials use can make an enormous difference, and that was even truer at the Treasury. I had to describe what was happening in Mexico accurately without being inflammatory. A meltdown, though, is precisely what we were worried about—and not only because of its effect on current economic conditions. With the implementation of the North American Free Trade Agreement (NAFTA), Mexico was hailed as a role model for developing countries pursuing economic reform. The public failure of that model could deal an enormous setback to the spread of market-based economic reforms and globalization.

But there were arguments against intervention as well, which we also laid out for the President. I emphasized that, for a variety of reasons, our rescue package simply might not work. What's more, intervention would almost surely be criticized as "bailing out" wealthy American and European investors who had speculated on developing markets. Putting public funds on the line was likely to be massively unpopular and politically risky. Leon Panetta, the White House chief of staff, was even more blunt in warning Clinton about the downside risk. Leon favored intervention, but he told Clinton that a failed rescue effort could cost him the election in 1996.

When we finished our presentation, the room was heavy with a collective sense of how big a problem this had rapidly become. Larry had tossed out a figure of $25 billion as the amount of U.S. assistance that might be necessary. George Stephanopoulos, a senior adviser to the President, said that surely we meant $25 million. No, Larry said, we meant "billion with a B." That was more than the annual budget of the Department of Justice, enough to buy a fleet of B-2 "Stealth" bombers.

Sitting on a sofa in the Oval Office during my first hour on the job, I was answering questions from the President that I had been asking others only a couple of weeks before. Larry had phoned me in December, while I was on vacation in the Virgin Islands, to bring me up to speed on the unfolding Mexican situation. I didn't know much about Mexico's economic problems, and I didn't understand why a peso devaluation was urgent enough to interfere with fishing. I assumed that Mexico was one of a large number of countries with similar problems and that Larry, a consummate professional in the field of international economics, would take care of whatever needed to be done. But I intended to be a hands-on Secretary, and I liked that Larry was including me, even though I was still in the netherworld of being designated but not yet confirmed as Treasury Secretary.

It didn't occur to me that day that Mexico's problems would shortly blossom into a full-blown economic crisis that embodied the heightened risks of a more global economy. In retrospect, the Mexican episode also offers much insight into the Clinton presidency. The Bill Clinton I watched come to the aid of Mexico was one the public too seldom saw. His seriousness of purpose, his depth of substantive understanding, and his keen intellectual quest for the right decision on Mexico are a continuing reminder to me of the way in which he remains, in important respects, a misunderstood figure. At a broader level, the dilemma Clinton faced with Mexico suggests to me that our politics may not be well suited to coping with the new risks of the global economy.

GETTING MY ARMS AROUND a problem like the Mexican crisis meant thinking about it as systematically and dispassionately as possible. The situation, as I rapidly came to understand following my preconfirmation conversation with Larry, was this: After the outgoing Salinas government had spent over $15 billion in a futile attempt to prop up the peso at the fixed rate of around 3 pesos per U.S. dollar, the newly installed government of Ernesto Zedillo had, in late December 1994, surrendered to overwhelming pressure in foreign exchange markets and allowed the Mexican currency to float freely. With only around $6 billion of its foreign exchange reserves left and far more than that in short-term debts coming due, Mexico had little choice. But with the government no longer providing support, the peso fell rapidly to around 5 pesos to the dollar. As the Mexican currency continued to slide, doubts grew about whether the government would be able to repay its debt, much of it very short term and linked to the dollar. Fearing a possible government default, investors were selling Mexican bonds, as well as the peso. In sum, Mexican authorities had lost control of their country's finances.

All of us working on the problem agreed that Mexico, now essentially cut off from private lenders, almost surely could not solve the crisis through its own policies alone. The Mexican government's bond auctions were attracting few bidders, even at dollar interest rates approaching 20 percent. In the short term, the private sector was very unlikely to produce loans on the scale needed to prevent default.

Nor, with requirements this large, could the international financial institutions—the IMF and World Bank—arrange a rescue on their own, as they had in many other cases. Michel Camdessus, the French managing director of the IMF, was unknown to most Americans despite his tremendous influence. Skillful and audacious, Camdessus was prepared to weather the anger of his organization's European shareholders to make a stabilization loan to Mexico of unprecedented size. But the sums needed exceeded the IMF's available capability. The only realistic chance of avoiding disaster was help from the United States. The questions for me then became the possible consequences of financial chaos and default in Mexico, the danger of the program failing, and the possible costs of that failure.

What has guided my career in both business and government is my fundamental view that nothing is provably certain. One corollary of this view is probabilistic decision making. Probabilistic thinking isn't just an intellectual construct for me, but a habit and a discipline deeply rooted in my psyche. I first developed this intellectual construct in the skeptical environment of Harvard College in the late 1950s, in part because of a year-long course that almost led me to major in philosophy. I started to employ probabilistic decision making in practice at Goldman Sachs, where I spent my career before entering government. As an arbitrage trader, I'd learned that as good as an investment prospect might look, nothing was ever a sure thing. Success came by evaluating all the information available to try to judge the odds of various outcomes and the possible gains or losses associated with each. My life on Wall Street was based on probabilistic decisions I made on a daily basis.

This was the background I brought to the question of whether we should intervene in Mexico. With an enormous number of competing considerations, the key to reaching the best possible decision was identifying all of them and deciding what odds and import to attach to each—probabilistic decision making at work. Doing that also meant recognizing that our knowledge would never be as complete or perfect as I—or the rest of the team at Treasury—would like. Moreover, even with the most systematic and thorough work, a decision, though informed by the facts and analysis, would never emerge automatically from the yellow pad on which I scribbled notes. The final component of decision making was the intangible of judgment. The process of decision making that we evolved in the Mexican crisis—and that I would use over and over again in my time at Treasury—was familiar to me from my life in the private sector. But the range of considerations was much broader. For example, we had to think about the damage that a failed intervention could do to America's credibility. If we attempted to help Mexico and did not succeed, our backing would be a less useful tool in some future crisis.

Success had dangers as well. Even if our efforts helped stabilize Mexico, we might create a problem of what is known as "moral hazard." Investors, after being insulated from the consequences of risk in Mexico, might pay insufficient attention to similar risks the next time, or operate on the expectation of official intervention. In Mexico, investors had become complacent, following a herd mentality in buying short-term dollar-linked bonds throughout 1994 without paying sufficient attention to the danger that the central bank's currency reserves might not be sufficient to maintain their promised convertibility into dollars. We worried that our program to prevent Mexico's failure might encourage investors to make similar mistakes again in the future.

It was my good fortune to be able to think through these issues with Alan Greenspan and Larry Summers. In our backgrounds, our professional training, and our temperaments, the three of us were alike and very different. Alan is a conservative free-marketeer and an economist grounded in both macro policy and an acute empirical understanding of the American economy. Before entering government, he had his own private-sector consulting firm and traded actively for his own account. He is a precise man with an exceedingly good and understated wit. Larry, whose parents are both Ph.D. economists and who has two uncles who won Nobel Prizes in economics, was one of the youngest professors ever to receive tenure at Harvard. He is a forceful, self-assured theoretical economist with a good feel for the practical, both in politics and in markets. I had a pretty good conceptual understanding of economics, had spent a career in trading operations and management on Wall Street, and had been involved in Democratic politics. People who know me are familiar with my distrust of definitive answers and my habit of asking questions. While our personalities differed, they meshed—perhaps because our analytical approaches to a problem like Mexico proved highly compatible. Equally important was the spirit in which we worked. Though none of us is without ego, there was a remarkable lack of it in our meetings. Each of us tried to work with the others to find the best answer, not to show off his intellect or defend preconceived notions. Another crucial component of our relationship was the mutual trust we developed. For four and a half years, Alan, Larry, and I had breakfast or lunch at least once a week, along with many other meetings and discussions. After I resigned in 1999, Larry and Alan continued the tradition. To the best of my knowledge, nothing any of us said in any of those private meetings ever leaked out. (For this book, they gave me permission to refer to these conversations.)

I had seen Greenspan periodically during my time at the White House but hadn't known him very well before I became Treasury Secretary. When we were both thrown into the peso crisis, we got to know each other rather quickly. I was deeply impressed with the way he thought about the problem. Alan, who believes strongly in the discipline of markets, was very focused on the issue of moral hazard. This was why he had opposed the government rescue of the Chrysler Corporation in 1979. But, despite his opposition to the idea of government intervention in markets, Alan weighed the moral hazard against the risk of having Mexico go into default. He was a pragmatist, trying to find the best way to balance competing considerations.

ALAN, LARRY, AND I AGREED about what had caused the crisis. Mexico, despite reforms in many areas, had made a serious policy mistake by borrowing too much in good times, leaving it vulnerable when sentiment shifted. And when markets began to lose confidence, the government put off facing reality for as long as possible. It borrowed still more, at shorter and shorter terms, issuing dollar-linked debt and spending its limited dollar reserves on holding up the peso, which had an exchange rate fixed to the U.S. dollar. At the same time, creditors and investors—both Mexican and foreign—were paying little attention to the buildup of economic imbalances. Their continued financing allowed the problem to become almost unmanageable when the crunch finally came.

The trouble really began in the early 1990s, when Mexico's current account deficit—basically the trade deficit plus net interest payments and some similar items—began expanding rapidly. To cover this gap, the country needed dollars, which it attracted by issuing government bonds. At first, it sold peso-denominated assets. But later, as investors became less willing to take on the exchange rate risk, the government started issuing large quantities of Tesobonos, short-term obligations whose value was linked to the U.S. dollar. For a while, these bonds proved attractive to Mexicans and foreign investors. But Mexico's large current account deficit combined with a fixed exchange rate was not sustainable indefinitely. To make matters worse, Mexico's banking system was weak and under strain.

Underlying imbalances like Mexico's are the real cause of resulting crises, but often some event that might otherwise not have created trouble serves as a trigger. In this case, a violent insurgency in the Chiapas region at the beginning of 1994 and the assassinations of two leading Mexican politicians created a deep sense of alarm in financial markets. Mexican bonds began to look much riskier and started to trade at steep discounts. Domestic and foreign investors became less willing to keep money in Mexico. The central bank had to sell more and more of its foreign exchange reserves as it struggled to meet the demand for dollars while holding the exchange rate unchanged. At the same time, the Mexican government found it more and more difficult to roll over its debt, despite offering higher and higher interest rates.

As so often happens in financial markets, these negative effects became self-reinforcing. As investors feared that the exchange rate might fall, they moved into dollars and drove the government's reserves down still further. This in turn made a peso decline more likely and exacerbated fears of a government default. The promise to repay Tesobonos with however many pesos were required to keep investors whole in dollar terms came to look less and less credible. With the foreign exchange reserves running out, the authorities made a last-ditch attempt to save the fixed-exchange-rate system with a partial devaluation, but that didn't stem the tide. Domestic capital continued to flee, foreign market confidence plunged, and the government was forced to let the exchange rate float freely. Market attention shifted to the huge quantities of Tesobonos coming due in the weeks and months ahead. The demand for new bonds had dried up. So the government would have had to flood the market with pesos to pay off the maturing Tesobonos—which would send the exchange rate down further.

The Mexican crisis is usually viewed as a failure of Mexican policy. But it was, crucially, also a failure of discipline on the part of creditors and investors—a point about crises that would become very important a few years later, when we faced the return of the same kinds of problems elsewhere and on an even larger scale. Lured by the prospect of high returns, investors and creditors hadn't given sufficient consideration to the risks involved in lending to Mexico. Once investors became nervous, however, their reaction was swift and unforgiving. Mexico promptly lost access to international capital markets and couldn't refinance the short-term Tesobonos. Most observers believed that in the long run Mexico would be able to repay its debts. But in the short run, with less than $6 billion left in foreign currency reserves and almost $30 billion in dollar-indexed bonds coming due in 1995—$10 billion in the first three months—Mexican and foreign investors wanted out. For better or for worse, there's no international law enabling countries to reorganize their debts in bankruptcy court. Thus, our declining to intervene would likely have led to the default of a country that mattered to us in many ways.

Mexico is a good example of a situation—often encountered by policy makers as well as by those in the private sector—in which all decisions had the potential for serious adverse consequences and the key was to find the least bad option. In this case, the dangers of not acting were severe economic duress in Mexico, a contagious decline in emerging markets, and a setback to American growth and prosperity. The risk of acting was failure—potentially endangering repayment of billions of dollars of tax-payer money—or, if we succeeded, moral hazard. Alan, Larry, and I all opposed making the holders of Tesobonos whole. But we concluded—I think rightly—that Mexico couldn't be rescued without the side effect of helping some investors.

We also worried that the Mexican crisis could affect the global movement toward trade and capital market liberalization and market-based economic reforms. NAFTA had just gone into effect on January 1, 1994. If Mexico went into default a year later, in part for failure to properly manage the influx of foreign capital, the case for further reform might be set back in the United States and abroad. Larry, who had served as chief economist at the World Bank before joining the Clinton administration, was especially concerned with this problem. "Letting Mexico go," he argued, would send a discouraging signal to other developing nations— such as Russia, China, Poland, Brazil, and South Africa—that had been moving forward with market-oriented reforms. Though we took turns playing devil's advocate, Larry, Alan, and I all came to a rough consensus in the days before my swearing in. All of us came to think that the risks of not acting were far worse than the risks of acting. Alan captured all of our views when he called a support program the "least worst" option.

On the afternoon of January 10, the three of us, joined by a number of others, including my successor at the NEC, Laura D'Andrea Tyson, had our last meeting to confirm our recommendation to the President while waiting for my confirmation papers to arrive. Larry and I shared Alan's view that we should put up a substantial amount of money, significantly more than we thought would be needed. In this, we were employing a corollary to Colin Powell's doctrine of military intervention. The Powell Doctrine, which became well known during the Persian Gulf War, says that the United States should intervene only when American interests are at stake and that intervention must be with an overwhelming level of force.

Of course, no one could say with certainty how much force would be needed to overwhelm the problem in Mexico. One benchmark was the total value of the outstanding Tesobonos, which at that point was about $30 billion. Even that might not be enough, taking into account other government debt, the external debt of Mexican banks, and the potential for "capital flight" as domestic holders of pesos converted them into dollars. Knowing the IMF would also put up a significant amount of money, we proposed $25 billion in U.S. loan guarantees—which had the same financial risk to our government as loans but with some technical advantages.

No "right answer" or formula can exist for how much money is enough in such circumstances, because restoring confidence is a psychological matter that varies from case to case. In this instance, Tesobonos were on the minds of market participants and we decided to make available more than we thought Mexico would actually need. Like a big military arsenal, a large financial one can make a considerable psychological difference to the markets. If investors believe that a government has sufficient resources to right itself and that reforms are in place to deal with the underlying problems, the outflow should stop.

WHEN WE GOT THE MESSAGE that my confirmation papers had arrived, Larry and I bundled up our notes and hurried over to the White House. We could not have been bringing the President a more difficult decision at a worse time. Only nine weeks before, he had been dealt a severe political blow—the Democrats had lost both houses of Congress for the first time in forty years. Newt Gingrich and his Contract with America were gracing every magazine cover, and President Clinton was fighting to reestablish himself politically. And here we were, coming into his office on January 10 asking him to make what was likely to be an unpopular and politically risky decision—which also had a real risk of not succeeding—based only on the policy merits.

As usual, it didn't take Bill Clinton long to grasp the situation. He had a few questions for Larry and me. Is there a real risk of cataclysmic consequences if we don't do this? Clinton asked. We said yes. Second, the President wanted to know whether there was a good chance our program could prevent those consequences. While there was no guarantee of success, I repeated, the chances were good. Finally, the President asked how much money we could lose if the rescue didn't work. Larry explained that the loan guarantees would be offered in increments of about $3 billion at a time. If the medicine didn't seem to be helping, we should be able to stop our losses short of the full $25 billion.

Once he heard our analysis and the seriousness of the situation, Clinton responded without hesitation that he would have to live with the political hazards. "This is what the American people sent us here to do," he said. I also remember the President saying that he wouldn't be able to sleep at night if he didn't come to Mexico's aid. Often, when I've heard criticism of Bill Clinton as indecisive or driven by politics rather than policy, I've remembered and cited that night as a response. He gained nothing politically by helping Mexico and risked much at a time when his political capital had already been greatly diminished.

When our discussion was done, Clinton walked over to his desk, picked up the phone, and asked to be connected to the congressional leaders of both parties. Within a couple of hours, Senators Bob Dole (R-KS) and Tom Daschle (D-SD) and Representatives Newt Gingrich (R-GA) and Richard Gephardt (D-MO) all promised to back his emergency request for the loan guarantees. Larry and I went to see them all on Capitol Hill the next day, to solidify their support. At the outset, even Alfonse D'Amato (R-NY), the new chairman of the Senate Banking Committee, who had been investigating Clinton relentlessly over Whitewater, was supportive. D'Amato said we ought to put up more than $25 billion, so that the financial markets wouldn't think they could "overpower" us. With that encouragement, we increased our proposal to $40 billion. A critical component of the proposal also required Mexico to commit to various economic reforms and to pledge its oil export earnings to assure repayment.

Despite this support from the congressional leadership, the reaction when Alan and I went to Capitol Hill to explain the plan was overwhelmingly negative. Meeting with more than a hundred legislators from both parties on January 13, we got our first taste of just how difficult getting Congress to act was going to be. Several members asked for a promise not to put U.S. tax dollars at risk. Some questions were very sensible but hard to answer. Senator Joseph Lieberman (D-CT) pressed us on why the Japanese and Europeans weren't sharing the risk with us. I responded that our allies were making their contribution through the IMF. A less diplomatic response would have been that I believed our allies should have also contributed bilaterally, because a crisis in Mexico and possible contagion would have affected them as well. But they weren't going to, perhaps in part because they considered Mexico our problem but also because they didn't share our judgment about the global danger a Mexican collapse would create. In any event, none of this changed the fundamental point: acting was in our interest. Afterward, Larry and I went on a full-scale media and political blitz to press our case. Among the calls I made was to the governor-elect of Texas, George W. Bush, who offered his support for our effort. Like many border-state politicians, Bush instinctively grasped what was at stake and became a strong public supporter of our aims and efforts.

I'm still not sure I fully understand the depth of the negative reaction to our package in Congress. At one level, congressional opinion simply mirrored public opinion. Xenophobia may have explained some of this opposition, but many people just didn't see any need to risk our tax dollars on this effort. Perhaps we could have done a better job of making the case. But the situation was probably too novel and too complicated to be assimilated quickly. In 1995, the notion that a poor country's macroeconomic miscalculations could affect the largest economy in the world simply didn't register with a lot of people. A few years later, when the Asia crisis took hold, it still didn't. For most Americans, the global economy remains an abstraction, with little meaning in their daily lives.

The opposition we encountered in Congress also seemed to reflect entanglement with other issues. Many Democratic legislators had bucked their supporters in organized labor to vote for NAFTA. Now the opponents of NAFTA were taunting them—*look, we told you so.* On the Republican side, some of the new group of highly energized freshmen were eager to fight the President and skeptical of international engagement. Why help a country that sends us narcotics and illegal immigrants, especially when that help would benefit Wall Street at the same time? I tried—with little success—to explain that our purpose was not Mexico's or Wall Street's well-being but America's. A Mexican default would exacerbate the very problems they were concerned about. But my arguments made little headway.

Some members of both the House and Senate—such as Senators Chris Dodd (D-CT), Paul Sarbanes (D-MD), and Robert Bennett (R-UT)—understood the issues and worked to help us at many critical junctures. But most members willing to support the package wanted conditions that were either politically impractical or not germane to reestablishing stability, or that simply couldn't be worked out with Mexico as part of this program. For example, some Democrats insisted on new labor standards to protect Mexican workers. Jim Leach (R-IA), the conciliatory and internationalist-minded Republican chairman of the House Banking Committee who supported our proposal, was willing to accept some Democratic demands as the price of passage. But that incensed Leach's colleagues, who didn't see why Democrats should be calling the shots now that Republicans ran Congress. Some of them said they wouldn't support any rescue package with labor standards. This messy conflict provided a foretaste of future battles over globalization, including trade liberalization. The constituency for free trade wasn't large to begin with—but if we were going to have it, everyone wanted his particular interests protected.

As the negative reaction mounted, congressional leaders who had agreed to support us at the outset seemed to grow more wary. They weren't persuading skeptical colleagues and appeared to be reducing their efforts to do so. Even some of our committed backers seemed worried about looking too enthusiastic. One prominent supporter kept sending us letters raising "concerns" about our proposal. I later realized that this was a paper trail qualifying his endorsement that he could point to if we failed. But for Greenspan's credibility, the reaction from the GOP would have been even more negative.

One legislator who did grasp the full dimension of the problem was the new Speaker of the House, Newt Gingrich. Gingrich was concerned enough about populist opposition to the rescue that he asked Alan to phone Rush Limbaugh on his behalf, which Alan did. When Larry and I went up to Capitol Hill to meet with him the first time, Gingrich really seemed to get it. Toward the end of our meeting, he described Mexico as "the first crisis of the twenty-first century."

———

GINGRICH MAY NOT HAVE BEEN the first to use such a phrase—the IMF's Michel Camdessus described the crisis using the same words—but he effectively captured the reality we faced. Many elements of the Mexican crisis had been present in previous events, such as the Latin American debt crisis of 1982. Then, as in 1995, the Mexican government essentially ran out of foreign reserves. In 1982, Mexico's default triggered an economic decline that spread throughout much of Latin America and beyond. Banks that had lent heavily to developing countries in the preceding years pulled back dramatically, pushing one country after another into default. We did not want Mexico's difficulties this time around to precipitate another global debt crisis. But the world had changed over the preceding dozen years in ways that made this crisis very different and, in some respects, even more dangerous and difficult to contain. The international financial system had grown in scale, complexity, and velocity, so that the developed and developing worlds were now tied together as never before. Simply put, the potential for financial contagion across developing countries seemed considerably greater, and their economic health affected ours in more complex ways.

The most obvious change was the growth of international trade with developing countries. Many people don't realize that these countries purchase 40 percent of our exports. As a result, millions of American jobs now depend on the ability of consumers in the developing world to buy what we produce. Capital flows have increased even more dramatically. It's no longer just banks but investment banks, endowments, pension funds, mutual funds, and, through them, retail investors who have assets in the developing world. In the twelve years from 1982 to 1994, private capital flows to emerging markets had increased more than six times, from $24 billion to $148 billion. I had been at Goldman Sachs during the earlier crisis in 1982 and it had barely registered with me. The 1995 Mexican crisis was a high-profile event throughout the financial system.

By 1995, global finance had become immensely more complex than in 1982, as emerging-market debt shifted from banks to widely held securities. The 1980s debt crisis took considerable arm-twisting by the United States and other governments to make commercial banks renegotiate their bad loans to Mexico and other debtors. But that was in many ways a large-scale version of a "workout" session that banks hold all the time with troubled borrowers. With Mexico in 1995, some people proposed that we again "coordinate the banks," but the banks were now far from the only creditors. In place of bank loans, a vast variety of debt instruments and derivatives had been devised in the intervening years. Mexican debt was diffused, with bearer bonds—which are not registered in the name of the owner, thus making the owners difficult to identify—held privately by various institutional and individual investors all over the world. In addition, portfolio investors held stock in Mexican companies, which few had in the early 1980s.

With many participants in the financial system, including the big investment banks, holding an array of emerging-market securities, a financial crisis in Mexico could spread much more widely and less predictably, creating a potentially powerful ripple effect. People facing large trading losses in one emerging market might suddenly decide that other emerging markets seemed more risky and liquidate positions in all their securities, even if the countries were apparently unrelated, such as, for example, Mexico and Poland. Firms might also have to raise capital to cover the initial losses, forcing the sale of other positions. Massive downward pressure could develop in other developing markets and even create pressure in industrial-country markets.

A final change was the extraordinary acceleration of market reactions. Throughout most of the 1980s, emerging-market sovereign debt had been illiquid, changing hands only in privately negotiated transactions with large point spreads. In 1995, highly liquid capital moved at the speed of light through fiber-optic cables. Traders had an array of terminals on their desks, with complete information about all prices at all times. Orders could be executed at any hour. The result was that developments in markets in one place could have instantaneous effects in any other place, and crises could spread much more rapidly.

The combination of these factors made the Mexican crisis different in kind from anything anyone had experienced before and made Gingrich's phrase memorable. Almost as soon as the crisis broke, I began picking up reports that the loss of confidence was affecting markets as far from Mexico City as Warsaw and Bangkok. There was no rational economic tie between Mexico's liquidity crisis and the Eastern European financial markets. But the psychology of markets is that investors who are far too complacent one day may quickly change and become a stampeding herd the next. In a world of instantaneous reactions, the tendency to react rather than to think is not necessarily irrational. In the race to an exit that not all will fit through, speed can be lifesaving.

In describing what was happening, I found myself trapped in a kind of Catch-22. On the one hand, I needed to underscore the dangers in order to motivate reluctant legislators—and the public—to support our rescue package. On the other hand, frank talk about what might happen could provoke the very reaction we most wanted to avoid. Explicitly raising our worst fears about global contagion could create a self-fulfilling prophecy. Some people at the time pointed out that I lacked the experience of my predecessor, Lloyd Bentsen, in dealing with Congress. That was true but not my real problem. My real problem was relinquishing our strongest tool: fear. The only way to navigate the twin hazards of complacency and panic was by choosing my words very, very carefully, softening concerns and using calculated ambiguity.

When Alan Greenspan, Secretary of State Warren Christopher, and I testified before the House Banking Committee on January 25, the hostility was typical of the whole process. I had to answer charges that our proposal was a bailout for Wall Street and big investment banks disguised as help for a neighbor. Bernie Sanders (I-VT) said I should "go back to your Wall Street friends, tell them to take the risk and not ask the American taxpayers." I tried to explain that I wouldn't spend a nickel of taxpayer money for the sake of rescuing investors. Again and again, I returned to my arguments that our proposal to help Mexico was driven by our national interest. These numbers are always hard to calculate, but we made a rough judgment about the potential costs of a prolonged Mexican crisis to the United States—700,000 jobs affected, a 30 percent increase in illegal immigration, and so on.

Ross Perot, who testified to the Senate the following week and danced on what he took to be NAFTA's tomb, received a much warmer reception. And Senate Banking Committee chair D'Amato had gone from supportive to antagonistic. It was around this time that Pat Griffin, the White House's highly capable liaison with Congress, expressed annoyance with me at a meeting in the chief of staff's office for putting the President in a box. He felt that the decision to help Mexico had been made without adequate focus on the political risks and had left Clinton in an untenable position. I answered that the President had understood the political risk and decided to take it. As markets began to recognize the extent of congressional opposition to our proposal, they weakened further, not only in Mexico but also in Argentina, Brazil, and other emerging-market countries that tended to move in sympathy. And again, emerging-market countries as far away as Asia and Eastern Europe were affected.

In my office at Treasury, we embarked on a constant process of analysis and discussion. Included in our regular meetings was a group of officials who would become the core Mexican team: Jeff Shafer, David Lipton, and Tim Geithner, as well as my chief of staff, Sylvia Mathews, and Dan Zelikow, who became head of our Mexico task force. I got in the habit of referring to this group as "we" and "us" because in most cases our decisions were reached together after long days and nights of vigorous exchange of views. The Fed's top international official, Ted Truman, often joined us, as did Greenspan at important moments. Treasury and Fed officials were in turn consulting closely with top IMF officials, especially Michel Camdessus and his highly respected deputy, Stanley Fischer, a former chairman of the Economics Department at MIT.

Our Treasury meetings were characterized by searching questioning and debate, all for the sake of the fullest possible exploration of alternatives. This was a discussion, rather unusual for Washington, in which rank hardly mattered. A thirty-four-year-old deputy assistant secretary and the Treasury Secretary both felt fully entitled to express their views. That informality reflected my experience both on Wall Street and inside the White House about what kind of discussions tended to be the most illuminating and productive. So if someone, particularly someone junior, who was often closest to an issue, seemed to be holding back, I tried to draw out his or her view. What mattered to me was the merit of the argument, not the title of the person who made it.

Meetings produced the best results if those who disagreed with the accepted view were encouraged to speak out. So if a meeting seemed to be moving toward a consensus, I would make a point of soliciting dissenting views. Disagreeing with me was socially approved rather than discouraged. If no one disagreed, I would encourage someone to play the role of devil's advocate. I might say, "This is where we're heading, but we need to know the contrary view so we can consider it." And I, or someone else, would take up the other side. Just as important as the freedom to disagree, I think, was that this group of high-powered intellects in large measure avoided investing their egos in their arguments. It was a common search for the best answer in the midst of a worsening crisis.

As congressional opposition solidified, our group naturally began to consider alternatives. One possibility was acting unilaterally, without a vote by Congress, by drawing from the Exchange Stabilization Fund (ESF), the pot of money that the Treasury uses for currency interventions. Congress created the ESF at the time of America's departure from the gold standard in 1934 to allow the Treasury to stabilize exchange rates. At that time, no one envisioned a crisis like Mexico's, but in our view responding to the Mexican crisis fit within the purpose of the ESF. The fund had about $35 billion and, as Treasury Secretary, I had considerable discretion over when and whether to use it, subject to the President's approval.

Senator Bob Bennett—who supported us throughout this crisis—had suggested the ESF early on, but we had initially decided not to use it in part because we thought Congress should be involved in a decision of this magnitude for the country. However, as Congress clearly showed no disposition to endorse our decision, we belatedly focused on the ESF as a potential alternative. Some in Treasury captured one problem in this approach with the phrase that the ESF was "a weapon you could use only once." Our concern was that members of Congress might be so outraged by unilateral action that they might legally disarm us from using the ESF again. But with the package we called "Mexico I" struggling in Congress, the option of tapping the ESF gained force.

As this discussion continued at Treasury, I was in frequent contact with my Mexican counterpart, Guillermo Ortiz, who had been brought in after the managed devaluation had failed in December. I had gotten to know Ortiz a bit in the late 1980s, when, as an official at the Hacienda, as the Mexican Finance Ministry is known, he had handled bank privatizations. Like many of Mexico's senior economic officials, he was a highly capable economist, with a Ph.D. from Stanford University. A thin, serious fellow with a taut demeanor, he looked even thinner and more serious than I remembered when he visited the Treasury as the newly installed Mexican finance minister. Ortiz was not given to overstatement or self-dramatization, so when he told me on January 28 that despite the formal announcement of a $7.8 billion IMF program two days earlier, the situation was worsening, I took him very seriously. More than a billion dollars' worth of Tesobonos were coming due the following week, and the Bank of Mexico's currency reserves were running out. That meant default was getting very close.

Tony Lake, the President's national security advisor, had deputized Sandy Berger, his number two, to take the lead for the National Security Council (NSC) on dealing with Mexico. That evening, Sandy, Leon Panetta, and I met in Leon's office in the West Wing. After some discussion, we decided to press ahead with our effort to rally congressional support, setting a deadline of Monday, the thirtieth. On Sunday, when he got back from church services, Clinton again made calls to leaders in both parties. We still thought we might be able to convince Congress to act.

I woke up on Monday with a sense of deep concern. As I had feared, the Mexican markets began to sell off sharply, with the peso dropping almost 10 percent to more than 6 pesos per dollar, its lowest level yet. We had originally assumed that Mexico could remain solvent at least through February. But despite the assumption many people make that government has better information than the private sector, the opposite is often true. Mexico informed us that its reserves had fallen to around $2 billion on the same day the *International Herald Tribune* reported it. That could have meant a generalized financial collapse within days in Mexico.

That evening, Sandy, Leon, Larry, and I again gathered in Leon's office. As we considered our options, Gingrich phoned from Capitol Hill with bad news. The best-case scenario, in his opinion, was that congressional passage would take another two weeks. A few minutes later, Guillermo Ortiz called from the Hacienda and spoke to Leon. He delivered a message we already understood: The Mexicans were out of rope; we were the only hope. At about 11:00 P.M., the President, just back from a fund-raising dinner, joined us in Leon's office. As the meeting had stretched into the evening, someone had sent out for Domino's Pizza. The President, still in his tuxedo, gazed longingly at the grease-spotted pizza boxes. The Secret Service didn't like him to eat food brought in from the outside. The rest of us took our chances.

Once again, Larry and I presented the possible consequences of a Mexican default to the President. We proposed abandoning the effort to get loan guarantees through Congress and instead tapping the Exchange Stabilization Fund for loans. Partly because the ESF had only about $35 billion and needed a cushion for other possible needs, and partly because the IMF was willing to increase its contribution, we lowered our U.S. proposal to $20 billion. Michel Camdessus, in a moment of daring unusual even for him, had promised to find or provide another $10 billion on top of the $7.8 billion the IMF had previously committed. That brought the total amount available, including a bit more from other sources such as Canada, to just under $40 billion. Sometimes the press referred to our proposal as a $50 billion package, but we avoided using that number because it included other short-term contributions from the Bank for International Settlements that Mexico couldn't practically use to pay off Tesobono holders or finance imports.

The essential goal remained the same: to allow Mexico to restructure its debt from short term to long term and to implement reforms in order to reestablish financial stability and regain access to private capital. By acting on the basis of executive authority, we would avoid the problem of satisfying the immense range and number of conditions proposed in Congress. However, as under the previous proposal, Mexico would have to agree to significant policy reforms negotiated with us and with the IMF, including stronger fiscal and monetary policy, important structural measures, and fuller and timelier reporting about its financial condition. The Bank of Mexico would also be required to pay significant interest on the loans and to make revenues from oil sales available to the United States in the event of nonpayment.

This time we were even more specific with the President about the political risk. A poll published in the *Los Angeles Times* a few days before had showed that the American public overwhelmingly opposed our efforts to help Mexico, by a margin of 79 to 18 percent. I cited these numbers. And I stressed, once again, that the plan might not work. No precedent existed for action of this kind on this scale, and none of us could predict with substantial confidence what would happen. All the choices were bad. But the alternative to intervention remained much worse.

Despite the way opposition had solidified, Clinton's hesitation was no greater than the first time we had gone to him, three weeks earlier. "Look, this is something we have to do," he said. Once again I was deeply impressed not only by his willingness to take on a big political risk but by how relaxed he seemed about doing so. Leon Panetta also made the point later that Clinton seemed to welcome being able to do something difficult and important for the country on his own.

After the meeting, I went back to my Treasury office and called Alan to relate the President's decision, which Clinton discussed with the four congressional leaders at the White House early the next morning. Because the decision was made when it was the middle of the night in Europe, we didn't have time to consult most of our Group of Seven (G-7) allies in advance of announcing our new proposal. The next day, they were furious at Camdessus for offering another $10 billion without consulting them, and very upset with us too. Six countries were angry enough to abstain from the official IMF vote of approval. When German Chancellor Helmut Kohl met with President Clinton a few days later, he said the G-7 finance ministers were all irritated with me and that I should send them each a bottle of whiskey as a peace offering. I didn't send any whiskey, but Larry and I did try to make amends for the lack of consultation, both over the phone and when we met our G-7 colleagues at a meeting in Toronto a week later. Relations were repaired, and all eventually endorsed the IMF program.

For me, it was the first of many experiences of dealing with the ambivalence of our allies about U.S. leadership and the difficulties of exerting that leadership effectively with sovereign states that have agendas and political needs of their own. The lesson I took from that episode was the great importance of working with other countries to build support for what we thought was the right path on international policy. Thereafter, we spent considerable time and effort consulting with our counterparts around the world, especially through a process that brought Larry together with the deputies of the other key finance ministries.

THE PESO and the Mexican stock market, the Bolsa, climbed 10 percent following our announcement of "Mexico II" on January 31. Markets in Brazil and Argentina moved in sympathy. But the respite didn't last long. As we'd feared, some in Congress were furious that we'd made what amounted to the largest nonmilitary international commitment by the U.S. government since the Marshall Plan without their consent. And Mexican markets, realizing that Congress might not allow us to proceed, soon resumed their decline.

When I went up to Capitol Hill to testify before the House Banking Committee a week later, members of both parties blew off steam. Representative Maxine Waters (D-CA) asked whether the bondholders who would be made whole were my "Wall Street buddies." Beyond the hearing room, the reaction was even harsher. A group of Republican freshmen in the House tried to find a way to forbid us from extending loan guarantees without congressional approval. Although Gingrich was still personally supportive, he clearly understood the political realities well enough to conclude that he couldn't turn his caucus around.

In retrospect, it seems to me that many members of Congress probably meant to oppose us without actually stopping us. They didn't want to be blamed for failure. Gingrich was quoted in one newspaper article telling Panetta that if the President took responsibility for the rescue plan, he would hear a "huge sigh of relief" from Congress. The legislators understood what needed to be done but didn't want to have to vote for it. But even such halfhearted opposition was not without cost. Attempts to criticize the program without actually stopping it created market concern that the program was at risk, thus working against the objective of reestablishing confidence and perhaps putting more taxpayer funds at risk than would otherwise have been necessary.

Other attacks were truly meant to stop us and were getting quite ugly, especially a concerted effort at personally vilifying me. One rumor was that I had a secret account somewhere holding Mexican securities. The nastiest official statements came from a Republican freshman congress-man from Texas named Steve Stockman, who accused me of various "sus-picious" conflicts of interest and called for an investigation into whether I had arranged the rescue package for my own benefit. He said Goldman Sachs, which had underwritten the privatization of some of Mexico's na-tionalized industries, now might face liability from investors who lost money there. When I had joined the administration in 1993, my equity in Goldman Sachs had been converted into debt, and I had gone far beyond the requirements of the Office of Government Ethics—and paid a signifi-cant amount of money—to neutralize my position so that I had neither benefit nor risk tied to the success or failure of the firm.

To me, the attacks were an illustration of how harsh and ugly the po-litical process had become. Critics weren't content to disagree with our policies; they impugned my motives and asserted hidden conflicts. At that point, I was still somewhat surprised that opponents would make ad hominem attacks as a way of dealing with policy disagreements. As time went on, I came to recognize that, to some extent at least, Washington un-fortunately functions this way.

In February, the daily reports Dan Zelikow prepared on Mexico made for gloomier and gloomier reading. Alfonse D'Amato, by now a relentless critic of ours, said our approach had "all the potential of being a very real debacle." Bob Dole, who had signed a statement favoring our use of the ESF, was also in the process of revising his position, albeit more quietly. In a word, the political situation looked grave.

Guillermo Ortiz spent much of early February in Washington. He was negotiating the details of the new IMF program with Stan Fischer and others at the Fund, and also negotiating with Larry and his team on our bilateral program, which required Mexico to follow the IMF program and had some additional elements. Meanwhile, Mexican markets were uneasy and deteriorating. Ortiz was spending days and nights talking to the IMF and to us about conditions and difficult policy measures, all the while wondering whether he could sell the agreements to a suffering public back home. He looked ashen and exhausted. As great as the stakes were for us, we could only imagine what the crisis felt like for him.

A few of our own officials with primary responsibility for the problem also showed the pressure in their faces. I remembered similar stressful reactions from traders at Goldman Sachs when losses mounted. At one point Jeff Shafer, who was conducting our negotiations along with Larry, looked so distressed that I told him what I had told traders many times in the past—that a thousand years from now none of this was going to matter much. I told Jeff that he was extraordinarily capable and doing his best in difficult circumstances—and that was all anyone could ever do. One way or another, we'd make our way through this.

One source of remaining uncertainty was the new president of Mexico, Ernesto Zedillo. Zedillo was an economist, educated in both Mexico and the United States, with a doctorate from Yale. But I had not met this man to whom we were about to lend $20 billion, and no one in the administration knew him well. We didn't have a sufficient sense of how committed Zedillo would be to following through with the difficult reforms that were going to be required for the program to work. And we needed to be sure that Ortiz was speaking for him in all cases in our negotiations. So in a phone conversation with Zedillo, I proposed sending Larry down to meet with him. Zedillo thought that was a good idea.

This trip involved dilemmas of substance and perception in both countries. At a substantive level, our economists had a series of proposals to reform aspects of Mexico's economic policy and reestablish confidence. But the program would never work if we imposed these measures. We had to reach a meeting of the minds with Mexican officials, and they had to take ownership of the program. The problem of public perception was related but distinct. On the one hand, we didn't want the Mexican public to feel we were infringing on their sovereignty. On the other hand, we wanted the American public to feel precisely that we were imposing strict economic conditions on Mexico to protect taxpayer money. The tension between these contradictory demands pervaded our discussions. We spent countless hours fine-tuning the wording of our public statements to avoid erring in one direction or the other.

We solved the perception problem around the trip with a cloak of secrecy. We put in a presidential order for an Air Force plane, and before dawn Larry and David Lipton were off on a mission. We made every effort to keep their trip quiet, and luckily no one saw them slipping in and out of

Los Pinos, the President's dwelling in Mexico City. More important, our substantive concerns were eased. Larry came back deeply impressed with Zedillo. The new president of Mexico understood exactly what he was doing. Moreover, Zedillo clearly had full confidence in Ortiz. We didn't need to worry about his negotiator getting out ahead of him.

Furthermore, President Zedillo was firmly committed to economic reform despite the difficulties that lay ahead for his country. The single most important aspect of this reform was interest rates. The IMF had negotiated that the interest rate would be about 2 percent per month. However, inflation was expected to be 4 or 5 percent or higher. We wanted to restore confidence in the peso and knew that no one would hold pesos if their position lost value because the rate of return was negative in real terms— that is, if interest rates were lower than the rate of inflation. But the Mexican team negotiating in Washington had rejected higher interest rates. In the meeting with Zedillo, Larry raised this problem after forty-five minutes of polite conversation on the full range of issues regarding the rescue. Zedillo thought for only a moment, then said, "I spent my whole career at the Bank of Mexico writing articles saying that Mexico should have positive real interest rates. Now is not the time to abandon that idea." Although some critics take issue with the need for high interest rates in a financial crisis, this approach was absolutely essential in Mexico for two related reasons. It created confidence that credible policies were now in place to restore stability and, in the context of that confidence, it offered investors an attractive rate of return to induce them to hold pesos.

On February 16, I hosted a dinner at the Jefferson, the pleasant old hotel on Sixteenth Street that served as my home in Washington for six and a half years. In a private dining room at the back of the restaurant, Panetta, Berger, and the rest of our group at Treasury convened for one last examination of the program about to begin. In a few days, I was expecting to sign an agreement that would commit us to lend $20 billion to Mexico. Though we retained the power to withdraw unilaterally at any point, this was our last real chance to change our minds.

In previous discussions, Larry had laid out the analysis—and the risks—very clearly. In theory, if Mexico offered a high enough interest rate, then people—whether ordinary Mexicans or foreign investors—would choose to hold pesos rather than buy dollars at a particular exchange rate. The greater the confidence that the government's policies and IMF-led financial support would succeed in restoring financial stability, the lower the interest rate that would be needed to persuade investors to hold pesos. But if people feared that the program would not work—that their pesos might quickly lose their value as the exchange rate plunged further and inflation accelerated, putting more pressure on the peso and creating a vicious cycle—they would demand a terribly high interest rate to compensate for that risk. And as interest rates climbed, we might reach a point at which higher rates could actually become counterproductive in attracting capital. Rather than attracting capital and increasing the demand for pesos, higher rates could reduce the demand for pesos by threatening to push the government's debt burden to a level where default seemed inevitable, or trigger a collapse in the already weak banking system. In that case, the plan would fail and our billions of dollars in loans from the ESF would merely have helped finance some of the capital flight as money poured out of Mexico. Larry, Alan, the rest of the team, and I had spent endless hours trying to gauge how high interest rates could go without being too high. But what if no interest rate existed that was high enough to attract capital before rising above the level that would scare capital away?

Interest rates were the most critical issue, but other policies were also crucial to reestablishing confidence and therefore growth. These included a commitment to a floating exchange rate to avoid a rerun of the previous crisis; a budget plan that showed that the government could tackle its debt burden; reform of the banking system, revealed by the crisis to be close to insolvent; and much greater transparency so that investors felt adequately informed. The more credible the government's commitment to a strong reform program, the less pressure there would be on the exchange rate and the more leeway Mexico would have on interest rates.

As we sipped our coffee at the Jefferson, I went around the dinner table and asked all present what they thought the odds were that the plan would work. Dan Zelikow, who had seen real economic dysfunction as an adviser to the first democratically elected government in Albania, thought the odds of success were only one in three. Larry thought our chances were substantially better but didn't offer precise numbers. David Lipton gave the most optimistic specific prediction: better than a 50 percent chance. What was striking was that everyone agreed we were taking a significant risk.

In a sense, the plan had two distinct, but intertwined, risks. The first was that the Mexican government would simply be unable to follow through on the tough steps needed to rebuild confidence and attract private capital again. The second was that official money—from the United States and the IMF—would not be sufficient to provide the breathing space needed while policy reforms took hold. Ironically, the bigger and more certain the promise of official money, the less was likely to be needed.

Making matters more complicated, our G-7 allies were still protesting Camdessus's decision to add another $10 billion from the IMF. In response, Camdessus suggested restructuring our deal. On the morning of February 21, the day for signing our agreement with Mexico, Camdessus told me that the IMF could provide only $7.8 billion, plus contributions from elsewhere. That was inconsistent with his original commitment; now he wanted to go ahead with the extra $10 billion only if it came as bilateral loans from other countries, similar to our ESF commitment. That was a problem for us, since Mexico needed to have the entire $17.8 billion available and I had always told Congress that the total IMF contribution would be $17.8 billion. I sympathized with Camdessus's difficult position. But for him to do this now would harm the program and seriously undermine our credibility in Congress.

Camdessus had provided strong leadership in difficult circumstances and I had great respect for him, but this wouldn't work. With Leon sitting in my office, I called back and said, "Michel, this is not what we agreed to. And if you insist, I am going to go out and make a public statement. We are going to hold a press conference and announce that you have changed the deal. And I'm not going to go ahead with the Mexican program."

Michel said, "You can't do that."

I replied that, in fact, we could. The moment was dramatic, but in the end, Camdessus came around, and our strong relationship with him—so important in the years ahead—was not harmed. My approach in general is to try to see both sides and work to find common ground. But sometimes there is no good alternative to an adamant stand calmly taken.

We signed the Mexican rescue agreement as planned that day in the Cash Room at the Treasury Building. The Cash Room was where citizens once came to trade paper dollars for gold. The location seemed appropriate, since the closing of the gold window and the creation of the ESF in 1934 had made the action we were about to take possible. But we were all concerned. After the signing, I walked back to my office in worried silence with Sylvia Mathews and David Dreyer, another senior adviser. David tried to cut the tension with humor. "I guess we'll never see that money again," he joked. Sylvia and I didn't smile. It's funny to me now, but it wasn't then.

A night or two after that, when the positive market reaction to the agreement had already dissipated and markets were once again dropping, Larry came into my office and offered to resign. It was about eleven in the evening, and we were both still at work. Larry felt personally responsible for an effort that might well fail. I told him that his talk about resigning was ridiculous. While I understood how Larry could feel his responsibility so keenly, I told him he wasn't any more responsible than the rest of us and he was taking the matter much too personally. What we were doing was right, and we were all in it together. We'd just have to hang on and get through it, one way or the other.

In the next few weeks, we all felt the pressure. Jeff Shafer told me a story somewhat later about having a drink with friends before a baseball game at Camden Yards in Baltimore on a rare evening off. When a friend asked him something about the Mexican "bailout," the term that most irritated us, Jeff's response—"It was *not* a bailout!"—was loud enough to stop conversation in the crowded bar.

I didn't discuss my own feelings with anyone at work, but I too had focused on what the possibility of failure could mean for me. Losing $20 billion in public funds, especially on such a controversial and high-profile matter, could substantially taint how I would be seen as the Secretary of the Treasury. But even if I had to step down, I could deal with that. I felt better thinking that I'd helped set up the National Economic Council at the White House, which was working well. No one could take that away from me, no matter what happened afterward.

As markets continued to fall, Larry and I had a difficult phone call with Guillermo Ortiz. This was after we had signed the agreement but just before the first disbursement of funds. As we explained how bleak the situation looked, Guillermo, though sounding overwrought, tried to paint a rosier scenario for us. We weren't persuaded, but I understood he could do little else. After the call, we went right over to the Roosevelt Room in the White House for a meeting with Panetta and Berger. I felt, in light of the circumstances, that we had an obligation to raise the question of whether to exercise our right to withdraw from the arrangement unilaterally.

"Letting Mexico go" at this stage would turn the possibility of default into a virtual sure thing—but I thought I should raise the issue even though I personally believed we should still proceed. My question was greeted with surprise. Only Erskine Bowles, the deputy chief of staff, who, like me, had worked as an investment banker, related to why I was even posing the possibility of not following through on this program we had already agreed to. Leon said that he didn't think that option was viable. The administration was committed to a plan of action and had to stick with it even if the chance of failure had increased. The cost to the administration of reversing course—in terms of lost credibility—would be enormous. I, on the other hand, imagined the congressional hearing where I'd be called to account, with one of our very vocal critics leading the inquisition. *So, Mr. Secretary, you thought that there was only a small chance that sending billions of dollars of American taxpayers' money would help? And you sent the money anyway?*

That discussion illustrates a difference between making decisions on Wall Street and in government. There is a strong impetus to stick with presidential decisions, even when circumstances change, because the world is watching to see if you keep your commitments. Credibility and reliability are powerful values. Thus, changing direction may sometimes be worse than proceeding with something that could be wrong. In the private sector, reliability and credibility are also very important, but you can change course much more easily. When a Wall Street trader decides to cut his losses or a corporate head cuts back in a troubled business, no one complains about inconsistency. Nonetheless, there are times when high-profile government decisions should be reversed despite the damage to credibility. I didn't think that was the case here, but I did think the issue should be raised.

On March 9, the day we were to release the first $3 billion loan, the peso fell dramatically, closing for the first time at more than 7 pesos per dollar. Rumors—in this case accurate—circulated on Wall Street that we were contemplating not releasing the money on schedule. Despite the commitment of additional funds from the World Bank and the policy reforms that Ortiz was about to announce in Mexico City that evening, we were all deeply concerned that market confidence simply wasn't going to rebound. But when the time came to decide, we approved the release of the money.

The roller-coaster quality of that period was caught for me by the visit Larry and I paid the next day to the hearing room of the Senate Banking Committee. As I was answering questions, including hostile ones from Senators D'Amato and Lauch Faircloth (R-NC), my staff kept slipping me notes about the peso, which was rising even more dramatically than the prior day's fall. Larry, who was testifying alongside me, passed me a note saying, "I think this thing might actually work." While one of the senators was talking, I scribbled back a response: "I think it might." Once again, though, our optimism was short-lived. The March 10 rally was followed by a steady decline. A month later, we went through the same agonizing decision again about whether to disburse the second $3 billion loan.

By mid-May, the Mexican central bank data we saw showed the first, very tentative signs that the program was beginning to work, although markets didn't seem to reflect much progress and still looked fragile. We sent a memo to the President that pointed to some encouraging indicators. The Mexican economy was in a severe recession, but the country's trade deficit had turned into a surplus, the stock of outstanding Tesobonos had been reduced substantially, and the peso had recovered somewhat. Anticipating the success of our rescue package, Thomas Friedman, the Pulitzer Prize–winning *New York Times* columnist, described it in his May 24 column as "the least popular, least understood, but most important foreign policy decision of the Clinton presidency."

Alas, Friedman was getting ahead of himself just a bit. The roller coaster continued for the next few months. With the policy measures imposed by Zedillo, the financial and economic situation looked more stable by the end of the summer. But unemployment was growing, real wages had fallen significantly, and bank balance sheets were severely impaired. Chafing under the duress—and encouraged by signs that the program was taking hold—the Mexican government moved prematurely to lower interest rates. Markets resumed their slide, but the Mexicans quickly reacted and tightened policy to halt the slide.

Despite another rocky period in November, by the end of 1995 the program was taking hold. Investors started to put some money in; foreign exchange reserves started to build up; exchange rates stabilized; interest rates came down a little bit. Everything just started to work. The private sector had begun lending Mexico money again. By the beginning of 1996, the Mexican economy was growing again. The Zedillo government began to repay the U.S. and IMF loans, rolling them over into less conditional private-sector debt.

The speed of the response was remarkable. The 1982 crisis led to what has been called a "lost decade" of negative growth, financial instability, and political and social unrest throughout Latin America. The 1995 crisis caused real suffering on the part of the Mexican poor and middle class—and real wages were very slow to recover—but only one year of economic growth was lost. After the 1982 crisis, Mexico took seven years to regain access to capital markets. In 1995, it took seven months.

In August 1996, Mexico prepaid $7 billion of the $10.5 billion still outstanding from the United States and IMF. When the Zedillo government completed the repayment in January 1997, more than three years ahead of schedule, an anonymous aide of mine was quoted in *The New York Times* as saying, "This was Bob Rubin's Bosnia. And today he got the troops out." Mexico paid us $1.4 billion dollars in interest and left the ESF with a profit of $580 million—the excess over what our money would have earned in U.S. Treasury notes. Senator D'Amato, who had already called the program a "failure," put out a one-line press release saying he was "pleased" our program had been successful—thanks to "vigilant congressional oversight."

IT SEEMS TO ME that the Mexican crisis has much to teach us about the global economy, new and heightened risks that our country is likely to confront in the future, and the challenges we face in trying to deal with these hazards. These challenges are complicated by volatile financial markets and by our own political processes. I've drawn out many of those reflections in the context of my narrative, but a few final observations depend on the whole story.

The first lesson is that our ability to address economic crises beyond our borders is limited. The money we lent to Mexico could not have had the desired effect without the policy choices the Mexican government made. This was the crucial element, both because of the effects of individual policies—especially on interest rates—and because of the confidence engendered by the more amorphous cumulative sense that the Mexicans were serious about getting their act together.

As an episode in public policy making, our decision making in the face of a highly uncertain situation and considerable political pressure showed that the probabilistic thinking that I internalized so deeply in the financial world had real applicability in Washington. And that process was ongoing, as we reevaluated options and policies when the facts changed on the ground in Mexico and in the financial markets. I think, too, that our work demonstrated the value of robust and open intellectual interchange in making government decisions.

Yet in other ways the episode showed me just how challenging decision making is in the context of government. Good decisions are much more difficult to make when disagreement is not just about means but about objectives. The private sector often focuses intensely on customers and employees, but in the final analysis everything comes back to serving the overriding objective of profitability—except perhaps for the relatively small portion of corporate activity devoted to philanthropy and other public purposes. The public sector, by contrast, operates with many equally legitimate objectives. For many in Congress, narcotics and illegal immigration mattered far more than economic issues in dealing with Mexico, and these legislators were not persuaded by our argument that the former problems would get far worse if Mexico defaulted and suffered from severe and prolonged economic duress.

Mexico also demonstrated the difficulties our political processes have in dealing effectively with issues that involve technical complexities, shorter-term cost to achieve longer-term gain, incomplete information and uncertain outcomes, opportunities for political advantage, and inadequate public understanding. Unfortunately, many of the most important economic, geopolitical, and environmental challenges of today's complicated world fit this profile, raising the question of how effectively our political system will be able to deal with them.

Having said that, the Mexican crisis also showed the strength of our system. Congress, while not able to act itself and often complicating our efforts, also induced greater focus on some important issues, such as moral hazard, and helped assure that all points of view were considered, a value often lost in a more monolithic system. In addition, some individual legislators were tremendously helpful. As I discovered, finding effective legislative allies is key to navigating our system successfully. At one point, Senator D'Amato had proposed measures that would rule out future Treasury use of the ESF in this type of situation—which would have severely hampered us in dealing with the Asian crisis two years later. But Senators Dodd and Sarbanes, who had a deep understanding of the benefits and risks of the global financial system, filibustered D'Amato's language, which led to a more limited constraint. I also remember an act of graciousness of the kind that occurs too seldom in any walk of life. Frank Murkowski, a Republican senator from Alaska and a former banker, who had opposed our rescue package as unlikely to work, went out of his way when I was testifying later at a hearing on another matter to say that he had been wrong—a gesture unusual in Washington and most other places.

However, Murkowski's prediction could have turned out to be right.

Our program could have been undertaken only by a President—and an administration—willing to take a major calculated risk, substantive and political. We could have failed because of a mistake in our analysis, but also because of unforeseeable circumstances, or simply the foreseeable risk actually occurring. If the odds are calculated accurately at three to one, you'll lose one time in four. Unfortunately, Washington—the political process and the media—judges decisions based solely on outcomes, not on the quality of the decision making, and makes little allowance for the inevitability of some level of human error. This can easily lead to undue risk aversion on the part of public officials. The same issue exists in the private sector—in my own experience, most seriously in judging trading and investing results. But the private sector somewhat more frequently recognizes the need to look beyond the outcome to reach the most sensible and constructive evaluation.

Some years later, Paul O'Neill, the Bush administration's newly appointed Treasury Secretary, said he liked the Mexican program because it worked. "We gave them money, it stabilized their situation, and they paid back the money ahead of schedule," he said. "I like success. I'm not a real fan of even well-meaning failure." Where O'Neill said he liked what worked, my view was that decisions shouldn't be evaluated only on the basis of results. Even the best decisions about intervention are probabilistic and run a real risk of failure, but the failure wouldn't necessarily make the decision wrong.

Finally, what concerns me most is how little the public understands the impact that all of the issues around globalization and economic conditions elsewhere have on jobs, living standards, and growth in this country and how critical U.S. leadership is on these international economic matters. The result, as I realized over and over again during my six and a half years in Washington, is that public support—and thus political support—for trade liberalization, international financial-crisis response, foreign aid, funding for the World Bank and the IMF, and the like—is at best very difficult to obtain.

At one point during the second term, Secretary of State Madeleine Albright and I discussed holding joint public meetings around the country to try to improve public understanding of how global issues, both economic and geopolitical, affect people's lives. Regrettably, we never did this, but some kind of ongoing public education campaign is badly needed to change the politics around all these concerns, which are so critical to our future. On trade, for example, dislocations are very specific and keenly felt—and lead to strong political action—but the benefits of both exports and imports are widely dispersed and not recognized as trade-related, and thus haven't developed the level of political support they require.

We also face significant challenges when it comes to the international politics of economic leadership. In Mexico, and later in the Asian financial crisis, U.S. leadership, exercised in correlation with the G-7, the IMF, the World Bank, and others, was necessary for effective response. But even our closest allies are ambivalent about the role of the United States. We are criticized if we don't lead and resented if we do. At Treasury, the lesson we took was to work all the more energetically with other countries to reach consensus whenever practical, which often meant making accommodations on our part. But we also recognized that at times we would feel a need to push beyond where others wanted to go.

In 1995, I referred to the Mexican crisis as a "very low-probability event." But my view later changed. The likelihood of a contagious crisis emanating from problems in any one developing country may ordinarily be small. But modern capital markets—with their many interrelationships, size, and speed—combined with the inherent human tendency to go to excess, create a seemingly inevitable tendency toward periodic destabilization that is difficult to anticipate and prevent. Indeed, only a couple of years later, I found myself immersed in another global financial crisis—one far more threatening in its scale, complexity, and potential consequences than what had happened in Mexico.

CHAPTER TWO

A Market Education

I WAS AN ODD CHOICE for Goldman Sachs when the firm hired me, at the age of twenty-eight, to work in its storied arbitrage department. Nothing about my demeanor or my experience would have suggested I might be good at such work. The stereotypical personality type of the arbitrageur was, in those days, forceful and confrontational. I was then, as now, a low-key, not manifestly aggressive person. As for my qualifications, I don't think I'd even ever heard the phrase "risk arbitrage" before I started the job search that led to Goldman Sachs. But as it happened, arbitrage and I turned out to be a pretty good fit.

Arbitrage in its classic form is nothing more complicated than attempting to profit by buying something in one market and then selling it at the same time in another market for a price differential. As practiced in the years before the Second World War, when communication advantages were still possible, classic arbitrage meant trying to capture discrepancies in different financial markets. To take a simple example, the British pound might have been trading at $2.42 in London and $2.43 in New York. If an arbitrageur could buy pounds in London and sell them in New York simultaneously, he would be assured a profit of $1 for every $242 he put up. The only risk in this kind of arbitrage is not completing the transaction fast enough. During the first half of the century, many firms made a steady income from the minor price differentials for the same currencies and securities trading in different markets.

As global communications improved, however, the profit went out of traditional arbitrage. Once everyone knew in real time what the pound was trading at on various markets, the discrepancies became, for the most part, too small to be worth exploiting. But in the years after the Second World War, Gustave Levy, the man I would work for a couple of decades later at Goldman Sachs, helped develop a new business known as "risk arbitrage." In classic arbitrage you buy and sell the same thing simultaneously. In the simplest form of risk arbitrage, you buy one stock—call it A—that will be converted into another stock—B—once an already announced event, such as a merger, is completed. At the same time as the purchase, you sell B in order to "hedge" the transaction and lock in your profit. There's an element of risk, because the conversion of A into B isn't certain—the deal might fall apart rather than close.

Since the 1950s, risk arbitrage on Wall Street has meant buying securities that are the subject of some material event, like a merger, a tender offer, a breakup, divestiture, or a bankruptcy. As a hypothetical example, Big Company might announce a friendly takeover of Acme Industries at the price of one half of a share of BigCo's stock for every Acme share. Say BigCo is trading at $32 per share. The stock of the target company was trading at $13 before the deal was announced and rose to $14.50 after the announcement, based on its being worth $16 per share once the deal is completed (one half of BigCo if it remained at $32). In a risk arbitrage transaction, you would buy shares of Acme and "sell short" the number of BigCo shares you would receive when the takeover closed. Short selling in this context means selling something now that you don't yet own to hedge against market risk—in other words, to protect yourself against the possibility that by the time the item you're buying (A) is converted into the item you're selling (B), B will have gone down in value. (To sell something you don't own, you have to borrow it for a fee.) Then when the deal closes, you simply take the shares of BigCo you received in exchange for your Acme shares and deliver them against the short, replacing what you borrowed and closing out the position. Your profit is the difference between the transaction price and the price you initially locked in. Movements of the BigCo stock subsequent to your short sale don't matter—if BigCo goes down 5 points, it doesn't affect you because you've already sold the BigCo stock short, locking in the spread against the Acme stock you've bought.

However, you receive the profit only *if* the transaction goes through. If the deal breaks up, you are left with a position that you bought at a deal premium (Acme) and a short position (BigCo)—with almost certain losses on one or both. In this type of transaction, the potential profit is much larger than in a classical arbitrage trade—$1.50 for every share costing $14.50 in my hypothetical example. But the risk is also much greater, since the takeover might fail to close for any number of reasons. In practice, such transactions become enormously more complicated and more interesting.

Gus, a great financial innovator with the gentle disposition of an active volcano, had developed this kind of transaction after World War II in response to anomalies produced by the wartime boom. During the Great Depression, a number of railroads had filed for bankruptcy, leaving the prices of their shares and bonds badly depressed. During the war years, however, the railroads had been operating at full capacity and, as a result, were flush with cash. Coming through bankruptcy court, they were due to be reorganized in ways that would unlock their real value. Arbitrageurs like Gus would buy the stock of such technically insolvent companies and wait for them to be restructured.

By the end of the 1950s, that kind of opportunity was also becoming rare. But in the mid-1960s, around the time Gus and his protégé L. Jay Tenenbaum hired me as the junior man in the arbitrage department at Goldman Sachs, the risk-arbitrage business was picking up again, thanks to a wave of takeovers and mergers. By the end of the decade, Goldman Sachs was making significant profits in the context of the times—several million dollars a year—using its own capital for these transactions. Because the work was risky, complicated, and highly profitable, it had also acquired a certain mystique. Firms like Goldman didn't want their competitors to know how they went about the arbitrage business. In 1966, the year I was hired, L. Jay was quoted in *Business Week:* "Asking about our arbitrage operations is like walking into a couple's home and asking about their sex life." While arbitrage is still a big business on Wall Street, it has become much less secretive.

I'll try to explain what we did in those days by describing an arbitrage transaction I actually worked on in 1967. Although this deal was in many ways typical of the hundreds I was involved in during my first several years at Goldman Sachs, I remember it well for reasons that will become clear. It was a merger of two companies that were traded publicly: Becton Dickinson, a medium-sized manufacturer of medical equipment, and Univis, a somewhat smaller company that made eyeglass lenses. Under the terms of an announced friendly takeover, Becton Dickinson would buy all outstanding shares of Univis for about $35 million in stock. Shareholders in Univis would get a .6075 share of Becton Dickinson for each share of Univis they held.

At the time the deal was announced, on September 4, 1967, Becton Dickinson was trading at around $55 a share and Univis at around $24½. If the merger was to be completed, A, or Univis, would become B, or Becton Dickinson, and a Univis share would be worth $33½—at the price of Becton Dickinson when the deal was first announced (.6075 × $55). To decide whether to engage in arbitrage, we had to estimate the odds of the merger coming to fruition, what we would make if it did, and what we would lose if it didn't—my framework, you might say, for dealing with most decisions in life.

Such an announced merger could fail to be completed for any number of reasons. It might be called off after either side performed its "due diligence" of examining the other's books in detail. Or the shareholders of either company might reject the terms of the transaction as not favorable enough. The Justice Department or the Federal Trade Commission might decide that a combination of the two companies was anticompetitive. Regulatory issues might surface. One of the firms might have a history of announcing deals and not completing them, and simply change its mind or be too unwilling to make accommodations on specific matters that arose after the initial agreement in principle. We would weigh and balance the different factors to decide whether or not to take an arbitrage position.

The first order of business was rapid, intensive research. I had to examine all the publicly available information I could obtain. I had to talk to proxy lawyers and antitrust lawyers. Then I had to speak to officers at both companies, much as a securities analyst does. I almost never had all the information I would have liked. Seldom did I have enough time to think everything through.

But even with as much information and time as I might have hoped for, risk arbitrage would have fallen far short of science. Many of the notes I put down on my legal pad weren't quantitative or measurable points of data. They were judgments. And once I finished all my analysis and reached a point of relative clarity, a correct answer wouldn't simply present itself. The final decision was another judgment, involving my sense of a situation. We might pass up a transaction where the numbers looked promising simply because of a feeling that two companies didn't make a good match or because we didn't trust some of the people involved.

But recognizing the essential component of experienced feel in this kind of judgment is different from not having a framework and making decisions in a nonsystematic way or on the basis of instinct. Some arbitrageurs at other firms operated on a far more ad hoc and subjective basis, their decisions driven by bits of information, trading activity, and gossip. At Goldman, our decisions were driven much more by analysis. We always tried to think of everything that could possibly go wrong with a deal and then tried to evaluate how much weight to accord to such risks in our analysis. Despite the all-too-human tendency to lose sight of one's own disciplined framework, we tried our best to be cool and hardheaded. Emotion, like instinct not moored in analysis, could be misleading. If you became frightened easily—or were greedy—you couldn't function effectively as an arbitrageur.

In merger transactions such as Becton-Univis, our projected loss would typically be much larger if the deal fell apart than our projected gain if it went through. That meant that the odds had to be substantially in our favor for us to choose to participate. But how greatly did they have to be in our favor? Someone who had been to business school would have recognized the charts I made on my yellow pad as expected-value tables, used to calculate the anticipated outcome of a transaction. After a while, organizing my analysis according to these tables became second nature and I'd do them in my head. But I still constantly scribbled notes and numbers on a legal pad—a lifelong habit with me.

The basic inputs in an arbitrage expected-value table are the price you have to pay for a stock; what you will get for the stock if a deal goes through (the potential upside); what you will have to sell it for if the deal doesn't go through (the potential downside); and finally—the most diffi-cult factor to assess and the heart of risk arbitrage—the odds that the transaction will be completed. With the help of some papers from Gold-man's archives, I've re-created an expected-value table for Becton-Univis. After the merger was announced, Univis stock traded at $30½ (up from $24½ before the announcement). That meant the upside potential from an arbitrage trade was $3, because a Univis share would be worth $33½—.6075 of a share of Becton Dickinson—if the deal went through. If the deal didn't go through, Univis would be likely to fall back to around $24½, giving our investment a downside potential of around $6. Let's say we rated the odds of the merger being completed as slightly better than six to one (about 85 percent success to 15 percent failure). On an expected-value basis, the potential upside would be $3 multiplied by 85 percent. The downside risk would be $6 multiplied by 15 percent.

$$\$3 \times 85 \text{ percent} = \quad \$2.55 \text{ upside potential}$$
$$-\$6 \times 15 \text{ percent} = -\$0.90 \text{ downside risk}$$

$$\text{Expected value} = \quad \$1.65$$

The $1.65 was what one could expect to earn by tying up $30.50 of the firm's capital for three months. That works out to a return of approxi-mately 5½ percent, or 22 percent on an annualized basis. A lower rate of return than that would have been a red light. We figured that it wasn't worthwhile to obligate the firm's capital for a return of less than 20 per-cent per annum.

I'm simplifying in a variety of ways. You also had to factor in the risk that a merger would break up under conditions that would cause the target stock you'd bought—in this case Univis—to fall lower than its pre-announcement floor or that would drive the acquiring company's stock—

the Becton Dickinson shares you'd sold short—higher. Or, even worse, both could occur at the same time. And you wouldn't just make the decision to invest in this sort of deal and wait for the result several months later. The odds of a merger reaching closure changed constantly over time, as risks emerged and receded and share prices fluctuated. We had to stay on top of the situation, recalculating the odds and deciding whether to commit more, reduce our position, or even liquidate it entirely. And, of course, an arbitrageur would be involved in many such deals at any one time. You had to do a lot of them, because arbitrage is an actuarial business, like insurance. You expect to lose money in some cases but to make money over the long run thanks to the law of averages.

In the case of Becton-Univis, the positive expected value prompted us to take a position—we sold short 60.75 shares of Becton Dickinson for every 100 shares of Univis we bought. As I explained, selling short the acquiring company—which we'd do by borrowing shares for a fee—was a hedge against the market risk. If the stock prices of both companies went down while the merger was under way—perhaps because the sector or market weakened—our profit would still be locked in, as long as the deal went through.

Goldman's trading records—which the firm graciously made available to us for this example—show that on my recommendation, we initially bought 33,233 shares of Univis at an average price of $30.28 and a total cost of just over $1 million—a significant amount at that time. We also sold short 19,800 shares of Becton Dickinson, into which the Univis shares would be converted. After increasing our positions in the interim, we stood to make around $125,000 if the merger closed. By the end of the year, Becton had risen to around $60, causing Univis to climb to $33¾.

Unfortunately, the deal didn't work out as we hoped. The merger fell apart in January because an unexpected decline in quarterly earnings at Univis prompted Becton Dickinson to pull out. When the merger went sour, the stock of Univis fell, not only back to its preannouncement price of $24½ but all the way down to $18. As a result, we suddenly had a loss on our books of $485,000. We also faced a second loss on our short position, because Becton Dickinson shot up to $64 after the deal fell apart. We would have to buy Becton shares for $64 in the open market to replace the ones we'd borrowed and sold short at $55, which was going to cost us an additional $190,000. Everything that could go wrong had gone wrong. This was it: the dreaded arbitrage perfect storm.

By the end of January, we were down some $675,000 on the deal. That was a lot of money back then, more than we made on any other arbitrage transaction that year and a noticeable slice out of the firm's yearly profits. Gus Levy, who always had terrific insight into deals in retrospect, was furious. He stalked around the trading room muttering that we should have known better than to think a merger like that would go through. L. Jay joked afterward that he'd been to "Univis University."

But a critical point was that while the result may have been bad, the investment decision wasn't necessarily wrong. After a deal broke up, we'd always reexamine it, looking for clues we might have missed. But even a large and painful loss didn't mean that we had misjudged anything. As with any actuarial business, the essence of arbitrage is that if you calculate the odds correctly, you will make money on the majority of deals and on the sum total of all your deals. If you take a six-to-one risk, the foreseeable risks will occur and you will lose money every seventh time. Other times deals will break up for reasons that you could not reasonably have foreseen (a potential that also needs to be worked into your calculations). To an outsider, our business might have looked like gambling. In fact, it was the opposite of gambling, or at least of most amateur gambling. It was an investment business built on careful analysis, disciplined judgments—often made under considerable pressure—and the law of averages.

Flux and uncertainty made arbitrage quite nerve-racking for some people. But somehow or other, I was able to take it in reasonable stride. Arbitrage suited me, not only temperamentally but as a way of thinking—a kind of mental discipline. I took naturally to being rigorously analytical in weighing probabilities. I described this as being like a mental yellow pad. Risk arbitrage sometimes involved taking large losses, but if you did your analysis properly and didn't get swept up into the psychology of the herd, you could be successful. Intermittent losses—sometimes greatly in excess of your worst-case expectations—were a part of the business. I accepted that, though some in our business did seem highly stressed much of the time. Having Gus Levy remind you of all the reasons you were a moron wasn't always the most pleasant way to begin a day. But not only could I live with risk without becoming a nervous wreck; risk taking actually comported with my way of looking at the world.

Did arbitrage suit me because I instinctively thought the way an arbitrageur thinks? Or did I learn to think in terms of probabilities by practicing arbitrage? Arbitrage certainly reinforced my instinct to look at issues probabilistically. But that instinct had been formed long before I got to Goldman Sachs. The arbitrage business I learned there was consistent with the way I thought about life, as a process of weighing odds in a world without absolutes or provable certainties. This outlook was rooted in my basic temperament and shaped by the intellectual influence of various teachers and friends. Looking back at my life up to that point, I think you could trace the development of the mental processes and temperament of an effective arbitrageur.

I GREW UP with the influence of my two grandfathers, Morris Rubin and Samuel Seiderman. As I look back, I think both of these men affected me in ways I wasn't really aware of while they were alive.

Morris Rubin was my paternal grandfather. He was born in 1882 in Minsk, Russia, from which he fled as a teenager to avoid being drafted into the Czar's army—somehow, as a young Jew, he didn't think the Russian military would be a terrific career choice. Morris arrived at Ellis Island as a penniless immigrant at the age of fifteen. The first question he asked was *Where can I learn to speak English?* He found work delivering milk and in 1906 married Rose Krebs, my paternal grandmother. Born in Poland, my grandmother Rose was the opposite of my grandfather Morris in every apparent respect—taciturn where he was exuberant, a worrier where he was a perennial optimist. They began their married life in a tenement on the Lower East Side of Manhattan.

Sometime after their first child, my father, Alexander Rubin, was born in 1907, Morris and Rose moved to Flatbush, Brooklyn, a rung up the socioeconomic ladder from the Lower East Side. The family did well until the early 1920s, when my grandfather became gravely ill with an infection contracted following a tonsillectomy. After he was on disability for a couple of years, Rose felt that her husband was dying. A doctor told her that his only chance of survival was to live in the sun. So the Rubins picked up and moved to Miami, Florida. After just a few months there, Morris completely recovered.

My grandfather was a little man with a huge force of personality and tremendous commercial instincts. His arrival in Miami coincided with a big Florida land boom and he quickly made a good deal of money speculating in real estate with large leverage. For a short time in the 1920s, Morris Rubin was a wealthy man. Then came the Florida land bust, which preceded the stock market crash of 1929 by a couple of years and wiped him out. This was an enormous psychological blow. In 1930, he arrived at my father's Columbia Law School graduation unshaven and unkempt, having driven from Miami with a pistol in the glove compartment of his Chevy. Financially ruined and distraught that he couldn't help his eldest son open a law office in New York, he couldn't decide whether to attend my father's graduation or shoot himself.

This story makes Morris Rubin sound like someone for whom financial success was terribly important. But having gotten past that crisis some years before I was born, my grandfather developed an extraordinary sense of equanimity about his lost fortune. By the time I was a little boy, everyone knew him as an irrepressibly affectionate little man with a thick European accent and a joyful attitude toward life. He greeted everyone with a bear hug. Most days, Morris would be out in the garden in back of his house on Prairie Avenue, just a mile from ours in Miami, tending his mango and avocado trees. After his crisis, he still dabbled in the stock market and real estate. But he had somehow changed his way of thinking so that his happiness wasn't contingent on being wealthy or successful. My grandfather transformed himself into someone whose identity wasn't tied to his net worth. Though he would never again be rich, he didn't lament his losses. He had enough to live on, and there were greater pleasures in life.

My mother's family had been in the United States for many generations. My grandfather Samuel Seiderman was a lawyer, an investor in real estate, a political activist, and a major figure in his Brooklyn world. He knew everyone; his close friend Emanuel Celler was elected to Congress in the 1920s and remained there for five decades. My grandfather was also a founder of a synagogue in Crown Heights, where he lived. Samuel's wife, my grandmother Ella, presided over the proper Victorian house they built for themselves. Her parents, my great-grandparents, the Schneiders, had been very successful in their own right and lived in the house next door.

My grandfather Seiderman's great love was politics. He was closely involved with "Boss" John McCooey, the power broker who controlled Brooklyn's Democratic political machine for the first few decades of the century, through the Madison Democratic Club. At the club's headquarters in Crown Heights, McCooey would hold court several nights a week, receiving supplicants for jobs, union cards, health care, or other kinds of assistance. He dispensed favors and collected votes in return.

After McCooey died in 1934, he was succeeded by my grandfather's friend Irwin Steingut, the Speaker of the New York State Assembly and a close ally of New York's governor, Herbert Lehman. When Irwin Steingut died in 1952, his power and positions passed to his son Stanley Steingut. For many years, my grandfather ran the club for the Steinguts while they were away at the legislature in Albany. Family legend has my grandfather and his colleagues sitting around in the basement of what I remember as their enormous house at 750 Eastern Parkway and choosing judges.

My grandfather Seiderman died in 1958, when I was a sophomore in college, but his influence remained with me: he had made politics seem appealing and his example had helped seed my desire to become involved in the world. I always had a sense of my grandfather as a large presence in his community, mostly from my mother, who admired him enormously. My parents made the point that he was deeply engaged in politics but never dependent upon it financially, and they thought he was effective in his political work partly because he didn't need anything from it.

I remembered this years later when I became involved in politics, although my focus was on psychological rather than financial independence. Relying on politics for your sense of who you are greatly impedes your ability to remain true to yourself, your views, and your values. Feeling you can walk away allows you the freedom to decide how much to accommodate to the demands of a political environment. And financial freedom—though neither necessary nor sufficient—can help contribute to psychological autonomy.

My mother grew up in her father's Democratic political milieu. She saw Franklin D. Roosevelt inaugurated in Washington, D.C., in 1933—staying during her visit at the Jefferson Hotel, where I subsequently lived for my six and a half years in Washington. Unlike my father, my mother had a stable, cosseted childhood. The family was prosperous enough to send her on a trip to Italy during the summer of 1930—though by the time my grandparents died, the family money had been greatly diminished.

My mother met my father at a dance at the Waldorf-Astoria hotel in 1933. As he tells the story, he was there with a law client of his who was being honored for a large donation he was giving to a hospital. He and his client were sitting at the head table, and the client was saying that he had made a big mistake by not marrying. My father should avoid such a mistake—in fact, he should ask this young woman sitting nearby to dance. My father looked at the woman and said he didn't feel like dancing.

Then he looked up at the balcony and saw my mother. "Now, there's a girl I'd like to dance with," he told his client. My mother's father, who was also at the head table, overheard this remark.

"You'd like to dance with that young lady?" Samuel Seiderman said. "That's my daughter."

My parents are in some ways an example of opposites attracting. My mother has a positive outlook and a comfortable sense of self. When problems arise, her attitude is that everything will work out for the best. My father has a strong and incisive analytic mind, and he is confident in what he does, but he is also something of a worrier. He doesn't like to leave important details to others, whether they're about business, health, or family. These descriptions are as accurate about them in their nineties as I gather they would have been in their thirties. They've been happily married, despite the differences in their outlooks on life, for nearly seventy years.

I WAS BORN IN 1938, when my parents were still living in Neponsit, Queens. When I was three, we moved to an apartment in Manhattan on West Eighty-first Street across from the American Museum of Natural History. I went to Walden School, a progressive private school on Central Park West, a few blocks from our apartment building. Walden stressed creative expression, cooperation, and social concern. It was the kind of place where the students called their teachers by their first names. My third grade teacher, whom I remember fondly, was Thora.

After graduating from Columbia Law School, my father joined the law firm of the father of one of his classmates, which became Rubin & Hetkin. The firm specialized in real estate but also had as a client *The New Yorker* magazine, whose board my father's partner came to join. My dad's specialty was challenging property-tax assessments. My father also kept a hand in what little was left of his father's businesses after the crash. One of these was a money-losing mica mining operation centered in the town of Sylva, North Carolina. Mica was an essential strategic mineral used as a wire insulator for airplanes. In the 1930s, it came cheaply from the East Indies and so wasn't worth much. But when World War II broke out in Europe, that supply was threatened. My father wrote to the War Department, offering to give the mines to the government for free. After Pearl Harbor, the War Department got in touch with my grandfather, asking him to go to North Carolina to run the mines. He volunteered my father, who had spent several summers working in the mines, and my father's job for the duration of the war became running the operation, supplying sheet mica to the government at a fixed price. When I was four, we moved to the nearby town of Asheville, North Carolina.

The North Carolina Highlands was a beautiful place, but poor and remote. The people in the town called my father "Jew man" and "Mr. Jew." It was a bit much for my mother, who felt as if she'd woken up in the wrong century. She rather quickly moved back to Manhattan with me and my sister, Jane, who was born in 1942. My father would come home by train every few weeks for a visit. The mining operation roughly broke even, and my grandfather sold it for a pittance after the war.

When I was nine, we moved from Manhattan to Miami Beach, Florida meant a calmer, more pleasant life for my father, who also wanted to be nearer to his father. After we moved, he continued to do some legal work, built a shopping center, studied stocks and investments, and played golf. My mother also played, and she had a shelf full of local club trophies.

I have only dim memories of not wanting to change homes and of trepidation about my new school. At North Beach Elementary, my new teacher, Miss Collins, introduced me as the new boy. "Robbie Rubin has gone to a private school in New York and has never learned script," she announced to the class. "So let's all be very nice to him." As a result, I assume, of this suggestion, I was elected president of my fourth-grade class on my first day. My protests that I didn't know how to be class president fell on deaf ears. Far-fetched though it may sound, I think you can draw a line from that day to my becoming Secretary of the Treasury forty-eight years later. I wasn't the class president type, but in a funny way the designation stuck with me. Though I was never a class leader, I held class positions intermittently throughout my school years, including senior class president—which later helped me get into Harvard, and so on down the line.

For a kid like me, Miami Beach was an easy place to grow up. I rode my bike a mile to school every morning and added to my enormous collection of painted lead soldiers. For a while, I had a morning paper route delivering *The Miami Beach Sun.* I read Hardy Boys mysteries and listened to *The Lone Ranger, The Phantom,* and *The Shadow* on the radio. I was a regular participant in basketball and baseball games at Polo Park. To this day, I can summon the starting lineup of the 1954 Brooklyn Dodgers: Roy Campanella, Gil Hodges, Jackie Robinson, Pee Wee Reese, Carl Furillo, Duke Snider, Junior Gilliam, Don Hoak, and whoever might be pitching— Don Newcombe, Preacher Roe, or Carl Erskine.

The rabbi at our temple was an interesting man named Leon Kronish, who tried to get a group of us involved in Jewish thought when I was a junior in high school. Rabbi Kronish told us he didn't believe in God in a conventional sense. His point wasn't to shock us, but rather to engage us in ethical and philosophical debate. Those discussions were my first exposure to the term "humanism." But more than any specific ideas, what I took away from talking to Rabbi Kronish was a sense of questioning and of intellectual exploration—qualities that would become core to my being in later years.

People seldom think of Miami Beach as being part of the Deep South. Yet, growing up, my sister, Jane, and I attended segregated schools and our Woolworth's had "colored" and "white" water fountains. Jane registered her protest by drinking from the "colored" water fountain and sitting in the back of the bus. I can't remember ever hearing expressions of racial prejudice from the people I grew up with, but neither was there any evident awareness of the immense injustice being done to so many.

My parents are sociable and always had a large circle of friends in Miami Beach. They enjoyed the kind of social life that was then normal there, playing golf and cards and spending time at the cabana club at the Roney Plaza Hotel. Yet both of them are thinking people, interested in politics and the wider world. We always had a lot of books around the house.

Then as now, I was an avid and eclectic reader. Even at the busiest times, when I was at Goldman Sachs or in Washington, reading has been an integral part of my daily life—history, biography, unusual voyages or lands, or whatever caught my imagination at our local bookstore. For example, not too long ago, I picked up Adam Nicolson's history of the King James Version of the Bible, which provided a graphic look at an era and described a deep commitment by many people, and Simon Winchester's book about the creation of the *Oxford English Dictionary*. I'm usually reading two or three books at the same time and often go back and reread parts of books. When I went down to Washington to join the Clinton administration in 1993, for instance, I took with me two famous books about Africa that I'd read a decade earlier: *The White Nile* and *The Blue Nile* by Alan Moorehead, as well as *Philosopher's Holiday*, a collection of lively essays by Irwin Edman, which I first read as a teenager. Edman was a professor of philosophy at Columbia when my father was a student there in the 1920s.

By the time I entered Miami Beach Senior High School, I had begun to fish. My friend Bobby Birenbaum and I used to fish in creeks and canals—mostly in places that are dense with hotels and condominiums now. As we got a bit older, we took our rods and tackle all over the place. Most often, we'd drive down to the Florida Keys. The Keys were different then—we could fish off the old bridges for mangrove snapper and sometimes catch something more exotic. My mom didn't want our fish in the house, but when we caught enough, we'd sell them to a local smokehouse for pocket money.

Fishing became a much more important part of my life in the late 1980s, when I first visited Deep Water Cay on Grand Bahama Island and saw people casting with fly rods. Fly fishing has been a passion of mine ever since—it gives me a feeling of total absorption and removal from the here and now. I can spend eight hours stalking bonefish on the saltwater flats in the Bahamas, or casting to trout on a river or creek, and the time just disappears. My mind focuses completely on the wind, the water, what kind of flies to use, and where to cast. Whatever external concerns I bring with me quickly evaporate.

Back in Florida, we fished with old-fashioned spinning rods. On weekends, Bobby and I would sometimes rent a small skiff with a 10- or 15-horsepower engine to cast for barracudas and dolphin in the Gulf Stream. Or we'd go around the mangrove swamps and back into the Everglades to fish for snapper or sea trout. Once we motored far in and then ran out of gas. Instead of the motel where we expected to be sleeping, we spent the night in the boat, fighting off mosquitoes and wondering how we were going to get back to civilization. The next day, the people we'd rented our boat from sent out a search party that found us. Luckily, no one phoned my parents until after we'd been rescued.

ANYONE WHO IS HONEST about having done well will acknowledge the enormous role played by chance. Chance certainly played a big part in my getting into Harvard. My grades were good but not outstanding, and I came from a regular public high school. I've always had the feeling, though with no substantiating evidence, that a particular fortuitous incident may have made the difference. My father and I ran into a lawyer he knew at a Harvard Glee Club concert. And this friend of my father's introduced me to his friend, the Harvard dean of admissions, who was passing through Miami.

When I arrived at Harvard in the fall of 1956, I felt overwhelmed. Half my class came from academically intense prep schools that were feeding grounds for the Ivy League. And much of the other half came from top-notch public high schools. I, on the other hand, had taken four years of French in high school, and when I got to Harvard I couldn't pass the exam to get out of the entry-level course. In math, I couldn't even get into the entry-level course because I hadn't had calculus, and I had to take reme-dial math.

On the first day of orientation the freshman class met in Memorial Hall. The dean of freshmen tried to reassure us by saying that only 2 per-cent of our class would fail out. I looked around and thought that every-one else was lucky, because I was going to fill the entire quota by myself. One of the first people I met was a kid from Staten Island whom I saw look-ing through the course catalogue. But he wasn't looking at courses. He was looking at the prizes listed at the end of the book, to see which ones he might win. I thought, *What a curious way to go through life.* I was looking through the same catalogue for courses I might be able to pass.

The dominant emotion of my freshman year at Harvard was anxiety. For solace, I read a little inspirational book that my dad sent me, *A Way of Life* by William Osler. The book was an address that Osler, a professor of medicine, had delivered to students at Yale in 1913. Osler's message was that the best way to deal with the fear of failure was to live your life in "day-tight compartments." At some point, you should climb to the "mountaintop" and engage in self-reflection. But on a daily basis, you should close the door to your larger worries and focus on the task at hand. I tried to take this advice and block out questions about whether I was ca-pable of doing the work at Harvard.

To everyone's surprise, especially mine, my grades that year were good—so good that my academic adviser called me in for a meeting. He asked if I was okay.

"Why shouldn't I be okay?" I asked him.

"Well," he responded, "you've done very well and nobody thought you would. Are you sure you're not overstraining yourself?"

Even after freshman year, I still had a tenuous feeling about being at Harvard. At the beginning of my second year, the teacher of an English

literature class was trying to figure out what books to assign that everyone hadn't already studied. He asked for a show of hands of those who
had read various books—classics of English literature by Charles Dickens,
George Eliot, and William Makepeace Thackeray. The other students,
graduates of places such as Groton, St. Paul's, and Andover, put up their
hands as he named more and more obscure titles by these authors. My
hands remained in my lap. It wasn't only that I hadn't read these books; I
had never even heard of most of them.

For most of those who came from prep school, Harvard was just the
next step in their intellectual development. For me, it was all so new, so
completely different, that I was forced to rethink everything. Sophomore
year, I took a yearlong introduction to philosophy course with Raphael
Demos. Professor Demos was a genial little Greek man with white hair
and a wonderful gift for engaging students in basic questions. His style
was unadorned simplicity. Demos would walk onto the stage in the lecture
hall, turn over a wastepaper basket on a desk, and use that as his lectern.
He communicated a feeling of vast respect for those philosophers he regarded as great thinkers, such as Plato, Aristotle, Kant, and Spinoza. Trying to understand what these authors were saying was very challenging
for me. Then, some way into our yearlong course, Professor Demos as-
signed the work of several authors whose thinking was not so rigorous.
They were easier to understand, but we quickly became aware of the fault
lines in their logic. We then went back to Aristotle and Kant with new appreciation for their intellectual power.

Although Demos revered philosophers such as Plato who believed in
provable certainty, he instilled in us the view that opinions and interpre-
tations were always subject to revision and further development. He
would turn to Plato or one of the other philosophers to demonstrate to us
that proving any proposition to be true in a final or ultimate sense was impossible. Demos encouraged us not only to understand the logic of the
analysis but to find the point at which the edifice rested on hypothesis, assumption, or belief.

These ideas struck a chord with me; I even considered majoring in philosophy. Although I didn't ultimately do that, my year with Demos
spurred my developing tendencies toward skepticism and critical think-

ing. I often encapsulate my Demos-inspired approach by saying, "There are no provable absolutes"—a stance bolstered by the larger Harvard ethos of that period. The mind-set among my classmates was one of not accepting dogma, of questioning authority—and in retrospect, I'd say the most valuable development I took away from college was the attitude of never taking propositions at face value, of evaluating everything I heard and read with an inquiring and skeptical mind. But the seed that Demos cultivated and that Harvard nurtured didn't lead to just skepticism. Once you've internalized the concept that you can't prove anything in absolute terms, life becomes all the more about odds, choices, and trade-offs. In a world without provable truths, the only way to refine the probabilities that remain is through greater knowledge and understanding.

Years later, when I discussed this with Alan Greenspan, he told me that the assertion "All is uncertain" is inherently contradictory because it asserts that uncertainty itself is certain. I didn't choose to debate the matter with Alan at the time, but one answer is that he was right—the basic assertion of uncertainty is unprovable. But that just leaves us back where we started—nothing is provably certain.

Academically, my plan at Harvard was conventional. Most people who were headed for law school, as I loosely assumed I was, majored in government. I started doing that and then switched to economics. In those days, the focus in economics was largely conceptual, and I found it difficult but engrossing; later, when the field had become much more rigorously econometric, I would not have had adequate math to major in it.

My senior honors-thesis tutor was Thomas Schelling, the economist famous for applying game theory to international relations and thereby explaining the doctrine of nuclear deterrence. Schelling had just come to Harvard from Yale, and I was his only tutee. I spent the summer between my junior and senior years in Cambridge with no job, sleeping on a broken couch in the living room of a shared apartment, and working on my thesis to get a head start. Researching and writing in the stacks of Widener Library every day were among the few projects I really enjoyed at Harvard. My paper was about the relationship between inflation and economic development in Brazil—a subject that attracted me in part because Latin America seemed a potentially fruitful area for entrepreneurial involvement. I found plenty of data and analysis from English-language sources to test various hypotheses about inflation. In 1995, when I met the Brazilian finance minister, Pedro Malan, he'd done his research. He said that his ministry had looked up my Harvard thesis and that my conclusions were largely on the mark.

Socially, Harvard was made up of subcultures. I wasn't really a part of any of them, but I liked to think of myself as someone who hung around coffeehouses—which in those days didn't mean Starbucks but places with a bohemian atmosphere and not particularly good coffee. I didn't actually go to coffeehouses very much, but occasionally I would stop by the Club Mount Auburn 47 or some other club, where people would sit around and some would-be Joan Baez would sing. I liked the sit-around-and-ponder-the-issues-of-life atmosphere.

One of the intellectual movements swirling around in the coffeehouse culture of those days was existentialism, and I related to that in some way. But my version of existentialism didn't have much to do with whatever I read of existential philosophy. Instead, I would describe it as an internalized sense of perspective. During my years at Harvard, I developed a feeling that, on the one hand, the here and now mattered a great deal, while on the other hand, in the totality of time and space, in some ultimate sense, that significance shrinks. How much will anything that happens today matter a hundred thousand years from now? Somehow, this internalized duality allowed me to maintain an intense involvement in whatever I was doing, while at the same time retaining a sense of perspective and a feeling that I could always opt for an entirely different kind of life.

Not until senior year did I really develop some sense of belonging at Harvard. In reality, my anxiety proved to be unrealistic early on in my college career. But holding on to it, while detrimental in some ways, may have been useful in others. Worry, if it doesn't undermine you, can be a powerful driver. After thinking I wasn't going to cross the finish line, I graduated from Harvard in 1960 with the unexpected distinctions of Phi Beta Kappa and summa cum laude, as well as a summa minus on my senior thesis.

After graduation, I sent a tongue-in-cheek letter to the dean of admissions at Princeton, to which I had not been accepted four years earlier. "I imagine you track the people you graduate," I wrote. "I thought you might be interested to know what happened to one of the people you rejected. I just wanted to tell you that I graduated from Harvard summa cum laude and Phi Beta Kappa." The dean wrote me back, "Thank you for your note. Every year, we at Princeton feel it is our duty to reject a certain number of highly qualified people so that Harvard can have some good students too."

DURING MY SENIOR YEAR, I had applied to Harvard Law School as well as to the Harvard Ph.D. program in economics. I was admitted to both but couldn't decide which to do. In fact, I wasn't at all sure I wanted to do either, at least just then. I went back up to Cambridge in the fall and spent three days at the law school, but I wasn't ready to roll up my sleeves and cope with the stress of it after having just finished four intense years of college. Everyone else was buying books and looking serious, and that wasn't for me. So I went to speak to the assistant dean of the law school and told him that I was going to leave.

"You just started," he said. "You can't just drop out. You've taken a place somebody else could have had."

I told him that I was dropping out anyway.

"If you drop out, I won't readmit you unless there are some extenuating circumstances," the dean said.

We talked some more, and the dean said that if I'd go to see a psychiatrist and the psychiatrist said that I was making a reasonable decision, he would readmit me the following year.

So I went to see the psychiatrist. He told me that when he had been about to begin medical school, he had taken a year off instead and traveled abroad. He said that I was fine—but that perhaps the dean ought to come see him if he found what I wanted to do so troubling.

A few days before law school started, I had run into some college classmates who were on their way to England for a year. One was going to study at Oxford, which sounded appealing. I was too late to apply to

Oxford or Cambridge, but I discovered that I might still get into the London School of Economics for that year. I applied by cable, emphasizing my Harvard credentials. The LSE cabled back, accepting me. Then I called my parents and said I had a surprise for them. I was dropping out of law school and going to London.

The only impediment to my immediate departure was that I had to go home to Miami first to meet with a representative of my draft board. Graduate study provided a military service deferral, but the school had to be recognized. My interviewer at the draft board was a southern businessman of an earlier era.

"Well, I don't know anything about the London School of Economics," he said. "The trouble with boys of your race is they don't want to go to war."

"I have no objection to war," I told him obsequiously. "I just want to study at the London School of Economics."

"How do I know this is a respectable institution?" he said.

I offered to get him a letter. So the chairman of the Harvard Economics Department, Arthur Smithies, had to write a letter stating that the London School of Economics was a recognized academic institution.

Before arriving in England, I had never been abroad, unless you count one family trip to Mexico and an elementary school excursion to Cuba. My year in Europe was enormously enlarging—and I'd recommend a postcollege year abroad to anyone who has the opportunity. Just before I left, I had a conversation with a worldy woman in Miami who was a friend of my parents. She told me that I should just open my pores and absorb everything I could. And that, in some reasonable measure, was my approach.

Harvard was an American culture, albeit a cosmopolitan one with quite a few foreign students, especially in the graduate schools. The LSE, on the other hand, was a truly international culture, with students from all over, especially from Commonwealth, former Commonwealth, and soon-to-be former Commonwealth countries. I met Indians, Africans, Australians, and West Indians. The political spectrum these students represented was much wider than what I'd encountered previously. Many described themselves as socialists, reflecting the broad-based support socialism had in both the developed and developing worlds at that time. I thought then, as I do now, that the concept of state direction of economic activity and state ownership of economic resources was likely to be highly inefficient. But debates around those issues also helped form my own interest in the problems of poverty and income distribution.

Meeting people with experiences and opinions so different from what I'd been exposed to was mind-opening. Issues that people at Harvard took to be about standards of living and economics, my Third World friends took to be about dignity and respect as well. For instance, people from the developing world wanted their own steel mills and airlines in order to show that they were just as good as the English and Americans, despite arguments that this was an economically inefficient allocation of resources for low-wage countries. Such arguments were a lesson in how fundamentally different an issue can appear from different perspectives. But the more important lesson, which would strengthen for me as time went on, was the overwhelming importance of recognizing and respecting the dignity of the individual. That respect is a fundamental value in itself. And sensitivity to the basic psychological need for such recognition is also essential to dealing effectively with all sorts of management and policy problems, whether in running a Wall Street trading room or in constructing and implementing international economic policy.

I was enrolled in the LSE as what was delightfully known as an "occasional student." Working toward a certificate rather than a real degree, I had no real responsibilities at the university. I would go to lectures and write papers for a tutor, but I spent most of my time just talking to people. The sense of freedom was marvelous. In my lodgings on Earl's Court Road, I could make dinner at midnight, sleep late, and then wake up and read all day if I felt like it. Or I could go to a lecture that looked interesting and then meet a friend and play squash. I worked on my French, carrying a little vocabulary booklet with me on the Underground. I was also a bit of a political tourist, going for instance to a rally in Trafalgar Square for a protest of the assassination of Patrice Lumumba, who'd been elected Prime Minister of the Republic of Congo. I didn't join in the protest, just watched with interest.

I also got to know an international crowd of people my age who lived in the neighborhood around Earl's Court Road. There were some faux aristocrats and a few real ones from places like Malta and Poland. With my LSE friends, I sat around and talked about politics, economic systems, and the meaning of life. With the Earl's Court crowd I went to parties, and once boating on the Thames. I went to Austria as part of an inter-university ski trip with students from Oxford, Cambridge, and Trinity College Dublin—the first and last time I skied. At the same time, I also continued to explore—in my own limited way—the strain within me that identified with the beat generation and its expatriate predecessors of the 1920s and '30s in Paris. I read a bit of Jack Kerouac and a lot of Henry Miller, which seemed especially fitting in Paris over the six-week-long Christmas vacation. I checked into a cheap hotel on the Left Bank, where some people I knew from Harvard were staying. During the day, I'd go to cafés and sit around talking or reading.

I've always thought—probably quite incorrectly—that if my life had taken a different turn, I could have lived the kind of life that those weeks in Paris, or the pre-1960s coffeehouse culture of Cambridge, represented. As the years went by, even as I became part of the establishment, I continued to feel that I could always opt out of the system if I wanted to. I could just say good-bye, put on a pair of frayed khakis, and check into a little hotel in St.-Germain-des-Prés. People who have never seen me without a pinstripe suit may find this somewhat incongruous, but I felt then, and feel even now, that I could comfortably opt for a more relaxed, unstructured existence. That feeling may not be realistic, but my belief in this possibility has been a mental escape hatch in times of pressure. At stressful times in my career, I've returned to that idea of sitting around in cafés, reading, and having long discussions about philosophy and life. Sometimes even now I think I could just spend my life fishing, reading, and playing tennis.

Over Easter I went to Italy, and in the summer I drove around Norway, Denmark, and Sweden with a friend named David Scott. I was considering the possibility of staying in Europe for another year when I read a passage by a onetime expatriate, who wrote something to the effect that "if you're abroad too long, you start to rot." That, combined with the possibility that my parents wouldn't be too keen to underwrite another year of undirected foreign activity, made me think it might be time to come home. I said good-bye to Europe when David's red Austin Healey was stolen in Frankfurt while we were having lunch.

Part of the reason I had such a good time living abroad was that I wasn't particularly worried about the future. In the back of my mind, I knew I would probably go to law school, either at Harvard or at Yale, where I had also applied and been accepted. I didn't necessarily want to be a lawyer, but law school seemed to keep a lot of options open. Thanks to that psychiatrist, Harvard had readmitted me. But I ended up enrolling at Yale, which seemed broader and more interesting, and also less intense. My idea, which was somewhat of an exaggeration, was that at Harvard Law School you sit around and discuss contracts and at Yale you sit around and discuss the meaning of good and evil.

IN FACT, my experience at Yale Law School, where I enrolled in the fall of 1961, did have some of that quality. In addition to classes and the library, I spent a lot of time discussing issues ranging from the Vietnam War to the nature of the good life. In law school, I had more than ample opportunity to apply the view I had developed at Harvard that all propositions were, when driven back to their core, unprovable. You can have strong moral beliefs developed through your upbringing or education, or through intense religious faith, but none of them are provable.

You can never tell who may come along in life to influence you. Early in my first year, I ran into a third-year student, George Lefcoe, whom I had met briefly when we both lived in Miami. He stopped his bicycle on the street during orientation week to offer me a bit of upperclassman's advice. George said that doing well in law school was important because it brought recognition, and recognition brought happiness.

I thought that understanding of human nature had the disadvantage of being wrong. "You're telling me that doing well and getting recognition makes you feel good," I responded. "But my experience is that it doesn't work that way." I told George that I had graduated from Harvard with strong credentials, which had brought one kind of satisfaction, but not the feeling of wholeness or fulfillment he was describing.

Years later, I would still be making the same point in job interviews at Goldman Sachs. When I'd ask interviewees why they wanted to work for us, the more honest ones would admit that at least part of the reason was to make money. I cautioned that they would find that making a lot of money might satisfy them in some ways but wouldn't fulfill whatever had driven them to want that money in the first place. Few of them paid any attention. But years later, some of them came to me after doing very well financially to complain of being bored or unsatisfied with their lives.

Every place I've worked—Goldman Sachs, the White House, Treasury, and now Citigroup—I've seen people who seem to be seeking the Promised Land of satisfaction through some kind of position or accomplishment. Most often, what I was trying to say to George Lefcoe all those years ago still seems to me to have held true. The only place people find fulfillment is within themselves. And too often, that's the last place they look.

That argument with George was the beginning of a yearlong dialogue. We spent endless hours walking the streets of New Haven, talking about law, philosophy, and life. George had a much more developed philosophy than I did at that age, and he loved to be cynical and provocative. Another participant in some of these conversations was Leon Brittan, a graduate of Cambridge University who was studying at Yale on a fellowship. After returning home, Leon went on to become a prominent Tory politician. The three of us once took an especially long walk in New Haven, with George arguing that reading fiction was a waste of time because whatever was gained could be learned more efficiently from nonfiction. Leon responded that fiction can often capture reality better than nonfiction. The argument became heated, and although my view was closer to Leon's, I tried to keep the peace.

George sympathized with an approach to legal analysis called legal realism, which was very influential in shaping the ethos of Yale at that time. Legal realism held that the language of statutes or prior decisions didn't dictate outcomes because it could be interpreted in different ways. Judges' decisions were a product of policy views, beliefs, biases, and all sorts of subjective influences—the famous formulation being that decisions were dictated by what the judge had eaten for breakfast that morning. With this approach, you'd consider the statute, the facts of the case, and a judicial decision. When you asked whether the language of the statute had dictated the decision the judge had made, the answer would almost always be no. The words of the statute could fit two or more different conclusions. Legal realism was another way of challenging certainties and reexamining assumptions, and the atmosphere at Yale furthered my own intellectual development along these lines.

At Yale, I made a group of lasting friends who also enjoyed lengthy discussions of the issues of the world. Leon Brittan, for example, had a much more nuanced view of the earliest stages of the Vietnam War than anyone else I knew. He believed that the United States should stand up to communism but was afraid that our involvement would be so divisive as to create serious social disruptions at home, and that the negatives of American involvement might outweigh the positives. That was a remarkably astute analysis, especially in 1962.

Toward the end of my year at LSE, I had briefly met a junior at Wellesley named Judy Oxenberg, who was passing through London with a girl I'd been dating back at Harvard. They were on their way to spend a summer in France. When I arrived at their boardinghouse to take her friend out to dinner, Judy answered the door and I thought to myself, *My God, she's beautiful.* The next evening I fixed her up with a friend from Canada, and the four of us went out.

When Judy arrived at Yale to do graduate work in French, at the beginning of my second year at the law school, I invited her to dinner. Judy's real passion was for the performing arts, and, in addition to her French studies, she was taking classical voice lessons at the Yale School of Music. I decided that holding on to such an accomplished and attractive woman in the graduate environment of Yale—which in those days had few women—was unlikely. So I decided to fix Judy up with friends of mine, on the theory that they would return the favor by fixing me up with women more on my own level.

Luckily, that plan never went into effect and we ended up seeing each other exclusively. Judy had different interests from mine; she was immersed in theater, music, and literature, and in that context I was a bit of a heathen. But both of us shared something more important—a sense of curiosity about everything around us, from the people we knew to world affairs to the books the other person had read. We also tended to have the same reactions to people and shared a somewhat irreverent sense of humor. People's interests often evolve in unexpected ways. Over the years, Judy developed a good sense of politics and spent four years as New York City mayor David Dinkins's commissioner for protocol and friendly confidante. Meanwhile, I became a bit of a theatergoer. And there is something else we have in common: while both of us have led active civic lives, we are both relatively private people and have not taken much part in the social whirl.

By November, Judy and I were engaged. We were married that March, at the end of Easter break, in Branford Chapel at Yale. There were fourteen people at the wedding, including both sets of parents. We took a one-day honeymoon—borrowing a car from my law school classmate Steve Umin, whose devotion to music and theater matched Judy's and who has become a lifelong friend. The next day I was back in the library, preparing for exams.

I ENTERED LAW SCHOOL not really intending to practice law but feeling that it would be good training for whatever I might do and would help to keep open a broad array of options. I didn't have any career path in mind, but I had a vague sense of wanting to do something financial and entrepreneurial. In the back of my mind was the idea that I might eventually return home to Miami and go into the real estate business, perhaps drawing on my father's knowledge in some way. But I felt I should go to a big law firm for a time, to see what it was like. Lots of our friends were headed to New York, and Judy and I never really considered moving to any place else.

I interviewed at several firms, and decided to go to Cleary, Gottlieb, Steen & Hamilton because it had a more comfortable environment and was somewhat smaller than most major firms, but with an establishment practice. I thought the hours would be a little shorter, and Cleary had a reputation for paying higher bonuses in addition to the starting salary—

that year, $7,200—that was uniform across the major law firms, antitrust laws notwithstanding.

That wasn't much to live on, even in those days. Judy and I had to get help from my parents to pay the rent on what our landlady called a "garden" apartment—in reality a basement in Brooklyn Heights. But living in the city suited us. We spent a lot of time wandering around, going to restaurants and attending theater. Judy had some parts in musicals. The job at Cleary worked out well for me. I liked the people and the atmosphere, which did turn out to be relatively collegial and less formal than those of its counterparts. Working at such a firm also had a certain cachet; I liked being part of an establishment organization—a predilection that coexisted, for the most part peacefully, with my sporadic countercultural inclinations.

I worked as an associate at Cleary for two years, doing research for big litigation, tax analysis on an estate issue, and background work on some corporate matters. I saw how this type of law could be highly engaging, but it wasn't for me. Also, realistically or not, I figured my odds of making partner weren't great. I still wanted to do something more entrepreneurial and have the possibility of major financial reward. When I look back, I'm surprised that I wasn't more involved in the larger social and political issues of that time. In law school, I had engaged in endless discussions about Vietnam, civil rights, and problems of poverty. But it would be a few more years before I would become actively involved.

My career epiphany came while I was working, at a junior level, on behalf of a client called Hayden Stone, a Wall Street investment firm that no longer exists. Hayden Stone was the lead underwriter helping to take public a company called COMSAT. In meetings, the investment bankers were the ones figuring out how to do a big deal. *When I'm forty, I thought, I want to be doing what those guys are doing, not what we're doing.*

I had also begun to pay more attention to the stock market, applying in a limited way my father's highly analytical approach to investing. It was based on the method laid out by Benjamin Graham—probably best known for his disciple Warren Buffett—in *Security Analysis*, the classic book Graham wrote with David Dodd in 1934.

Graham and Dodd believed that, in the short term, the stock market is a "voting machine," reflecting emotion and fashion more than rationality, but over the long term, the stock market is a "weighing machine," valuing securities based on earnings prospects, assets, risks, and other fundamentals. They argue that you should invest only for the long term, and then only when the price is below the fundamental value calculated on the basis of these factors. My father analyzed securities this way and invested with the expectation of holding for a long time. If he sold a stock after only a few years, it indicated that something had gone wrong, or that the stock had risen so much as to be highly overvalued.

Today I believe even more strongly that this is the only sensible approach to investing in stocks. You should analyze the economic value of a share of stock the same way you would think about the economic value of the whole business. A stock, whether in a steel plant or in a high-tech firm, is worth the present value of the company's expected future earnings, adjusted for risk and for other fundamental factors such as hidden assets on the balance sheet. Over the long run, the price of a stock will reflect this economic value, although the price can deviate dramatically from it for an extended period. Investors seem to lose sight of this reality periodically, with predictable results. Most recently, a large number of people incurred huge losses by following fashion, rather than valuation, in the period leading up to the dot-com and telecom collapses of 2000 and 2001. A separate but related point is that the greatest opportunities often lie in going against trends.

As a way of thinking about the market, the Graham-Dodd approach also played to my Harvard skepticism. To look at the market and try to find securities whose prices didn't reflect prevailing views appealed to me. A well-established academic doctrine argues that markets are efficient, meaning that the price of a stock fully incorporates all known information and judgments about that stock. A corollary to this Efficient Market Theory is that nobody can outperform the market over time. But everything I've seen in my years on Wall Street—and a lot of more current thinking on finance theory—says that that is simply not so. By definition, most investors, even most professionals, are not going to be able to outperform the market. But a few will be able to, through some combination of better analysis, better judgment, and greater discipline.

All this interested me far more than the practice of law, so I sent my résumé to several investment firms. But I didn't receive a single response, not even a note. Back then, a law degree didn't mean much in the financial world. The dominant traders on Wall Street had gotten where they were on the basis of street smarts and savvy, while the investment bankers mostly came from society backgrounds or business schools. Moving from a law firm to an investment bank was a strange choice in those days. Although it was a step up in income—when I eventually found a job, my compensation went from less than $13,000 to $14,400 a year—some people told me that it was a step down on the social scale.

A month or so after my applications vanished into the void of Wall Street's leading firms, my father was in town and I had lunch with him and a stockbroker he knew. The stockbroker mentioned that he had a friend at Goldman Sachs who was looking for a junior associate. That turned out to be L. Jay Tenenbaum, the partner who ran Goldman's arbitrage department. So I went to meet L. Jay. Since I wanted to learn more about investing in companies, I told him that I was interested in either Goldman's research department or its corporate finance department. He very accommodatingly sent me over to both departments. But as I later learned, he told the people who interviewed me there to discourage me from those areas because he wanted to hire me for arbitrage.

Through another friend of my father's, I received a second introduction, which led to an offer from Lazard Frères to work in its arbitrage department. So by sheer coincidence, two firms offered me jobs doing something I'd never heard of. I had some doubts about whether I'd be suited to arbitrage. My understanding was that an arbitrageur, like a securities analyst, had to get on the phone and interview executives at companies about transactions. I wasn't sure I could be so audacious. But those were the two offers I had, and I wanted to try something new. I chose Goldman over Lazard mostly because Goldman was considered the top firm in the arbitrage field—Goldman's renowned partner, Gus Levy, had built the department—and also because the pay was slightly better.

In arbitrage, you might end up learning about subjects that a week before you'd known nothing about, such as political unrest in Libya, if that affected the prospects of a transaction involving one of the big oil

companies. One deal we analyzed was the proposed liquidation of a holding company called the Roan Selection Trust. When you bought the
stock, you were due to get about five or six different securities if the deal
went through. You got cash, a warrant on stock in an American mining
company, common stock in a Botswana mining company, and a Zambian
6 percent bond. We had to calculate not only the odds of the deal going
through but what value to attach to each of those pieces, and how to
hedge them to the fullest extent possible. When we first heard about the
liquidation, we didn't even know where Zambia was—because until a
couple of years earlier it had been called by its colonial name, Northern
Rhodesia. So one of the fellows on the trading desk called the consulate
and asked, "Where are you?"

"Fifty-seventh and Madison," came the reply.

And our trader said, "No, I mean where is your country?"

L. Jay Tenenbaum, who taught me the business, wasn't intending to
stay at Goldman Sachs forever. He was trying to clear the way for his own
eventual retirement, even though he was only forty-four when he hired
me. And his deputy, Bob Lenzner, who went on to a distinguished career
in financial journalism, left shortly after I came. So everything sort of fell
into place for me. If L. Jay had wanted all the credit for himself, he could
have hidden me under a bushel. Instead, L. Jay looked out for my interests,
and took every opportunity to promote my career with his partners at the
firm until he retired in 1976. L. Jay took great pride in helping younger
people he respected advance in the firm. Later, I felt exactly the same way
when I had the opportunity to help talented people who worked with me
at Goldman and in Washington.

L. Jay had learned the arbitrage trade as a gofer working for Gus Levy,
who was an almost mythical figure by the time I joined the firm. Gus had
grown up in New Orleans and had had to drop out of Tulane to help support his family when his mother could no longer pay the tuition. He'd
made his way from being a Wall Street messenger to a job in the bond department at Goldman Sachs during the Depression. From those humble
origins, he became the heir apparent to Sidney Weinberg, the legendary
figure who had steered Goldman Sachs since the 1930s. Gus became a
legend in his own right—senior partner of Goldman Sachs, chairman of

the New York Stock Exchange, a major Republican fund-raiser, and a pillar of many New York civic institutions. What his list of accomplishments doesn't fully explain is that from the mid-1960s until his death in 1976, Gus was almost surely the single most important person on Wall Street.

In the 1950s, Gus was one of the inventors not only of risk arbitrage, but also of block trading for institutional clients. Before that, an institutional investor who wanted to sell 50,000 shares of Coca-Cola—a small block by today's standards—would sell them piecemeal on the open market, putting downward pressure on the price of the stock. Gus's innovation was for Goldman to buy a whole block of shares, which might cost $10 million or $20 million, with customer commitments to buy some of the block and the rest taken into inventory for subsequent resale. The firm would take more risk by actually owning some of the stock on its books for a time. Per-share profit may have turned out to be lower, but Goldman's trading volume and market share increased tremendously.

L. Jay and Gus were both men with tempers, which was pretty normal for trading rooms in those days, when most of the familiar Wall Street names were private, a large firm had a few hundred people at most, and few traders had college degrees. The environment was highly entrepreneurial and often seat-of-the-pants. For Gus, management was accomplished by yelling—all day long. The legend was that a decade earlier, he would regularly fire everyone in his office at the end of the day—but they'd all be back at work the next morning.

By the time I got to know him, Gus had calmed down somewhat, but he was still quite a challenge. He had a sliding glass window in his office that looked out onto the trading floor at the old Goldman office at 20 Broad Street. Gus would slam open the window and bark out orders— or abuse, if he found out that Salomon Brothers had done more block trades than we had that day. Then the window would slam shut again. I once started explaining something to Gus with the words "I assume . . ." "Don't assume anything!" he barked at me. "Find out!" Or he'd snap, "Do it now, you may not be able to later!" Of course, anyone might make such a comment. But coming from Gus, with his enormous intensity, such admonitions burned themselves into my soul, and I cite them to this day. Another time, soon after I'd arrived at Goldman, Gus called me into his office to discuss a memo I'd written proposing an arbitrage transaction. He dismissed it with a one-sentence remark that I didn't understand. When I asked him what he meant, he snapped back, "We don't have time for on-the-job training here."

Gus also had enormous charm, which he would employ with the firm's clients. One of the few times I was invited to a dinner at his apartment, he was hosting the visiting chairman of a major corporation. To hear Gus talk, you would think the chairman was the greatest genius in the history of American business and Gus's best friend. But I'd heard Gus heap similar accolades on other CEOs. In a taxi on the way home, I asked Ray Young, one of the firm's senior partners, "Ray, do you think Gus will remember those comments the next time he says the same thing to another big client?" Ray answered that Gus was being absolutely sincere— he meant everything he said when he was saying it. For that evening, the CEO in question was the center of his universe. That's why Gus's charm was so effective. Many years later, I met another person who had that kind of ability to focus his attention completely on someone without being insincere. That other person, even more persuasive in such moments, was Bill Clinton.

Despite his temper, Gus was a great leader who was truly supportive when times were tough. About individual transactions he could go absolutely crazy, as he did when we lost more than half a million dollars on the Becton Dickinson–Univis deal. "Anybody could have seen that was going to happen!" he'd shout. But those of us in the trading room knew that at the end of the day he would be fair about compensation and promotions. Gus understood that we were in a risk-reward, probability-based business and that a trader would do badly at times, either because the dice came up wrong or because people make mistakes. That made Goldman Sachs an environment where you could take rational risks. With all the ranting and raving—and there was a lot of it—in the final analysis, Gus supported risk taking and assessed people fairly based on their overall performance.

Gus himself was famously superstitious. You could hear him coming on the trading floor because of the "lucky" coins jangling in his pocket. Although one of his mantras was "It's better to be lucky than smart," Gus didn't rely on luck. He began his workday at 5:00 in the morning and got to the office before 7:30, well ahead of everyone else—a point he was kind enough to remind us of from time to time—and then went to client dinners or charitable events every night. After Gus died, I always regretted that I'd never asked him what he, driving himself all day long every day, thought life was all about. I don't know if he would have had an answer, but one answer I don't think he would have given was money. By the time I knew him, he didn't need more for practical purposes, and I don't think his sense of self resided there. In fact, he gave away much of what he made.

The big crisis in those years was the Penn Central bankruptcy, which hit in 1970, the year after Sidney Weinberg died and Gus's first year as senior partner. Goldman had sold commercial paper—short-term debt instruments—on behalf of the Penn Central railroad. When the railroad surprised everyone by declaring bankruptcy, investors who had bought Penn Central's paper accused us of inadequate disclosure—because of negligence or intentional failure—about the company's financial condition. The bondholders sued us for an amount that exceeded our capital. The claims may have been weak but they were not frivolous, and the partners' entire net worth was at stake. I was not yet a partner, but I had ideas about how to respond to this crisis and told Gus, though this may have been presumptuous given my limited experience, that I thought we should consider whether our regular outside counsel was well suited to the rough-and-tumble of a jury trial. He decided to stay with our regular counsel, but to use a different lead litigating partner than would ordinarily have done our work, someone who was better suited to this situation. Thereafter, he used me occasionally as something of an unofficial adviser. That was my first experience dealing with a critical institutional crisis. Since then I've had to help manage through a number of these events, not just at Goldman Sachs but later in Washington and at Citigroup.

For a period of more than a year, Penn Central created immense anxiety at Goldman. As a private partnership, we faced unlimited liability, and some people worried whether the firm would survive. When the firm's outside counsel, Sullivan & Cromwell, provided a letter saying it didn't think damage payments would materially impair our capital, Gus carried it in his jacket pocket as a kind of talisman. I thought of that letter when I had to face the same concern about the firm's survival after one of our partners was charged during the insider trading scandal of the 1980s and we obtained a similar letter from Wachtell Lipton, our counsel. In the end, the Penn Central matter was settled on terms that the firm could absorb. In fact, the settlement cost Goldman Sachs less than we eventually made in risk-arbitrage trades involving claims in the Penn Central bankruptcy.

Although some people found Gus impossible—and at times he *was* impossible—he was a giant figure for all of us who worked with him, and I still think of him often. He was less difficult with me than with the trading-room partners more directly under him—possibly because I was younger. After he died, Larry Tisch, a friend of his, told me that Gus had thought I'd run the firm someday—an idea that seemed far-fetched to me at the time.

Why did the arbitrage work at Goldman suit me? I think that there is an emotional answer and an intellectual answer, though the two are connected. The emotional answer is that my temperament was simply a good fit. Arbitrage was enormously intense; people at the firm used to think the stress was overwhelming and could drive a person insane. And there was immense pressure. But I was able both to apply myself intensely and, at the same time, to maintain a reasonable degree of equanimity. In my mind was the notion that I could walk away if I had to and go back to cafés on the Left Bank and read Henry Miller. Another calming thought was that a thousand years hence, no one would care whether some deal had gone through or whether my arbitrage career had worked out. Meanwhile, I was glad that other people at Goldman Sachs thought my job was so pressured. It meant respect from my colleagues, even though we traders didn't have to work at night like the investment bankers.

The intellectual answer relates to the questioning and probabilistic mind-set I started developing at Harvard. In 1975, a colleague of mine at another firm explained an investment that he believed to be a sure bet. He was making a massive purchase of shares of Anaconda, a mining company whose shares were to be bought by Crane, another company that wanted to enter the copper business. I agreed that the proposed deal looked extremely likely to reach closure. However, not believing in certainties, only in probabilities, I made a large investment, but with a loss potential Goldman could readily absorb in the highly unlikely event the deal didn't go through. Then the unexpected did happen—antitrust issues blocked the merger, and the deal fell apart. We took a big loss. But my friend took an unacceptably large loss, which included his job.

My approach grew from my basic makeup, from Raphael Demos's approach to philosophy and my whole Harvard experience, from my debates with George Lefcoe in New Haven, and the ethos of Yale Law School. In arbitrage, as in philosophy, you analyze, look for holes in the analysis, and seek conclusions that hold together. However, while analytic rigor may be sufficient for philosophy, it's not enough for arbitrage. In arbitrage—as in policy making—you also have to be able to pull the trigger, even when your information is imperfect and your questions can't all be answered. You have to make a decision: Should I make this investment or not? You begin with probing questions and end having to accept that some of them will be imperfectly answered—or not answered at all. And you have to have the stomach for risk.

As well as my career was going at Goldman during my first several years there, I nevertheless felt that my prospects for partnership were slight. I thought I'd make some money, learn a good deal, and take my newfound skills to a smaller place to capitalize on them. But then life took one of its unexpected twists. In 1970, I was recruited by White Weld, one of the old-line Wall Street firms. A friend from law school worked there, which led the company to interview me when the fellow who ran its arbitrage department left. I called my parents and told them about the offer, which I assumed I would take. My father was unhappy about my leaving Goldman Sachs. "Maybe they'll offer you a partnership," my father said. "Dad," I said, "you just don't understand. They're not going to offer me a partnership at Goldman Sachs." Becoming a partner of the Goldman of that time was like catching the brass ring—a very low probability bet.

So I went to speak with L. Jay, who was upset that I might leave. And he went to Gus Levy. Gus wasn't happy about having to deal with this problem, but after consulting with the firm's management committee, he came back and offered to make me a partner at the end of the year. I was, to say the least, surprised. Becoming a partner at Goldman Sachs was not in what I considered the realm of realistic expectations. But on the first day of fiscal 1971, I found that I was one.

CHAPTER THREE

Inside and Outside Goldman Sachs

T HE IMAGE OF my grandfather Samuel Seiderman's life was very powerful in forming my own ideas of how I wanted to live mine. My grandfather was successful professionally and financially, and he had a recognized and respected place in his community. His broad range of involvements—especially in politics—made his life more varied and interesting.

Gus Levy was another model of a multifaceted, externally engaged professional life. Gus's day job was running Goldman Sachs, but he had worlds outside the firm. Gus served as chairman of the board at Mount Sinai Medical Center, sat on the boards of cultural organizations such as Lincoln Center and the Museum of Modern Art, and was a major fundraiser for and confidant of Republican politicians. His range of friends and contacts was enormous; Gus knew, or appeared to know, everyone who was anyone in business and politics, including President Richard Nixon and New York Governor Nelson Rockefeller. "There are really six Gus Levys," the CEO of a major bank said. "At night they put on their tuxedos and fan out around the city." I had no desire to emulate Gus's peripatetic social life. But I was drawn to the kind of career that enabled Gus to contribute to causes that he cared about and earned him the same sort of place in his much larger world that my grandfather had in his. The various facets of Gus's life were synergistic, with efforts in one area contributing to accomplishments in others. The variety of his involvements gave his career a meaning beyond the considerable achievements in his day job.

A third example for me was Bernard J. "Bunny" Lasker, a legendary arbitrageur of Gus's generation. Despite an almost thirty-year age gap and vastly different political and social views, Bunny and I became close friends; perhaps, in some fundamental respects, we were on the same wavelength. A self-made man who had started on Wall Street as a messenger, Bunny was a vivacious, larger-than-life figure—one of those people who fill up a room just by entering it. Some people looked askance at Bunny because he lacked a certain polish, but that didn't mean he wasn't smart. Bunny never went to college, but he had a practical sense that Harvard Business School cannot teach. I used to say that if Bunny and our best MBA simultaneously started from the same point in a race that involved complicated practicalities, Bunny would run the course, have dinner, go to bed, and get up the next morning before his credentialed competitor reached the finish line.

Like his good friend Gus, Bunny knew everybody and was deeply involved in what he called the three great passions of his life—the Republican Party, the New York Stock Exchange, and West Point, where he served as a trustee despite having been rejected in his youth. He guided the New York Stock Exchange through hazardous times as chairman in 1970, when the investing public's confidence was probably at its lowest level since the Depression. Richard Nixon publicly credited Bunny with saving his career by persuading him not to try for the presidency again in 1964, when Nixon almost certainly could not have won.

Another person I sometimes think of as a professional role model was someone I never met: Armand Erpf, a partner in the then well-established investment banking firm Loeb, Rhoades and Company, who was involved in an array of cultural and civic activities. I remember reading an article in *The New York Times* in 1967, shortly after I started at Goldman Sachs, about a chair being established in Erpf's name at Columbia Business School. "My main interest is Loeb, Rhoades," Erpf said. "After all, everything starts from there."

That's it, I thought when I saw the story, which crystallized a thought that had previously been inchoate in my mind. And in fact, Erpf's line is not a bad description of my life over the next two decades, or at least what I tried to make it. Goldman Sachs was my fundamental and overriding involvement. From that strong base, I was able to reach out in various directions—nonprofit and charitable organizations, professional associations, politics, and, eventually, a second career in Washington.

Until the end of 1992, when I left Wall Street to join the Clinton administration, my inside and outside careers ran on parallel tracks. Inside Goldman Sachs, I was learning not only about markets, finance, and economics but also about management and human nature. Outside Goldman Sachs, I was learning about management and human nature in a variety of other contexts. These two careers developed side by side, each contributing to the other. Over many years, in a variety of disparate settings and institutions—Goldman Sachs, the White House, Treasury, Citigroup, Mount Sinai Medical Center, and the Harvard Corporation—what I learned in one place about working with people and how they think and react usually held true in another.

THE ANALYTIC MIND-SET I further developed doing arbitrage led me to look for inefficiencies or discrepancies elsewhere in the relative value of different related securities, and thus to the arcane business of stock options. Like arbitrage, options trading is a risk-reward, probability-based business, although more directly quantitative. At the time, even most people on Wall Street knew little about it. I read quite a bit on the topic, including a newsletter about opportunities in warrants. A warrant, similar to a "call option," is a security that conveys the right to purchase a share of stock at a set price for some period of time, usually a certain number of years.

One article in the newsletter said that warrants in Phillips Petroleum were overpriced—based on valuation models—relative to the price of the Phillips stock. That created an opportunity in what is often called relative value arbitrage or relationship trading. Relative value arbitrage means going long one instrument—a security or a derivative—and short another related instrument, when one of these instruments is considered undervalued relative to the other. The bet you're making is that the prices of the two instruments will return to their proper relationship and provide a profit from that movement. The instruments might be a common stock or bond and a "derivative"—an option or future that is convertible into the underlying stock or bond on some basis.

Not yet a partner at that point, I wrote a complicated memo recommending that we go short the Phillips warrants and long the common stock, betting that the price of the warrants would go down relative to the price of the stock. I gave the memo to L. Jay, who agreed with the recommendation. The warrants were overpriced relative to the stock, but the short position could still lose money if the stock price rose, so that the long position was an essential hedge. With that hedge, one would make a profit regardless of what happened to the price of the stock, as long as the discrepancy in relative value disappeared. L. Jay gave my memo to Gus, and Gus called me in.

"Ahh, I don't want to do all that," Gus said of my proposal to hedge. "Let's just go short the warrants."

"Gus," I said, "you know we have to be hedged."

Gus responded with a five-word sentence conveying that he didn't care about hedging, didn't care about my memo, and didn't care about explaining the matter—because if I didn't know this stuff, I shouldn't be at the firm in the first place.

I went back to L. Jay, concerned about what to do. L. Jay said, "You better just go short the warrants, if that's what Gus wants to do." So we went short the Phillips warrants, and fortunately the stock didn't run up while we were holding the position.

The same thinking that drew me to that transaction—and a lifelong tendency to restlessly reach into new areas—led me to other kinds of options. Stock options—instruments that allow, but do not require, an investor to buy shares at a prearranged price during a fixed period of time—had long existed but had always been extremely illiquid. To buy an option, you went to one of several small put-and-call houses, which ran ads in the newspapers and had a slightly questionable reputation. They traded options "over the counter," which meant not listed on any exchange. Prices were nontransparent, to say the least. I thought that perhaps relative value arbitrage transactions could be done against these over-the-counter options. As I became increasingly involved, I saw that Goldman Sachs might well do what the put-and-call houses did—trade stock options directly with our clients, other brokerage firms, and the options dealers themselves.

My proposal met some resistance at the firm. During the Depression, stock options had led to vast losses on Wall Street. As a result, I was told, Sidney Weinberg had a rule against Goldman Sachs being involved with them. But by the time I first discussed this with Gus, Mr. Weinberg had died. At the end of our conversation, Gus said, in his gruff way, "If you want to get involved with options, go ahead," and he got my proposal approved by the firm's management committee.

Options are one type of derivative—a security, such as a warrant or a future, whose price depends on the price of an underlying instrument like a common stock or bond—and this was the beginning of Goldman Sachs's trading in derivatives on securities. That business eventually became massive at our firm and across Wall Street as ever more new instruments developed that were based on equities, debt, and foreign exchange. But at the time, the options business was still at a primitive stage. Traders grasped that prices of options should reflect the volatility of the stock but as yet had no system for calculating values. However, an unpublished paper by Fischer Black and Myron Scholes was circulating that detailed a valuation formula based on volatility. For their work on option pricing, Scholes and another colleague, Robert Merton, won a Nobel Prize in 1997. Sadly, Fischer Black died too soon to share it.

The now famous Black-Scholes formula was my first experience with the application of mathematical models to trading, and I formed both an appreciation for and a skepticism about models that I have to this day. Financial models are useful tools. But they can also be dangerous because reality is always more complex than models. Models necessarily make assumptions. The Black-Scholes model, for example, assumes that future volatility in stock prices will resemble past volatility. I later recruited Fischer away from a full professorship at MIT to Goldman, and he subsequently told me that his Goldman experience caused him to develop a more complex view of both the value and the limitation of models. But a trader could easily lose sight of the limitations. Entranced by the model, a trader could easily forget that assumptions are involved and treat it as definitive. Years later, traders at Long-Term Capital Management, whose partners included Scholes and Merton themselves, got into trouble by using models without adequately allowing for their shortcomings and getting heavily overleveraged. When reality diverged from their model, they lost billions of dollars, and the stability of the global financial system might have been threatened.

What made options trading possible on a large scale was the Chicago Board Options Exchange, the first listed market for stock options, which opened in 1973. The key was the creation of standardized terms for the listed options and a clearing system, so that options could trade in a secondary market. I remember Joe Sullivan, the first head of the CBOE, coming to Goldman to tell me about his plans. I took Joe to meet Gus, who listened to him and said, with a twinkle in his eye, that this was just a new way to lose money, and then offered his support. I joined the founding board. Joe called the day before the CBOE first opened to say that he was afraid nobody would show up to trade. In fact, 911 contracts traded the first day, on 16 different stocks. Within a relatively short period, options trading turned into a genuinely liquid market and led to the creation of larger markets in listed futures on stock indices and debt.

I began as a Goldman partner during a period of ups and downs for Wall Street. The year 1973 was the first year the firm had lost money in many years, and 1974 wasn't much better. Our chief financial officer, Hy Weinberg, told me that we junior partners would be unlikely to ever do as well financially as the older partners had because there would never be another period as good as the one that had just passed. That seemed highly plausible at the time, but turned out not to be the case.

During one particular bad stretch in 1973–74, the stock market fell 45 percent from its high. We had very large losses in risk arbitrage and block trading. We were still holding the acquiree stocks in several deals that broke up—contrary to our usual practice—because they seemed so badly undervalued. But as the market continued declining, these stocks' prices kept falling. We thought our positions would eventually come back, and so we held on.

But sometimes, even if the market has gone way down and positions seem cheap, holding on may not make sense. I remember a customer who had a big position in a commodities arbitrage transaction. He bought soybean mash and sold soybeans because the mash was cheap relative to the soybeans. He expected to profit when the inefficiency corrected and prices converged. Instead, the spread widened and he had to put up more cash margin to creditors. As the spread kept widening, he ran out of cash and couldn't put up more margin, so his positions were liquidated to meet obligations. Eventually the prices did converge. But by that time our client was bankrupt. As John Maynard Keynes once reportedly said, "Markets can remain irrational longer than you can remain solvent." Psychological and other factors can create distortions that last a long time. You can be right in the long run and dead in the short run. Or you can be wrong in your judgments about value, for any of a whole host of possible reasons.

In that 1973–74 slump, we, like the trader with the soybean mash, were overextended relative to our staying power. In our case, the issue wasn't solvency but the limits on our tolerance for loss. I finally went to Gus. We reexamined the merits of each of our holdings and how much risk we were willing to accept going forward, and we decided to sell about half of our positions.

Looking back at that episode, I realize that we hadn't really been reevaluating our positions as the economic and market outlook changed. Holding an existing investment is the same as making it again. When markets turn sour, you have to forget your losses to date and do a fresh expected-value analysis based on the changed facts. Even if the expected values remain attractive, the size and risk of your portfolio must be at levels you can live with for a long time if conditions remain difficult. Praying over your positions—a frequent tendency in trading rooms during bad times—isn't a sensible approach to coping with adversity.

AROUND THE TIME L. Jay Tenenbaum retired from Goldman Sachs in 1976, Ray Young, who was in charge of equities sales at the firm, gave me some advice. He said that now that L. Jay was leaving, I had to make a choice. I could continue to act in the manner I had developed working in a trading environment—focusing intently on my business, being short with people, and projecting an impersonal attitude. If so, Ray predicted, I would continue as a successful arbitrageur. But as an alternative, I could start thinking more about the people in the trading room and in sales—about their concerns and views—and how to enable them to be successful. In that case, Ray said, I wouldn't be limited to arbitrage but could become more broadly involved in the life of the firm.

Ray Young's advice pointed me toward a whole new world that I hadn't thought much about. My tendency to be abrupt and peremptory—characteristic of Wall Street traders of that era—is exemplified by a typical episode: a colleague from investment banking came to ask me about the market impact of a deal she was working on. She had trouble explaining the deal to me, and I told her I was busy and didn't understand how someone could work at Goldman Sachs and not understand some basic corporate finance. I dismissively suggested she go back upstairs and return when she was properly prepared. Ray made me understand that that kind of attitude limited how far I would go at the firm and how interesting my career there would be.

My general experience in life has been that most people can change only within a narrow range, if at all. Many people can acknowledge criticism and advice, but relatively few internalize it and alter their behavior in a significant way. Sometimes someone can change in one respect but not in another. I was involved in many discussions at Goldman over the years that centered on the question of whether a person who was highly capable professionally, but limited in some way, could grow to assume broader responsibilities. Often the limitations revolved around the ability to work effectively with colleagues and subordinates.

I've often asked myself why this advice affected me so much. Perhaps I simply responded when someone whom I respected, who clearly had my best interests at heart, raised a problem I hadn't thought about and opened up new vistas. Judy's view was that the harshness of manner Ray critiqued was a superficial attribute. Most likely, both reasons were true. In any case, my mind-set did change and I began to listen to people better, to try to understand their problems and concerns, and to more appropriately assess and value their views. And as I've since said to others, this not only had the effects in my business career that Ray had suggested but gave me something I hadn't expected, a new satisfaction in the accomplishments of others.

I also connected what Ray told me with a comment that Richard Menschel, another more senior colleague who took a supportive interest in my career, had made a couple of years after I arrived at Goldman. Dick said that early in your career you may be concerned about bringing strong, younger people into your world. For some, that feeling remains; they continue to think that bright, more junior people threaten to outshine them in some way. But after a certain point, Dick predicted, I would become comfortable enough in my own position to eagerly seek out extremely capable young people for the arbitrage department.

He was right. Initially I felt uneasy about bringing a strong junior associate into the arbitrage department. But soon that changed and I wanted effective, aggressive people working with me in order to get the job done better. Moreover, as I found in everything I did thereafter, sharing credit with others didn't mean less credit for me. To the contrary, I got credit not only for the results being better, but also for sharing the credit. I also enjoyed the recognition given to people I worked with. Dick was right that a lot of otherwise successful people never figure this out. They view smart junior associates as a threat rather than as a reflection of their own capabilities as managers.

I'd never given one second of thought to management as such. Once I began to think about these issues, however, I found them engrossing. How do you get people to work well with one another? How do you attract and keep strong people? How do you motivate them to do their best? How do you get a whole organization to be strategically dynamic and to act on difficult issues? I'd never been to business school or even read any books about management, but I developed views on all of this through experience.

JUDY CONTINUED in the theater and became a member of the actors' union—Actors' Equity Association—when she was cast in an Equity production. But she ended this nascent career when she became pregnant with our first child. Thanks to Judy we went to quite a bit of theater and dance, and I particularly enjoyed ballet. (Concerts and opera she did on her own.) Sherwin Goldman, who had been at Yale Law School with me, had become deeply involved with American Ballet Theatre (ABT) and had seen us at a number of dance performances. So he assumed I liked dance and asked me to join the ABT board. At that point I wasn't in a position to raise much money, but I think Sherwin was trying to create a younger cadre on the board for the future.

Earlier, I said I thought you could draw a line from my election as fourth-grade president to the cabinet, showing how large a role chance and incident play in life. You can draw an even straighter line from my joining the board of ABT to subsequent opportunities, because being on the board of an arts organization caused people to view me as someone who was involved in civic activities. Soon thereafter, Gus asked me to help raise money for Lincoln Center, where he was treasurer. After Gus died in 1976, Bunny Lasker, who was always promoting my interests, got me on the board of Mount Sinai Medical Center. And so it went, with one involvement leading to another. The key was to get in motion to begin with. Also, at least for me at a number of critical junctures, some other person—for example, my fourth-grade teacher or Bunny—provided the critical impetus.

From the beginning, I had hoped to get involved outside the firm, and that desire never flagged. I wasn't bored or awash in spare time, especially after our sons, James and Philip, were born in 1967 and 1971. But out-side involvements added other dimensions to my life, providing a glimpse of what other people's jobs and lives were like and an opportunity to con-tribute to purposes beyond my work. What's more, outside involvements helped my Goldman Sachs career, as I met well-established people who were also clients or potential clients of our firm. Finally, these outside ac-tivities began to create a place in the community for me—though I may have set that back slightly at ABT when I suggested, at a time when the company was facing a 10 percent deficit, that nobody would notice if *Swan Lake* were performed with 10 percent fewer swans.

My real desire, however, was to get involved in politics. I'd done some work in a few New York campaigns, but that didn't amount to much. An avenue for larger involvement opened in 1969, when Henry Fowler, who was Secretary of the Treasury under Lyndon B. Johnson, joined Goldman Sachs. "Joe," as everyone called Fowler, was a courtly Virginia lawyer whose ancestors had come to America in the seventeenth century.

Many people at Goldman were not that interested in what Fowler had done in government. But to me, Joe was a fascinating figure—someone who had gone to Washington during the New Deal and served in every Democratic administration thereafter. I took every opportunity to talk politics with him and at some point mentioned that I would like to become involved. Joe called Robert Strauss, who had recently become treasurer of the Democratic National Committee.

Strauss had a different kind of charm from Fowler. Rather than flattering you, Bob insulted you. When I met him in New York in 1972, he told me that if I wanted to be involved in policy, I was of no use to him. But if I wanted to raise money, we should talk. He said that Nixon was going to be reelected, so he was focusing on senators and congressmen to make sure the Democrats retained control of Congress. Then Strauss said something I took to heart: in politics a lot of people promise to do something, but very few actually do it. If you don't want to do what you're asked, just say no. But if you say you're going to do something, following through will set you apart. Then Strauss told me, "You know, you look good on paper. But now that I've met you, I don't think you'll amount to much. So you better work hard." That seemed an odd way to get somebody to help you, but, in fact, it was the beginning of a great friendship.

I took off a week from work to call on people I knew and ask them to contribute to Bob's effort. While I don't have the personality ordinarily associated with fund-raising, I was determined to do it anyway. I called mainly on people in and around the arbitrage fraternity, only a few of whom were in any way sympathetic to the Democrats. I didn't raise more than $25,000. But in those days, that wasn't a bad start.

Even in his eighties, Bob has a magnetism that reminds me of Gus and Bunny. When he walks into a room, the effect is electric. With a twinkle in his eye, he continues to win people over through effrontery. "You must be the stupidest person alive," began a letter he recently sent me about a business matter. He's shrewd yet somehow the least cynical of cynics. I remember some of his early political advice: "Let me tell you about Washington, Bob. I could call President Carter once a week and just say anything—even talk about the weather. And after that, I could walk around town telling people that I had just been talking to the President today and, while it would mean nothing substantively, it would have meaning in Washington. That's just the way this city works."

From time to time others in the financial world have asked me for advice on how to get involved in politics. You can most readily acquire a place at the table by raising money, I tell them. And once you have a place at the table, you get to know people who work on campaigns. If those people think you have useful thoughts on politics, message, or policy, you can develop a broader involvement, at least informally. But there are actions and attitudes that can militate against crossing that line. One is if you appear to be trying to use politics to further your business or financial interests. Another is an attitude of self-importance. Many people assume that business success qualifies them to opine authoritatively about politics, but while business experience can be useful, politics and government differ in many ways.

Toward the end of the Carter presidency, Josh Gotbaum, who worked for Alfred Kahn, President Carter's "inflation czar," approached me about directing the Council on Wage and Price Stability, administering the price guideline program. Few notions were more appealing to me than seeing the world from inside the White House. But after going to Washington to meet the relevant people, I was left with the impression that that job wasn't positioned to work, in terms of either its staffing and authority within the administration or its conceptual approach. In addition, I had a great deal to lose by leaving a partnership at Goldman Sachs.

In any case, the issue was academic. Shortly before this, I had been playing tennis in Westhampton when, for the first time in my life, my back started hurting. Instead of getting better, it got worse, and I went to see the chief of orthopedics at Mount Sinai, Robert Siffert. He looked and looked and couldn't figure out my problem. Nor could others he referred me to. Nothing appeared on the X rays. After a while the pain was so severe that I couldn't sit up or stand for any length of time.

I was intent on not letting my back pain interfere with either Goldman or my outside activities, so I did everything I could to keep functioning. For many months, I'd have to lie down at the office on a couch. Some days, people at work would have to help me into a car to go home at two or three in the afternoon because the pain was so severe. I was in the hospital three times—for bed rest and diagnostic procedures—and each time I ran the arbitrage business from my bed. I was on the board of Studebaker-Worthington, and I participated in one meeting lying on the conference table. Once, the chief executive officer of the company, Derald Ruttenberg, called and asked me to meet him at his office on a Saturday to talk about selling the company. I thought, *If I don't go, he'll hire Felix Rohatyn*—the renowned investment banker from Lazard whom Ruttenberg had also mentioned. I couldn't walk for more than a few yards at the time, or even sit, but I went to Ruttenberg's office and lay on his window seat. We got the business, though much to my dismay, Ruttenberg gave Felix part of the fee. (It's more than twenty-five years later, but I still remember the amount.) Ruttenberg said he wanted Felix to be satisfied, given his importance in the world. Since stress is not good for a back problem—as my doctors reminded me from time to time—trying not to miss a beat by working from a horizontal position probably wasn't the ideal way to get better.

On the one hand, I was concerned the condition would remain undiagnosable and I wouldn't get well. On the other hand, I woke up every morning hoping and almost expecting that that day would be better. The then chief of neurosurgery at Mount Sinai wanted to operate on what he thought was a disc problem. But Bob Siffert wasn't sure he was right and told me to hold off. Months went by. Eventually, Siffert took another kind of X ray and found a barely discernible crack in a vertebra, the result of a genetic defect, which is apparently quite rare except in Eskimos. I had to have a spinal fusion, an operation in which bone from elsewhere in your body is used to mend the crack in your vertebra.

It was major surgery. I wore a brace for six months afterward and full recovery took about a year and a half, but the operation worked. Ever since then I have played tennis, fished, and done whatever I wanted to physically. But my back problem meant that I couldn't even consider the Carter position. When I saw the article in *The New York Times* about the person chosen for the job, I thought, *That could have been me*—though I also recognized that I almost surely wouldn't have taken the appointment anyway.

GUS LEVY SUFFERED a massive stroke in November 1976 and died shortly thereafter. He was sixty-six, young enough that he'd been able to ignore the issue of succession at the firm. However, shortly before the stroke, he had told George Doty, a senior member of the Management Committee, that he was going to name John Whitehead and John Weinberg co–vice chairmen of the Management Committee, and to George it was clear that Gus viewed them as his successors.

"The two Johns," as we called them, were the logical heirs in any case. John Weinberg, Sidney's son, was warm, not openly assertive, but highly effective and a great culture carrier in the firm. Born into the business, he had his father's touch with clients, who loved him for his straightforward good sense. John Whitehead was extremely bright, lucid, and self-confident, and had a powerful strategic focus. He was central to converting the investment banking department from a highly individualistic operation, with Sidney Weinberg as the extraordinary star at the center, into an effective organization. Whitehead also began orienting the firm much more toward the world outside the United States. Our continued movement toward global involvement during my time at Goldman stood me in good stead during my years in Washington, when I looked at many of these same issues through the lens of public policy.

I learned a lot about management from both men. From Whitehead, I learned how to focus on being strategic despite the pressures of day-to-day business. He was always thinking in terms of where Goldman Sachs wanted to be years into the future. From Weinberg, I learned about working with people, both clients and colleagues, and how to treat the perspectives of others seriously and respectfully even when I disagreed with them. From both, I learned how to deal with joint management. There was initially much skepticism at Goldman about whether a co-CEO arrangement could work. When the Johns disagreed in a Management Committee meeting, there was no clear way to resolve the issue. But they figured out a way to function effectively that reflected their personalities. They talked to each other every weekend before the Monday morning Management Committee meeting and went through a list of issues. Weinberg was willing to let Whitehead take the lead on most, but if Weinberg felt strongly, he would assert himself. Though a problem would occasionally remain unresolved for an extended period because of their differences, their chairmanship showed me that a co-CEO structure can work—though I later came to believe that successful joint management is the infrequent exception, not the rule.

Ray Young represented all of the firm's equity trading and sales activities on the Management Committee. In 1980, he retired, and I was one of three people who replaced him on the committee. Somewhat thereafter, I was asked to take on the problem of J. Aron & Company. A few years earlier, working with George Doty, I had tried to extend the arbitrage mind-set and our experience with trading in derivatives into building a commodities trading operation. Then, the year after I joined the Management Committee, Goldman bought J. Aron, its first acquisition since the 1930s. A hugely successful, family-owned commodities trading firm, Aron had sophisticated, well-established commodities operations, with connections all over the world. What neither we nor they realized, however, was that, because of various changes taking place, it didn't have a viable business model for the future. Aron's profits, which had been $60 million in 1981, fell to $30 million in 1982 and then to nothing in 1983.

Doty had responsibility for J. Aron and took the first difficult step of downsizing. With that done, the two Johns and George asked me to take charge of the problem. I could have said to myself that this might not work and could upend my position at Goldman Sachs. At the very least, I might have done some probabilistic analysis. But here, as in other major career changes that strongly attracted me, I didn't calculate. I wasn't at all cocky about my ability to turn Aron around, but neither was I anxious. Once I had the job, I just focused on trying to do what needed to be done. And I very much wanted the responsibility, because it was interesting and would enlarge my role at the firm. Moreover, Aron was a trading business with a strong arbitrage bent, so I felt suited to the task.

I walked around with my yellow pad for two or three months, just taking notes and trying to learn about the business before actually taking over. In the course of my inquiry, I found that the people doing the work had many thoughtful ideas about how to revise our strategy and move forward. After a while we changed the leadership, putting Mark Winkelman, who had been in the fixed-income department, in charge, reporting to me. Winkelman, who was born in Holland and worked at the World Bank before coming to Goldman, was extremely sophisticated about the developing business of relationship trading in bonds and foreign exchange. He had both the substantive background to understand Aron's problems and the managerial skills to help set them right.

Together Mark and I worked with the Aron people to rethink the business model. Aron had been doing classic arbitrage, buying a currency or a commodity—such as gold—in one place and selling it as close to simultaneously as possible somewhere else. Aron was imaginative in crafting opportunities for classic arbitrage, for example by maintaining open phone lines to Saudi Arabia to trade gold and silver. This kind of trading had little risk, and Aron was intensely risk averse—so much so that when it lost track of its transactions, it would close in the middle of the day, to sort everything out and make sure it wasn't holding an extra hundred ounces of gold on its books. The only exception to this model was coffee, where Aron acted as a large importer and trader.

One of the first conclusions others led me to see was that the relative stability of commodity prices, improved communications, and increased competition had eliminated the meaningful profit opportunity in Aron's traditional business. Spreads were being squeezed, a reality that the Aron leadership seemed to have missed because of its great success in the past. I found over the years that the Aron experience was quite typical. Success often leads businesses and individuals to fail to notice change or to adapt to it, and so, eventually, to falter.

Mark and I determined that Aron needed to make several basic changes. The first was to focus on relative value arbitrage, or relationship trading, which Goldman was already doing in fixed income and equities. In the Aron context, that meant looking for distortions in the price relationship between different commodities or currencies, or between them and derivatives based on them, using interest rates and other factors to estimate the appropriate relative values. For example, short-term gold futures could be traded against long-term gold futures to profit when prices that seemed out of whack converged. That meant taking risks that the Aron people had always been proud of not taking, and with the firm's own money. We decided to abandon the sure thing that no longer existed in favor of calculated risk taking. We also decided to greatly expand Aron's foreign exchange trading, going from a pure arbitrage operation into relative value arbitrage, outright position taking, and increased client business—for example, helping businesses and individuals hedge against currency risk, which added to the services that Goldman could offer clients. Somewhat later, we went into trading oil and petroleum products, adding a vast new arena to our business.

These transformations at Aron required certain personnel changes, our most delicate undertaking. After extensive observation, we concluded that Aron had some extraordinarily capable people—who had already contributed greatly to rethinking the strategy—but that some others were so steeped in the old, risk-free way of doing business as to be unable to make the transition to a risk-based approach. We had to find places for those people elsewhere at Goldman or encourage them to move on. And we needed a process for recruiting. Hiring at the old Aron had been based on horse sense—somebody seemed as though he might make a good commodities trader. We formalized the process, looking for people whose experience and qualifications met our new needs. With all of these changes, we had reengineered Aron and the business started to work again— though in a very different way. We didn't reach our ambitious $100 million goal the first year, but we exceeded it the second year and created a base from which Goldman earned enormous profits in the years after.

Like arbitrage, commodities and currency trading was an example of a good business based on calculated risk taking and that involved living with the large losses that sometimes—and inevitably—ensue. But the Aron transformation was also an illustration of how difficult change can be at big organizations. Michael Porter, a professor at Harvard Business School, argues that great institutions fail because, once successful, they become satisfied with themselves and stop changing, and the world passes them by. That was the case with Aron, which had lost its strategic dynamism. But even with an effective business model and a dynamic, strategic mind-set, a company needs a structure that works, a system for attracting capable people and putting them in the right jobs, and a culture in which people work together in a mutually supportive way.

But perhaps the most important management point about Aron was that the ideas for remaking its business came largely from the people who worked there, exemplifying my career's experience that the people in the front lines of a business often have a better sense of what's happening and what to do about it than the top executives. Our success at Aron was more evidence of Ray Young's and Dick Menschel's advice that to be most effective I was best off being surrounded by strong people, listening to them, and being sensitive to their concerns and quirks of personality—just as they had to be sensitive to mine.

AT THE SUGGESTION of Bob Strauss, the Democrats asked me to chair their 1982 congressional campaign dinner in Washington. Never having done anything like it, I wondered whether I would be able to raise enough money. Instead of saying yes or no immediately, I tried to get a better idea of how much I had to raise personally to be viewed as successful. People I spoke to named a figure of $100,000. So I called a family friend in Florida who had made a lot of money from my arbitrage advice. He and his partner said they'd each put up $20,000. With the $20,000 I could contribute under the legal limits and a few other ideas about where to raise money, I felt close enough to the $100,000, and I said okay. The dinner was successful: I raised much more than $100,000 on my own, and the dinner took in more than $1 million—large numbers by the standards of that era. Bob Strauss had told me that chairing that dinner put someone in a different position in the party. He was right. Soon after, both Walter Mondale's and John Glenn's campaigns sought my help for the 1984 election.

Substantively, I felt that the Reagan administration's budget deficits created a serious threat to future economic conditions and that sooner or later we would pay the price. I remember speaking at a House Democratic Caucus meeting in the late 1980s. Congressman Barney Frank (D-MA) said, pointedly, that although I had been concerned about deficits for some time, the economy had continued to grow reasonably well. I replied that the laws of economics hadn't been revoked. The timing of any market impact can be complicated, but the inevitable would surely occur at some point—as, indeed, happened not much later.

Many conservatives shared this concern. Martin Feldstein, the distinguished economist who was Ronald Reagan's second chairman of the Council of Economic Advisers, argued strongly against large budget deficits, but his arguments were unsuccessful and he stepped down near the end of that administration's first term. Gary Wenglowski, Goldman's highly regarded chief economist, said he thought Reagan's economic policy was the worst since Herbert Hoover's. At that time, some conservatives argued that tax cuts should be accompanied by commensurate reductions in the cost of running the federal government. But that would have required program reductions that neither party was prepared to support, especially during a period when defense and entitlement spending were rising at a rapid rate. Another view was that tax cuts would generate sufficient additional growth to pay for themselves, which George H. W. Bush referred to in his 1980 presidential primary campaign against Reagan as "voodoo economics"—which seems to me about right.

The other aspect of Reagan's policy that most concerned me was the failure to address the country's social problems, many of which were clearly getting worse. Around that time, I read Ken Auletta's book *The Underclass*. In vivid fashion, Auletta described the replication of poverty through generations. The book crystallized a lot of my thinking on the topic—though later, when I worked in a Democratic administration, I learned that the term "underclass" is no longer politically correct. (I was told that the acceptable alternative is "people who live in distressed areas, rural and urban.")

I had some direct exposure to the problems of inner cities at meetings of a neighborhood group called the 28th Precinct Community Council in central Harlem in the 1970s. In searching for a way to get involved with these issues, I had met Warren Blake, an African-American police officer in charge of community relations for the precinct. Warren, a huge man with a personality to match, had strong ties to the community and cared deeply about what was happening to it. His wife's family had run a prosperous funeral business in the neighborhood for many years, and the Blakes lived nearby in a large Victorian house that had once belonged to James A. Bailey of Barnum & Bailey Circus. When he was off duty, Warren sometimes drove a hearse. I remember a dinner Judy and I went to at their home. One of the other guests was a political activist from Papua New Guinea who proposed that Goldman Sachs finance a revolution in exchange for some of the country's shrimp and timber concessions. I didn't pursue this.

What I saw and heard at the 28th Precinct Community Council gave me a more personal feeling that it is just wrong that a country as wealthy as ours does not provide the resources to successfully address poverty that passes from generation to generation. The more I learned about these issues, the more I was convinced that there were approaches that would work if adequately supported. I also came to believe that the problems of the inner cities greatly affect all of us—no matter where we may live or what our incomes may be—through crime, the deterioration of public schools, the costs of social ills, and the lost productivity of a large group of people who are not being equipped to realize their potential. The belief that affluence can insulate is illusory.

And that helps explain why I am a Democrat. If you put all my views on public policy issues together, I wouldn't fit neatly under any political label. In fact, many of my views, such as the importance of fiscal discipline to our country's future growth and the centrality to our own well-being of American leadership on global issues such as trade liberalization, poverty, the environment, and terrorism, don't really fit into any political camp. But when I look in both directions from the center, I find concerns that echo my own to a greater degree on the Democratic side, which has long seemed to me more committed to using government to meet the needs of middle- and lower-income people that markets by their nature will not adequately address.

However, I wasn't necessarily in full agreement even with those who shared my concerns. Roughly twenty years ago, I heard Senator Ted Kennedy (D-MA) give a speech advocating a whole host of government programs that sounded worthwhile to me. The address was powerful and well delivered. But as much as I agreed with Kennedy's goals and respected his commitment to them, I wondered, *How are we going to pay for this?* The focus by some social advocates on problems and programs—but not the means to fund those programs—bothered me. My deep involvement in the 1984 presidential campaign was largely driven by the conviction that we needed a President who combined Kennedy's social concerns with a sense of fiscal responsibility.

Walter Mondale seemed to fit that bill. I met Mondale through his campaign chairman and former White House aide, Jim Johnson, who later became the CEO of Fannie Mae. Through Jim, I also met Mike Berman, the treasurer of Mondale's campaign and a man wise in the ways of Washington. As I got to know Mondale better, he seemed to be very practical, with a well-known commitment to the plight of the poor, joined with a deep concern about our growing fiscal disarray. When the Mondale people asked me to be his New York State finance chairman, I accepted, after initially hesitating because once again I wanted to be sure I could raise enough money to be successful.

Though my place at the Mondale table came from fund-raising, my conversations with Jim Johnson, Mike Berman, and others in the campaign often shaded into economic policy and politics. Some people like opera. Some like basketball. I like policy and politics. Somewhere in the back of my mind, I also knew I wanted to work in the White House if the right opportunity should ever arise.

After Mondale's defeat, gloom pervaded the Democrats. The party was widely seen as being in trouble and needing to reassess its direction. Some thought it was in thrall to the labor unions and interest groups, and that more centrist positions would be both better policy and more attractive to middle-class voters. Others felt just the opposite—that the focus needed to be on what they referred to as the "base." I remember one dinner discussion at the house of Roger Altman, a fellow Wall Streeter who had served in the Carter administration and had worked with me on the Mondale campaign. Two other political strategists, Tom Donilon and the late Kirk O'Donnell, were also there, as was Jacob Goldfield, a colleague at Goldman Sachs. The focus of the discussion was that Reagan's position was too simplistic to be serious policy but was easy to grasp and good politics: fight communism, cut taxes, and reduce government. How could views that reflected the true complexity of the issues be framed with enough political resonance to respond to such bumper-sticker simplifications? By the time dinner was over, no one had any very promising thoughts. In the years since, I've had many such conversations about this same conundrum.

THE ELECTION HAD consequences inside Goldman Sachs as well. In 1985, John Whitehead resigned and soon became George Shultz's number two at the State Department, leaving John Weinberg as the sole senior partner. That same year, Steve Friedman and I became co-heads of the fixed-income division. We were roughly the same age and each of us had moved from a law firm to Goldman Sachs at about the same time, when that was rarely done. Steve and I became partners and joined the Management Committee within two years of each other, and we worked on many client assignments and firm matters together. Steve, a former national wrestling champion, was relatively conservative and a Republican. (Curiously enough, Steve assumed the same position in the White House at the beginning of the third year of the George W. Bush administration that I had at the outset of the Clinton administration.) Despite our differences—and perhaps despite our commonalities—we worked extremely well together for twenty-five years.

The fixed-income division at Goldman traded all kinds of interest-bearing instruments—government debt, corporate and high-yield bonds, mortgage-backed securities, fixed-income futures, options, and other derivatives. The business was big, with a lot of risk. And shortly after we arrived, the trading operation developed serious problems. Our traders had large, highly leveraged positions, many of them illiquid, meaning that they couldn't be sold even at generous discounts to the price of the last trade. As losses mounted, Steve and I tried to figure out what to do.

I tend to think about fixed-income trading in three categories, although any single trade or position often involves two or even all three of them. The first is flow trading. You buy on the bid side of the market from clients and sell on the offer side, earning the spread between the two. The second is directional trading, based on judging the short-term direction of the market. You expect weaker economic numbers or a stock market dip to push bond prices higher. So you buy at $98¼, expecting to sell at $99 or even higher. The third is relative value trading, or fixed-income arbitrage. You decide that the relationship between two different securities is out of line and likely to return to form, based on valuation models, historical experience, and judgment; for example, the five-year Treasury bond is trading at an unusual discount to the ten-year. So you buy the relatively cheap bond and sell the relatively expensive bond, anticipating that their normal relationship will return.

Relationship trading was at the heart of the trouble that developed in the fixed-income department. Bonds and derivative products began to move in unexpected ways relative to each other because traders hadn't focused on how these securities might behave under the extremely unlikely market conditions that were now occurring. Neither Steve nor I was an expert in this area, so our confusion was not surprising. But the people who traded these instruments didn't fully understand these developments either, and that was unsettling. You'd come to work thinking *We've lost a lot of money, but the worst is finally behind us. Now what do we do?* And then a new problem would develop. We didn't know how to stop the process.

We had lost about $100 million. Today that wouldn't mean much, but in that world at that time, it was very meaningful. And it wasn't just the losses to date but also a question of what those losses portended for the future. You have no way of knowing when a downward spiral will end or if the next period will be even worse. The fixed-income division had contributed greatly to Goldman's overall profitability. Suddenly, our biggest trading operation had gone sour, and we didn't understand why or what the future might bring.

Steve and I went into the trading room and said, "Let's all sit down and try to understand what we're holding. If we have positions we shouldn't have, let's get rid of them." Leaving aside the psychological factors that incline most traders to resist taking losses, what soon became clear was that they hadn't fully anticipated the behavioral characteristics these securities could have when conditions changed substantially. Many of these bonds had embedded or implicit options. As a simple example, the firm was trading mortgage-backed securities that represented the loans people take out to finance homes. As interest rates declined, people refinanced 13 and 14 percent mortgages at 9 and 10 percent. That meant that our bonds didn't rise in line with the fall in interest rates and in some cases were paid off early—creating a loss on a position that had been hedged with Treasury bonds. A similar problem affected corporate bonds. As interest rates declined, bond prices rose to a point where the corporate issuers might exercise call provisions—the right to pay off an outstanding bond, usually to refinance at lower rates. When a bond was at $80, the borrower's right to redeem at $102 was often ignored. Then, when the bond market had a massive rally, the call provisions did begin to reduce the otherwise expected premium, while the short position rose and created a net loss. What happened to us represents a seeming tendency in human nature not to give appropriate weight to what might occur under remote, but potentially very damaging, circumstances.

Another lesson in these 1986 bond market losses—which I had learned through mistakes made in arbitrage years earlier—was to think not only about the odds of making a profit on each trade, but the limits on tolerance for loss in the event market conditions became much worse then expected. The issue wasn't simply financial staying power. A trader and his firm had to know the outer limits of what they were willing to lose relative to their earnings and balance sheet. A related problem was liquidity. Traders tend to assume that their positions will always be salable at very close to the last market price. When markets are doing reasonably well, they say, "Well, if I don't like something I've bought, I'll just kick it back out." But when conditions deteriorate severely, liquidity diminishes enormously. Traders often can't sell bad positions except at enormous discounts, and sometimes not at all. Then they may be forced to sell good positions to raise money. Thus, during periods of great market duress, investments can react in unexpected ways. Securities that have no logical relationship may suddenly move in tandem while securities that do have a logical relationship may diverge. Unexpected losses can develop rapidly and be huge.

Dealing with the 1986 meltdown in fixed income probably helped reinforce the position Steve and I had acquired as heirs apparent, and in

1987, John Weinberg appointed us co–chief operating officers of Goldman Sachs. Even after we assumed our new positions, however, I remained co-head of trading and arbitrage and the Management Committee member responsible for J. Aron—albeit with many fewer day-to-day responsibilities in each of those areas. Steve, on the other hand, chose to relinquish his position as co-head of the investment banking division, although he remained very involved in it.

Beginning in early 1987, we became embroiled in a crisis which—painfully—prepared me to help manage several other high-profile crises in subsequent years. A partner of ours, along with two people from another firm, was arrested for insider trading in a highly controversial case. Based on our counsel's investigations, we believed our partner was innocent, and we stood by him through the entire ordeal. All the original charges were dropped. No new charges were ever brought against the other two. Our partner ultimately pled guilty to a single count unrelated to the original charges. His counsel advised him that he shouldn't be found guilty but that, with a wealthy defendant in a jury trial in a matter of this sort, there were no guarantees.

For almost two years, Steve and I were engaged with this case and the issues it created for the firm. In dealing with this problem, we learned a number of important lessons. First, in managing a crisis, it is crucial that you not allow it to interfere significantly with conducting your business. One way to minimize this risk is to designate a small team to deal with the crisis. Steve and I told everyone else at Goldman that we'd keep them posted, but that their responsibility was to remain focused on their work. Second, we learned the importance of getting out and seeing your clients during a crisis. Clients have a lot of questions and the firm has to answer them. Third, you have to communicate with your own people frequently, especially since the media is likely to emphasize the negative. Fourth, regarding the media, my own experience over many years, in a number of crisis situations in both the public and private sectors, has convinced me that you simply have to grit your teeth and live through the rough early coverage—you ordinarily can't affect the initial firestorm. What you can do is be candid about whatever the situation may be, affirmative with respect to your commitment to address your problems—if that is relevant in the particular situation—and confident about the future. Over time, your answers should begin to get more attention and the coverage should become more balanced. Finally, in all of this, you need to resist the tendency to become a little paranoid, thinking that people are looking at you differently when, in most cases, they're not. It's important not to be oversensitive, and to treat everyone normally. With all of the potential for something to go wrong in any big company, no matter how well run, and with the attendant media and political firestorms that can erupt in short order, knowing how to cope with a crisis can quickly become critically important for any senior manager.

At the end of 1990, John Weinberg stepped down, and Steve and I were named co-chairmen. Following the Weinberg-Whitehead example, we didn't try to divide up responsibilities or subject areas. We told everyone to assume that either of us could speak for both and that touching one base was sufficient. This worked because we shared the same fundamental views about the firm, trusted each other totally, kept in close touch, and were both analytically minded in our approach to problems. When this structure does work—and that is a rarity—the advantages are substantial: there are two senior partners to call on clients and two people who can work together on issues with no hierarchical baggage, and who can reinforce each other in discussions with the rest of the organization. Also, when difficulties arise, having a partner reduces the feeling of loneliness at the top.

Absolutely key to our partnership was that when we disagreed, neither of us had his ego invested in winning. Steve and I had a rule that the one who felt more strongly would prevail, or at least have the decision more toward his direction. If one of us felt 80–20 and the other 60–40, the 60–40 one would say, "I sort of disagree, but if you're eighty–twenty we'll do it your way—or someplace in between, but more your way than mine." In the rare cases when we disagreed and both felt strongly, we worked it out. Another proviso was that we usually—although not always—deferred to the more risk-averse position.

On maintaining a meritocracy, protecting the culture of the firm, and focusing on our customers, we agreed. But within those parameters, our views sometimes differed. As an example, Steve strongly favored greater differentiation in partnership shares, based on meaningful distinctions in performance. I, on the other hand, thought the possible ill will of those not favored outweighed the benefit of favoring the best performers—except where the difference was truly major. Over the years, I had seen partners who earned millions of dollars a year become deeply unhappy over tiny distinctions in partnership shares. (Bob Strauss once captured this dynamic when he said that a lawyer at his firm earning $90,000 a year—this was some time ago—and offered a $10,000 raise with the stipulation that a peer next door would get a $20,000 raise would prefer no raise at all to someone on his own level being paid even more.) Steve referred to my inclination to avoid conflict-provoking distinctions as "solving for maximum social harmony." Because he felt more strongly than I did, we agreed to increase differentiation, although less than Steve would have done on his own.

My partnership with Steve was in some respects a forerunner of the relationship I had as Treasury Secretary with Larry Summers and Alan Greenspan. None of these people is a shrinking violet. But because of mutual respect, trust, and our analytic approach to issues, these relationships worked. Alan had somewhat different starting points on some issues, but through financial crises, G-7 meetings, currency interventions, and much else, we almost always analyzed our way through to agreement. Steve and I didn't worry that someone might consider one of us weak because the other's view had prevailed, nor did Larry, Alan, or I. The overriding drive in both relationships was to reach the best decision.

WHEN STEVE AND I first became co-chairmen, I found the difference between the senior position and what we had been doing far greater than I had expected. With John Weinberg as senior partner, the ultimate approval and responsibility were his, even if we had operating responsibility. Once Steve and I became senior partners, the ultimate responsibility was ours. Larry Summers said the same thing to me about becoming Treasury Secretary. When he was deputy secretary, he felt that the difference between his job and mine was small. After becoming Secretary, he realized that the difference was enormous.

In those days, Larry Tisch, the CEO of Loews Corporation and later of CBS, used to tell me, "Bob, you worry too much." I'd say, "Larry, you don't understand. There's a lot to worry about." One worrisome issue was Goldman's lack of a permanent capital base. A firm like ours needed a lot of capital to support what had become a massive global trading operation, to withstand difficult times, and, later, to be competitive in investment banking with the commercial banks. As it was a private partnership, each new retiree could withdraw his share of the capital within a relatively brief period. In a public company, capital remains in the company, and a retiree simply sells his stock on the public market. If conditions were difficult and partners became nervous, Goldman could face a run on the bank. Building capital is thus far more difficult in a private firm. And finally, the partners were at risk not only for the money in the firm but for their entire net worth—a source of great concern in the Penn Central bankruptcy. For these same reasons—as well as the simple desire to cash out—all of our major competitors had already gone public or merged into larger concerns. Steve and I were convinced that the way to deal with these issues was to become a limited-liability corporation and sell stock to the public.

One argument against going public was the flexibility of being able to periodically adjust partnership percentages among the partners, to reflect performance and changes in seniority. Another was the mystique of being private—especially after all the other big Wall Street firms had gone public or merged. The initial public offering proposal presented in 1986 was rejected, largely because the younger partners wanted to preserve flexibility so their stakes could grow more easily. And that structure continued to work for more than a decade. Years after both of us had left, the inevitable eventually happened and Goldman finally did go public.

IN EARLY 1988, I met Governor Michael Dukakis a few times and was impressed with his intelligence. Although I shared the popular view that he was somewhat stiff as a candidate, I raised money and contributed a bit of advice to his campaign. At one point, Dukakis was way ahead of George Bush in the polls, and after his defeat many in the party felt bitterly toward him for the way he had handled his candidacy. Issues about his campaign aside, I still thought that expressing moderate Democratic views—or, for that matter, any sensible views that reflected the complexity of the underlying issues—in ways that resonated politically was extremely difficult. The political system's bipartisan failure to address the growing deficit demonstrated the imperative need to figure out how to do so. The country remained in denial about serious social issues as well. Our public education system was deeply troubled, and life in the inner cities was getting worse. I wondered whether the country would muster the political will to address its problems. The alternative to facing up to these problems, as I discussed at a dinner Bob Strauss held for me in Washington after I became co-head of Goldman Sachs, was the risk of inexorable national decline.

I hadn't decided among the Democrats who were considering running in 1992, but I was looking around. I hosted—along with David Sawyer, a well-known Democratic political consultant and Oscar-nominated documentary filmmaker who died at a young age—a series of small dinners at which roughly fifteen business and media people talked with candidates and potential candidates. Among others, we had Senators Tom Harkin (D-IA), Dale Bumpers (D-AR), Joe Biden (D-DE), and Bob Kerrey (D-NE). Bill Clinton was our guest at dinner in mid-1991 and was enormously impressive. I've been to many events where a candidate spends much of the time talking. For more than three hours, Clinton engaged in a real dialogue—a serious give-and-take—on the issues important to us. At the end of the dinner, I said to Lew Kaden, a New York lawyer and Columbia law professor deeply involved in Democratic politics, "This guy Clinton is amazing. It's remarkable how well he understands this stuff." But Clinton expressed uncertainty about running because of the effect a campaign might have on his family.

Almost a year later, in May 1992, when Clinton had not only decided to run but had pretty much locked up the nomination, he drew together a few so-called advisers in Little Rock to discuss economic issues. The group included several Wall Street investment bankers—Roger Altman and my fellow Goldman Sachs partners Ken Brody and Barrie Wigmore—as well as a centrist economist named Rob Shapiro and three friends of Clinton's,

Robert Reich, Ira Magaziner, and Derek Shearer, who had well-developed views on an active role for government. I had no illusions about our position as "advisers." We were mainly surrogates intended to lend credibility to Clinton's economic policies, which, in reality, were set inside the campaign organization. But at this meeting, Clinton took the extraordinary step of taking a day off from the campaign—with no media coverage—to assess his economic proposals and see whether positions developed under the pressure of the campaign made sense for governing. He wanted to stop running for a day in order to check his course.

Doing that showed remarkable seriousness of purpose for a candidate in the midst of a campaign. The group of us flew to Little Rock and spent a number of hours with the governor and Hillary, whom I had never met before. Our group had a range of opinions, but we agreed on the most important issues—the importance of deficit reduction, the need for greater investment in education and health care, and the benefits of trade liberalization. These remained the central components of Clinton's economic strategy for his eight years in office. Within the context of that consensus, there were differences in emphasis. Ken Brody, Rob Shapiro, Roger Altman, and I emphasized reestablishing fiscal discipline more strongly. Reich, Ira Magaziner, and Derek Shearer tilted somewhat more toward investment in education and training.

Our group was asked to draft an economic statement that subsequently evolved into the economic section of the campaign platform, "Putting People First." I suggested that Ken Brody, who shared my focus on deficit reduction, draft the document. But Gene Sperling, who had just joined the campaign and instantly became its economic engine, became the chief draftsman, with some input from the rest of us. I'd known Gene slightly from the Dukakis campaign, where he had played a more junior role. Gene was bright, knowledgeable about economics, extraordinarily productive, and highly adept at crafting a message. He was also slightly disheveled and almost impossible to get on the phone except in the middle of the night. When, or whether, he slept was a great mystery. But on a substantive, as opposed to a stylistic level, Gene was well ordered. He understood what an economic platform for a campaign should look like and how to meld economic policy, politics, and communication.

Gene would sometimes have the "outside advisers" talk to the press when Clinton discussed economic issues or announced a new proposal. And so I began learning how to engage with the media in a Washington context. Gene told me that it was crucial to get my points across in my response to questions—in effect, to be responsive but from my point of view. Throughout my years in Washington, I never lost my wariness of the media, developed from my earlier experience in crisis response at Goldman, but I did develop great respect for many of the people who covered us and tried to respond seriously to those who were serious with us. One of the ironies of my time in Washington is that by the time I left, I felt that some of the most knowledgeable and interesting people I had gotten to know there were journalists, while at the same time I continued to have reservations about the way the media as a whole functioned.

I spent election night in Little Rock, celebrating Clinton's victory. A couple of weeks later, I was summoned back to meet with the President-elect. His mood was upbeat, and he jokingly said, "I'm the leader of the free world," as I shook his hand. We talked for a couple of hours, hardly at all about economic policy, which I told Judy seemed rather peculiar. I wasn't even quite sure what his purpose in seeing me had been. Later I realized that this had indeed been an interview and served a less obvious but important managerial purpose: Clinton was getting a sense of what I'd be like to work with and how I would work with others—a sensitivity about personalities and the interaction of administration members I would observe many times in the years ahead. I remember Clinton noting that despite being a senior partner at Goldman Sachs, I'd developed very comfortable working relationships with Gene and other younger people on the Little Rock campaign staff, such as Gene's deputy Sylvia Mathews. In fact, I liked working with more junior people, who were often closer to the specifics of what was going on and had more time to speak with me. I thought—correctly—that I had much to learn from Gene and Sylvia about politics, campaigns, and much else.

I left the meeting more impressed than ever with the President-elect, but without any idea of what, if anything, would happen next. Clinton did ask who I thought should be Treasury Secretary. I felt I didn't have the experience in dealing with Congress, the media, policy, or politics to handle the job at that point and I recommended Senator Lloyd Bentsen (D-TX), whom I knew pretty well and respected, and who as chairman of the Senate Finance Committee was well equipped for the job. I also remember talking to Clinton about coordinating the many offices and agencies that participate in economic policy. Clinton wanted to create an Economic Security Council—renamed the National Economic Council after the campaign—to do for economic policy what the National Security Council did to coordinate foreign policy.

Shortly thereafter, Warren Christopher, the head of Clinton's transition team, called to sound me out about jobs. I wasn't at all sure I would be offered a position, although I was certainly interested. Christopher, whom I already knew from being on the board of the Carnegie Corporation, which he chaired, said, "If you don't become Treasury Secretary, would you be interested in running the National Economic Council at the White House?" I told Chris, as everyone calls him, that I would. Some time later, I was in Frankfurt, Germany, on a business trip, when the phone rang in my hotel room at 2:30 in the morning. Chris was calling to formally offer me the NEC job. Without any further deliberation, I said yes. Then I went back to sleep.

Christopher had seemed surprised that I'd been receptive when he first raised the NEC job. He may have thought that, as a senior partner at Goldman Sachs, I would consider a staff position at the White House, as opposed to a cabinet post, a step down, even though all economic policy was to be coordinated through the NEC. In retrospect, although not for reasons of status, I might have been wiser to think more seriously about the pluses and minuses of the NEC job before agreeing. For starters, Judy and I hadn't fully discussed this—she was more surprised than Christopher when I called from Germany and told her I'd accepted the job. Beyond that, a rigorous weighing of all factors might have led me to conclude that the odds of succeeding were not so high. The NEC was a new idea, and I was untested in Washington. Many cabinet officers and senior White House staff could view the NEC as an added layer or a diminution of their authority.

But I just said yes. I've been asked a few times how this decision squared with my probabilistic approach to decision making. The answer, I think, is that I responded based on years of wanting to be part of an administration. However, a thorough probabilistic analysis would almost surely have come out the same way, because of the overwhelming positive weight I would have placed on this opportunity. My fascination with Washington and the political process—and my desire to get involved in issues I cared about—overrode all other considerations, and an unconscious probabilistic process may well have underlain my decision. As concerned as I was about the difficulty of making the NEC effective, I didn't focus on the hazards; I focused instead on how much I wanted to do it.

Leaving Goldman Sachs after twenty-six years wasn't easy—for me or for the firm. At a hastily convened partners' breakfast meeting in our conference room on the thirtieth floor, I said good-bye. The company had had 650 people, all in the United States, when I had started in 1966 and had grown more than tenfold by the end of 1992 into a global institution. I said the firm was in extremely good hands—Steve, the others on the Management Committee, and the larger partnership. I also tried to explain something of what the firm had meant to me. I didn't mention the story that had caught my attention in *The New York Times* all those years before, but it came to mind as I left. Goldman had given me a career filled with interest and challenge on the inside—with people I respected and whose values I shared—and a base for involvements on the outside. Armand Erpf—this man I'd never met—was right about what it meant to have that kind of base. Everything started from there.

CHAPTER FOUR

A Political Education

O N DECEMBER 10, 1992, I FLEW to Little Rock for the announcement of the first members of President Clinton's economic team. The group included me as director of what was to be the new National Economic Council, Lloyd Bentsen as Treasury Secretary, Roger Altman as deputy secretary of the Treasury, Leon Panetta as director of the Office of Management and Budget, and Alice Rivlin as Panetta's OMB deputy. Before we walked out for the press conference, Gene Sperling warmed us up with some practice questions. When he got to me, Gene asked, in a very serious tone, "How can a wealthy guy from Wall Street possibly relate to the problems of working Americans? Aren't you just totally unsuited to understanding the problems of ordinary people?"

"Well, I think you've got a good point," I deadpanned. Everyone broke up.

"Bob, you and I are going to have to keep a lighter touch around here," the President-elect said, laughing.

Clinton's comment made an important point that many of us would lose sight of from time to time under the pressures of the next several years. The prospect of all we had to do weighed heavily on our shoulders, especially at that moment, when we were just beginning. It's right to be serious about serious matters—but you also need an ability to escape the intensity. People deal with stress in different ways. My own steam valve was that existential sense I've described. I was highly focused on the policy issues we faced and the problem of making the NEC work. But I also tried at the same time to maintain a sense of perspective. I had to call upon that perspective with some frequency as I figured out my new job. My most urgent assignment during the transition was organizing the decision-making process around the President's economic program. It would involve making critically important choices, and we needed the best process possible.

The catch was that I had no idea what to do. I had experience with financial markets and management, but I didn't know the first thing about process inside a presidential administration. I had no idea how a body like the NEC might be made to function, who I would need on my staff, or what kinds of difficulties I might encounter. I'd never heard of a "decision memo." Put bluntly, I didn't have the foggiest notion how to conduct myself in the White House. I figured that once you got to your new office, you'd call your family and say, "I'm here in the West Wing!" But what were you supposed to do after that? Many of the biggest government programs were barely familiar to me. I'd heard of Medicare, but I couldn't have explained it. In the NEC transition meetings we held at the Washington office of the accounting firm Coopers & Lybrand, people were talking about "discretionary caps," "pay-as-you-go rules," "CBO scoring," and something called the "unified budget." At times it felt like being in a foreign country with people speaking another language.

As I had done at Goldman Sachs, when I showed up for my first day of work not knowing what an arbitrageur did, I started writing down questions. How had other Presidents coordinated economic policy? What had worked and what hadn't? What would make this new body succeed or fail? How could we get cabinet members and senior White House staff to buy into the NEC process? What should my substantive role be? I had other questions about how to function in Washington. How could I be seen to have authority without behaving in an authoritarian manner? How could I follow my inclination to maintain a low profile but deal effectively with the media? How should I allocate my time? How could I do my job and still have time to think?

Legal pad in hand, I made the rounds and interviewed people. A few, such as Bob Strauss, I already knew well. Others, such as Brent Scowcroft, who had been national security advisor to Ronald Reagan and George Bush, I didn't know at all. What they had in common was knowing a lot about life and work in the White House. While some of the advice didn't work for me, my semi-legible notes from those conversations make an interesting primer on the ways of Washington. As much as I would have to learn from my own mistakes in subsequent years, I'm lucky to have been able to begin by learning from other people's.

Bowman Cutter, who had worked as Jimmy Carter's chief deputy director of OMB and who would become one of my two NEC deputies, told me to expect constant infighting. Bo's experience had been that vendettas in the White House were continual and that getting something done often meant battling the cabinet agencies. He said that intergovernment networking would be essential in my job and warned that even if I got along with other top-level people, turf wars among more junior officials could cause serious problems.

Stu Eizenstat, who had been Carter's chief domestic policy adviser, warned me about the potential frustrations of managing my time. He said I'd need to make twenty-five or thirty calls a day, which meant learning to be efficient on the telephone. I should always return calls from members of Congress and the cabinet first, on the same day if possible. In terms of managing my own team, he suggested that the time blocked out for weekly staff meetings should be inviolable.

Others had useful advice on dealing with the press. Roger Porter, who had been the assistant to the President for economic and domestic policy in the Bush administration, told me he had arrived thinking that White House staff should maintain a low profile in dealing with reporters. Over time, he began to feel that invisibility could make someone in his position less effective. Porter was unsure whether he had found the right balance. This conversation left me wondering how I could deal with the press without having a higher public profile than I felt comfortable with. Jody Powell, who had been Carter's press secretary, suggested I spend time talking to reporters on background instead of for quotation. That would keep me out of the limelight, save me from gaffes, avoid offending the journalists I chose not to talk to, and enable me to help advance our views and to create a sense of my relevance. Jody said that departing officials such as Scowcroft, Secretary of State James Baker, and Secretary of Defense Dick Cheney were good models for media relations. Scowcroft, in particular, had never sought attention, yet everyone knew he had been a major presence in the Bush White House.

Ken Duberstein, who had been Ronald Reagan's chief of staff, advised me on a staff person's relations with the President. He suggested that I always be in the room whenever the chief of staff spoke to the President about economic policy and also that I shouldn't go to see the President unless I had something substantive to say to him. At the same time, I should make sure to meet with the President regularly. Ken also gave me a sense of what my working life in Washington might be like. He said I should plan on a twelve-hour day, with an additional hour and a half of reading time at home at night. I should expect to work at least half a day on Saturdays but should try to avoid working on Sundays. And remember, he said as I left, the White House operator can find you wherever you are. Scowcroft made the workload sound even more overwhelming. He said he worked ninety-hour weeks and went jogging at midnight. I found all this alarming, because I knew I couldn't live that way. I need at least seven and a half hours of sleep a night, and time to read and relax.

Jim Johnson, my friend from the Mondale campaign, told me what a decision memo was and gave me advice about how to prepare one for the President. Jim said that such documents shouldn't be long or frequent and should always be channeled through the chief of staff. He also said that the staff person who prepared the memo should be in on any meetings with the President about the decision.

I also went to see Kirk O'Donnell, a highly respected Democratic political hand whose death at a young age in 1998 was a great personal tragedy and a heavy loss for the party. Kirk, a big, ruddy-faced Boston Irishman who had politics in his bones, told me he thought the Clinton administration would succeed or fail as a result of how it approached the economy in its first nine months. He also offered me some practical wisdom about Washington: I should cultivate relationships with six or eight key congressional figures who would serve as advocates for me on Capitol Hill. He also said I should operate on the assumption that anything I told anyone, even in a social setting, would be repeated. (This was, if anything, an understatement. I got to the point where I felt that if I talked to myself, it would leak.) Kirk also told me I needed someone to "watch my back." I said I was probably going to hire Gene Sperling. O'Donnell, who had worked with Gene on the Dukakis campaign, said I'd be okay, since Gene had immense political savvy as well as valuable relationships in the press corps.

My job didn't require congressional confirmation, but I took the opportunity nevertheless to pay a couple of courtesy calls in the Senate. When I visited New York's senior senator, Democrat Daniel Patrick Moynihan, he offered a bit of historical perspective. Anything truly important in Washington took thirty-five years to accomplish, he said. Obviously Moynihan was speaking figuratively, but he was also making a useful point about the difficulty of making major changes through the political system—a lesson we would learn for ourselves when trying to reform health care.

If I'd been more attuned to Washington, I think I might have picked up the question that some of these people had about whether the NEC was likely to be successful. Six months later, Walter Mondale told me that when he'd first heard I had taken the job, he'd had his doubts: the other top people in the new administration, he'd felt, could see the NEC as threatening their own authority and direct access to the Oval Office. I did worry about some of these obstacles, but I didn't dwell on them, perhaps because I didn't understand that much about how government worked. Had I fully understood the pitfalls, I almost surely would still have taken the job, but with more trepidation.

As I considered all the advice I'd received, I realized I had two intertwined challenges. The first was to make the NEC an effective White House process. The second was to work with the President and the rest of the economic team to make sound and sensible economic policy decisions. Concentrating my mind on both issues was the President's directive to have an economic recovery program ready for public release within a month after his inauguration on January 20. Gene Sperling likes to remind me that when I was unable to convince him and others to skip the President's swearing-in, I called a meeting about the budget for 2:00 P.M. that day.

The NEC did have one indispensable asset: the President's intention to use it. From the start, Bill Clinton signaled clearly to the members of his economic team that he wanted to use this instrument to harmonize their efforts and coordinate policy. I remember Clinton commenting during my "job interview" in Little Rock on the harsh observations that were attributed to President Bush's budget director, Richard Darman, about some of his colleagues in a Bob Woodward series published in *The Washington Post* shortly before the election. Clinton thought that the Bush team's "frenzied strife" had greatly undermined his predecessor's effectiveness in dealing with economic issues.

By contrast, Clinton thought that Bush's effectiveness in foreign policy had been due in some fair measure to successful coordination by the National Security Council. Through the NSC, Scowcroft, Baker, and Cheney had successfully worked out their overlapping roles in foreign policy and military affairs, and had functioned as a team. The President-elect wanted the NEC to do the same for economic policy, which lacked an institutional mechanism for coordination. Different administrations had tried different approaches. When economic policy had been run from the White House, cabinet officials had often proved uncooperative. When the Treasury Secretary had assumed a coordinating role, he had often run into conflict with the other cabinet officials.

Clinton appeared to have a vision of good process that resembled the way Steve and I had functioned at Goldman Sachs. As a decision maker, Clinton wanted his aides and advisers to present him with the widest possible range of views and alternatives. He liked to encounter those views not just in memo form, but actually to hear people on his team discuss and debate the options in front of him. Clinton felt that live debate best enabled a decision maker to test and sharpen various options. Moreover, people sometimes persuade one another by discussing their differences, or generate new ideas. My experience in Washington strongly reinforced my view that good process makes good policy. And a fair, open process is more likely to result in participants buying into decisions with which they may differ.

I knew the NEC wouldn't work for five minutes if I tried to be autocratic. Although Clinton wanted economic issues to be presented to him through the NEC, I couldn't simply announce that I was in charge and declare myself the President's gatekeeper—and that would not have been in my nature in any case. I had to think of the other members of the economic team as my clients; they had to feel better off having the NEC than not having it. At times they might have preferred to go to the President directly on the issues they had primary responsibility for. But the advantage, which I think everyone came to see rather quickly, was that they would be at the table when all economic issues were discussed, and decisions on their issues, once made, would be far less subject to attack or reversal within the administration. To work, the NEC had to serve as an honest broker, summarizing everyone's positions and always presenting all sides of an issue fairly. In addition, I had as much right to express my views as anyone else did, but not to give disproportionate weight to my own opinions. So I would wear two hats—one as the neutral manager of a process, the other as a substantive participant. And I would have to clarify which hat I was wearing at any given time. The process had to be run with an integrity that won and maintained the trust of the other participants, or it wouldn't work.

I FLEW TO Washington on a Sunday night with a few suits and a bunch of books and checked into a suite at the Jefferson Hotel. Leaving home gave me a strange, hollow kind of feeling. Judy had no enthusiasm for living in Washington, and our plan was for her to come down one night a week and for me to return on the weekends. We had little idea of how soon I'd move back to New York. For twenty-six years, my two abodes had been my office at Goldman Sachs and my apartment uptown. Now I was stepping into a largely unknown world, moving from an established position as co–senior partner of Goldman Sachs & Company to a job that had never before existed in a world that was new to me in many ways.

My most immediate problem was choosing a staff that could put the concept of the NEC into practice. My first hire was Sylvia Mathews, who had been Gene's deputy on the campaign. I had started talking to Sylvia on media matters when I couldn't get Gene on the phone and had found her well informed and exceedingly adept at crafting comments. A former Rhodes Scholar and consultant for McKinsey & Company, Sylvia came from a small town in West Virginia and had the accent to prove it. In a short while, Sylvia, with her strong organizational skills, became the NEC's de facto chief of staff, organizing me and everything we were doing.

Next, on the recommendation of Vera Murray, Bob Strauss's Washington-savvy executive assistant, whom I had known and respected for twenty years, I met Linda McLaughlin. Linda, who had been working at the World Bank and had long experience in public-sector institutions, became the NEC's second employee. She was my secretary, scheduler, and all-purpose administrator and turned out to be indefatigable, effective, and consistently good-humored in an environment that often could strain anyone's patience.

Following Stu Eizenstat's advice, I decided the NEC should have two co-deputies, with one taking primary responsibility for domestic issues and the other for international ones. I approached Bo Cutter about becoming the international deputy. Bo had an excellent reputation for his intellect and good sense and four years of experience—in President Carter's OMB—with governmental process. I was also interested in hiring Gene Sperling on the domestic side because he knew the issues, knew all the Clinton people, had strong political and message capabilities, and had been extremely effective during the campaign. I wound up with enormous respect for Gene, but at the time I still had some qualms. With his penchant for calling meetings at one in the morning (returning calls sometime thereafter) and an office piled high with paper, his habits could be viewed as a bit chaotic. On the other hand, his work seemed highly disciplined. I couldn't figure out what he was all about. So I called a few people who knew Gene or had worked with him in the past, including then New York governor Mario Cuomo and Guido Calabresi, the dean of the Yale Law School. Both recommended him highly, though Guido did mention that Gene had spent part of his law school career living in his car.

(Gene claims this was just a joke about the messiness of his backseat.) Gene and Sylvia both stayed with Clinton through two terms, in a variety of capacities. Over that time, Sylvia developed great substantive expertise and Gene became skilled at process as well as economic issues. Over the course of the eight years, they were two of the brightest stars in the administration.

With Bo, Gene, Sylvia, and Linda on board, we went about hiring a professional staff. Bo's analysis of NEC subject areas suggested we needed a professional staff of approximately two dozen people. We were already interviewing applicants for those positions when Harold Ickes, who was helping to run the transition and would later become deputy chief of staff at the White House, called to say that we could have no more than twelve people. I told Harold I didn't think the NEC could work with so few people, but he said the administration was hemmed in by a Clinton campaign promise to cut the White House staff by 25 percent and twelve was it, period.

After conferring with Bo and others, I called Mack McLarty, the incoming chief of staff. I had only recently met Mack, but I told him that the NEC wouldn't work without an adequate staff, which I judged to be at least twenty people. If the budget was too constrained to provide that many positions, they should give up on the idea of the NEC and find another way to coordinate economic policy. That was a bleak moment for me. I had given up a major position on Wall Street, which was irreversible, and I was on the verge of winding up with nothing at all.

Mack didn't have any immediate solution. But the next day, he called to say they'd make room for more staff people—not as many as I wanted, but enough to make the NEC work. I subsequently heard from Ken Brody, a Goldman partner who was an important early Clinton backer, that Mack had called him to ask what to do about me. Ken told Mack I probably meant what I said. Ken was right. I believe strongly in trying to reach a reasonable accommodation in the face of disagreement, but I also believe in not crossing what I view as fundamental lines and accepting the possible consequences that may ensue. I didn't think the NEC could work without adequate staff, and I wasn't going to do what didn't seem to me to make sense.

A similar episode occurred later in the first term, after I had moved to the Treasury Department and was negotiating with OMB about the size of our budget. I understood the need for budget cuts but felt that if our funding fell below a certain level we could not run the department effectively. My position was that if our budget had to go below that level, I would understand the budgetary exigencies, but the administration would have to find a Secretary who felt comfortable running the department under those conditions. When others sense your willingness to walk away, your hand is strengthened, and in this instance we received our minimum acceptable level. Afterward, Sylvia and Larry Summers said that they were trying to understand how I had managed the negotiation. "For that to work," Sylvia said, "you must be prepared to die." As Sylvia pointed out, my stance had been effective precisely because I hadn't been negotiating but stating my commitment to a fundamental position.

WE WERE SUPPOSED TO BE developing an economic plan—but I had no idea what a presidential economic plan was or how to assemble it. I consulted Leon Panetta, who had been chairman of the House Budget Committee, who said we had to present the President-elect with a budget, which sounded right. So Leon drew up budget options, and we focused on framing them as alternative fiscal and programmatic paths for Clinton at an all-day meeting to be held on January 7 at the governor's mansion in Little Rock. Everything became focused around this meeting.

Making a budget raises every question about how to allocate the resources of the federal government—what new programs to fund, which old ones to reshape or terminate, what deserves more or less, and—very important—who should pay. The budget also brought us face-to-face with what rapidly emerged as the essential question: how to balance all of Clinton's potentially costly proposals—universal health insurance, welfare reform, a middle-class tax cut, education and job training programs—with the reality of an unsound and worsening fiscal situation. Obviously all of these proposals could not be fully implemented during the first year while we were simultaneously trying to accomplish significant deficit reduction, working toward Clinton's campaign pledge to cut the deficit in half in four years. I sent a memo to the President-elect to prepare him for the meeting, saying that he could not significantly reduce the deficit and do all that he had proposed during the campaign.

We divided up the presentation among the various economic officials. Leon was responsible for the budget; Lloyd Bentsen for taxes; Laura D'Andrea Tyson, the incoming head of the Council of Economic Advisers (CEA), for the economic outlook and the impact of various policy options. My role would be to keep the meeting on track. But how to do that? This would be the President-elect's first working experience with his incoming cabinet members and their first experience working together in his presence. The economic plan was due only weeks after the inauguration, and we had five hours to cover an enormous amount of material. When the two of us met beforehand in a small dining room, I told Clinton he should pose whatever questions he wanted but that we needed to keep the meeting moving along. He laughed and patted me on the shoulder, promising to "be good."

George Stephanopoulos, who for some reason I had never met during the campaign, stopped me on the way into the meeting and said that the President-elect was in a real bind. If Clinton decided on a significant deficit reduction target, he couldn't follow through on his middle-class tax cut and various domestic proposals. George said the President-elect couldn't be expected to make such a momentous decision in this first meeting and moreover wasn't likely to. I couldn't tell whether George didn't want Clinton to make such a momentous choice that day or simply didn't want me to get upset when it didn't happen.

In any case, George was wrong. What I remember best about that meeting was that after less than an hour, as Leon and Alice Rivlin were laying out the details of the worsening deficit, Clinton stopped the discussion and said, "I get it." Deficit reduction, he said, had become the "threshold" issue. "I know it won't be easy," he continued. "But I was elected to deal with the economy and this is what we need to do to get the economy back on track." I've since felt that Clinton might already have had that view coming into the meeting, so quickly and decisively did he state this position.

The rest of the session substantiated Clinton's view. An intellectual

framework was provided by Laura Tyson; Alan Blinder, a Princeton economist who was to be Laura's deputy at the Council of Economic Advisers;
and Larry Summers, the chief economist at the World Bank who was
slated to become undersecretary for international affairs at Treasury. The
three of them explained that according to the familiar laws of Keynesian
economics, cutting the deficit by reducing government spending or increasing taxes should slow the economy. But this time the situation might
be different, because the growing deficit had been keeping interest rates
high, a phenomenon I referred to as a deficit premium. Then and in many
subsequent meetings, we debated just how much effect deficits have on
the bond-market interest rates that drive the economy. There was a great
deal of uncertainty on this issue. As one input, Alan Greenspan had told
a number of us that, citing the published deficit impact model of the Federal Reserve Board's staff, he projected a reduction of $1/10$ of one percentage point in long-term interest rates for each $10 billion in annual deficit
reduction, with GDP then around $6.6 trillion. (As an aside, that trans-
lates into a reduction in bond-market interest rates of 0.66 percent for
every 1 percent of GDP of deficit reduction.) Clearly, the Fed's actions
would be one important factor, among others, in determining market interest rates, and knowing Greenspan's views helped us gauge his likely
reaction to our fiscal choices.

Interest-rate effects are only part of the argument for fiscal soundness—
an analysis I'll lay out more fully later—but they were our focus at that
moment. Bondholders were demanding a higher return, based both on
the longer-term fiscal outlook and on the risk that the politics of reestablishing fiscal discipline would be too difficult and that, instead, our political system would attempt to shrink the real value of the debt through
inflation. We thought that lowering the deficit and bringing down long-
term interest rates should have an expansionary effect that would more
than offset the contractionary Keynesian effect and that, conversely, the
expansionary effects of continued large deficits would be more than offset
by the adverse impact on interest rates. In Japan, Europe, and the Middle
East, as well as in the United States, investors would increase their demand for dollar-denominated bonds if they believed that a sound fiscal
pattern was going to be reestablished. And lower interest rates should spur

consumers to spend and businesses to invest. This seemed our best strategy for stimulating the economy and promoting a strong, sustainable recovery at a time of pervasive uncertainty, with business and consumer confidence still soft, unemployment above 7 percent, and the resumption of growth tentative.

Many people might have been surprised to see a group of Democrats sitting around a table in Arkansas talking about the international bond market. And that our focus was the international bond market rather than just the U.S. market was a sign of how far the globalization of financial markets had already come by 1993. I think historians looking back on this period some decades hence are likely to see the Clinton administration as deeply engaged with global integration, the emergence of new technologies, and the spread of market-based economics. I don't know what they'll call this era, but I think they may draw the conclusion that Bill Clinton was the first American President with a deep understanding of how these issues were reshaping our economy, our country, and the world.

My role in the meeting was to make sure that all views got a fair airing, but I also made my own opinions plain. For us to achieve those lower interest rates that Laura, Alan, and Larry were talking about, financial markets would have to believe that the administration was serious about deficit reduction. More than a decade of promises that hadn't materialized had led to an understandable skepticism. I was concerned that creating credibility with financial markets might take longer than one would hope. I remember saying that there was nothing scientific about how much deficit reduction would have credibility and create a real economic impact. In a $6.6 trillion economy, a few billion dollars more or less—a small fraction of 1 percent of GDP—shouldn't make a big difference. But I'd learned on Wall Street that relatively small differences in absolute amounts could make a big difference in market psychology: the difference between a bid for a block of stock at $34⅞ and a bid for the same stock at $35 could be a lot more than 12.5 cents. Or, as my former partner at Goldman Sachs Bob Mnuchin used to say, we were better off paying someone $250,000 than paying him $240,000, because the psychological impact of earning a quarter of a million dollars was greater to the individual than the financial impact of another $10,000 to the firm. The difference between small amounts of deficit reduction over a five-year period was like that—minor in economic terms but potentially great in terms of the market's reaction.

In retrospect, the effect of the Clinton economic plan on business and consumer confidence may have been even more important than the effect on interest rates. In important ways, the deficit had become a symbol of the government's inability to manage its own affairs—and of our society's inability to cope with economic challenges more generally, such as our global competitiveness, then much in question. The view that fiscal discipline was being restored contributed to lower interest rates and increased confidence, and that led to more spending and investment, which in turn led to job creation, lower unemployment rates, and increased productivity. Some have argued that the productivity surge of the 1990s was merely a delayed reaction to the new digital technologies that arrived in the 1980s. But that view overlooks what happened in Europe and Japan, where the same access to new technology failed to result in a similar sustained productivity surge, probably because businesses didn't invest in technology to the same degree. That paucity of investment may well have been due to the structural rigidities in the labor and capital markets of Europe and Japan, but even with the flexible economy of the United States, investment, and therefore productivity, probably would not have surged as they did without that increased confidence as well as lower interest rates.

In an economic boom, as in a decline, cause and effect can become difficult to distinguish. The restoration of business and consumer confidence, combined with lower interest rates, created a virtuous circle, a positive feedback loop. Deficit reduction contributed to economic growth, which, through increased government revenues, contributed to further deficit reduction, which in turn led to more growth, and so on. The fiscal effect of the plan was thus a function both of our policy measures and of the growth those policies fed. We didn't design the plan around the potential effect on the stock market, as we had with the bond market, but in fact a similar phenomenon occurred as improved fiscal and economic conditions contributed to a rising stock market, which in turn fed back into deficit reduction and the economy.

While I don't think any of us fully foresaw the impact that restoring fiscal discipline would have on economic confidence, everyone in that room in Little Rock accepted the argument about what a credible plan was likely to do for interest rates. Contrary to some subsequent reports, everyone agreed that a serious deficit reduction program was absolutely necessary. I remember Lloyd Bentsen, the incoming Treasury Secretary, arguing persuasively that we had to do the tough things in the first months, when credibility was highest. Once we were in the White House, some political advisers—such as Paul Begala, James Carville, Stan Greenberg, and Mandy Grunwald—expressed serious concerns about the politics of our program. James Carville even took to calling me "Nick"— referring to Nick Brady, Bush's Treasury Secretary—because of my concern with the bond market (though James always said this with a twinkle in his eye, and I still smile when I remember that nickname). They felt that deficit reduction had no political constituency and that the President's political interests would be better served by following through on the middle-class tax cut and other campaign proposals. And in fact, in one sense their concerns turned out to be well warranted. In the longer run, there is no question in my mind that this program was right not only economically but also politically, because it was essential to the strong economy that helped reelect Clinton in 1996. But the economic benefits were not felt on a sustained basis by the time of the 1994 midterm election, and had we listened more to the concerns of the political advisers, we might have focused better on framing our deficit reduction message in a more politically effective way.

DESPITE CONSENSUS ON the broad goal of serious deficit reduction, there was no immediate agreement in Little Rock on the amount of deficit reduction or how to achieve it. At one end of the spectrum, Alice Rivlin advocated the most strenuous program of deficit reduction. Of the same general orientation, although slightly less hawkish, were Al Gore, Lloyd Bentsen, Leon Panetta, and myself. Among the others in the room that day, Bob Reich, Laura Tyson, George Stephanopoulos, and Gene Sperling suggested a more moderate position. While the hawks were focused on our plan's credibility with markets, Gene, Bob, and George wanted to preserve more of the campaign proposals. The new, higher deficit projection the Congressional Budget Office had issued in late December 1992 had made trade-offs between credible deficit reduction and these proposals even more difficult, and everyone understood that new programs in education, job training, health care, and welfare reform would have to be substantially constrained, at best, and that the middle-class tax cut was no longer feasible.

At some point, Leon and Alice presented five options—alternative amounts of deficit reduction, ranging from merely meeting the Bush administration's existing "baseline" deficit projection to cutting it in half over five years. Each option was combined with a commensurate level of investment. We disregarded the extremes at either end and focused on three options, all of which included significant deficit reduction. None eliminated the structural deficit over the five-year period—that was more than was practically possible, given the starting point. But we thought that health care reform's effect on Medicare would mean further reduction and that future budgets could continue the program.

I had told Clinton this wasn't supposed to be the "decision" meeting, merely a first airing of big issues. But as we discussed these options, he indicated support for a strong level of deficit reduction. After the inauguration, our group met in the Roosevelt Room over a period of several weeks to set the exact level of deficit reduction, priorities for allocation of budgetary resources, and the specifics of our tax proposal. Clinton remained intensely involved in the specifics. Throughout the process, his essential view—and the administration consensus—never faltered. The President adhered to a strong deficit target number despite the concerns of his political advisers, pressure from some Democrats in Congress, and the complaints of constituencies that were important to him politically. When the plan ran into serious political trouble, he persisted, and while he sometimes complained and even on occasion lost his temper about the fiscal problems he had inherited, he put tremendous energy into getting his plan passed. This was my first real experience with presidential decision making, and it left me with a respect for Clinton that has continued through the years. Like the Mexico decision, deficit reduction involved exchanging near-term political pain for the potential, not the guarantee, of long-term economic gain.

The decisions the President made in this process marked a dramatic change in fiscal policy. The opponents of that change—especially supply-side advocates who vehemently objected to including tax increases in our deficit reduction program—predicted that our program would lead to increased unemployment, higher deficits, and economic stagnation or recession, or worse. Republican Representative Dick Armey of Texas, chairman of the House Republican Conference, said the plan would be "a disaster for the performance of the economy" and warned that "no deficit reduction, no good can come of it." His colleague from Texas, Republican Senator Phil Gramm, called it "a one-way ticket to a recession." Instead, the country had the longest period of growth in its history, massive new private-sector job creation, low inflation, higher incomes across all income groups, increased investment and productivity growth, and lower deficits, eventually followed by surpluses. That has been a great and enduring frustration to supply-side advocates, who first predicted that our policies would cause great economic injury and then, when the opposite happened, argued that sound fiscal policy had nothing to do with economic conditions they had predicted would not occur.

Economic causation is complex and many factors contributed to the strong economy of the 1990s, but I think the evidence strongly supports the conclusion that deficit reduction was, as President Clinton said in our January 7 meeting, a threshold act. Without the policy changes ushered in by the 1993 economic plan, I don't believe that the sustained, robust recovery of the 1990s would have occurred. In our January 7 meeting, Alan Blinder argued that without restoration of fiscal discipline, the recovery could be "choked off" by higher interest rates. A few years ago, the Congressional Budget Office put out a paper arguing that the surplus that arrived in 1998 derived one third from policy decisions and two thirds from economic growth. But in reality these factors cannot be distinguished, since the growth was, to a considerable degree, a product of the policy.

What presidents do and say can have a substantial impact on the economy. So can what they don't do and don't say. On the affirmative side,

Clinton maintained consistent focus on fiscal soundness throughout his time in office, as part of a broad-based domestic and international economic policy agenda. On the do-no-harm side, Clinton avoided trying to "jawbone" markets and resisted politically appealing measures that might have had a negative effect. For instance, he often came under pressure to constrict the flexibility of labor markets in various ways, such as proposing plant-closing notification laws. He advocated mitigating the consequences of economic dislocation—through measures such as worker training and universal health care—rather than restricting the workings of the free market.

OUR ECONOMIC POLICY DEADLINE was February 17, the date of the President's scheduled address to a joint session of Congress. The first draft of the speech I saw had a lot of language designed to resonate with the public but lacked a tightly reasoned discussion of our economic strategy with regard to deficit reduction and long-term interest rates. So I drafted a few short paragraphs attempting to explain our strategy with some rigor. In a speech frequently punctuated by wild applause, my neat little explanation—"It has an investment program designed to increase public and private investment in areas critical to our economic future. And it has a deficit-reduction program that will increase the savings available for the private sector to invest, will lower interest rates, will decrease the percentage of the federal budget claimed by interest payments, and decrease the risks of financial market disruptions that could adversely affect our economy"—was greeted by zero applause. So much for my future as a speechwriter, but I still thought that having a brief but serious reference point in the President's speech could be useful in the subsequent political debate.

I assumed, as many of us did, that the economic plan, once finished, would pass in due course. After all, our party controlled Congress with a comfortable majority in both houses, and we were standing for a reestablishment of fiscal discipline long advocated by many Republicans. In February 1993, there were already indications that the plan was having an effect, even before it passed. In one of our morning briefings, I told the

President that the bond market was reacting more quickly and strongly than I had anticipated. In a recovering economy, interest rates might have been expected to rise in response to improved business and consumer demand and the expectation of future demand. Yet the yield on thirty-year Treasury bonds, 7.4 percent on December 31, 1992, had actually declined, quickly falling by more than half a point to 6.83 percent on February 23, 1993. That suggested to us that the markets were beginning to believe that our deficit reduction plan would work. (By mid-August, immediately after the plan was passed, long-term rates dropped by a full percentage point to 6.37, even though recovery was continuing.)

In monthly lunches the President held in the dining room in the White House residence, corporate leaders began to speak more positively about the economy. Most who came to these sessions were Republicans and hardly sympathetic to the new administration. After spending an hour and a half with the President, however, they often said to me that they thought he was smart, understood their issues, and really listened to them. Many continued to disagree with the tax piece of our plan, but as the months passed, it became clear that business leaders were gaining confidence in the country's economic prospects. I repeated to President Clinton a bit of sage advice Bob Strauss had given to President Carter: there are many people in the business community who probably won't ever support a Democrat for President, but he can take the energy out of their opposition with sound economic policies.

Confident that our plan was right, we put it out and moved on. As Clinton later said to me, this was a crucial tactical mistake. He should have been out talking about his economic program every day. He told me he would never again attempt a major policy initiative without an integral and forceful communication and political strategy. He also said he should have made an intense effort to frame the debate from the very beginning.

I learned through this episode that from the moment a President presents an important proposal to the nation, he has to spend time painting a picture of it his way. Otherwise, his opponents will color it their way and put him on the defensive. Our opponents went right to work casting our plan as a tax increase—a grave distortion in relation to the vast majority of taxpayers, who saw no increase in their income taxes and a gas tax estimated at only $36 a year for an average family of four. We, on the other hand, spent little time explaining how few people were affected by the tax increase or, more important, painting our own picture of the program as a restoration of fiscal discipline to create jobs, increase standards of living, and promote economic growth. Clinton subsequently came back into the debate very vigorously. But because he was largely absent from it for some time, our opponents had a big lead in creating the prism through which our economic plan was viewed. We had to fight against that prism and were never entirely successful. Senator Dianne Feinstein (D-CA) told me that when she ran for reelection in 1994, a poll showed that 42 percent of the people in California thought their income tax rates had been raised in 1993.

That's a good example of how distortions can stick when they aren't immediately and decisively rebutted. In reality, the income tax hike in our plan affected the top 1.2 percent of Americans and, I imagine, a somewhat similar proportion of Californians. The tax that did affect middle-income Americans—the gas tax—was tiny. I remember thinking at the time that a small energy tax could give us credibility in the markets, precisely because of the conventional wisdom that it was dangerous politically. But I hadn't realized how that very small gas tax could be used—or, more accurately, misused—to portray our program as a middle-income tax increase. Most of my colleagues also missed it, although George Stephanopoulos and some of the other political advisers had been very concerned about precisely this point.

One political issue we faced was whether to use class-laden language to sell our program. My view was that such rhetoric was inadvisable for multiple reasons. A key episode in that debate occurred when I saw a draft of the President's address for the joint session of Congress. I was disturbed by the tone of some of the rhetoric and went to Hillary, my office neighbor on the second floor of the West Wing, to make my point. Hillary not only agreed, she marched me down to the Roosevelt Room, where Paul Begala was working on the speech. She stood over Paul's shoulder as he rephrased the problematic passages.

Even talking about "the rich," it seemed to me, had an unnecessary normative connotation, suggesting that there was something wrong with having been successful financially. This objection was not an expression of class solidarity on my part; I thought that discussing tax issues in terms of who should pay was entirely appropriate and a necessary part of any serious tax debate. My only issue was the choice of language; polarizing rhetoric could undermine business confidence in President Clinton and his policies. That confidence was crucial to achieving strong economic performance. And while no political expert, I felt that the politics wouldn't work either, because middle-income people didn't respond well to disparagement of economic success, and such language risked alienating the economically most successful as well.

My alternative way of presenting our tax increase was to argue that the affluent had done very well in the 1980s, while middle-income people had actually lost ground. The best-off should therefore bear a substantial part of the burden of reducing the biggest negative economic legacy of that decade, namely the deficit. And in fact, the upper-income individuals whose taxes were increased seemed for the most part to take it in stride. I remember telling the President that I knew many people with large incomes, and when I went back to New York, I didn't hear much objection. Nobody likes to have his taxes go up, but I was surprised at how little complaint there was.

In contrast to wealthy individuals, the business community did object vigorously to a 2 percent increase in corporate rates included in the original proposal. I remember in particular one visit I paid that spring to the Business Roundtable in Washington, D.C. I told these corporate leaders, quite a few of whom I knew personally from my days on Wall Street, that we were doing exactly what the group's members had long advocated—reducing the deficit. But most of these business people believed that deficit reduction should come largely or exclusively from spending cuts, with very little, if any, increase in taxes. I argued that we had to operate within a political system in which existing programs had powerful constituencies and often served important purposes, even if most business people didn't rate those purposes highly. As a result, there were limits on how much spending could, or should, be cut. Without help from the revenue side, powerful deficit reduction simply wouldn't happen. We expected further spending reductions through greater efficiency, but that was a longer-term process being pursued through the Vice President's Reinventing Government initiative and, we hoped, through reforming government health care programs.

This reaction was, in a way, typical. Business people often have unrealistic expectations of how much the outcome of a political process can—or should—resemble their ideal solution. If you offer business people 75 percent of what they want—on trade, workplace safety regulations, taxes, or whatever else—they'll tend to focus on the 25 percent they can't have. They may be willing to strike a bargain in the end, but they often don't tend to recognize either the validity of objectives different from their own or the realistic political limits. And the same is generally true for interest groups of all kinds.

More surprising to me than the Business Roundtable's response was the reaction of some in Congress who did understand the political process and who had always been strong advocates of fiscal discipline. Instead of crediting our attack on the deficit, they tended to dwell solely on the tax increases they didn't like. In fact, the deficit reduction in our plan came half from spending cuts (including interest saved by reducing the level of national debt) and half from tax increases. In our Roosevelt Room meetings, we had struggled to maintain this principle of balance. But to many of the longtime deficit hawks in Congress, the tax increase was all that mattered. The gas tax was a particular point of contention. I remember one Democratic senator telling me that a gas tax any higher than 4.2 cents per gallon would lose his vote for the plan. Practically, that didn't make any sense—why support a four-cent increase but not a five-cent one? The price of gas could fluctuate more than a nickel in a week of free-market movement. But politically, people were scared to death of the issue.

The first sign of serious trouble was Congress's defeat of the President's stimulus package in April. The stimulus package played a useful role in a deficit reduction program, because the deficit reduction measures in the budget could take quite some time to develop credibility and have an impact on the economy. Compared to the deficit reduction, the stimulus package was tiny—$16.3 billion versus $496 billion—but the stimulus provided a near-term insurance policy if the program wasn't succeeding quickly enough, in which case Congress might lose patience with deficit reduction and reverse course. I argued that the more you cared about long-term deficit reduction, the more you should be in favor of the short-term stimulus package. As it turned out, we didn't need the insurance. Economically, the defeat was relatively insignificant, but politically it was perceived as a major setback for Clinton. The President had asked for something, and Congress, controlled by his own party, had refused his request.

The defeat of the stimulus package cast some doubt on the prospects of our larger economic plan. The story of that legislative battle, culminating in a two-vote victory in the House and a fifty-fifty tie broken by the Vice President in the Senate, has been well told elsewhere. As those votes were being taken, a group of us including the President, Bentsen, McLarty, and Panetta crowded around the TV in the President's private study off the Oval Office, unsure of how the House would vote. The next day in the Senate, the fiftieth yea was that of Bob Kerrey of Nebraska. The last holdout in such a situation has considerable power: typically someone in that position will ask for some tangible benefit for his constituents. But Kerrey wasn't looking for anything like that. His demand was for a presidential commission to study the future of entitlement spending. We agreed and breathed an enormous sigh of relief. Had the President lost on his initial budget, not only might economic recovery have been stymied, but, as Mack McLarty said, the whole Clinton presidency might have been imperiled.

CHAPTER FIVE

White House Life

WORKING IN THE WHITE HOUSE sometimes felt surreal. With the exception of the Oval Office and a few other key spaces, such as the Vice President's office and the Cabinet Room, much of the West Wing was cramped and shabby. Our NEC offices on the second floor were nondescript, lit with fluorescent lights and filled with ragtag office furniture that looked secondhand. But the people who met in the West Wing were the key officials of the U.S. government. I'd be having a normal discussion with some people around a conference table and it would strike me that this nice man, Warren Christopher, bore the title Secretary of State; that fellow whom I'd known for years, Lloyd Bentsen, was Secretary of the Treasury; and that bright, argumentative fellow over there was the Vice President. And what we were discussing didn't affect just my company, but the fate of the country and the world. Every so often I'd stop and think to myself, *My God, I'm sitting in the Oval Office having an argument with this guy I know, Bill Clinton, who is President of the United States.*

After a few seconds, though, that slightly otherworldly sensation would pass and I'd return to the discussion as if these people didn't have those titles. Even though the stakes were enormous and I cared greatly about the issues, I generally went to work and did my job, as I would have anyplace else. But then I'd pass by South African President Nelson Mandela in the hallway or see PLO Chairman Yasser Arafat shake hands with

Israeli Prime Minister Yitzhak Rabin and be struck all over again. Then Gene Sperling would wander in with a decision memo and the spell would be broken.

In an environment where many tended to push themselves forward, my natural inclination was to stand back a bit. Erskine Bowles, who joined the White House as a deputy chief of staff in 1994 and tended to take an anthropological view, told me that what happened inside the Oval Office was sort of a rugby scrum to get up next to the President. Even in the smaller meeting in the chief of staff's office that followed the large morning staff meeting in the Roosevelt Room, some people would cluster as close to the head of the table as possible. I always liked to be away from the center, whether in the Oval Office or the chief of staff's office, where my regular seat became the foot of the table. That little bit of physical distance felt more comfortable to me, and let me read the room and comment from a perspective ever so slightly removed. I didn't worry about being overlooked. No matter how far away you were sitting or standing, you could always just say, "Mr. President, I think this, that, or the other."

This distance afforded a clearer view of Clinton's relations with others inside and outside the administration. Evident to me from the first was Clinton's unusual skill as a listener. He could relate to someone else's point of view in a way that made that person feel not just heard but understood. Listening in that way was more flattering than ordinary flattery; here was the President of the United States, and he really cared about what you had to say. And this was not calculated or phony. Clinton was like Gus Levy with clients at Goldman Sachs, able to make people feel like the center of his world because they were the center of his world while he engaged with them. The President's charm, like Gus's, lay in the fact that he meant it. Moreover, Clinton processed what he heard. He would make comments referring to what someone had told him days or weeks before. And his views reflected his considered reactions.

This is part of what could captivate people about Bill Clinton but could also lead to a certain amount of misunderstanding. Clinton listened so sympathetically that people who were unaccustomed to him often took it as duplicitous when he later came out against their positions, as with Newt Gingrich in the crucial budget negotiations of 1995, when the

Speaker mistook Clinton's comprehension and engagement for assent. By that time, I had seen enough that I could tell where Clinton really was. Sitting in White House meetings over the years, I would say to myself or to someone next to me, "That person is going to think Clinton is leaning toward his position. But he's going to get a big surprise, because Clinton doesn't agree at all—that's just how he listens."

From his own staff, the President expected candor, and my approach was to tell him what was on my mind—though in some cases diplomatically. Clinton specifically told us during our Little Rock transition meeting, "If you all don't tell me what you really think, I'm dead."

That comment reminded me of what John Weinberg had once said to me at Goldman Sachs: as a CEO, you have a special place in the minds of your subordinates. People in your own organization have a natural tendency to pull their punches around you, to soften the bad news and try to tell you what they think you want to hear. Because you're a bit of a king, you can easily get an unrealistic sense of the wisdom of your own views and your merits as a leader. (Walter Mondale once told me that when he was Vice President and then his party's presidential nominee, everyone laughed uproariously at his jokes. Then he lost the election and realized he wasn't so funny after all.) To keep a realistic sense of yourself and to make well-informed decisions, you have to go out of your way to make people feel comfortable disagreeing with you.

A President faces these problems in the extreme. But Clinton meant what he said in Little Rock and worked to draw out disagreement with his own views. And contrary to what I've heard and read about some administrations, the people around Clinton generally said what they thought. The instinct to pull punches was often present, but most of us resisted it most of the time—although some more than others.

People outside the administration were a different matter. From time to time, business leaders would meet with me and express strong criticism of one or more of the President's positions—and on some issues (tort reform, for example) I agreed with them. But when the same people met with Clinton in the Roosevelt Room or in the dining room in the residence, they often either muted their opposition or even sounded supportive of those policies. Then, when I'd later tell Clinton that the business community disagreed with those positions, he'd respond, "Bob, what are you talking about? So-and-so was here last week, and he didn't say that." I always encouraged those who met with him to be frank, and he encouraged candor as well. But frequently that didn't work.

Disagreeing with the President may also have been harder for people who joined the administration later. Some of us who had known him as governor of Arkansas remained comfortable approaching him in a certain way. But a President acquires an aura that can inhibit challenge, and some of those who signed on in later years seemed more affected by it. Midway through the second term, when I directly and strongly expressed disagreement with the President in a Cabinet Room meeting over his reservations about applying conditionality to debt relief in Africa, I caught a look of sharp surprise on the faces of some officials who had little contact with him.

One of Clinton's characteristics that could be upsetting to people who weren't used to him was his temper. Once when I was in the Oval Office, the President blew up at Roger Altman over a health care issue. A few minutes later, the two of them were talking as calmly as ever. People who worked in the White House soon learned that Clinton sometimes vented his frustration in an explosive way, but that those outbursts didn't mean much. His anger was like a tropical storm. It blew up suddenly and then went away.

Despite working closely with Clinton for six and a half years, I never developed the kind of close personal relationship with him that others in the administration such as Mickey Kantor, Ron Brown, Vernon Jordan, and Erskine Bowles had. We had an easy, informal working relationship, but I was never somebody the President called late at night or palled around with on the golf course. This measure of personal distance never interfered with our working relationship and, in Judy's view, might even have been helpful in some ways.

WORKING IN THE White House was preoccupying like nothing else I'd ever done before, in part because it was always with me. The issues I was dealing with were often on the nightly news and in the newspapers. While at Goldman Sachs, I hadn't exactly left my cares at the office when I went home at the end of the day, but I hadn't had to live with the ever-present public focus and spotlight of Washington.

And that spotlight has a strong tendency to be critical. On any issue, partisan opponents might be trying to make my job more difficult, in part through ad hominem attacks. On top of this, the media tended to be critical and emphasize conflict. Tony Lake, President Clinton's first-term national security advisor, who had served in two prior administrations, told a group of us early in the first term to expect the press to write stories—whether well grounded or not—about who was up and who was down, which could create divisions among us. Tony said we had to keep working together and not to let those stories get to us.

But that was sometimes more easily said than done. Howard Paster, the administration's highly effective first congressional liaison, made a very shrewd point after he was criticized in a few stories. Recalling Tony's comment, I told Howard that such stories come and go and that he shouldn't be concerned. But Howard, who had been a very successful lobbyist in Washington for many years, said that once the press views you in a certain way, that view tends to stick. Being human, none of us was able to put media criticism completely out of mind, but different people reacted to this media environment in different ways. Some became highly focused on how they were perceived and seemed largely driven by a focus on perception—which, ironically, seldom worked. Others were better at putting issues of perception into perspective and concentrating on their substantive and political objectives. I was generally fortunate in my press coverage at the NEC, which may have made it easier to absorb the criticism we did get.

Washington's critical spotlight added to the stress of an inherently uncertain White House role. At Goldman Sachs, Citigroup, or any other company, you have a job and a role. Whatever your title may be, whether CEO or clerk/typist, you have an idea where you fit into the organization. Positions may have some fluidity, but they also have fairly clear definitions. For someone working in a senior position at the White House or one of the cabinet agencies, by contrast, it was never entirely clear what your role—or anybody else's—was.

On a daily basis, this uncertainty could manifest itself in the question of what meetings you were going to be in. Struggles about who would be in the room were frequent and sometimes ferocious. I once called Sandy Berger, who succeeded Tony as national security advisor, about a meeting I hadn't been invited to. Sandy, who sounded stressed, said it was fine for me to come. Then he sighed and said that he sometimes thought his main job was deciding who got into meetings.

The larger uncertainties related to what effect you would have in your job. An administration is a President-centered universe; your title didn't define your influence on the President's decisions—and that influence could change at any time. That ambiguous and unstable structure may help explain the constant, intense jockeying that seems endemic to most administrations (though ours probably had less than most). Everyone felt it, although people reacted in different ways. For me, an additional issue was whether people native to the political world would think that I "got it." The President said to me shortly before his inauguration that the health care task force was going to operate under Hillary and Ira Magaziner. "You're going to be the strongest person in the White House, and you've got to help me make this thing with Ira work," Clinton said. And I thought to myself, *You know, that's a ridiculous thing to say. I don't know about the White House; I don't know about Washington; I don't know how to do any of this stuff. I'm just hoping to be relevant and have an impact.*

I was not a fan of efforts at formalized camaraderie within the administration. In the middle of our putting together the economic plan, the Clintons invited the entire cabinet and the most senior White House staff to Camp David for a weekend of bonding and discussion of strategy. The concept—which was the Vice President's—might well have been good, but the event itself was pretty awful. Saturday night, after dinner, we sat around in a circle, and each of us was supposed to talk about something the others didn't know about us. The President talked about having been overweight when he was in school and how everyone had made fun of him. When my turn came, I said I didn't have anything I particularly wanted to share. By that point, Lloyd Bentsen had wisely gone home for the evening.

I arrived in Washington knowing a good bit about how Wall Street worked, and some of what I knew was very useful. But I also had a strong appreciation for how much I didn't know about the ways of Washington. My chief asset in navigating this unknown terrain was recognition of my shortcomings and a readiness to learn. I subsequently saw others pay a price for having a different attitude. Sometime during the transition, I took a walk down Pennsylvania Avenue with another new administration official who had never been in government before and was coming from the private sector. I was talking about how difficult and complex this new world was and about how much we outsiders had to learn about it. My future colleague said, "Bob, you and I know how to do things. We'll do them the same way down here that we did them at home." Applying the rules of business to politics was his formula for success. I told him that I didn't think our life in Washington was going to work that way. As useful as our background was likely to be in certain respects, much in Washington was very different.

Steve Silverman, a staff member who worked in Cabinet Affairs, once said to me, "You know, some of us from the campaign were afraid that people like you, who came from big positions in the outside world, would be the big feet and that we'd be kicked aside." He was pleased that the administration hadn't turned out that way, but I would never have dreamed of thinking like that. I was an amateur coming into a world of professionals. People such as Gene Sperling and Sylvia Mathews were impressive to me because they knew so much more. In this new realm of government and politics, I was, in a way, their considerably older junior associate.

My modesty about my skills in this world was frequently reinforced. In May 1993, as we were struggling to get our economic plan through Congress, I appeared on *The MacNeil/Lehrer NewsHour* opposite Pete Domenici, the ranking Republican on the Senate Budget Committee. I spent considerable time preparing with Gene. My opening comment was that our deficit reduction plan was real and serious.

"Frankly, it is predominantly a tax plan," Domenici replied.

I responded by talking about the "trust fund" we had proposed so that monies set aside for deficit reduction would go to deficit reduction.

"If the American people think there's too much taxes and not enough spending cuts in the plan, please don't think that calling the taxes a trust fund changes it," Domenici said.

I responded that Leon Panetta and Alice Rivlin felt very strongly that the numbers in our plan were real.

Domenici responded that the defeat of our "tax plan" would be the best thing that could happen to the country.

I fired back with more specifics. The numbers produced by the non-partisan Congressional Budget Office were close to those produced by OMB. Both agreed that the ratio of tax increases to spending cuts in our plan was approximately 1 to 1.

Domenici responded that our tax plan would hurt the economy.

I thought I'd done pretty well and was very pleased to say so to Gene after the broadcast. They had asked me various questions, and I had come back with good, detailed answers. Domenici had just kept repeating the shibboleth that our plan was a tax increase. Gene had a different take. He said that people who saw the program would think that "you seemed like a nice, smart man who wanted to raise their taxes." Domenici's performance demonstrated both how effective a simple message could be on television and how effectively our plan could be attacked. My response demonstrated the difficulty of crafting an effective, simple defense of our substantively complicated strategy.

Of course, part of the problem simply may have been me. Shortly after that episode, I spoke to Ricki Seidman, the deputy communications director, before I was scheduled to go on CNN's *Capital Gang.* Ricki told me quite bluntly that I needed some help in dealing with the very particular medium of television. Maggie Williams, who was Hillary Clinton's chief of staff, had said something similar a month or two earlier, so I decided to act. I got Leon Panetta, who was highly skilled at television, to substitute for me on CNN, and I made an appointment to see Michael Sheehan, a media coach who worked with President Clinton, among others.

I was skeptical about going to see Sheehan, because I knew I couldn't be anything other than myself, on television or anyplace else. I told Sheehan that, and he responded that I should indeed be myself but that I should also try to understand a few basic points about the medium and how it works. For instance, you can attack a question, but you should never attack a questioner, since TV tends to make a personal challenge look more hostile than intended. You should boil down your points and avoid long, discursive answers. You had to be somewhat more animated than in normal conversation just to seem natural, because TV tends to deenergize you. And most important, you have to go in with a clear sense of what you want to accomplish and respond from that perspective.

Over time, I developed some additional pointers about television, sometimes from watching tapes of my appearances with Gene and Sylvia—and later at Treasury, with Assistant Secretary for Public Affairs Howard Schloss, David Dreyer, or Linda McLaughlin. For instance, Sheehan was absolutely right about the importance of being sufficiently energetic on television, but energy with an edge could make you seem strident—which was Judy's comment after seeing me once on *This Week with David Brinkley.* And boiling complex ideas down into simple formulations could lead to a stronger statement than intended or than the subject matter warranted. I often dealt with that problem by adding a qualifying phrase—such as "at least it seems to me" or "the chances are very good that"—which reflected my approach to life anyway. I had no interest in becoming polished at television appearances—nor, I suspect, the capability to do that—but I did want to learn enough about the medium to be myself on TV and to get my points across at least somewhat more effectively. I also took Sheehan's rule about not attacking the questioner a step further and decided never to make ad hominem comments in any public appearances, even when someone criticized me in a personal way. But that was a matter of how I felt public discourse should be conducted and had nothing to do with television as a medium.

Another rule of mine was to talk about policy, not about politics. I wanted to engage substantively, not as a political pundit, and in most cases I wasn't qualified to make political forecasts anyway. So if someone asked me about the administration's chances of getting renewed funding for the IMF, I'd say we would ultimately be successful because the merits were on our side and then I'd set out our case. If that sometimes made me a less interesting guest, so be it. I avoided the most combative talk shows—which focused largely on conflict and predictions. In general, I found that, like most else in life, you got better at TV by thinking about what you were doing and preparing. I didn't rehearse answers since that seemed artificial and would undercut the responsiveness and engagement with questioning that is the whole point of television interviews. Instead, I got ready by trying to frame my views in ways that would work on television. I often found that this preparation was valuable in other ways. Thinking about how to express points succinctly often forced me to face contrary views and vulnerabilities in my positions, which sometimes led me to think them through more clearly or even to modify them. A commonplace in Washington is that a lot of policy is made through the speechwriting process. In the same way, I found that my policy thinking was sometimes affected as I prepared for television interviews.

I learned a great deal that first year about dealing with the print media as well. When I first visited newspaper editorial boards, Gene would come with me. We would sit there together, and I would answer a question. Then Gene would amend my answer—saying that what I had actually meant was slightly different from what I'd just said. In retrospect, this may have seemed slightly bizarre to the journalists in attendance. But it did help me learn how to respond to questions with an awareness of how my answers might create problems for me later.

Gene also taught me how a telling detail could turn into a useful symbol. He once mentioned to a reporter who was writing about the NEC that I often gave up my scheduled time with the President when I didn't have any pressing issue. That didn't seem like a big deal to me; on other occasions, I didn't insist on being present at briefings Gene would give Clinton in preparation for meetings and interviews. Gene was the appropriate person, and the President deserved to have as few people in the room as possible. I didn't feel cut out of the picture. To the contrary, I felt that the President's decision to have someone from the NEC brief him reflected well on the value of the NEC. But Gene's giving-up-time-with-the-President anecdote had salience because it cut against the familiar clichés about people jockeying for power and "face time" in the White House. As the story got repeated in other profiles, it helped to get across what the NEC was trying to accomplish in terms of creating a fair and open process.

I realized from the start that the NEC effort would surely go astray if I took advantage of my position or my access to the President to try to promote what I believed personally. So I always bent over backward to be fair to those with opposing points of view. Even when I was alone in the Oval Office telling the President what I thought, I would go out of my way to say that while I thought *X*, Bob Reich thought *Y*, and Laura Tyson thought *Z*. Sometimes, when I had my regularly scheduled time with Clinton, I would ask people who disagreed with me to come along to the meeting to present their views themselves. People in Washington often assume that effectiveness in a presidential administration depends on maximizing your access and exercising your power. But I found that by not seizing all the face time I could, I was more effective. By cultivating a sense of teamwork and fair dealing, I persuaded colleagues to work within the NEC process—and also, in the end, I think, enhanced my standing with the President.

This kind of teamwork contributed greatly to the development of policy and to internal support for our policies, as shown by the 1993 economic plan. Another memorable illustration was the way we handled trade negotiations with Japan. The members of our economic team had a variety of views—though all were basically committed to trade liberalization. At one end of the spectrum were those who thought that Japan would never open its markets to American competition without extreme pressure. At the other end were the more doctrinaire free traders who felt that our trade deficit with Japan was more a function of our own problems, including our low savings rate, and that, in any case, we benefited from the imports. For my part, I believed that the second-largest economy in the world having significant trade impediments was a major problem for the global trading system, and I supported strong efforts to pry open the Japanese markets. But the point is that in our process, everybody had a fair and full say. Not only did that lead to better decisions because all views were considered, but the participants also bought into those decisions, despite their reservations, because they felt fully invested in the decision-making process. That meant that, despite internal differences, the administration spoke with a single voice in taking a tough stance when the trade issues came to a head at the G-7 Tokyo summit in 1993. One cabinet member reported back a conversation with the Japanese ambassador. In previous administrations, the ambassador said, Japanese officials could visit with administration officials and identify differences among them, which was then helpful in defending Japan's trade policies. He was amazed that under Clinton, no cracks appeared; every member of the administration hewed seamlessly to the decision that had been made.

Of course, every rule has exceptions. In a few areas, I thought the free play of internal debate wouldn't be constructive. Occasionally, someone in the administration would suggest discussing dollar policy or Federal Reserve Board decisions on interest rates. I was able to persuade the others that these two issues should be exceptions to our NEC process. If the outside world knew that our strong-dollar policy or support for the independence of the Federal Reserve Board was subject to internal debate, confidence could be shaken and the markets seriously affected. If others had expressed strong concerns, perhaps some kind of quiet process would have been needed, but that didn't happen.

THE CLINTON ADMINISTRATION is widely viewed as having gotten off to a rocky start. Throughout the first year, the press focused heavily on flare-ups over the $200 haircut, the Travel Office firings, Whitewater, and so on. These incidents may well have reflected a shortfall in White House organization and discipline, but the coverage and the impression of chaos seemed to me greatly overstated.

For chaos was certainly not what I experienced. To the contrary, in the early months of the administration, I saw people working together in an effective, productive way. I used to make that point, and others would look at me as if I'd been spending time on another planet. Clearly, the White House was perceived as less than effectively organized in dealing with communications, media, and political relations—despite very good senior people. But most of that wasn't really part of my world. I now think that Clinton's tardiness, his taste for open-ended discussions, and a few other stylistic hallmarks of his first year created a powerful impression at odds with the reality I knew. What I didn't grasp at the time but have come to appreciate in retrospect is how powerful an influence this kind of style and symbolism can have on how an administration is seen. But however many meetings ran late, work on the vast majority of the substantive economic issues was both organized and effective—and led to major legislative accomplishments. What might have looked messy to outsiders was actually a process of deliberate and open discussion, of smart, committed people engaging in debate as a way of getting to the best decision.

Some people said that the President shouldn't be involved in a lengthy discussion of whether the Coast Guard should have a little more or a little less in the budget. My view is that the President's hands-on involvement in drawing up his first budget in the fifteen or so presidential meetings between January 22 and February 12 contributed enormously to making all of the very difficult decisions necessary to produce a $500 billion deficit reduction plan in such a brief time. What's more, from then on Bill Clinton possessed a detailed, practical understanding of how the budget process works, and of a vast number of programs in the budget, that provided him with strong grounding for eight years of annual budget making. Another advantage was that Leon and the rest of us knew in considerable detail what the President's views on various programs were. Many of the important decisions that Clinton made in his first six weeks were issues that remained settled business within the administration for eight years. Moreover, Clinton wanted to be deeply and personally involved in the budget, and I'm not sure anyone could have prevented that.

Mack McLarty, Clinton's boyhood friend who became his first chief of staff, took a lot of criticism for our early troubles. Again, my view is somewhat at variance with the conventional wisdom. The press tended to apply a Washington template that judged the chief of staff's effectiveness on the basis of the President's approval rating and the appearance of order—or the lack of it. But it seemed to me that the key issue was whether the head of an organization created an environment that produced substantive results (although appearances can affect the ability to achieve results, especially in Washington). In substantive terms, I viewed Mack as successful. Mack wasn't a type like John Sununu, President Bush's chief of staff, who I gather would lay down the law for others to follow. Mack would never try to dominate. Instead he focused on developing an atmosphere in which people could work together effectively, which was what Clinton wanted, rather than spending time and energy on infighting. Mack achieved something that Washington didn't quite know how to deal with: the creation of an environment with a good measure of mutual support and respect, in which for the most part people functioned well together.

My own position in the first year was entirely contingent on Mack's attitude. Another kind of chief of staff could have seen my authority as a threat and taken charge himself, crowding me out. Instead, Mack made room for the NEC process. A reporter once made an observation that I didn't understand at the time but was absolutely right—the NEC could not have worked unless Mack had let it work.

As the first-year difficulties mounted, Mack came to feel that the White House needed to take a more strategic approach, a view I shared. Mack suggested to the President bringing in David Gergen, who had worked in four previous administrations, as a high-level adviser with authority over the communications office. I thought that made sense; David brought a strong and experienced strategic perspective. He was very thoughtful about questions such as: How should the President use his time? How much exposure should a President have? How should he present himself? We didn't have people with the experience to think about those issues in quite the same way David did. But because he was a Republican and had worked for Richard Nixon and Ronald Reagan, Gergen was never really accepted by some who worked in the Clinton White House.

Bringing in Gergen was seen as a demotion for George Stephanopoulos, who was reassigned from his position as director of communications. George is immensely talented and wonderfully persuasive, but this situation was beyond even his powers. He told me that for a while he tried to explain to reporters that his new role still involved constant proximity to the President. But the assumption that he was being brushed aside in the shake-up was so powerful that after a while George realized that he couldn't counter it and could only wait until the wave passed. That has been my experience as well. During a media storm, you have to put aside the idea of a balanced presentation of both sides. But you should still try to get your version of events included in a story, even if only in the twenty-second paragraph, because at some point, those efforts might start to have some effect. And that's what happened here. Once the hullabaloo over Gergen's arrival died down, reporters realized that George was still central to what was happening and revisited the issue with more balance than in the initial stories.

As much as Gergen helped, he wasn't in a position to address the larger organizational problems around the White House. Toward the end of 1993, Mack decided to try to prioritize more effectively, with what came to be known as the "legacy project." As part of drawing up the President's second budget in the fall of 1993, Mack asked various members of the administration what they would like to see as Clinton's major accomplishments, looking back from a notional perspective of either 1996 or 2006. This effort didn't have any immediate consequence, but it's interesting to look back at it now, both for my perceptions that first year and as a yardstick to measure the Clinton legacy.

In addition to health care, which we took as a given, my memo listed five "legacies": (1) an effective human capital program of high-quality education and training; (2) progress on the problems of the inner city; (3) deficit reduction; (4) an expansion of global trade; and (5) implementation of a rational approach to regulation. Revisiting that list, which reflected my own ambitions for the administration, I'd argue that we accomplished a great deal. Deficit reduction was enormously successful, due to our policy choices and the growth those policies helped promote. Trade liberalization was powerfully advanced by passing NAFTA, strengthening the General Agreement on Tariffs and Trade (GATT), and laying the groundwork for China's accession to the World Trade Organization, and we were active more generally on international economic matters, including crisis response and prevention.

On the other issues, the picture is more mixed. The strong economy made a real difference for inner cities, and our policies, including the expansion of the Earned Income Tax Credit (EITC) and increased funding for Head Start, helped reduce poverty. (In the view of many, welfare reform had a significant impact as well, although I had serious reservations about this legislation.) But the fundamental problem of an urban underclass cut off from the mainstream of American society remains, and we still lack a federal effort commensurate with the problem. In terms of "strengthening human capital," we substantially increased spending on education and worker training. But our public education system still falls far short of what is needed. I think we took the right approach to rationalizing regulation—from reducing export controls and simplifying loan applications for small businesses to banking reform and resisting calls to regulate the Internet. And on a related issue of great importance, we unfortunately did not address the excesses in the tort arena that are such an abuse of our legal system and so adversely affect our economic well-being. I concluded my memo with some observations based on my not-quite-a-year in Washington. "Our political system is too cumbersome to deal effectively with decision making on the complex problems of the modern world," I wrote. "This problem may be irresolvable, but over the very long run, could overwhelm everything else."

This last statement didn't mean that the more top-down business model of business management could or should apply to government. To the contrary, I've developed a deep respect for the differences between the public and private sectors. In business, the single, overriding purpose is to make a profit. Government, on the other hand, deals with a vast number of legitimate and often potentially competing objectives—for example, energy production versus environmental protection, or safety regulations versus productivity. This complexity of goals brings a corresponding complexity of process. Our constitutional system of checks and balances has multiple decision centers—Congress, the Executive Branch (with all its own internal complications), the courts, and state and local governments. Often the relationship among these participants is one of conflict, and, with respect to some issues, the balance of power is ambiguous. Moreover, many participants face electoral accountability. And finally, all important decisions—and even many less important ones—are made with an awareness of how they will be presented in the media.

In the corporate world, power is far more centralized. Unless trouble develops, a CEO almost always has a relatively good relationship with his company's board of directors, even as it performs its oversight function. Media scrutiny is far less of a factor, except, again, when problems occur. A successful CEO is far freer to say whatever he wants about politics, his colleagues, or his competitors, at least within reasonable limits. This simpler model might sometimes look appealing for the public sector. But in reality an immense complexity is inherent in the circumstances of a modern, democratic government. Making government more businesslike can improve efficiency—in both processes and operations—but the inherent complexity would remain.

WHEN I THINK ABOUT what I wish we had accomplished in our administration and didn't, broad-based health care reform ranks very high. Our country's health care system remains an inefficient mixture of market and nonmarket forces that leaves large numbers of people inadequately covered and at the same time consumes a much larger portion of GDP than competitor nations spend. At the start of our administration, I shared the conventional view that the prospects for health care reform looked good. The campaign had built a mandate for reform and there was widespread public and congressional support for it.

My own involvement was limited, but I came away from our failed effort at comprehensive health care reform with several observations. Most fundamentally, the sheer magnitude of the endeavor—a major policy shift in an area encompassing 14 percent of GDP—made health reform extremely difficult to pass. The larger and more complicated the public policy undertaking, the more special interests there are that may take umbrage and organize against it.

In this case, massive forces arrayed against this effort, many with a vested interest in the status quo, and spent tens of millions of dollars to defeat the President's efforts. One example of this was a huge multimillion-dollar national advertising campaign against the plan that proponents lacked the resources to counter. And these ads weren't constrained by the truth. I turned on the TV late one night in my room at the Jefferson and saw one of the "Harry and Louise" ads. *That isn't what our proposal says,* I said to myself. But these ads were highly effective.

The politics were also very complicated, and I thought Lloyd Bentsen, who had been the savvy chairman of the Senate Finance Committee before becoming Treasury Secretary, made a lot of sense when he said that the President's deficit reduction plan and health care reform were simply too much for our political system to process at one time. Also, over time, my colleagues working on health care told me that the initial Republican support they had expected slipped away. Watching members in both parties who had publicly espoused support for health care reform "to and fro"—rather than work with each other and compromise to reach a conclusion acceptable to the majority—was a crash course in the realities of politics. The lesson I took from that was that the politics is as important as the policy, because if the politics doesn't work, the policy—no matter whether the decisions are sensible or not—won't be implemented.

Undoubtedly, there were other factors militating against the success of health care reform. For example, some argue that the program itself was too complicated or just substantively wrong. My own view—though I was not expert in this area—was that the underlying, market-oriented approach of the bill made sense in many respects, but various of the specific provisions were open to question.

One factor I did feel able to judge was the internal White House process, and that to me seemed flawed. The President, having decided on the broad parameters of the policy, set up a project run by the First Lady and Ira Magaziner, an extremely bright, very intense management consultant who had known the President since their student days. But giving the Health Care Task Force a hundred-day deadline to submit legislation was probably unrealistic. More significantly, health care cuts across much of the domestic side of the government, and significant participants inside the administration—including the members of the economic team, even though most agreed with the general approach—didn't think, at least until nearer the end, that this process aired their views in a way that seriously affected decision making. Consequently, people whose internal backing was crucial too often felt somewhat disaffected, and cooperation was less than it could have been. At one point, for instance, Lloyd Bentsen said he couldn't produce cost estimates because he didn't feel adequately informed. Also, important arguments and criticisms weren't exposed in the way that would have occurred in an NEC-type decision-making process.

And, of course, the health reform process had the additional complication of having the First Lady in charge. In Little Rock, during the transition, the President-elect asked me what I thought about having Hillary head his health care task force. I told him I liked the idea—she was smart and effective and clearly knew the subject well. As I had gotten to know Hillary during the transition, I even had the naive idea—perhaps augmented by a feeling of rapport with her that I never lost—that she could be involved some way in running the White House. What I didn't understand at that stage was how being the President's wife would complicate her role. Nor, apparently, did the President, with all of his political savvy. People tend to pull their punches and to be less forthcoming in dealing with a President's family member. What's more, the assumption that a close relative of the President has a back channel in daily life would always render such a process suspect to some degree.

One irony is that Hillary, contrary to some impressions, was amenable to challenge and debate. At some point, for instance, a number of us came to believe that a more limited and less costly benefits package would be preferable for fiscal and economic reasons. Although this was a very central issue and Hillary believed a more comprehensive benefits package was worth the cost, she was receptive to airing the issue fully. Someone suggested that knowledgeable proponents of each side present their views in a debate for the President. She agreed, and a candid and vigorous debate in front of several dozen people in the Roosevelt Room ensued. Unfortunately, details of that debate leaked and appeared on the front page of *The New York Times* the next day. Leaks, and the damage they can do to internal communication and the ability of an administration to implement a political strategy, are a frustrating reality of Washington life, and it is almost impossible ever to know—as opposed to suspect—who a leaker is.

Health care not only competed, politically and internally within the administration, with the economic plan in the first half of the administration's first year—usually considered the most propitious time to accomplish large purposes—it then competed with NAFTA in the second half of 1993. After the economic plan passed in the summer of that year, the President had to decide whether to give precedence to health care reform or NAFTA. Fighting on both fronts would spread our political operations too thin, creating a greater risk that both would fail. The President convened a small meeting in early September that Mack McLarty and I organized in the White House residence. Warren Christopher, Lloyd Bentsen, and I all spoke in favor of putting NAFTA first, arguing that this was our only real chance because, as the midterm election drew nearer, the odds of passing such a controversial trade bill would diminish. Hillary and Ira spoke in favor of putting health care first, both to maintain momentum and because the election posed a problem for health care as well. In hindsight, I think both sides were right. The President decided to proceed with NAFTA first, but also to continue some political effort on health care until NAFTA passed and health care could get the highest priority. That seemed to me both a good decision and an example of good White House process. Of course, that was easy to say when the decision came out the way I wanted.

Although our broad effort at health care reform was not successful, the administration was later able to pass important smaller pieces of legislation—including an expansion of health care coverage for children and portability of health insurance for people changing jobs. I also think that many of the insights, much of the analysis, and some of the specific proposals developed by the health care reform project will be useful in future reform efforts, and I believe at some point circumstances will force the political system to make major change.

MY SON JAMIE'S marriage to Gretchen Craft in 1994 was wonderful for them, but also a respite for Judy and me. They had met while both were students at Yale Law School and now were going to be married in Gretchen's hometown of Kansas City, Missouri. Many of our friends flew in from New York City and elsewhere for a lively weekend of parties. Gretchen's parents, Jack and Karen Craft, and her sister, Elizabeth, have become not only relations but friends. Jack is deeply engaged with Republican Party politics— both Republican senators from Missouri were at the wedding—but I think he has adjusted to his daughter's apostasy. Jack is also an enthusiastic (and quite skilled) fly fisherman, and on our various trips we've managed to discuss both politics and fly selection without difficulty.

A particularly memorable event at the wedding that weekend, at least for Judy and me, took place at the rehearsal dinner. Shortly before our irreverent younger son, Philip, was supposed to give a toast, Judy saw him scribbling on a napkin. She asked what he was doing and was horrified to hear that he was just then composing his remarks. When he got up to speak, Judy was in a state of anxious anticipation. He started by saying that his remarks were going to be about cynicism and I thought she would collapse. But Philip's turned out to be the best toast of the evening: a very thoughtful and moving commentary about how Jamie and Gretchen's relationship was the antithesis of cynicism. And so another potential pothole in life was safely avoided.

I then returned to Washington and a world of potholes. On election day in 1994, Democrats lost control of both houses of Congress for the first time in forty years. Not a single Republican incumbent lost a race for congressman, senator, or governor. No independent observer had predicted such a stark result, nor had anyone in the White House. A shell-shocked feeling pervaded the West Wing. I was surprised but not so emotionally engaged to have that kind of reaction myself—my life was economic policy and trying to make the NEC work. Also, I didn't begin to foresee the full consequences of a Republican-controlled Congress.

But I was keenly interested in the arguments about why this had happened and what the administration should do. The day after the election, some of the political people got together in the office of Mark Gearan, the communications director. I wondered if I would be welcome—I wasn't really qualified to comment the way people such as political director Rahm Emanuel, chief speechwriter Michael Waldman, or others were. But someone invited me, so I went.

The essential debate in that meeting, and for some time after the election, was whether to take a more populist or a more centrist tack. Shortly after the election—following a meeting on health care conducted by a new joint process of the Domestic Policy Council and the National Economic Council—I had a discussion with Bob Reich and Hillary about all of this. Bob said the election had shown that the Democratic base wasn't motivated and we needed to move in a much more populist direction. My view was that some of the policies and much of the language that Bob called populism was unwise economically. I respected—and had learned from—Bob's insights on the importance of education and training and addressing inequality, but I felt strongly that the language he and some of the political advisers were eager to use, terms such as "corporate welfare," could adversely affect the business confidence requisite for economic growth. Nor did I think populism would be effective politically. Hillary agreed, telling Reich, "Bob, the polls and political intelligence we have say that the people we need to reach don't respond well to that kind of populist approach." She was very pragmatic—she didn't think the approach would work and said so.

But if Reich's interpretation was wrong, what *was* our problem? My own view of the 1994 debacle emphasized five factors. First, by the time of the election, the economy's strength and the contribution made by Clinton's decisions were not yet clear. The second was the mischaracterization of our deficit reduction as a tax increase on the middle class, which proved extremely hard to shake. Related to that was a third factor: the misimpression, fueled by the health care plan, which itself was misleadingly described by opponents, that Clinton was an old-style, big-government liberal. Fourth was the effect in some elections of Clinton's advocacy of gun control legislation. A fifth and final factor was a series of issues and episodes, mostly minor but blown out of proportion by the press, manipulated by political adversaries, and, as a contributing factor, sometimes mishandled in some respects by the White House.

Preeminent among these was Whitewater, a numbingly complicated story about a money-losing real estate investment the Clintons had made in Arkansas in the 1980s. For years after *The New York Times* broke the story during the 1992 campaign, investigations by the press and congressional committees cast a shadow over the administration. These inquiries damaged lives and careers and provided an endless supply of ammunition to the President's opponents. But after the expenditure of tens of millions of dollars, the conclusion most sensible people reached—as did, ultimately, the independent counsel—was that the original Whitewater charges against the Clintons had been unsubstantiated. Many felt that the way the White House dealt with the issue made matters worse, although I could understand the Clintons' frustration.

My two years in the White House were a deep immersion course in politics and the workings of Washington. Early in the administration, Clinton said to me that his gays-in-the-military position was really going to hurt Democrats in the South for many years to come.

"Mr. President, that can't be," I replied. "I mean, that's what happened today, and they don't like it. Tomorrow you're on to the next thing."

And Clinton responded, "No, this is going to affect how people look at us for a long, long time."

That's a good illustration of how a decision can have political consequences far beyond what most people could anticipate, and of how someone with political sensitivity can see possible effects that others miss. Bob Strauss once said to me that either you have political feel or you don't. I think that I had some when I began in Washington and that it developed over my time there—though it was never near the President's level or that of some others in the White House.

When I suggested to the President—in various meetings when the 1994 election came up—that health care or gun control had been involved in the debacle, he would remind me of the tax increase or our failure to get our economic message out effectively. I never heard his more considered diagnosis of what went wrong. In the immediate aftermath of the election, he seemed off stride in a way I hadn't seen before. Around that time, I watched him prepare for a press conference. George and others were throwing him questions in the small dining room off the Oval Office. Usually a master of such situations, he wasn't knocking back the warm-up pitches. He seemed down and a little disoriented.

I identified with Clinton based on a feeling that dated back to troubled times in arbitrage or in fixed-income trading at Goldman Sachs. What had worked to make money had stopped working, just as Clinton's political strategy had stopped working, and for a time my Goldman colleagues and I felt we had lost our grounding. It was a sense of bad news compounding, of unanticipated losses on top of unanticipated losses with no end in sight and no clear sense of a strategy for going forward. That feeling eventually gave way to a sense that we were getting a grip on our problems. But as I prepared to move to a new job at the Treasury, Clinton hadn't regained his footing. He hadn't figured out how to operate in this new political environment. And the rest of us hadn't either.

CHAPTER SIX

Confidence and Credibility

I N AUGUST 1994, LLOYD BENTSEN called to tell me that he was planning to resign as Treasury Secretary after the midterm election in November. "I haven't told this to anybody else," he said. Lloyd explained that he was telling me because he was afraid I might be thinking about leaving the administration as well. If I went to the President with my resignation first, it would make it harder for him to go. Lloyd said he was going to recommend that I take his place at Treasury.

The only person I told about Lloyd's call was Judy. She had mixed reactions. She was pleased that I might have the opportunity to do something I wanted to do. But she had been hoping that after two years in the administration, I might leave and rejoin her in New York full-time. She was also afraid that the job of Treasury Secretary would impose a new kind of formality on our lives. Judy wanted to know if I'd still be able to walk down Park Avenue in an old pair of khakis. I said that whatever happened, I had no intention of changing because I had the job of Treasury Secretary.

Some weeks thereafter, the President asked me to come to his office. He told me what I already knew—that Lloyd was leaving and had suggested that I be named as his replacement. Clinton said something that indicated that he was inclined to take the recommendation—but not without some concern about my leaving the job I was in. He said he felt the National

Economic Council had worked well in a White House that continued to face problems of process and organization. For that reason, he had mixed feelings about sending me elsewhere. "You'll be over there, and I'll still be stuck here in the White House," he said somewhat ruefully.

Shortly thereafter, Leon Panetta, who had only just succeeded Mack as chief of staff, had me over to his office. He said that if I moved to the Treasury, it would leave a problem at the White House, but that he thought the choice would be mine. I responded that I wasn't so sure about that, since the President hadn't yet offered me the job. I was encouraged that Leon thought it would be up to me, but I wasn't going to say I wanted the job until I was certain it was being offered. Instead, I told Leon that I had to think about my own life and what I wanted to do next.

The situation remained ambiguous for a long while. A number of people who knew Lloyd was leaving assumed that I would replace him. But weeks and then more weeks went by and for some reason nothing happened. I never found out if the delay was because Clinton was considering other candidates for the Treasury job, deciding what to do about the NEC after I moved, trying to figure out how to get me to stay where I was, or simply dealing with more pressing matters. The President may also have been avoiding an issue that he wasn't eager to face. Eventually, Leon called to tell me that the President wanted me to take the job and that was that. Clinton himself never formally offered me the position. Erskine Bowles, Leon's then deputy and later White House chief of staff himself, used to joke some years later that if things kept going well for me as Treasury Secretary, maybe one day the President would offer me the job.

I did have a variety of concerns about becoming Treasury Secretary. I had learned in my two years at the White House that, while the substance of the issues was most important, presenting positions in a way that was clear and precise and would also resonate with the public was also critical. At the NEC, I'd noticed that those who were really skillful at framing issues often didn't just have a gift for communication. They were people such as George Stephanopoulos, Gene Sperling, and Sylvia Mathews, who also understood policy and were able to think several chess moves ahead, anticipating the likely reaction to a comment and the possible reactions to that reaction.

One of my biggest worries in moving to Treasury was how to find that quality of advice about communications and political strategy away from the White House. To be fair to the NEC, I had said I wasn't going to take anyone but Sylvia with me to Treasury. But that meant I would have to build an entirely new team. I was especially concerned about how I was going to function effectively without Gene, the person I relied on most heavily in those areas. As it turned out, Treasury had a number of people with strong political and communication skills combined with policy expertise. But I didn't know that before I got there.

When I discussed this problem with Leon, he suggested that I take along David Dreyer from the White House communications office because he was unusually bright and had an especially good feel for framing issues. With his beard, ponytail, diamond-stud earring, and American flag necktie (usually worn with a denim shirt), David was not your typical Treasury official. What's more, he had a reputation as being one of the more liberal members of President Clinton's political team. I once gave Alan Greenspan a good fright by introducing David—who was dressed even more outlandishly than usual that day—as a close adviser of mine. The chairman stared at David as if he were a visitor from another planet.

I found that Treasury was different from the White House in all sorts of ways. At one level, my role, while broad, was more defined. I was the head of an immense enterprise that, while obviously answerable to the President, also functioned in many respects as a freestanding subsidiary, with established statutory responsibilities. These included supervision of (though with varying degrees of authority over) large agencies, including the Internal Revenue Service, the Customs Service, the Bureau of Engraving and Printing, the Secret Service, and the Bureau of Alcohol, Tobacco and Firearms. Much more central to the life of the Secretary, Treasury also has several big policy shops. International Affairs deals with international economic policy and with representing the United States at the IMF, World Bank, and other multilateral institutions. Domestic Finance handles debt management, oversight of bank and regulatory functions, and much else. Tax Policy is central to any administration's economic strategy. The Economic Policy Group provides analysis on a broad range of issues. All told, I was now in charge of 160,000 employees.

In another sense, though, my position as head of a cabinet department was much more exposed and precarious. At the NEC, I had been one member of a group of people who helped to formulate and advocate the administration's economic policies. Now I was publicly and politically accountable in a way I hadn't been at the NEC. Because of his extensive knowledge and deep involvement, Bill Clinton remained the real leader of his own economic team—as well as being the decision maker with the ultimate responsibility. That notwithstanding, I was now also in some measure the personification of the administration's economic policies. That meant that if the performance of the U.S. economy deteriorated in any way in terms of inflation, unemployment, productivity, trade, or the strength of the dollar, I would be viewed as in some sense responsible—certainly for the policy response and probably to some extent for the problem as well. It also meant that those who objected to the administration's economic policies now saw me as the personal expression of them, not just as a part of a White House process that devised them. In short, I was now in the line of political fire in a way I hadn't previously been and hadn't really recognized as part of the Treasury Secretary's job until it became mine. And just when I took that job, the fire became a good deal more intense, thanks to the Mexican crisis.

The experience of serving as Treasury Secretary brought me closer to two related concepts that had already become central to my Washington experience: confidence and credibility. At the NEC, I focused on confidence and credibility as they related to the President and his policies. My first job at the NEC had been to assist in designing an economic plan that would lead to the kind of business, consumer, and financial market confidence that were necessary for Bill Clinton to succeed in his economic goals. I also helped advise him on ways to increase—and avoid diminishing—his public credibility as an economic policy maker and leader. An administration's policies are by far the most important determinant of its economic credibility. But how an administration speaks about economic issues, both in tone and in substance, affects its reputation with businesses, consumers, and markets as well. And that reputation is important. If an administration is viewed as generally sensible on economic matters, that contributes to confidence. If, on the other hand, an administration is viewed as not sensible economically, that diminishes confidence.

At Treasury, I retained those same responsibilities as part of the President's economic team. But I had a new role as well. The most important factor in an administration's economic credibility is what the President does and says. But how the Treasury Secretary handles himself in office is also meaningful. As the administration's lead economic spokesman—a role long enshrined in practice—I had direct, as well as indirect, responsibility for furthering confidence in the U.S. economy. That meant that my credibility now mattered for more than personal reasons. And, as I quickly discovered, my credibility was at constant risk from substantive mistakes or careless words—or even from carefully crafted words that people didn't relate to in the way I had anticipated. I also faced the new hazard of what were sometimes harsh personal attacks as an inherent part of my new job.

There was a critically important paradox at the heart of my new role, one that unfortunately is not always well understood. At one level, confidence and credibility are issues of perception—perceptions about how strong economic conditions are, how well an administration is handling economic policy, how successful the President is in his job, and how effective the Treasury Secretary is in his. But to say they are perceptions does not mean that they're based on illusions or that they can be manipulated for any length of time. While economic confidence and an administration's economic credibility might at times and in certain ways diverge from reality, they are ultimately grounded in reality. For that reason, pursuing confidence and credibility as goals in themselves is largely futile. Trying to create an impression of economic strength will almost surely backfire. Public relations efforts or attempts to "jawbone" the economy or markets don't change the underlying realities. They only diminish the credibility of anyone who tries—whether a President or a Treasury Secretary—and erode his ability to instill confidence.

In other words, while confidence and credibility were constant concerns, they weren't objectives that someone in my position could pursue explicitly. Ultimately, confidence would come from the policies we pursued. And managing the politics well would be critical to what we could accomplish in an era of Republican control of the legislature.

THE STRUGGLES THAT PLAYED OUT in the course of 1995 and early 1996 between President Clinton and the new majority in Congress were about issues of great and fundamental importance: What functions should government perform? How large a role should government play in society? How much should the government help the poor? In retrospect, what was happening in those days is much clearer. Bill Clinton was in the midst of turning back a powerful antigovernment effort by the victors in 1994 congressional elections. At the time, however, it just felt like bitter fighting over everything.

Internally, the Clinton administration continued to face a conflict over how to respond to the Republicans. On one side was the argument that we needed to be more populist, to energize the Democratic Party's base. That view was best exemplified by Secretary of Labor Robert Reich, who was now speaking publicly about the need to cut what he termed "corporate welfare." I shared the view that public subsidies for profit-making enterprises, many of which were embedded in the tax code, were often wasteful and unjustified. But I also thought that using the term "corporate welfare" was inflammatory and could adversely affect how the President was seen and, as a consequence, the economy itself. In addition, I had sat in on enough discussions about swing voters to feel that this crucial section of the electorate reacted badly to anything that sounded like class warfare. President Clinton had gone a long way toward countering the old stereotype of Democrats as being antibusiness. To a surprising degree, he had gained the confidence of the business community and financial markets. Using language that sounded hostile to business could undermine that confidence, harming both the economy and the administration.

On top of these substantive and political disagreements, there was a process issue. Throughout the first two years of Clinton's first term, Reich had been an especially good team player inside the administration. As someone who had a close personal relationship with Clinton going back to their days together at Oxford, he could easily have gone around the NEC process. As far as I could see, he never did that. But now he was venturing into new rhetorical and substantive territory on his own, without any internal debate. To me, that seemed inconsistent with our understanding. Our agreed-upon process was that if people on the economic team differed and couldn't work out their dispute on their own, they should take the issue to the President, through an NEC process, for him to decide. Then we could all publicly support whatever the decision was. What Bob was now doing left me, as someone who strongly disagreed with him, in a troubling position. If he alone spoke about these issues, he would appear to represent the administration's position. But if I spoke on the other side, it would look as though the administration were divided. Process can be a fragile thing; I couldn't do what Bob was doing without creating a mess. After some discussion, Bob—who, like the rest of us, was very supportive of our all working as an economic team—agreed not to use that kind of language. We agreed to conduct a public conference on the related issue of corporate best practices.

Around the time this was going on, debates inside the White House began to be affected by the invisible hand of Dick Morris. In the spring of 1995, people at the White House were stunned to discover that the President had created an entirely separate advisory team led by Morris, a pollster and political consultant who had worked for him in Arkansas. Though I didn't have much interaction with him, I thought some of Morris's perspectives, such as his focus on swing voters, made sense politically. But the problem once again was the need for a regular process. It made sense for the President to solicit views from whomever he found helpful. But there should have been a way to do that without circumventing the regular structure of the White House, which created all sorts of problems.

In April 1995, an act of domestic terrorism in Oklahoma City killed 168 people, including 18 Treasury Department employees and members of Treasury Department employees' families. I flew to Oklahoma City with the President and others in the administration to meet with the families of victims and attend a memorial service. President Clinton's words at that service movingly expressed the feelings of people throughout the country. I had groped for words when meeting with victims' families, so I not only appreciated but greatly respected the President's ability to comfort these families and the country at a time of shock and tragedy. Political analysts said that these terrible events—and President Clinton's response to them—did much to revive public respect for government in our society and were something of a turning point in the President's standing with the American people.

Clinton's political turnaround unfolded through the budget battle that culminated in two government shutdowns. I remember that at the outset of that conflict, George Stephanopoulos told me, as we were leaving a meeting in the Cabinet Room, that we were going to attack the Republicans over their proposed Medicare cuts. George said that Gingrich had made a big mistake by proposing drastic reductions in Medicare, and we were going to ride that mistake through to the 1996 election. Gene Sperling had described George as a political genius, but it seemed to me that George was just being ridiculous. That Medicare cuts could become the organizing principle of a presidential campaign seemed almost inconceivable. I remember laughing with Larry Summers about how small and insufficient that approach seemed.

I was, of course, wrong. Government spending in the abstract might not be popular, but specific programs resonated with people. The attempt to cut Medicare by $270 billion and reduce taxes by a similar amount, in a way that primarily favored the affluent, was an issue with special political force. The Clinton administration had learned a few things since 1993, when the Republicans had been so successful at casting deficit reduction as what it was not, a tax increase on middle-income people. This time, my colleagues weren't going to stand by while our opponents created the prism through which our policies were viewed. The President told me that in 1993 we had "left the field." In 1995, we stayed and played hard. Of course, there was much more at stake in the budget conflict than just Medicare, and the President cared passionately about many of these issues. "Medicare is the thing that matters politically," he said at one of our Cabinet Room meetings, alluding to the powerful lobbies that protected this health care program for the elderly. "But I'm not going to let them gut Medicaid just because no one cares about a program for poor people."

The President's defense of Medicare and his opposition to tax cuts aimed primarily at the affluent was only part of the reason he bounced back and won reelection in 1996. Another important aspect of his political recovery was that he was at last coming to be seen as a centrist. The prevailing view in the media was that this represented a change from his first two years in office. My view was that Clinton remained the centrist that he'd been all along, as evidenced by our original deficit reduction plan, his support for NAFTA, and a host of other issues. Although his health care reform was often touted as a big-government program, Clinton had proposed a private-sector solution—albeit with a significant government role—as opposed to government provision of health care. In 1995 and 1996, however, the President communicated this orientation more deliberately and effectively. The change in perception makes an important point that goes well beyond Washington politics. The President's policy choices remained on a largely consistent track, but it was only after the first two years that the perception of what he was doing began to accord with that reality.

In 1995, we put out a budget that continued deficit reduction as a proportion of GDP, but with a stable actual deficit number. Our congressional opponents kept hammering away at our budget's failure to balance. I remember that when I testified before the Senate Finance Committee, several of the Republicans on the committee wanted me to acknowledge that our proposed budget would mean $200 billion deficits "as far as the eye can see." I wouldn't describe the ongoing deficit in dollar terms because that could be used to argue—incorrectly—that we were not committed to deficit reduction. Instead, I responded by pointing out that our proposal would continue to reduce the deficit as a share of GDP. But the reality was that I was in a holding pattern I couldn't acknowledge. Our strategy was to put out a budget while at the same time we were working on additional spending cuts that would lead to much lower deficit numbers. In this detailed and painstaking work, we were lucky to have the help of one of the unsung heroes of the federal government, Alan Cohen, an indefatigable, disheveled Treasury staffer who had perhaps the greatest knowledge of and passion for the federal budget process of anyone in government. But we had not wanted to put in the cuts Alan helped us find in our original budget submission for fear that the Republicans would "pocket" them and then seek additional cuts that we objected to in negotiating a final budget. And so, for some time, we continued to work on developing what would be our real budget, but without any decision at that point on whether it had to go to absolute balance. In May, the congressional Republicans introduced their proposal to cut taxes, paid for with Medicare and Medicaid reductions, in a budget that went to balance.

From early on, President Clinton sensed that the persistence of a deficit, even a small one, created a major political problem for him. In our regular meetings in the Roosevelt Room and the Cabinet Room on the 1996 budget, he kept asking, "Shouldn't I come up with a balanced budget?" All of his economic advisers, myself included, responded that he shouldn't, because there wasn't any real economic difference between small deficits that continued to decline as a share of GDP and actual balance. We had successfully addressed the deficit problem in 1993 and intended to continue reducing the deficit. Going all the way to a truly balanced budget would require additional program reductions that would serve little economic purpose.

It was in a meeting in the Cabinet Room sometime in May that Clinton finally said to us, "If I'm going to get heard on anything else, I first have to show a balanced budget. Once I do that, I can talk about progressive programs. But if I don't show a balanced budget, they'll never listen to me about progressive programs." Basically, I knew what he was saying was right. We advisers were all sitting there telling him there was no economic difference between a few billion dollars and zero, which is true as an analytical point. But there was a much bigger point, the one Clinton was making: if we wanted to talk about spending money on education and programs for the inner city, people weren't going to listen to us unless we talked about those programs in the context of a balanced budget. The President realized that while fiscal responsibility was not itself politically resonant, balancing the federal government's books did resonate and was a goal that voters could relate to and rally around. In that meeting, the

President was pretty much alone in what really was an extraordinarily perceptive insight about what was needed to make his agenda work with the public. And I later realized that without the politically resonant goal of a balanced budget, fiscal responsibility itself becomes much harder to establish and maintain.

Clinton's point was an extension of the one I remembered him making in early 1993 at that initial Little Rock meeting about the economic plan. At the time, deficit reduction had been what he called a "threshold issue" to get the economy moving—a precondition for everything else he hoped to do. Now, a balanced budget had become a threshold issue, because it was a precondition for getting people to listen to us and hence for doing almost everything else the administration cared about. Proposing to balance the budget may also have been the only feasible way to defeat the pernicious idea of adding a balanced-budget amendment to the Constitution. Such an amendment would violate all known wisdom about economic policy. It could compel the federal government to cut spending or raise taxes in a recession, substituting "procyclical" policies (which would cause the economy to contract even more) for the "countercyclical" ones that a recession ordinarily calls for. Even after our decision to support a balanced budget, the amendment failed by only a single vote in the Senate in 1995, and it might well have passed if we hadn't persuaded people that Social Security benefits could be endangered by the spending cuts the amendment might at times require.

I learned a lesson from what Clinton said about balancing the budget at that meeting. Working in the White House, I had already come to understand that if you want people to listen to you, you have to express yourself in a way that connects with them. But sometimes even that isn't enough. On some subjects, people simply won't listen to you unless you say or do something that opens the door first—which was Clinton's point about the balanced-budget proposal. Conversely, on some subjects, certain comments close the door, and people won't listen to the rest of what you have to say. Thinking back to my days in New York, I was reminded of a dinner I'd been at years before with Bill Lynch, an African-American politician who had been a deputy mayor under David Dinkins. Bill had become a friend of ours when Judy had served under Mayor Dinkins—with whom she'd become friendly before he was mayor—as commissioner for protocol. Gathered around the table at the Regency Hotel were a lot of senior Wall Street figures, many of them Jewish. At that time, there was considerable controversy over whether Jesse Jackson had said something anti-Semitic. My own view was that the issue was greatly overblown and that the relationship between the Black and Jewish communities, which should have been very strong, had deteriorated around misunderstandings and unfortunate comments by some people in both communities. Lynch was terrific, smart, and interesting on a whole range of issues. Then at one point during the dinner, he cited Jesse Jackson for some proposition. He immediately recognized that with that comment the dynamic changed. He said to me afterward, "Once I said that, they stopped listening to me." I've observed the same phenomenon many times in the corporate world. Often a company will deal with a public relations problem by aggressively defending its actions. But even if its actions are defensible, no one really listens if the CEO starts with the defense. People listen only if he begins by apologizing or acknowledging mistakes. That can be hard to do when he believes that he didn't really make a mistake or that his mistake wasn't as it was portrayed, but it may be the only way to be heard.

Agreeing that we should have a balanced budget didn't mean agreeing with the Republicans on their specific proposals. Throughout the year there was a series of highly publicized negotiations, though most of the early White House–congressional meetings couldn't really be called negotiations. Pete Domenici, the chairman of the Senate Budget Committee, and John Kasich, his counterpart in the House, led the GOP forces into battle. Leon Panetta carried the banner for our side. The process started with disagreements over how many people could attend from either side, who they should be, and so on. Most of the substantive discussions, when finally addressed, were handled like a diplomatic summit meeting, at which the two sides essentially exchange talking points. The Republicans would express outrage that we weren't tough enough in our program cutting. We would respond by expressing outrage about their deep reductions in Medicare and other social spending to fund tax cuts for the affluent. Both sides were pretty shrill. These discussions were conducted in secret, but the same people were saying the same things in public. Neither side was trying to persuade the other side of anything or to reach an accommodation.

Even after Clinton offered some significant concessions, the two sides couldn't reach agreement. The Republicans could have declared victory at several points—particularly after Clinton proposed a ten-year balanced budget, or after he later proposed a seven-year goal in exchange for the Republicans' relinquishing big cuts in social spending. For some reason, they never did. The President's demeanor in the negotiations may have contributed to his opponents' disinclination to strike a deal. Based on the many hours I had spent watching Clinton interact with others, I could see that the Republicans were misreading him. They had the sense that he was sympathetic to their views, when I could see that he wasn't—he was just listening intently. Clinton may also have been telegraphing his own feelings, which were that he badly wanted a deal.

What he wasn't making clear was his commitment to his basic principles and his willingness to veto the budget if it didn't move a good deal closer to his position. I was afraid that once again Clinton's body language could be misinterpreted. When we went back to the Oval Office after one of these sessions, Clinton asked me how I thought he had done. "Mr. President, I used to sit in on a lot of negotiations at Goldman Sachs," I said. "And if you were my client and we came out of this meeting, I would say, based on the way you sounded to those people, they're going to think they can roll over you." Harold Ickes, who was then serving as deputy chief of staff, later told me that Clinton had repeated what I had told him. My impression was that before that the President hadn't realized the effect he had had in those meetings.

Gingrich and the others did misread Clinton in this way, taking his listening and his desire for a compromise as signs that he would give in on matters on which he never wavered. But in retrospect, the Republicans' misreading of Clinton's negotiating stance turned out to be helpful to us politically. After two government shutdowns, a threat of default on the federal government's debt, and endless meetings with congressional leaders, Clinton found himself in a greatly improved position. He ended up getting most of what he wanted, such as protecting Medicare and Medicaid, and preventing most of what he didn't want, such as large tax cuts favoring the best off. He did all this without ever making a deal. It's a useful lesson in negotiation. Sometimes you're better off not getting to yes.

THE LARGER ISSUES and principles at stake in the Clinton-Gingrich conflict were brought dramatically to the fore in the debt limit crisis that exploded in the autumn of 1995 and got woven into the budget battle and the two government shutdowns that took place over the winter. On the surface, this conflict involved a barely comprehensible dispute about technicalities of federal debt management. But the real stakes in this fight, as intense as any I had to face in Washington, were two fundamental principles. One was the obligation to pay debt. The other permeated the larger budget battle that enveloped the debt limit crisis: What are the responsibilities and role of the federal government? As this drama unfolded in late 1995 and early 1996, I experienced what it meant not just to be criticized harshly on the basis of policy but, even more than during the Mexican crisis, what it was like to be personally vilified.

Increasing the debt limit is a technical issue. I'll explain the background in brief. Throughout nearly all of American history, the federal government has carried a national debt, financed by issuing Treasury bonds. This debt has risen over time. Until the First World War, Congress directly approved each new issuance of debt. But that became impractical as a way to finance the war, giving rise in 1917 to the practice of authorizing an overall "debt ceiling." The advent of annual budgeting made the debt limit anachronistic, because now Congress would control federal spending directly through the budget process. However, the practice was never eliminated.

Over the many decades since, congressional approval of increased ceilings—which is necessary to finance the operations of the federal government—had sometimes involved fairly contentious disputes over budgetary issues, but never to the degree of the 1995 conflict or with an expressed willingness to default. But in the spring of 1995, while we at

Treasury were busy dealing with the Mexican crisis, conservatives were looking for a way to force Bill Clinton to sign their budget, with deep cuts in programs he cared about and large tax reductions favoring the most affluent. The debt limit became a lever. By attaching an increase in the debt ceiling to their bills for the 1996 budget—and refusing to authorize an increase in the debt ceiling otherwise—the President's antagonists in Congress thought that Clinton could be forced to accept the minimalist view of government built into their proposed budget.

The Speaker of the House, Newt Gingrich, began publicly to bring up the possibility of refusing to raise the debt limit in April 1995. He went on the ABC program *This Week with David Brinkley* and suggested that he and his allies might use the debt limit as a way of getting the President to sign a Republican budget bill. If the President refused and Gingrich held firm, this course of action would prevent the Treasury Department from borrowing and thus could lead to the government's failure to meet its obligations for the first time in the country's history. Gingrich was suggesting a deliberate financial default by the government of the United States, which could mean the cessation not only of payment on debt instruments but also of some operations of government—from sending out Social Security checks to paying doctors at veterans' hospitals. Clinton, Gingrich said, would then have to "decide how big a crisis he wants."

At the time, I didn't think that this threat was serious. Coming from Wall Street, I thought the notion that the government of the United States would choose, *as a political act*, not to meet its financial obligations was outside the realm of possibility. Publicly, I said that such a default was "unthinkable." The obligation to pay debt underlies our entire financial system and had to be maintained as a practical and moral imperative.

For the United States to choose not to pay obligations for political reasons would undermine that imperative. Such a message was especially troubling in the context of developing countries that were making enormous sacrifices to pay their debts in order to avoid the damage to living standards that could flow from default. During the not-yet-resolved peso crisis, we were essentially saying to Mexico what we would subsequently say to a number of other countries: debt default risks creating chaotic financial conditions and loss of access to capital markets for a long time. Instead, you need to implement reforms in conjunction with IMF assistance. How could we square that message with defaulting on our own debt for political reasons?

Moreover, a default would likely have harmed the perception of our country's reliability as a debtor, raising the interest rates the United States would have to pay on its debt, even if only slightly—not only in the short term, but for years to come. And this damage to our credit standing could be extremely damaging when we needed it most: if we ever faced real financial duress. Moreover, diminished confidence in our society's commitment to the moral imperative to repay debt might also raise borrowing costs for the private sector. I thought that defaulting on United States government debt, even for a brief time, would be a monumentally unwise and consequential act—so I didn't believe Gingrich could be serious.

My view was substantively right but seemed to be politically wrong. Gingrich and some members of his party claimed to be quite ready to court the unthinkable—default—to get Clinton to accept what he viewed as the unacceptable: their budget proposals. I underestimated the resolve of the President's antagonists, who, over the next several months, certainly seemed to be entirely willing to use this weapon. I was even more surprised when they found a few well-known figures from Wall Street who would support the idea. One was Stanley Druckenmiller, a hedge fund manager, who took the position that the markets would ignore a default if it helped to produce a balanced budget. In September, Gingrich gave a speech to a trade group called the Public Securities Association, in which he said that his side would not back down. "I don't care what the price is," Gingrich said. "I don't care if we have no executive offices and no bonds for sixty days."

Without an increase, the federal government would hit the debt ceiling before the end of 1995, possibly as early as October. Default and the President being forced to sign an unacceptable budget were both untenable. We needed to find a way out, rather than simply waiting and hoping that at the last minute the opposition would blink and increase the debt limit. We also faced a conundrum similar to one we had just experienced with Mexico. We had to avoid causing alarm in financial markets; but without raising an alarm, creating pressure on the President's opponents in Congress to abandon these tactics would be difficult.

But if default was unthinkable—something akin to nuclear war—and the Republican budget was merely horrible, shouldn't we accept the horrible to avoid the unthinkable? I never found an entirely persuasive answer to that question. When the issue would arise in media interviews, I would deflect it by saying that this wasn't how the legislative process was supposed to work. Something as important as the debt limit shouldn't be held hostage to another piece of legislation or be used to coerce a President into signing something else—especially not a major policy measure such as the budget. Hostage taking is frequently practiced in legislation, but my point was that it should not extend to such fundamental matters as default. Fortunately for me, no one in the media ever persisted beyond this discussion of legislative principles to force me to explain why I would risk the unthinkable just to avoid the horrible.

But the showdown did not unfold as our opponents expected. At first this was due to a simple misunderstanding. Republicans originally thought I had said that the debt ceiling would be reached in mid-November. In mid-October, we sent a letter to the Hill saying that the debt ceiling would be hit on October 31. The Republicans felt that I had intentionally misled them earlier. In fact, they had simply misunderstood a technical distinction about the dates that I had testified about several times. Although the debt ceiling would be hit on October 31, there was enough cash on hand for us to keep meeting obligations through mid-November.

This misunderstanding about the timing was the first of several events that fall that undermined their legislative strategy. As a result, attacks on me that fall and winter were angry and vicious—much more than during the Mexico crisis. I had never experienced anything like this before. This began when Newt Gingrich said on TV that I was playing games and was untrustworthy. "We have no belief that the Treasury has accurate figures," he said. "We have no belief that Rubin's advice is anything other than politics." Senate Majority Leader Bob Dole told reporters on Capitol Hill, "He doesn't have a lot of credibility up here."

Meanwhile, we still faced the prospect of running out of cash in mid-November. It was Ed Knight, our savvy chief Treasury counsel, who suggested borrowing from federal trust funds on an unprecedented scale to postpone default. Accounting for certain government obligations— such as pension benefits for government employees, highway construction, and Social Security—is separate from the rest of the federal budget. Ed argued that we had the legal authority to borrow from these funds in order to meet other pending obligations. By doing so, we could hold off default for a few months without a debt limit increase.

On November 12, three days before what would have been the first default by the American government in its history, we decided to borrow from the trust funds. We drew from two funds, the Civil Service Retirement Fund and a federal savings plan. We did not borrow from Social Security, in part for technical reasons and in part because it would be hard to persuade retirees that borrowing Social Security funds would not endanger their benefits. I think many on the other side were hoping that we would use Social Security funds, which would give them a chance to provoke outrage against us.

I never viewed our actions as an attempt to protect the President, though they certainly had that effect. I was simply trying to fulfill my statutory responsibility to pay the government's debts without causing some other unacceptable outcome. But Clinton's opponents were infuriated, because what we did to forestall default freed the President from the vise they thought they had him in. Using the debt limit to coerce his capitulation was their strategy. Our finding a way to get cash even though we were at the debt limit pushed them into a new, more explicit strategy of closing down the government to force Clinton's hand on the budget.

That strategy was highly damaging to them. Antigovernment feeling was not as deeply imbedded as some conservatives thought. The American public, for the most part, did not think that shutting down the federal government, even temporarily, was a good idea. And for a variety of reasons, most people blamed Congress and not the White House for the shutdown, driving the Republican Congress's popularity down and the President's up.

After we announced our decision to borrow from the trust funds, freeing the President from the threat of default as pressure to reach an agreement, some of his opponents became even more upset. James Baker, one of my predecessors as Secretary of the Treasury, was cited in the press as saying that I could be held personally liable for the amounts borrowed from the trust funds. (I'd done well on Wall Street, but not well enough to keep the federal government running for more than a few seconds.) Bill Archer (R-TX), the chairman of the House Ways and Means Committee, said that I was provoking a "constitutional and legal crisis" and introduced a bill to stop me from using the trust funds. Congressman John Mica (R-FL) testified that our use of the trust funds' cash made me a thief. Around that time, I remember Hillary telling me that she drew strength from seeing how I handled being vilified.

One morning, I woke up to a Robert Novak column in *The Washington Post* saying that Gingrich no longer "trusted" me and would not take my phone calls. Another report quoted Gerry Solomon (R-NY), the chairman of the House Rules Committee, as saying he was interested in trying to impeach me if I borrowed any more money. In a meeting I had on Capitol Hill, a Republican congressman mentioned talk about impeachment to my face. I was concerned about the totally unjustified attacks on my integrity, but in conversations with colleagues and friends—or even in off-the-record interviews—I treated it lightly, saying that Judy wanted me back in New York and that when she heard the threat of impeachment, she called to ask me how she could testify for them.

This harshness and personal vilification—which Washington too often resorts to when conflicts develop—can be hazardous to sensible choices. Decision makers can readily become excessively risk averse. In this environment, minor mistakes can have vast, distorting consequences. I was keenly aware that some insignificant, good-faith error that didn't matter in any substantive way could derail our entire effort. The pursuit of fewer errors is sensible; the insistence on none at all, counterproductive. Unrelenting criticism of people in public service—and the same is true on Wall Street trading desks or in any business—may well reduce the frequency of mistakes. But it does so at a great cost—chilling the willingness of individuals to act and to take worthwhile risks.

And you can never eliminate errors, even among the best-intentioned, most capable people. Due simply to oversight in the midst of managing complex matters, we discovered at one point that we had miscalculated some numbers. The difference wasn't substantively significant, but the political effect could have been immense. In another instance, we said that the Federal Reserve, which acts as agent for the Treasury in sending out checks, could not distinguish among different types of government payments. This would have meant that in the case of default, the government would have no ability to, say, withhold payments to defense contractors while continuing to send Social Security checks. But then we found out that may not have been entirely accurate.

I remember going out to dinner with Judy in Washington and agonizing over our quandary about whether we could send out Social Security checks in case of default. I thought the issue could blow up, and I told Judy that I might have to step down: "We made this assertion that we now realize may have been wrong." After talking it over with Judy, I went to Leon and told him about what had happened. "I don't know how we screwed this up," I told him, "but we did."

Leon agreed that it was a serious problem. Our opponents weren't going to view anything as an honest slip-up. I remember Pat Griffin, the White House legislative counsel, saying to me, in a not altogether joking way, that I might want to leave town for a while. In fact, our assertion was based on what Federal Reserve Board officials had initially told us and was probably right for practical purposes, although later the Fed's computer people said that, with sufficient notice, they might have been able to control who got paid. Thus, we may have somewhat overstated the case. In any event, there were no established legal criteria for prioritizing payments, so that actually having to do this would have been chaotic and rife with uncertainty, to say the least.

Neither of these relatively insubstantial mistakes became a public issue. If they had, the handling of the debt limit crisis and, in an environment in which my credibility was already being attacked, my position as Treasury Secretary might have been at serious risk. Or to put the matter differently, on such a highly charged, contentious issue, human error, which is inevitable, can readily be interpreted in the worst possible way and have a vastly disproportionate effect. The debt ceiling controversy remained highly unpleasant for several months. Our opponents continued to challenge my ethics and truthfulness. My concern was partly personal and partly professional. I didn't like having my integrity questioned with no justification. But the bigger concern was that if I came to be seen as not credible, it would be very difficult to function effectively as Treasury Secretary.

We continued to borrow from different trust funds, but by late January we had no more running room. Come March 1, we would not be able to send out $30 billion in checks due to Social Security recipients and military retirees. But before we got to that point, several things happened that reinforced our position and helped to bring the matter to a conclusion. Our opponents began to hear from some of their constituents in the financial community who didn't think a default—whether to retirees, contractors, or debt holders—was such a great idea. And then, fortuitously, Moody's, the bond-rating agency, issued a warning that the AAA status of federal government bonds could be at risk, which Standard & Poor's had done earlier. That made our expressions of concern about the consequences of a default more convincing—although some Republicans still didn't believe a default was imminent until Alan Greenspan told them privately that our projections were right.

The larger factor may have been a sea change in politics and public opinion. After the government shutdowns in November and December proved immensely unpopular, the idea of default became so politically charged that few people wanted to be associated with it any longer. A number of congressmen—including Charles Rangel (D-NY), Steny Hoyer (D-MD), Sandy Levin (D-MI), and Robert Matsui (D-CA)—had been actively making the case against default in the public domain. In addition, the media had become more focused on the consequences of default and had begun to examine the issue more critically. At some point, our opponents simply stopped fighting and, in a retreat with several stages, increased the debt limit. When all was over, I was surprised that the Republicans who had said such awful things about me didn't seem to retain any of their anger. I remember running into Gingrich a while after that and he said something about how they had been a little rough on me during the debt limit thing, but that's just how the game is played in Washington.

Gingrich was very friendly and so was I. But even after a few years in Washington, I couldn't relate to the idea that you shouldn't take it personally when someone calls you a liar and a thief. The propensity to convert policy and political disagreement into personalized assault can have consequences for decision making. Having some measure of psychological independence may have made it easier to make decisions that involved substantial risk. (Of course, financial independence may have also helped.) That my sense of self didn't come from my job meant that I could more readily take the chance of failing.

CHAPTER SEVEN

Talking Softly

I CONTINUED TO BE STRUCK by how different being at Treasury was from life in the White House. In many ways, heading a cabinet agency is like running a business, but someone who goes from the private sector to a cabinet position can easily be misled by the similarities and consequently fail to learn to deal with the differences. As a cabinet officer, you're the head of a large, hierarchically structured organization. As Bob Reich told me when I moved to Treasury, you get to "run your own show," much as a private-sector CEO does. In both worlds, setting objectives, establishing effective accountability, and having capable people are crucially important.

But the two worlds are different enough that the analogy to corporate structure can prevent a former CEO from being effective in government. In a noticeable sense, you don't run your own show; the White House does. Goals, as I had already discovered, differ in government and the private sector. In business, the chief focus is on profitability. Government, by contrast, has no simple bottom line but rather a vast array of interests and priorities, many of which exist in a state of tension or conflict. For that reason, decision making in government is vastly more complex.

At Treasury, I also found a difference from business in terms of authority. Many former business executives feel great frustration when they discover the limits on their ability to act in government. I had not been accustomed to, nor did I expect, a corporate-style hierarchical structure. But even I was surprised at what limited power I had in my own building. The various bureaus and agencies that are part of the Treasury Department operate with considerable independence. Just because you are dissatisfied doesn't mean you can make changes. Even with respect to the Treasury Department proper, many familiar management tools were not available. A private-sector CEO has the power to hire and fire based on performance, to pay top managers large bonuses, and to promote capable people aggressively. At Treasury, I had the power to hire and fire fewer than 100 political appointees among the 160,000 people who worked under me. Others could be dismissed for gross incompetence, but the practical obstacles to doing so made it seldom worth the effort. In general, the quality and commitment of many career civil servants was a great positive surprise during my time in government—but the rules were rigid and needed bold overhaul.

Furthermore, most structural departmental reorganization couldn't be done on my own, but required legislation. Even closing an inefficient IRS field office would mean a time-consuming and often unsuccessful discussion with that state's congressional delegation to avoid creating damaging political ill will. Luckily, as Roger Altman told me before I arrived, the organizational structure of the Treasury Department, which had been in place for many years, was basically sound.

The biggest difference in both process and authority is the organizational complexity involved in making major Executive Branch policy decisions. In the private sector, a CEO has more or less free rein. In a presidential administration, everything revolves around the White House and almost every major policy decision is brought into the White House, often through an extensive interagency process. Moreover, most significant decisions made at the cabinet level are reexamined at the White House not only for substance but for their "message" and political dimensions. As a cabinet secretary, you wear two hats at the same time—one as head of your agency, the other as part of an administration in which everything revolves around the President. And to be successful in the cabinet, you have to be skillful at working within the White House process on issues that affect you. The White House staff may have great and even decisive influence on policy decisions you think you should be making. Sometimes the cabinet agencies and White House work in harmony, sometimes they operate in ignorance of what the others are doing, and sometimes they go to war with one another.

Presidents have dealt with this problem in various ways. The National Security Council was created in 1947 to coordinate the different bodies involved in foreign policy. To deal with domestic and economic issues, Presidents have tried various approaches. Richard Nixon proposed having four cabinet supersecretaries, organized around subject areas, but never got to implement the idea. Some Presidents have tried to coordinate through lead cabinet members, but often not successfully. And President Clinton, as I discussed earlier, created the National Economic Council.

Clinton's Health and Human Services Secretary, Donna Shalala, had it right when she told me that the position of a cabinet secretary is, in a sense, schizophrenic. You're the boss in your own building—albeit with less authority than you'd have in the private sector. But when you come to the White House and sit around the table, you may have less influence than a thirty-some-year-old staff person, despite your august title and the trappings that go with being a cabinet member. For some, it's hard to keep these two roles straight, and the complexities can create considerable stress and tension. Longtime officials at the Treasury Department sometimes recalled one of my predecessors, who was notorious for threatening to resign every few days after blowups with the White House.

When I moved to Treasury, I had the advantage of having already developed a sense of the relationship between the cabinet agencies and the White House from the other side of the fence. Working at the NEC for two years, I had gotten to know the thirty-year-old staff people, respected their experience in policy and politics, and thought of them as colleagues. I also understood how the Clinton administration really functioned, including the importance of the daily early-morning staff meeting in the Roosevelt Room and the smaller meeting-after-the-meeting in the chief of staff's office. That's where the administration's agenda was set and all sorts of decisions about the interplay of policy and politics, including congressional strategy and media strategy, were made. I never relished showing up for work at 7:30 in the morning. But after my move to Treasury, I told Leon Panetta that I'd like to keep coming to the daily staff meetings because Treasury was involved in so many issues. Leon said okay, although no other cabinet members attended, other than those located in the White House complex.

Many of Clinton's cabinet secretaries were fully effective without being part of the daily White House process. But for me, attending those meetings addressed the "schizophrenia" problem and kept me in the thick of everything going on in the Clinton administration. Erskine Bowles, who succeeded Leon as chief of staff in 1996, agreed that I could keep coming. Having run the Small Business Administration during Clinton's first term, Erskine understood the problem of isolation inside the departments very well. He once said to me, "If you're running an agency, you feel like you're on the moon." Erskine has accomplished many things in his career, none of them more important, in my view, than moving the morning meeting to 7:45.

Becoming Treasury Secretary also enormously increased my activity on Capitol Hill. At the NEC, I had had some involvement with Congress, but only at Treasury did it become a part of my daily life. The first of those interactions was my confirmation hearing. Linda Robertson, then Treasury's deputy assistant secretary for public affairs, was the quarterback of this effort. She and her colleagues used this preparatory process to bring me up to speed on all of the many aspects of Treasury, to introduce me to the key people, and to discuss questions that might arise. At the hearing itself, before the Senate Finance Committee, both New York senators, Alfonse D'Amato and Daniel Patrick Moynihan, joined me at the table to make the formal introductions, and then I was on my own. On the one hand, I didn't anticipate any great difficulties; on the other hand, it was always possible that some senators might use the hearing—and me—as a vehicle for attacking the administration. And, since White House staff does not testify before Congress unless required to in some investigation, this was my first hearing as a public official and it was being nationally televised on C-SPAN. I felt some natural unease, but I remember feeling buttressed by thinking of my younger son, Philip, who was sitting right behind me, and his sense of perspective and wry, ironic view of life.

Committees that oversaw Treasury's budget could direct departmental management and might, in some instances, try to affect policy positions as well. And, of course, virtually all major policy decisions were subject to congressional approval, or at the least to congressional inquiry and hearings. And beyond the question of oversight, members of Congress tried to exercise influence over how we ran the agency and the scope of my job. I remember Trent Lott (R-MS), who was then the Senate majority whip, asking me to come to his Senate office that first year. When I got there, he told me that, as Treasury Secretary, I shouldn't be delving into social programs and the like. My job was worrying about the dollar and interest rates. I didn't know quite what to say, so I disagreed respectfully.

For all these reasons, one's relations with key members and congressional committees are key to being effective and require a great deal of time and thought. In testifying before Congress, my approach was to apply what I'd learned about client relationships at Goldman Sachs: be well prepared, responsive to their concerns, and highly respectful. The master at the art was Alan Greenspan. Alan would doff his cap in the direction of a question, even if, on occasion, it was somewhat off the mark. "That's an interesting observation you make, Senator, about the earth being flat," he'd say. "If I might, let me rephrase the question." Alan would then ask himself a completely different question and answer it with such complexity and finely calibrated nuance that the questioner faced a choice between nodding intelligently and acknowledging his own confusion. I must say that testifying next to the chairman, I was sometimes completely baffled myself.

Alan would then ask the House member or senator, "Does that respond to your question?"

And the interrogator would invariably say, "Yes, it does."

In many other instances, of course, congressional testimony meant a real dialogue—and sometimes disagreement—on serious issues, but even those exchanges were best conducted with a highly respectful tone toward the interlocutor.

Press relations also took on a different dimension after I became Secretary. Before moving across the street from the White House, I never thought about how much of a role the media plays in the daily life of the Secretary of the Treasury. As head of the NEC, I could speak for the administration, but I wasn't the point person. As Treasury Secretary, even though many others comment on economic matters, I was the administration's principal spokesperson on the economy. I was expected to represent the President's budgets, his tax proposals, and his views about any sort of economic crisis, problem, or event. I also represented the U.S. government at international summit meetings, such as the regular gatherings of finance ministers from various groupings of countries—the G-7, G-10, G-20, and so on. Because of this formal role, anything I said that had implications for financial markets could cause them to respond swiftly and powerfully. The markets might also react to comments by the NEC chairman or various other administration officials, but ordinarily not nearly to the same degree.

To avoid moving markets, I had to be consistent and highly disciplined in not only what I said but precisely how I said it. The most sensitive area was exchange rate policy. Because of Treasury's ability to buy and sell currencies for the purpose of affecting exchange rates, the markets would respond to almost anything I said that seemed to make intervention more or less likely. Affecting exchange rates unintentionally would make me look undisciplined and unsophisticated. My credibility, with respect to our currency, could be especially critical if at some subsequent time we had a weak dollar and faced the possibility of a dollar crisis.

My substantive view was that economic fundamentals determine exchange rate levels over time, and that we should focus our attention on strengthening U.S. economic policy and performance, not on influencing the level of the currency. I also believed that a strong U.S. dollar was very much in the national interest. This was different from the question of whether our exchange rate was overvalued, though people often had difficulty recognizing that distinction. My rhetorical position thus always adhered unvaryingly to that policy, both because that was substantially right and to maintain confidence in the currency.

A strong currency means that American consumers and businesses can buy imported goods and services more cheaply and that inflation and interest rates will tend to be lower. It also puts pressure on American industry to increase productivity and competitiveness. These benefits can feed on themselves as foreign capital flows in more readily because of greater confidence in our currency. A weak dollar would have the contrary effects. A strong dollar does make imports cheaper—and therefore more attractive—in the United States, and American exports more expensive overseas, tending to increase the current account deficit. However, that is a problem with many underlying causes, including the gap between savings and investment in the United States.

In my view, the sensible way to deal with the risks that can come with a large and sustained trade gap is not to promote a weak dollar as an instrument of trade policy, which, in addition to its other drawbacks, could set off competitive devaluations. Instead, we should act to increase savings in the United States, especially by improving the government's fiscal position, and to increase productivity to make American goods more competitive. At times, though, the dollar may trade for an extended period at a high degree of overvaluation relative to the fundamentals. An overvalued exchange rate that makes goods and services less competitive in world markets than warranted by comparative efficiency results in undesirable dislocations and will likely not be sustainable. Whether to try to correct this, and how to frame such action, is a very difficult judgment.

Some saw a tension between my basic stance in favor of a strong dollar and our action on rare occasions to spur a market correction of what seemed an undue rise in the dollar against a particular currency. But when we took this action, we were operating within the context of our strong-dollar policy. I was skeptical about the efficacy of currency "interventions" per se—that is, of governments trying to influence the exchange rate of a currency by buying and selling large quantities in the open market. My experience with foreign exchange markets at Goldman Sachs led me to believe that trading flows were simply too vast for such interventions to have more than a momentary effect, except in very unusual circumstances. Basically, currency levels reflect the market's expectations—and the realities—of a country's fundamental economic situation relative to the economic fundamentals of other countries: fiscal conditions, interest rates, inflation, and growth.

In any case, whatever my views were about whether the dollar at any given moment was too strong or too weak relative to economic fundamentals, I virtually always said exactly the same thing: "A strong dollar is in our national interest." A lot more thought went into that small phrase than was evident from my boring repetition. The repetition reflected not only my belief in a strong dollar, but also my belief in leaving markets to market forces. The slightest shading, such as going from "I believe a strong dollar is in our national interest" to "I believe it's in our national interest to maintain a strong dollar" could have market effects, even if no change in view was meant.

At press conferences at home or on the road, reporters from financial publications would try to engage me in a cat-and-mouse game. They would ask the same questions about the dollar and the stock market again and again, each time with some new twist, hoping to elicit something different from my standard response—a response that was always true on its own terms but not necessarily a complete answer relative to the circumstances at any given time. I had said a strong dollar was in our national interest when one dollar could buy 120 yen. Now the yen was at 130—was the stronger dollar better? How strong was too strong? Wire service reporters kept their cell phones on to broadcast my remarks directly to their news desks, in case I disgorged some unexpected nuance. But I became very adept at simply repeating my mantra—except in those rare instances when we deliberately used a slight shading, always built around commitment to a strong dollar, to convey a message. For example, my saying "A strong dollar is in our national interest, and we have had a strong dollar for some time now" created great excitement at a press briefing, as it was construed to mean that we wouldn't mind seeing the dollar remain strong but soften somewhat. However, I would never give any explanation for such a change beyond my prepared phraseology.

A good illustration of how sensitive markets can be is what happened when I was testifying before the Senate Finance Committee in June 1998. At that point, the Japanese yen had fallen to 141 to the dollar, its lowest level in eight years. The weak yen seemed to have reached a troubling extreme and was exacerbating our trade deficit by making Japanese imports cheaper in the United States and American exports more expensive relative to Japanese products in overseas markets. Of even more urgent concern at that moment was that the falling yen could worsen the economic crisis that had then been afflicting Asia for nearly a year, by putting pressure on the currencies of the troubled Asian countries and by motivating China to devalue its currency. When Senator Frank Murkowski asked me about the possibility of U.S. intervention to support the yen, I said that intervention was "a temporary tool, not a fundamental solution." Weakness in Japan's currency, I said, reflected the underlying weakness in Japan's economy. In order to raise the value of the yen, the Japanese would have to address their fundamental economic problems.

That was all correct, but in focusing on Japan, I mistakenly discussed intervention in an intellectually serious way. Larry, who was sitting next to me, passed me a note that read, "Bob—Yen has moved to 143.20 in last 15 minutes. I think we need a little more saber rattling." In other words, the foreign exchange markets were interpreting my remarks to suggest I had made the possibility of intervention to support the yen less likely, and were selling yen against the dollar. In fact, my policy views had not changed at all: I was never enthusiastic about currency interventions, but I didn't rule them out as an occasional tool.

After reading Larry's note, I hastened back to my normal level of opacity, offering the clarification that I didn't want anyone to infer that I was suggesting that intervention was not an appropriate tool to affect the short-term direction of currencies. "We have often said in the past, Mr. Chairman, that we will intervene when appropriate and not intervene when it's not appropriate, but it is always a tool that is available for the kinds of impacts that it could have."

This was not especially useful guidance, a point Senator Moynihan picked up on immediately. "And you will always know when it is appropriate and when it is inappropriate?!" he interjected.

But my clarification was unavailing. The yen continued to fall that day, to 144.75 to the dollar. We hadn't adjusted our policy on the yen-dollar relationship or on currency intervention in the slightest. But currency traders were reading nonexistent meaning into my comments, even after I said that I hadn't meant what they'd thought I'd meant. An episode like that demonstrated the value of discipline and, on exchange rates, of avoiding interesting discussions and sticking to carefully wrought stock phrases.

Having said all that, currency intervention can make sense on rare occasions. Just a few days later, with the yen continuing to fall against the dollar, I felt the conditions that can make a currency intervention effective might well be present. The first was that the yen-dollar exchange rate, now at 147 yen to the dollar, seemed to have gone to a real extreme—the yen was approaching free fall. American manufacturers, who were always worried about the level of the dollar, were becoming truly alarmed. The second condition was that the intervention would be supported by policy changes. Japanese officials were prepared to make a series of statements supporting economic reforms we were encouraging, such as closing insolvent banks. (Whether they would follow through with such promises was another question, but their going on the record seemed like progress.) The final condition was the psychological element of surprise. If the markets expected you to act, that would already be reflected in market positions and prices and tend to vitiate the impact of the action. My well-known bias against currency intervention—and even my unintentionally direct Senate hearing remarks—were helpful here. For this kind of move to be successful, surprising the market can be key.

But despite propitious conditions, I still felt that the odds of success might not be good enough to warrant intervention. Alan, Larry, several top Treasury officials, and I debated the pros and cons at length. Japan's economic slide urgently required economic reform that the government seemed unable to accomplish. How much reform commitment had to accompany the intervention for the market to react? And I was concerned, as usual, about the effect that an unsuccessful intervention might have on our credibility. But Larry and Tim Geithner made a strong case that intervening in support of the yen was a risk worth taking, largely because of what was happening elsewhere in Asia. After many, many hours of discussion, they persuaded me.

That decision illustrates another point about decision making. While keeping your choices open for as long as possible—a proclivity of mine that Larry termed "preserving optionality"—is desirable, the markets don't wait for you. As we continued our discussion into the early evening, in the Far East the new day was under way and we had to decide before the Tokyo markets opened. When the markets opened the next morning in New York, we would be too late. So rather than continuing our deliberations in the hope of new information or new insights, I had to make a decision without further delay.

In this case, the intervention worked—which is to say that the psychology of the foreign exchange markets was clearly affected. When the Federal Reserve Bank of New York, which acts as the Treasury's agent in the foreign exchange markets, converted $2 billion into yen, currency traders were caught by surprise and the exchange rate moved all the way back to 136 yen to the dollar. Although the larger issues related to Japan's economic weakness remained, the yen never again reached the lows of that summer. We intervened very seldom, and each of our interventions was successful.

ANOTHER CONSTANT FACTOR in the life of a Treasury Secretary is the stock market. As my time at Treasury went on, my personal view was that excesses were probably building. The U.S. bull market had begun in 1982. By the second half of the 1990s, investors were asking much less of a risk premium for investing in equities than they had historically. People had come to believe that stocks would bounce back reasonably quickly from any decline, as they had from the sharp drop in October 1987; that stocks always outperform bonds over the long term; and that stocks involve minimal risk if you hold on to them. The proliferating financial news on television and book titles such as *Dow 36,000*, published when the Dow was around 11,000, exuded financial market euphoria. The attitude of people who grew up in the 1980s and '90s was the mirror image of people I had known who grew up during the Depression. Whereas many people of my parents' generation never lost their wariness about investing in the stock market, many people of my generation and younger were equally conditioned toward complacency.

My view was that nothing had changed to reduce the substantial risk that has always been associated with stocks. From the last day of 1964 to the last day of 1981, the Dow Jones Industrial Average fluctuated a great deal, but the closing price was roughly unchanged—meaning it had declined substantially when adjusted for inflation. We were now in the midst of a bull market of similar duration that could potentially be followed by a long period of underperformance. In Japan, in admittedly different circumstances, the Nikkei average lost roughly three quarters of its value between 1989 and 2003.

Many new investors weren't knowledgeable about stocks and were investing based on theories that were oversimplified and, at worst, simply incorrect. Take the popular hypothesis that stocks outperform bonds over the long run. This has been true historically, though the assumption that the future will resemble the past remains exactly that—an assumption. Moreover, stocks might have ceased to be undervalued in relation to bonds once investors became aware of the phenomenon and priced it into the market. Leaving that issue aside, what's true of market aggregates is not necessarily true of any one portfolio, which is subject to the performance of particular companies. A preference for stocks in general doesn't help you understand valuation or choose investments wisely. Moreover, while buying stock index funds and holding shares for a couple of decades or longer may provide a good likelihood of a distinctly higher return than bonds, history also indicates that markets can provide subpar returns for lengthy periods. Even if the stocks-versus-bonds thesis is correct, not all investors have a time horizon of sufficient duration to benefit from what might be a very long run—for example, if you're planning to retire on your savings in five or ten years or don't have the psychological staying power to withstand a long drought. All of this was relevant—but ignored—in the subsequent political debates, at the height of the bull market, about reforming Social Security by creating individual equity accounts.

As it seemed more and more likely that stock prices were excessive—and that the NASDAQ was almost manic—I became increasingly concerned that a sudden return to historical valuation levels could do harm to the economy. My considered view was never to say anything about the level of the stock markets, but with possible serious overvaluation posing larger risks to the economy, was there anything I could do about it? Alan, Larry, and I talked about this issue as the Dow broke 5,000, 6,000, 7,000,

8,000, and 9,000. Warning off the investing public might have seemed tempting, but I thought, and still think, that public officials ought not to comment on the level of the stock market—and that applies when stocks seem undervalued relative to historical trends, just as when they appear overvalued. A Treasury Secretary serving as a market commentator and hoisting a green, red, or yellow flag depending on his current view is a genuinely bad idea for four reasons. First, whatever our opinions might be, nobody can say what the "correct" level of the stock market is—or whether the market is overvalued. My personal alarm bells started ringing thousands of Dow points below the peak, and I know very shrewd people who were bearish at many points during the great bull markets of the 1980s and '90s. Having been wrong then, I was reminded that I could well be wrong now.

Second, I think any comments I made probably wouldn't have had any effect. An object lesson occurred on December 5, 1996, when Alan Greenspan posed a rhetorical question in a speech: "But how do we know when irrational exuberance has unduly escalated asset values, which then become subject to unexpected and prolonged contractions . . . ?" I'm not sure Alan was even intending to express a view about stock prices. But markets thought the "irrational exuberance" phrase was deliberate and the Dow declined the next day, from 6,437 to 6,382. Then the bull market resumed its run—for another 5,000 points. The only lasting effect of Alan's comment was to win him a probable future entry in *Bartlett's Familiar Quotations.*

Third, I believed that attempts to influence financial markets through words not only would be ineffective but would harm the credibility of the individual making the effort—because knowledgeable people will understand that he has no special insight, and because he'll almost surely be wrong a good bit of the time. By undermining the credibility of policy makers, such attempts could erode confidence and damage the economy itself. Finally, a gradual decline of an overvalued stock market can be readily absorbed. But if an official's comments, for whatever reason, precipitated a rapid and substantial market decline, that could be economically disruptive.

On the other hand, I did, in speeches and television interviews, what seemed appropriate and useful, namely advise investors to focus adequately on risk and valuation, and express concern that these disciplines had flagged. That seemed to me a sound approach no matter what the state of the market might be and carried with it none of the disadvantages of comments on the level of the markets.

By mostly refraining from comment, Alan and I differed greatly from our Japanese counterparts, who tended to take the view that markets should be managed by policy makers. I remember one bilateral meeting with a Japanese finance minister where the issue arose of whether our stock market was too strong. The Japanese official said to me, "Why don't you bring the stock market down?" Obviously, government actions, including fiscal and monetary policy, do affect equity markets. But the Japanese view was that government can affect markets by providing guidance or, in the case of currency rates, through intervention. My view, and that of most American economists and policy makers, is that the impersonal judgment of a vast number of participants guides markets. Over the longer term, stock markets, like currency markets, tend to reflect fundamental economic conditions, although they often diverge from those averages and go to excess in one direction or the other, sometimes for extended periods. In any case, in the long term as well as the short term, markets are going to go where markets are going to go—with jawboning by government officials unlikely to have more than the briefest effect, at most. As I often put it to others in the Clinton administration, "Markets go up, markets go down." Some people viewed this as a profound observation. To others, it was the most obvious of truisms.

All that notwithstanding, in rare instances a Treasury Secretary probably does have to say something about unusually dramatic movements in the stock market. On October 27, 1997, the Dow Jones Industrial Average fell 554 points, its largest-ever single-day point drop at that time. The precipitating factor was a decline in foreign markets brought on by the Asian financial crisis, which created widespread concern in U.S. markets that the problems might spread to us. Adding to the psychology of the situation was that, just ten years and one week before, the Dow had suffered what was then the largest point drop in history, the 1987 stock market crash. People started referring to "Black Monday II."

Now, 554 points in 1997 was a 7.2 percent decline, far less significant than the 508-point, or 22.6 percent, drop on Black Monday in 1987. Moreover, ten years earlier, the crash had overwhelmed the systems that processed and cleared buy and sell orders. As a result, the New York Stock Exchange had temporarily ceased functioning in an orderly way. This time, the market's order-clearing and protective systems had worked much better. Trading had been halted before the end of the trading day by the so-called circuit breakers put into place after the 1987 crash. Nonetheless, the fall worried us, in the context of large declines and growing market volatility at home and abroad, and had been receiving intense media attention throughout the day.

I was torn about whether to say something publicly. On the one hand, I did not want to be in the position of cheerleading the stock market, since that is intellectually dishonest, very unlikely to work, and potentially counterproductive with respect to confidence. On the other hand, the great nervousness and uncertainty in the U.S. financial markets seemed to call for a reassuring presence. Larry Summers, Alan Greenspan, Gene Sperling, and I decided, after much discussion, that I should make some statement. We didn't want or expect to affect the market's direction, but we did want to try to diffuse a panicky environment. Our hope was simply that whatever was going to happen would happen in a calm, orderly fashion, as opposed to what had occurred in 1987.

With Greenspan at the Treasury, the four of us spent more than an hour with other Treasury officials constructing a brief statement. It said that I had been in touch with other officials, that we'd been monitoring developments closely, and that these consultations indicated that market mechanisms, such as the systems for settling trades, were working effectively. The statement continued, "It is important to remember that the fundamentals of the U.S. economy are strong and have been for the past several years." As a final note, we added that the prospects for continued growth with low inflation and low unemployment remained good.

The delivery of this statement was a dramatic moment. I walked down the steps of the Treasury Department and read the statement we'd worked out to a vast number of television cameras. Then I turned around and, ignoring the questions being shouted by members of the press, walked back inside. This was treated as a major news event; the networks broke into their regular programming to carry it live.

The next day, the stock market recaptured some of its losses, and the news media expressed a general view that my comments had served a useful purpose. Having somebody who is viewed as possessing some measure of credibility with respect to markets and economic matters speak in a calm and thoughtful fashion, even if he says nothing that is relevant to the immediate market phenomenon, probably does contribute positively to the psychology of a volatile situation. One advantage of avoiding frivolous market commentary is that one builds and maintains a credibility that can be drawn upon when it is really needed.

Given the remarkable rise in the Dow following Clinton's election in 1992, political people in the White House often wanted the President to take credit for the strength of the stock market. I argued that for Presidents to validate their policies by pointing to the stock market's performance was always a mistake. The stock market could fluctuate for all kinds of reasons and could overstate or understate reality for extended periods. I sometimes dissuaded Clinton's advisers by using the argument that if the President took credit for the rise in the stock market, he'd get the blame for the fall as well. Live by the sword, die by the sword.

BECOMING SECRETARY of the Treasury greatly increased my interaction with the Federal Reserve. At the NEC, I had always supported the Fed's independence with regard to monetary policy, and I continued to do exactly that at Treasury. The basic logic here is familiar: the head of a country's central bank has the job of acting countercyclically—prompting growth during economic slowdowns and constricting the money supply when strong growth threatens to produce inflation. The latter task is intrinsically unpopular. As the longest-serving Federal Reserve chairman in history, William McChesney Martin, famously said, the Fed chairman is the fellow who takes the punch bowl away just when the party is getting going. That's why the chairman should have a fixed term, which he does, rather than serving at the pleasure of the President. This helps insulate him from political pressure.

Before 1993, Presidents and Treasury Secretaries had sometimes opined on what the Fed should be doing with regard to interest rates and sometimes tried to lean on the Fed chairman in various ways. Bill Clinton, by contrast, always adhered to the principle of not commenting publicly on Fed policy. Whenever the contrary suggestion was made inside the White House, I argued that commenting was a bad idea for several reasons. First, and most fundamental, the Fed's decisions on monetary policy should be as free from political considerations as possible. Second, evident respect for the Fed's independence can bolster the President's credibility, economic confidence, and confidence in the soundness of our financial markets. Third, the bond market might be affected by any belief that the Fed chairman was under political pressure that could affect the Fed's actions. There was also another factor I came to recognize after moving to Treasury: we advised other countries around the world, such as Mexico during the peso crisis, that their central bank governors should be insulated from political pressure. Attempting to put political pressure on our own central bank could undermine that prescription.

Whatever a President's philosophy about publicly commenting on the Fed, every President probably complains about it privately from time to time. There's a natural tendency to second-guess any decision not to let the economy grow faster, especially when such a decision comes in advance of an election. Even with President Clinton, who respected the Fed's independence both in principle and in practice, behind-the-scenes discussions sometimes grew rather heated. In 1994, a few people in the White House suspected—totally wrongly—that Alan Greenspan, a Republican, might be raising interest rates more than necessary out of some kind of political bias. I responded that Greenspan seemed to me to be trying to extend the recovery by preventing the economy from overheating. That would ultimately benefit the President politically when he ran for reelection in 1996.

Greenspan's actions in 1994 were vindicated by subsequent economic developments. But such suspicions of political motivation, though not warranted in this case, leave nagging questions. What should be done if the Fed chairman is consistently wrong or ineffective or politically motivated, and who should make those judgments? We obviously never had to face those quandaries with Greenspan, but they have no easy answer.

At Treasury, my personal relationship with Greenspan also grew much more familiar. The Treasury and Fed staffs work closely together on a range of issues, despite what has historically been some degree of institutional competition. There is a tradition, maintained by Lloyd Bentsen before me, that the Treasury Secretary and Fed chairman meet on a regular basis. So I now got together with Alan at least once a week for breakfast either at my office or at his, and before too long Larry Summers also joined us.

Our discussions ranged all over the place. Sometimes we were dealing with issues of crisis, such as Mexico or Asia. Other times we would be preparing for one of the several different international meetings of finance ministers and central bank governors or considering some issue expected to arise in Washington. But many times, we simply debated and explored issues about the U.S. and world economies. These meetings were a cross between a graduate seminar in economics and a policy-planning meeting, with bits of gossip thrown in. We were looking at intellectually complicated issues in the context of immediate, practical issues and decisions. While these discussions were serious, they could also be very funny—assuming you shared Alan's taste for jokes about the yield curve.

One of the issues the three of us returned to again and again was the strong performance of the American economy. By mid-1996, the expansion was well established and still going strong. The growth rate was higher, and unemployment lower, than prevailing views would have said was possible without igniting inflation by putting upward pressure on wages and prices. People were throwing around the phrase "new economy," suggesting that advances in technology had revised the familiar rules and limits. Some investors appeared to be falling prey to the timeless boom-era temptation to believe that the business cycle had been tamed, that companies would never fail in their earnings, and that the next economic slowdown would never come.

Yet amid such indicators of what Alan called irrational exuberance, real signs suggested that something had indeed changed for the better. With unemployment so low, a Fed chairman's normal instinct would be to raise rates to prevent inflation. But there were no signs of increased inflation. The question was whether—as Clinton had intuitively argued in our internal discussions in 1994—the American economy could safely grow faster than during the previous few decades. Though there was no real evidence at the time, Clinton's instinct turned out to be correct.

This apparent change in the so-called speed limit of economic growth strongly suggested that productivity growth—which had greatly slowed from the early 1970s through the early 1990s for reasons not fully understood—had now picked up again. Productivity increases work wonders on an economy, allowing faster growth without inflation. Understanding why productivity growth first faded and then apparently returned would help us estimate future growth and develop policies to promote it.

Most economists were initially skeptical about increases in productivity. But as time went on, Alan said that the data he was poring over didn't reconcile unless productivity was substantially higher than was generally thought. One of Alan's great strengths is his wide-ranging focus on data and his insight in drawing inferences from it. He'd show up at breakfast and ask what I thought about the latest railcar shipments of some type of wheat I had never heard of. "Alan," I'd say, "I don't know how I missed that figure in the paper, but I did." He would have worked out a whole hypothesis around it. Greenspan was the first of the three of us to reach the tentative conclusion that productivity growth did explain the absence of expected inflation. That meant that the speed limit on economic growth was higher than we'd thought. Larry and I followed in agreement somewhat later.

In my view, a critical factor in the return of productivity growth was the restoration of sound fiscal policy. That helped catalyze productivity-enhancing investment by contributing to lower long-term interest rates, increased business and consumer confidence, and greater foreign capital flows into the country. Another key factor was advances in technology, which raised an interesting question. Europe and Japan had access to the same technologies we did in the 1990s but did not experience increased productivity growth. I think the explanation for the difference lies in a third factor: America's cultural and historical disposition to take risks and embrace change. That inclination helped to explain why American companies invested much more heavily in new technologies than companies in other countries. A fourth factor, related to the third, was our more flexible labor market, which meant that companies could more readily benefit from productivity-enhancing investment, and our greater availability of risk capital. Japan and Europe were and are far less change oriented, more mired in structural rigidities, and shorter on risk capital.

A fifth factor, also related to our cultural tendency to embrace change, was our relatively low trade barriers. My initial belief in open markets was based on the standard comparative-advantage argument that dates from the great nineteenth-century British economist David Ricardo—that all countries will benefit if each specializes in the areas where it is most efficient compared to the others and then trades with the others. But Alan once made another point that never had occurred to me until he said it. The biggest advantage of free trade, he said, is competitive pressure *within* the United States from foreign producers. Companies have to become more efficient in order to meet competitive threats from outside our borders. Trade drives companies to reorganize and invest in pursuit of increased productivity. Conversely, Japan's and Europe's relatively less open markets protected companies and reduced their incentive to become more efficient.

But did these seemingly real changes in America's productivity growth justify the tremendous rise in stock prices that was taking place? Again, Alan, Larry, and I reached a similar, tentative conclusion: something real was happening in the economy, but at the same time, the markets were probably overreacting to that real thing. That is what the great Austrian émigré economist Joseph Schumpeter said: almost every transformative, productivity-enhancing development also results in financial market overreaction. To me at least, that tendency seems grounded in human nature. Markets—which are expressions of collective behavior—tend to go to excess, in both directions, because human nature tends to go to excess.

Some of our continuing discussion was about what, if anything, people in our position could or should do to mitigate that inherent tendency to excess. As discussed earlier, none of us thought that economic policy makers should become market commentators, or that we could guide financial markets the way the Japanese and some previous administrations in this country had tried to do, by talking them up or down. I tended to believe, however, that regulatory measures might possibly have some effect in inducing investors to exercise discipline, and could certainly help protect the financial system itself. Disclosure requirements were obviously the place to start and were generally not controversial, at least in principle. But such mechanisms were like the old adage: you can lead a horse to water, but you can't force it to drink. All the disclosures in the world won't help if investors don't care about risks or valuation. The boom in Internet stock prices in the late 1990s occurred despite full disclosure by companies with no real earnings.

Given the limits on what could be accomplished through disclosure requirements, I thought limiting leverage was also necessary both to constrain market excesses and to mitigate the harm they can create. For many years, banks and registered broker dealers had lived with capital requirements, and all investors were subject to margin requirements when they borrowed against stocks. But other kinds of financial institutions, including hedge funds, had no regulatory leverage constraints other than the margin requirements, if any, associated with the instruments they bought or sold short. My own view was that it wasn't necessary to impose special leverage rules on hedge funds as a class of investor. I still think that is right, though as they become a larger and larger part of trading activity, policy makers may revisit that question, if some systemic risk is thought to be at stake. I do think, however, that derivatives, with leverage limits that vary from little to none at all, should be subject to comprehensive and higher margin requirements. But that will almost surely not happen, absent a crisis.

While economically useful under most circumstances for more precise risk management, derivatives can pose risks to the system when market conditions become very volatile. That occurs because of various technical factors that can cause derivatives users to suddenly need to buy or sell in the underlying markets to maintain appropriate hedge positions. With the truly vast increase in the amount of derivatives outstanding, it is at least conceivable that the effect on already disrupted markets could be vast. Some evidence of that potential appeared in the third quarter of 2003, when a rapid spike in interest rates changed the hedging requirements for mortgage-backed securities. The result was substantial exacerbation of that spike. Similarly, in 1987, some traders estimated that "portfolio insurance" selling of stock index futures added substantially to the October 19, 1987, stock market collapse. In a later speech at the Kennedy School at Harvard, Larry characterized my concerns about derivatives as a preference for playing tennis with wooden racquets—as opposed to the more powerful graphite and titanium ones used today. Perhaps, but I would still reduce the leverage allowed on derivatives substantially.

ANOTHER FOCUS OF MINE, which was less typical for a Treasury Secretary, was poverty and the distress of inner cities as critical economic issues. We set up, for the first time at Treasury, an office to focus specifically on these matters, headed by an extremely able and highly committed former Supreme Court clerk, Michael Barr. Such questions were often framed as debates about whether or not to help the poor. But, as important as moral and ethical issues are here, you don't need to rely on altruism to make the case for tackling poverty. It is in everyone's self-interest to reduce the societal consequences of deprivation. Poverty can foster crime and health care problems and in various other ways increase social costs and affect the lives of people who aren't poor.

I learned very quickly, however, that advancing programs to help the poor—especially for minorities living in inner cities—was very difficult. Many people object to the idea of government assistance for the poor on principle; even well-designed programs meant to encourage work instead of welfare faced strong opposition. And the poor are not easily mobilized to advance their own economic interests. All sorts of groups could bring great pressure to bear when their concerns were at stake: environmentalists, labor, the elderly, business, and many, many others—but not the poor. You couldn't count on a major letter-writing campaign in support of food stamps or inner-city job programs.

A significant accomplishment in this area by the Clinton administration was a large expansion of the Earned Income Tax Credit, a payment under the tax code to low-income working families to help lift them out of poverty. However, the EITC increase and other measures—though they had substantial impact—were not even remotely commensurate with the scale of the problem. But our ability to do more was limited. For our first two years, deficit reduction and health care reform were our highest priorities. For the next six years, control of Congress was in the hands of people who rejected most government involvement in these issues.

Nonetheless, real progress was made in combating poverty during Clinton's years in office, largely because of the strength of the American economy. As unemployment fell back to levels not seen since the 1960s, the number of Americans living below the poverty line dropped steadily and gains by minorities were very strong. Births to teen mothers, which had been rising for forty years, finally began to fall. Welfare rolls began to decline significantly, even before the passage of a welfare reform bill in 1996. In New York, as in other big cities, the homeless population declined visibly. Clinton used to say that the best social program is a strong economy, though he always added that that wasn't sufficient. He was right. Some people focus only on the economy and neglect the necessity of well-designed programs. Others focus on the programs and miss the central importance of a healthy economy.

Advancing new programs was not our only difficulty. Once we lost control of Congress, defending the effective programs already on the books, such as the EITC, became a major challenge. Without a large staff or a big bureaucracy, the EITC had made an enormous dent in the size of our poverty population by providing a subsidy to the working poor that was a powerful incentive for poor people to work full-time instead of getting by on public assistance. A group of conservatives in Congress, led by Senators Don Nickles (R-OK) and William Roth (R-DE), pointed to fraud in the program—people who weren't entitled to the credit were receiving refunds—and we had to threaten to veto the 1997 tax agreement with the Republicans to prevent damage to the program. Fraud was a serious issue, significant reforms had been made, and we were strongly supportive of further reform. But the EITC was an excellent concept—Ronald Reagan, not a leading advocate of social programs, had strongly endorsed it because of its focus on work. And we insisted that the program be fixed, not cut back or thrown out.

Another program under attack was the Community Reinvestment Act, passed in the 1970s to discourage banks from the practice of "redlining," or refusing to make loans in minority neighborhoods. The CRA required lending institutions, when seeking regulatory approval, to demonstrate that they had invested in their communities. This measure had greatly increased the availability and flow of credit in inner cities. After the 1994 election, however, we faced constant efforts to roll the program back in one way or another. One argument was that the CRA was simply a way for community and political groups to extort money from lending institutions. CRA almost surely had been misused in some instances—and we were again fully supportive of reforms. But, as with the EITC, we had to fight the all-too-common Washington strategy of using one rotten apple to proclaim the barrel spoiled. Our opponents seized on real issues about misuse in an attempt to eviscerate what had been, on balance, effective and valuable antipoverty programs. Happily, we were able to protect the CRA as well as the EITC. However, I'm not sure what would have happened absent our veto threat, and that is a sobering thought.

Welfare reform was the highest-profile issue in this area. In 1994, the administration had proposed legislation intended to replace welfare with work. But once Republicans took control of Congress, they passed a bill that was much more stringent. Inside the administration, feelings ran high. Some of us thought the bill Congress passed in 1996 was too severe and could create serious humanitarian and social problems. Others argued that the GOP bill was close enough to what Clinton wanted. Some believed that Clinton's reelection prospects could hinge on his signing the bill.

The President convened a meeting of relevant members of the White House staff and cabinet. George Stephanopoulos, who was one of the first to speak, set the tone for the discussion. George was against signing the bill, but he said—as I think everyone in the room thought—that this was an agonizingly difficult decision. A veto could have a decisive impact on the 1996 presidential election, and if that happened, the consequences for people on welfare could also be far worse. I had not been much involved in welfare reform, but I shared George's view that the President should not sign the bill. I felt strongly that some people on welfare are unable to work for reasons that are beyond their control, whether psychological, physical, or simply through a lack of work skills and work habits. This legislation didn't seem to me to address any of that sufficiently. What's more, the notion of cutting food stamps and other benefits to legal immigrants just seemed wrong to me. We needed more of a balance—not only stronger incentives for work, but also a greater effort at preparing and training people to work, and continuing to provide a true social safety net for people who couldn't work.

I never knew if that was a real meeting or if the President had already decided to sign the welfare reform bill and was merely mollifying those likely to disagree by allowing them to be heard. In either case, airing the issue in this way was an example of shrewd governmental process. Getting everyone into the room and giving us all an opportunity to speak on an issue about which people felt so strongly minimized subsequent leaks and carping to the press. A couple of well-respected subcabinet officials did resign over Clinton's decision to sign the welfare reform legislation. But had the President made his decision in a different way, the internal fallout could have been much heavier.

I never saw welfare as central to Clinton's reelection, but I understood its larger symbolic significance and the political concern. To me, the central issue was the economy. The country's continuing economic strength was obviously a powerful argument for giving the President a second term. Bob Dole, by contrast, seemed to me not to have a strong vision for his candidacy. I remember watching an interview with Dole on *This Week with David Brinkley* one Sunday, when I happened to be a guest. John Cochran asked him why he was running and what he wanted to do for the American people. Dole's response focused on the politics and the polls, instead of where he wanted to lead the country.

AT THE BEGINNING of Clinton's second term, I had to decide whether to stay or leave—possibly to become chairman of the Carnegie Corporation, a foundation involved in an enormous range of issues from education and civic participation to international security and development concerns. The President wanted to get together to discuss the issue and called me at the Jefferson one night at about 10:30 and asked me to come over. I was getting ready to go to bed but was happy to oblige. Since my Secret Service detail had turned in for the night, I went downstairs and walked over to the White House.

I went to the nearest gate, and the uniformed Secret Service officer inside the gatehouse asked if he could help me. "I'm here to see the President," I said, mentioning that I was Secretary of the Treasury.

The guard gave me a suspicious look and sent me to another gate, where they recognized me and let me in. Then I went upstairs to the second floor of the residence, where Clinton and I had a long talk about what I was going to do, interspersed with an open-ended discussion of politics, our views of other people, and the policy issues that animated both of us.

Sometime after 2:00 A.M., I finally said, "Mr. President, I've just got to go home. I need to get up and be at work tomorrow."

"Okay," Clinton said. "Thanks for coming over."

There was just one problem. I'd left home without my wallet.

"Can you lend me five dollars for cab fare?" I asked. "I'll pay you back tomorrow."

"Well, I don't carry money," Clinton said. "Maybe Hillary has some." But she was already asleep, and he didn't want to wake her up.

I suggested borrowing money from the Secret Service. So we asked them, and they immediately offered to drive me home.

There was another job possibility for me if I stayed. Leon Panetta was heading back to California and the President needed a new chief of staff to run the White House. Leon tried to convince me that I should take his place. For years, when I worked on Wall Street, I had always thought that being chief of staff to the President—which put you at the very core of the U.S. government and involved you in virtually all matters—would be the most compelling job in America. But now that this had—beyond my wildest imagination—become a real possibility, I knew I would pass.

While the job retained much of its appeal in the abstract, I didn't think my being chief of staff would actually work, either for the President or for me. When you're chief of staff at the White House, you can be an effective advocate for your own views, but you're ultimately a personal assistant to the President and you're deeply involved in all of his politics. I'd read some books about how previous administrations had functioned, and from them, as well as from working in the White House myself, I understood that an integral part of the chief of staff's job was taking calls at one in the morning about whatever was on the President's mind and dealing with complaints about newspaper articles he didn't like. As Erskine Bowles said to me once, you may be the "chief" but you're still "staff." I couldn't see being at the beck and call of anybody, even a President I liked and respected as much as I did Clinton. And after four years of commuting back and forth between Washington and New York, I didn't want a seven-day-a-week, twenty-four-hour-a-day job. Finally, the position involved more immersion in politics than I wanted. At Treasury I could focus more intensely on a host of policy issues that I felt deeply engaged with.

So I took my hat out of the ring. But that left the question of who should be Clinton's chief of staff. Erskine Bowles, who had resigned as Panetta's deputy to return home to North Carolina and his financial career, had called to try to convince me to accept the job. We went through an Alphonse-and-Gaston routine: Erskine thought I should take it; I thought Erskine should do it. He didn't want to come back to Washington. But Erskine has a strong sense of responsibility, and with Clinton leaning on him to return, he felt he either had to find someone else acceptable to the President or take the job himself. Somewhat reluctantly, Erskine agreed to become Clinton's third chief of staff. But there was a price for me as well: Erskine wanted my chief of staff at Treasury, Sylvia Mathews, to become his deputy at the White House.

At the same time this was happening, I knew Larry Summers was thinking about leaving as well. He had been offered a high-level academic job and was also a leading candidate to become chairman of the Council of Economic Advisers. That caused me to think seriously about resigning. The Treasury Department was a team run by Larry, Sylvia, and me. Sylvia was essentially our chief operating officer; Larry provided a lot of intellectual leadership for what we did and played a big role in management. Both were superstars, with the kind of political savvy that's critical in the ever-dangerous world of Washington, and, not unimportantly, we had a comfortable and good-humored relationship with each other. Perhaps I could have built a new team of equal effectiveness, perhaps not. In any case, my life at Treasury would be quite different, and I wasn't sure I wanted to start all over again. I was mindful that I had had four good years and that in Washington things can change completely at any minute of any day. New York also held many attractions for me, including the prospect of being home again.

If, however, I could convince Sylvia or Larry to remain at Treasury, staying would become much more appealing. Sylvia was willing to stay and Erskine would have let her—albeit with great regret—but I didn't want to hold her back from something she wanted to do. I thought the better alternative was to persuade Larry, whose importance to the administration was great and underappreciated, to remain in place. In government, as in business, the top person often has a complicated attitude toward the second in command. Some people think a powerful deputy will upstage them or make them look weak. I'd seen chiefs follow an instinct—conscious or unconscious—to prevent capable seconds in command from succeeding them. But I'd long had just the opposite view: having an extremely bright and skillful deputy greatly increased Treasury's effectiveness. I also thought it made me look good, just as I thought that Gene Sperling's prominence as my deputy at the NEC was good for the NEC and good for me. For two years, Larry and I had worked together as partners and shared credit for the department's accomplishments. If I left before the end of Clinton's presidency, I thought he would be the best possible choice to succeed me.

So I worked out a rather complicated proposal to make Larry comfortable with staying. I told him that my intention was to remain for two more years. I would try to get the President to agree that if I served two years into the second term, he would then name Larry as my successor—assuming, of course, that the President was still comfortable with Larry. If I left sooner, there would still be what lawyers call a "rebuttable presumption" in Larry's favor. If I decided to stay longer, Larry could do as he saw fit. Larry said jokingly that he would understand if something dramatic happened that made my leaving after two years impossible. We both laughed at that. As it turned out, there were two such events: a global financial crisis and the President's impeachment.

No guarantees were involved. I could decide to stay, or the President could simply say he wasn't comfortable with Larry as Secretary for whatever reason. But we had an agreement in principle. For it to work, though, absolute confidentiality was essential. The only people who knew about this arrangement, as far as I knew, other than the President, Larry, and me, were the Vice President—whose agreement was requisite and readily given—Erskine, Sylvia, and Judy. For two and a half years, no hint of this understanding ever leaked—which was remarkable.

With Larry in place, I asked Michael Froman to take over Sylvia's job as chief of staff. Mike had come to Treasury from the NEC staff some months after I had moved. He had a doctorate from Oxford, a law degree from Harvard, where he'd been an editor of the *Law Review,* a strong intellect, a deep interest in policy issues, and good practical judgment. Mike, like Sylvia, was straightforward, worked well with people, was highly effective managerially, and had an irreverent sense of humor—sometimes, alas, directed at the Secretary. One recent instance sticks in my mind. During the 2000 presidential campaign, my name briefly and implausibly surfaced as a potential running mate for Al Gore (along with all kinds of other people). Froman commented that it would be an interesting ticket: Gore and I would be on the stage fighting over who had to kiss the babies.

FOR THE TREASURY DEPARTMENT, the second term soon brought a crisis in one of the most basic functions of government: tax collection. The battle we fought with Congress—both Democrats and Republicans— over the Internal Revenue Service in 1997 stands in retrospect as a microcosm of much that I learned about Washington: the central importance of management; the complexity of managing effectively in government; the great difficulty in most circumstances of anticipating when matters will explode into political conflicts; the need to frame issues in ways that resonate; the power of the media to shape the political agenda and drive events; and, finally, the challenges of dealing with a political firestorm in the public sector.

Years before moving to Washington, I had clipped and kept an interview that Michael Blumenthal had given to *Fortune* magazine after resigning as Jimmy Carter's Treasury Secretary in 1979. Blumenthal said that management tends to be taken much less seriously in government than in the private sector. Unlike CEOs, Treasury Secretaries aren't remembered for how well they ran the place. Nonetheless, I had a strong interest in management and paid a lot of attention to management problems in the department. I was able to recruit Nancy Killefer, a partner at the consulting firm of McKinsey & Company, as assistant secretary for administration. Nancy brought great expertise and skill to issues such as the Treasury's own budget and created flexible rewards for employees within the existing rules, as well as improving training and personnel practices.

Our greatest management challenge during my first two years at Treasury was our largest agency, the Internal Revenue Service. At that point, the IRS's most widely publicized problem was an automation effort that in large measure hadn't worked. The technology failure related to more general problems in the way the agency was run. Since the Second World War, the commissioner of the IRS had always been a tax lawyer, someone capable of navigating the labyrinths of a tax code that had grown to 9,500 pages. Larry Summers, who convened a working group to focus on the wayward technology project, convinced me that an organization of the IRS's size, complexity, and importance needed a CEO experienced in management, not taxes. Larry and I spent a great deal of time at the beginning of Clinton's second term interviewing candidates for this post. The person we liked best was Charles O. Rossotti, who had run a large Virginia-based consulting firm and was an expert in information technology.

We worked hard to address Rossotti's concerns about the job, which included a fear that for political reasons we would commit ourselves to overhauling the IRS overnight. Rossotti knew what we knew: that the agency's problems were vast and serious. Morale among employees was low and sinking lower. We were concerned that because of its antiquated technology, the system—which processes 95 percent of the revenues of the federal government—might simply break down.

While we worked quietly on this effort, others were becoming more vocal. Senator Bob Kerrey had set up a commission on restructuring the IRS, and its hearings became a forum for using complaints against the IRS to argue against the progressive income tax itself. The House majority leader, Dick Armey (R-TX), came and testified in favor of his flat tax. The conservative activist Grover Norquist, who was chosen as one of the Republican members by Newt Gingrich, tried to turn the hearings into an investigation of whether the IRS had politically targeted conservative organizations such as the Christian Coalition—a baseless accusation. Around that time, bumper stickers that said SUPPORT THE IRS—VOTE DEMO-CRAT began to appear.

Senator Kerrey tried with mixed success to resist the effort by some conservatives to turn the hearings into an antitax, antigovernment platform. He also used it to promote one of his own favorite ideas: the separation of the IRS from the Treasury Department. Despite my regard for Kerrey, a man with enormous personal charm, this proposal appeared to me to be monumentally wrong. The notion, which reappears periodically, of breaking out discrete parts of government into independent units reporting to boards, seems to me to be a formula for less accountability and hence less effective government. In this case, a board would never have the knowledge or the continuity of focus that Treasury could have. And unlike a private-sector CEO—the argued analogy—a freestanding IRS chief wouldn't have to worry about his share price or stockholders. Kerrey and I had some fairly contentious meetings in which I failed to persuade him of my position and he failed to persuade me of his. I felt strongly enough to recommend that the President veto the reform legislation that Kerrey was planning to introduce on this issue.

With Rossotti signed on and the White House supporting our position on an outside board—although not to the point of agreeing to my veto recommendation—we began to feel that we were getting a handle on the IRS. It was far from my mind during our trip to China in September 1997. I was walking through Tiananmen Square late at night with Mike Froman and Bob Boorstin, who had moved from the White House to Treasury to advise me on political and communications issues, when Linda Robertson, by then our assistant secretary for legislative affairs, reached me on a cell phone to say that a storm had broken out in Congress. What flashed through my mind was a warning signal I hadn't recognized. Back in 1995, soon after I'd been confirmed as Treasury Secretary, I'd appeared on *This Week with David Brinkley*. Brinkley's first question had been about complaints he was hearing about the IRS. I'd been surprised that this legendary Washington journalist would waste valuable interview time on such an obscure topic, and I'd fobbed off the question with a kind of nonanswer. Now I thought that Brinkley might have had his finger on the political pulse after all.

We knew, of course, that Senator William Roth, chairman of the Finance Committee, was going to hold hearings to look into IRS abuses. But we had no idea of the media feeding frenzy that would develop. Opponents of the income tax had found—or created—a great political opportunity. Roth's staff gave an advance preview of the worst horror stories they had gathered to *60 Minutes,* which presented them on the Sunday before the hearings in a highly dramatized way that was lacking in balance. Clearly, the IRS had real and serious problems. But the *60 Minutes* presentation was misleading. Shortly after that, *Newsweek* published a cover story about the IRS that was also inflammatory.

Over a period of three days, the Senate Finance Committee had IRS employees testifying in hoods and people hidden behind partitions speaking into voice distortion machines for protection against possible retribution. We didn't even know who these people were. Those on the committee who were truly interested in fixing what was wrong with the IRS—as opposed to demonizing it—had no way to bring balance to the hearings.

We couldn't respond to the horror stories even if we had wanted to. A federal law forbids any release of private taxpayer information, unless the taxpayer waives his right to sue for violation of privacy. Such waivers ought to have been a condition of this sort of testimony before the Senate Finance Committee, but neither the committee nor the media required that of witnesses. As a result, the public had no way of knowing whether people who claimed to have been so abused were telling the truth.

In a more reasonable perspective, the IRS was a largely effective tax collection agency with some very real failings. One problem was that it had too much of a law enforcement mind-set and not enough of a customer-service mentality. But many people simply refused to acknowledge that law enforcement was necessary for our system of voluntary compliance to work. Some critics, such as Senator Charles Grassley (R-IA) and Representative Rob Portman (R-OH) were sincerely concerned with making the IRS more taxpayer-friendly. But throughout the hearings, others tried to turn a few abusive episodes into a misleading impression about the IRS as a whole. No one cared that 205 million returns were processed every year without any known dishonesty or corruption. Once the idea took root that the IRS was an out-of-control agency gratuitously abusing taxpayers, reason and proportion could not be brought to the issue. Republicans, Democrats, and the media piled on, without any serious focus on the larger picture.

I soon realized we had no way to effectively respond to allegations, let alone restore balance, in the midst of a political firestorm. David Dreyer told me that no one would listen to anything I said on the subject unless the first words out of my mouth were "There are problems at the IRS, and we're committed to reform." But this wasn't like Clinton and the balanced budget or Bill Lynch refusing to criticize Jesse Jackson at that dinner in New York. Even with that admission, which I made constantly, no one was interested in a balanced view of the IRS. I could have hired a marching band, and no one would have paid any attention.

The problem is that when one person is abused—and some people really were—a government official who tries to paint a more complete picture simply won't be heard. When a taxpayer gets up and tells a story about IRS agents acting like thugs, it wipes out everything else. Saying that the overwhelming preponderance of the 102,000 employees at the IRS are conscientiously applying a code of incredible complexity, and that some error, even some wrongdoing, is inevitable, gets absolutely no traction. The most courageous U.S. senator couldn't bring balance to such a discussion with the whole process lined up against him in this way. He would simply be overwhelmed by a bad process on its way to creating flawed legislation.

What I never understood in any of these firestorms is why some enterprising reporter didn't pursue the other side of the story out of self-interest. Someone attempting to be the voice of reason in a lopsided debate would seem well positioned to get onto the front page or appear prominently on television. Eventually a few journalists did write more objective articles about the IRS. But for the most part, the coverage seemed utterly one-sided, with at best an offsetting paragraph or two buried deeply in articles with sensational headlines.

In private, I did try to make the point about the inevitability of error. At one meeting with Senator Roth, he said that the IRS should have "zero tolerance" for mistakes. I'd say, "Bill, I don't know of a single day of my life with zero errors. There are a hundred thousand people at the IRS—how are you going to do that? I'll bet even you make mistakes sometimes." Roth laughed and said, "It's true we all make mistakes." But he didn't alter his course.

With these hearings and the surrounding media coverage, IRS reform legislation became veto-proof. When I got back from China and met with Erskine and a few others in the chief of staff's office, everyone there agreed that vetoing the GOP bill made no sense. But with the Democratic leadership in Congress signaling support for a law that was sure to pass and no threat of a presidential veto, we had little with which to negotiate. However, the Treasury team decided to persist. I steeped myself in the technical details and functioned almost as a senior staff person in working with congressional members and staff to try to improve the bill. Despite our lack of leverage, we were able to make a significant contribution to the legislation in the end, due in large part to the credibility that our prior work on reforming the IRS gave us with those legislators who took the problem seriously. In particular, after the political uproar had died down, I was able to work with the two House members most involved with this bill—Republican Rob Portman and Democrat Ben Cardin of Maryland—in a refreshingly non-political way on the key issues. The other congressman I remember most vividly from that episode was Democratic Representative Steny Hoyer, who supported us on principle at a time when few others were willing to do that.

We were also aided by the President's political deftness. After the House passed a bill in October, Senate Republicans gave the President an opening by not rushing the legislation through before the end of the fall congressional session. Their thinking may have been to keep the issue alive into 1998, closer to the midterm election. But holding the bill over to a new session defused some of the political energy behind IRS bashing.

After being sworn in by President Clinton (and Treasury counsel Ed Knight),
I said good-bye to my wife, Judy, and stayed behind in the Oval Office
for an emergency meeting about the financial crisis in Mexico.

My maternal grandparents,
Ella and Samuel Seiderman.

My paternal grandparents,
Rose and Morris Rubin,
and I in the early 1940s.

At home in
Neponsit, New York,
at three years old.

My family in our Miami Beach home in the mid-1950s. Standing: My grandfather Morris, left, and my uncle Joe. Sitting, left to right: my grandmother Rose; my mother, Sylvia; my father, Alexander; and my aunt Mitzi. Floor, left to right: my sister, Jane; my aunt Estelle; and me.

Bobby Birenbaum and I after a day of fishing in the mid-1950s.

JOHN O. FOX

"Two Harvard students need ride": Hitchhiking in England, 1961.

ROBERT A. DEFELICE

Judy and I on our wedding day, March 27, 1963.
There were fourteen people at the wedding,
including us and both sets of parents. The next day
we were both back in the library, studying for finals.

Our first apartment, on
Henry Street in Brooklyn.

JUDY RUBIN

A chat with my son Jamie, 1968.

JUDY RUBIN

Horsing around: Philip and Jamie,
ages three and six.

We all bring Jamie to Harvard, 1985.

On the Goldman Sachs trading floor in 1967,
during my first year. Left to right: L. Jay
Tenenbaum, Bruce Mayers, Bob Lenzner, Bob
Mnuchin, Jennie Gomez, Paul Levin, and me
in the back.

I don't think I had ever heard the phrase "risk
arbitrage" before I started at Goldman Sachs.
An early picture of me as an arbitrageur.

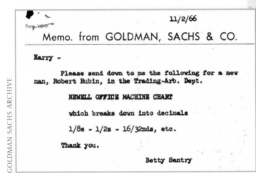

11/2/66

Form 1100

Memo. from GOLDMAN, SACHS & CO.

Harry -

    Please send down to me the following for a new
man, Robert Rubin, in the Trading-Arb. Dept.

    NEWELL OFFICE MACHINE CHART

    which breaks down into decimals

    1/8s - 1/2s - 16/32nds, etc.

    Thank you.

                    Betty Santry

Pre-"hi-tech": a memo from my
third day at Goldman Sachs.

The Management Committee of Goldman Sachs in 1967. Left to right: John Weinberg, Ray Young, Ed Schrader, Sidney Weinberg, John Whitehead, Gustave Levy, Walter Blaine, and George Doty.

Goldman Sachs senior partner and New York Stock Exchange chairman Gustave Lehmann Levy. From the mid-1960s until his death in 1976, Gus was almost certainly the single most important person on Wall Street.

The Management Committee of Goldman Sachs in 1985. Left to right: Jon Corzine, Bob Friedman, Jim Gorter, Steve Friedman, Fred Krimendahl, me, Bob Mnuchin, Richard Menschel, and John Weinberg (seated).

Steve Friedman and I, co–heads of the
fixed-income division at Goldman Sachs.

VERA E. MURRAY

The first time I met Bob Strauss, he told me, "You look good on paper. But now that I've met you, I don't think you'll amount to much." It was the beginning of a great friendship. In 1992, Judy and I visited Bob in Russia, where he was U.S. ambassador.

Never having done anything like it, I thought, *How do I know I can raise enough money?* Judy and I with legendary U.S. Speaker of the House Tip O'Neill at the 1982 congressional campaign dinner I chaired in Washington.

ROBERT KNUDSEN

President Clinton's new National Economic Council gets straight to work in early 1993. Left to right: Gene Sperling, me, Bo Cutter, and Sylvia Mathews.

The economic team meets with President Clinton in February 1993 to prepare his first budget proposal. Left to right: Roger Altman, Vice President Al Gore, Alice Rivlin, Greg Simon, George Stephanopoulos, Bo Cutter, Laura Tyson, Lloyd Bentsen, President Bill Clinton, Robert Reich, me, and Alan Blinder.

Gathering my thoughts during a meeting in the Oval Office. Seated, left to right: Larry Summers (hidden), Erskine Bowles, Bill Daley, Susan Brophy, Charlene Barshefsky, Vice President Gore, President Clinton, Jay Berman, Vicki Radd, and Thomas "Mack" McLarty.

Briefing the President. Left to right: me, Jim Steinberg, Ken Lieberthal, Lael Brainard, Gene Sperling, Steve Ricchetti, Charlene Barshefsky, and John Podesta.

Talking with
President Clinton
at Camp David in
January 1993.

A light moment with Hillary.

BOB MCNEELY/WHITE HOUSE PHOTO

Coming back late on Air Force One: the President talked with members
of his foreign policy team (Dennis Ross, Tony Lake, and Sandy Berger)
while Leon Panetta and I pored over some numbers.

RALPH ALSWANG/CLINTON PRESIDENTIAL MATERIALS PROJECT

Labor Secretary Robert Reich, CEA chair
Laura D'Andrea Tyson, and I relaxing in the Rose Garden.

STEPHEN CROWLEY/THE NEW YORK TIMES

Judy and I follow Lloyd Bentsen back into the White House after I was nominated to succeed him as Treasury Secretary in December 1994.

New York senators Al D'Amato and Pat Moynihan introducing me at my Treasury confirmation hearing in January 1995, with, left to right, Gretchen, Philip (hidden), Judy, Sylvia Mathews, and Linda Robertson in the front row for support.

MR RUBIN

TREASURY DEPARTMENT PHOTO

"The first crisis of the twenty-first century": signing the rescue plan for Mexico with finance minister Guillermo Ortiz and central bank governor Miguel Mancera, March 1995.

DAVID SCULL

Testifying with Alan Greenspan and Larry Summers.

TREASURY DEPARTMENT PHOTO

Circled by the
media at the
Marriott hotel.

The debt limit
announcement in
November 1995 that
led to such uproar.

Treasury chief of staff Sylvia Mathews briefing a senior staff meeting, 1996.

Preparing to testify before the House Banking Committee in 1995 with, left to right, Alan Cohen, David Dreyer, Penny Rostow, Linda Robertson, and Darcy Bradbury.

A "bilateral": meeting with Chinese finance minister Liu Zhongli and other U.S. and Chinese officials in November 1996.

G-7 finance ministers—representing the United Kingdom, France, the United States, Italy, Japan, Canada, and Germany (hidden)—trying to find their footing for an official photo, April 1998.

Judy and I talking with the women's users' committee at a World Bank rural development project in India in April 1995.

FEBRUARY 15, 1999 $2.95

TIME

The Clintons:
Their Future

Who Wrote
Shakespeare?

THE COMMITTEE TO
SAVE
THE WORLD

The inside story
of how the
Three Marketeers
have prevented a
global economic
meltdown—so far

Rubin, Greenspan and Summers
at the U.S. Treasury last Wednesday

www.time.com

Time magazine's 1999
cover story on the Asian
financial crisis called
Alan Greenspan, Larry
Summers, and me
"the Committee to Save
the World" and profiled
our "subcommittee,"
below. Left to right:
Edwin "Ted" Truman,
David Lipton,
Tim Geithner, Dan
Zelikow, Mark Medish,
Caroline Atkinson,
and Michael Froman.

"All the News That's Fit to Print"

The New York Times

Late Edition

New York: Today, mostly sunny and not as breezy, high 61. Tonight, clear and chilly, low 45. Tomorrow, mostly sunny, high 69. Yesterday, high 68, low 47. Weather map is on page A34.

VOL. CXLIX .. No. 51,688   Copyright © 1999 The New York Times   NEW YORK, WEDNESDAY, OCTOBER 27, 1999   If beyond the greater New York metropolitan area   75 CENTS

A *New York Times* article announcing my decision to join Citigroup. I am pictured with co-CEOs John Reed and Sandy Weill.

Former Treasury Secretary Joins Leadership Triangle at Citigroup

Jeffery A. Salter/The New York Times

Robert E. Rubin, right, the former United States Treasury Secretary, joins John S. Reed, left, and Sanford I. Weill at the top of Citigroup.

By JOSEPH KAHN

Robert E. Rubin, arguably the best-known financier of his generation and the recently retired Treasury Secretary, has taken a top position at Citigroup, the nation's largest financial services company.

Mr. Rubin, 61, a former top official of Goldman, Sachs & Company, said yesterday that he had joined Sanford I. Weill and John S. Reed, the chairmen and chief executives of Citigroup, in what Mr. Reed described as a "three-person office of the chairman" that will oversee what has become the first true American financial conglomerate since the Depression.

The appointment came less than a week after the Clinton Administration and Congress agreed on a compromise bill that would overhaul the laws that regulate the financial industry, a measure that removes

many of the restrictions preventing banks, securities firms and insurance companies from buying one another or engaging in one another's businesses. Both Mr. Rubin and Citigroup strongly supported the bill, which would greatly benefit the company. Mr. Rubin said he played a role in arranging the final compromise that will probably lead to the repeal of the so-called Glass-Steagall legislation. But he said that had nothing to do with his decision to join the company.

The appointment settles the speculation about what Mr. Rubin, who presided over the Clinton Administration's economic policy during one of America's longest economic booms, would do for an encore. Mr. Rubin also discussed jobs with

Continued on Page C15

Meeting with Chinese premier Zhu Rongji in 2001.

GRETCHEN CRAFT RUBIN

With Philip, Judy, Jamie, and our granddaughter, Eliza.

STEPHEN LOCKE

JUDY RUBIN

Jamie and Gretchen at their wedding reception, September 1994.

With Eliza in 1999.

Relaxing with Leon Brittan after a bit of hiking in Sicily.

A boat ride with family and friends. Left to right: Brandon Phay, Philip, me, two crew members, Steve Umin, and Alan Jacobson.

Fishing at Spruce Creek, Pennsylvania, an occasional
respite when I was at Treasury.

I'm holding a sea-run brown trout in Tierra Del Fuego
on a fishing trip with President Jimmy Carter in 2000.

Making some last-minute changes in my
commencement address on the steps of
Widener Library at Harvard University, June 2001.

Moreover, President Clinton seized upon the delay to co-opt the issue, saying the bill must not "languish" in the Senate, and calling on the Republicans in his State of the Union address to "pass the bipartisan package as your first order of business." That took some nerve and helped reduce the political heat.

The bill President Clinton signed in July 1998 still had serious flaws—especially the provisions that deterred or impeded enforcement. Since I left office, a cascade of news reports have appeared about the problems created by the reform legislation. People who had supported the bill at the time were now "shocked" to discover that enforcement was suffering seriously. Such a consequence may have been unintended, but it was entirely foreseeable. The very news organizations that had failed to bring balance to the debate in the first place were now complaining about the resulting problems, without acknowledging their own central role. One example was an editorial in *The Washington Post* that accused members of Congress of having "assaulted and weakened" the IRS—which was true—but neglected to mention how the *Post* itself and other news organizations had contributed to the process.

When the IRS battle wound down—and after Mexico, the debt limit crisis, and the battle over the budget—we thought that perhaps Treasury might enjoy a spell of relative normality. But that was not to be. Within a few weeks, we began to engage with a global financial crisis that turned out to be much bigger, longer lasting, more complex, and more threatening to the American economy than anything any of us had expected to encounter during our time in office.

CHAPTER EIGHT

World on the Brink

I HAD TOLD LARRY SUMMERS—and, more important, myself—that I was probably going to leave the Treasury Department in the middle of the second term, ideally sometime in 1998. As it turned out, two events prevented me from doing that. The first was the yearlong impeachment battle that began in January 1998. I didn't want to make the President's position any more difficult—and whatever I might have said to explain my departure, people would have read my resignation in 1998 in ways harmful to Clinton. My leaving could also have increased the general sense of uncertainty, which might have had adverse economic effects.

The other obstacle to my departure was the Asian financial crisis, an event that began several months before the impeachment conflict with a devaluation of an obscure currency, the Thai baht, in July 1997. From this seemingly unremarkable event in a country few Americans had thought much about since the Vietnam War, there unfolded a major financial crisis. Much of the practical work of handling the crisis fell to the Treasury Department. As Secretary, I was the public face of the U.S. response, and my leaving could affect confidence. With all of Larry's capabilities, the situation clearly called for both of us to remain fully engaged, and we were better off avoiding a change in leadership.

What people generally referred to as the Asian financial crisis was actually a global economic crisis that began in Asia in the summer of 1997 and spread for a period of nearly two years as far as Russia and Brazil. Aftershocks were felt across emerging markets and even in the industrialized world. Viewed in its entirety, this event posed an enormous threat to the stability of the global economy and caused great economic hardship in the affected countries. Here in the United States, in the fall of 1998, capital markets seemed in danger of seizing up. After a Russian default and the near collapse of a giant hedge fund—Long-Term Capital Management, which had bet heavily on a return to normalcy in the global markets—even the market in U.S. Treasury bonds, the safest and most liquid instruments in the world, was buffeted. For a brief period, all but those companies with the best credit were frozen out of the debt markets. This was perhaps the most dramatic of several moments when cascading financial instability appeared to endanger the entire global financial system.

In certain ways, the Mexican peso crisis of 1995 provided a template for understanding what was happening in the crisis economies. But our fears during the Mexican crisis—that a kind of financial contagion would take hold around the world—had not been realized. This time around, that scenario came true. From its beginnings in Thailand, the contagion spread violently and inexorably. But while our stake in what was happening was very great, the self-interest of the United States in dealing with the problem was even less obvious to Congress and to the American public than it had been two years earlier with Mexico.

Looking back with a few years' perspective, I've come to regard the global crisis of those years as more and more important. What happened to the world economy during that period—and, perhaps more important, what didn't happen—leaves us with a sense not only of how much damage was done but how close we came to even greater calamity. Financial markets are driven by human nature and have a propensity to go to excess. This means that periodic financial crises of one sort or another are virtually inevitable. Understanding what happened last time can help us better prevent and respond to crisis in the future. And that has tremendous importance for many people around the world. My primary focus at Treasury was on the financial aspects of the crisis and its ramifications for the American and global economy. But behind the facts and figures were enormous humanitarian costs—as people lost their jobs and their savings and were plunged into poverty in the worst-hit countries.

In each of the countries where the crisis focused with great intensity—Thailand, Indonesia, South Korea, Russia, and Brazil—the issue of restoring confidence, reestablishing financial stability, and returning to economic growth went well beyond the traditional realm of macroeconomics. As we worked with the IMF, the World Bank, and other nations on the unfolding problem, I found myself having to deal with issues that an American Treasury Secretary doesn't typically become involved in—the labor movement in South Korea, corruption in Indonesia, and the good faith of various members of the Russian government. In this kind of situation, distinctions between foreign policy and economic policy blurred, although decision-making structures inside the government (the State Department, the Treasury Department) were still defined by these traditional boundaries. Also, economic policy makers needed to understand all sorts of issues that weren't expected to be part of our purview. In a way, the need for a rapid education in unexpected topics took me back to my days as an arbitrageur, when I would urgently immerse myself in matters I knew nothing about, ranging from the condition of railroad beds to Rhodesian sanctions, that had the potential to affect big corporate mergers.

Of course, my perspective on the crisis remains an American one, based on my experiences at Treasury. As intense as our interactions were, the experiences and reflections of other key players—whether in the governments of other countries or in the IMF—would undoubtedly differ from mine. To me, the events of those years lead to four important points. The most straightforward of these is the international interdependence that results from greatly increased integration of trade and capital markets—and how little understood that interdependence is. I remember Pedro Malan, the finance minister of Brazil, telling me in October 1998 how difficult it was to explain to his people that their currency was under attack and interest rates were higher in part because the Russian Duma had failed to raise taxes. The global crisis underscored the reality that in an economically integrated world, prosperity in faraway countries can create opportunities elsewhere, but instability in a distant economy can also create uncertainty and instability at home. One country's success can enrich others, and its mistakes can put them at risk.

The reality of interdependence leads to a second point, namely the central importance of effective governance, both national and transnational. The familiar framing of conflict between "the government" and "the market" is in many respects a false one. A market economy needs a whole host of functions that markets by their nature won't provide effectively, including a legal and regulatory framework, education, social safety nets, law enforcement, and much more, and that only government can adequately address. Moreover, while we live in a world of sovereign nations, more and more issues are multinational in nature—for example, trade and capital flows, certain major environmental problems, terrorism, and some public health issues—and those too can only be dealt with effectively by government. Beyond this, some people argue that globalization means that national governments matter less, in the sense that forceful imperatives of the world economy take power away from them. To me, the opposite is true. The potential impact of any one country's problems on others means that national governments matter more—an ineffective government in one country can have a damaging impact beyond that country's borders. Moreover, the responsiveness of global capital markets to national economic policy, whether that policy is good or bad, magnifies the impact of government actions.

The third point is that when a crisis of confidence develops and capital starts to flee, neither money nor policy reforms alone can turn the situation around; both are required. Governments need to implement strong reform programs to convince creditors and investors—both domestic and foreign—that staying is in their interest, that growth and stability will return. In many cases this means addressing long-standing structural weaknesses that have finally become unsustainable and a focus of investor concern, such as a weak banking system or corruption. Also, exchange rates and interest rates must move to levels where both savers at home and investors from abroad feel confident of adequate returns going forward. But money is also needed. Effective international response to a financial crisis combines support for strong policies with enough funding to give those policies time to work—to stem unraveling in the markets and to create confidence—while still allowing governments to support essential programs, including social safety nets to protect the poorest. This is where official resources—from the IMF and World Bank and in some cases "bilateral" contributions directly from the governments of the United States and other countries—are also necessary.

The fourth and final point is that the tools available to deal with the crisis were not as modern as the markets. These tools included the resources and policy expertise of the IMF and the World Bank, the deep engagement of the U.S. President and administration and our G-7 partners, bold leadership in a number of the affected countries, and the ability of nations around the world to work together. And together we did eventually succeed in taming the financial market turmoil, but not before the crisis had wreaked great havoc on emerging economies around the world, causing deep hardship for millions of people. Changes were needed in what was called the "architecture" of the international system to deal more effectively with the risks of globalization by improving crisis prevention and response. The IMF, which was at the center of the crisis management, was founded nearly sixty years ago to promote stability in a world of fixed exchange rates where trade, not capital flows, dominated the international economy. It had adapted remarkably well to the challenges of globalization, but much more needed to be done. We expected this reform process—initiated while the crisis was still raging—to be complex and long term. While important progress has now been made, better approaches still need to be developed on a number of issues.

THE FIRST FLASH POINT in Asia was the collapse of the Thai baht in the summer of 1997. I say "flash point" because what happened in Thailand might just as easily have happened in a number of other countries. Throughout the developing world, imbalances had been building for the better part of a decade. Since the late 1980s, investment and credit flows from the developed world had been increasing rapidly in response to strong growth and steps toward economic modernization. Many developing countries had privatized state-owned industries and opened their markets to competition. But these flows were also a textbook example of the kind of speculative excesses that can take hold when investors become seized with some idea—whether an irrational idea like the scarcity of tulips or a sound concept such as the transformation of emerging-market countries—and lose their discipline.

Over time, those excesses became increasingly evident. The mentality that prevailed among emerging-market investors and lenders by 1997 was similar to the psychology of stock market investors in a bull market. Less and less thought was given to risk, which meant that credit and investment flowed into economies that still had many shortcomings. These shortcomings included some traditional macroeconomic problems, such as overvalued exchange rates that were effectively fixed to the U.S. dollar and inappropriate fiscal or monetary policy. But they also involved structural weaknesses, such as underdeveloped and poorly regulated financial systems, serious governance and corruption issues in some countries, lack of financial transparency, and various counterproductive regulatory, labor, and trade regulations. Excessive inflows into countries with serious vulnerabilities were an accident waiting to happen. Thailand simply happened to be the first place where that combustible mixture blew up.

Many of the particulars of Thailand's problems in 1997 echoed those of Mexico at the end of 1994. The country had a big current account deficit—its imports greatly exceeded its exports. Thailand was financing this current account deficit with a lot of short-term borrowing, which was then lent by Thai banks and finance companies for long-term projects, including an unsustainable real estate boom. The Thai baht was tied to the U.S. dollar. The dollar had begun to rise in value on the world market in 1995, and as that continued, the baht became more and more overvalued, worsening the current account deficit. Eventually investors became unwilling to continue financing it. Through the spring and summer of 1997, the Thai government repeated another one of Mexico's mistakes: instead of unfixing its exchange rate from the rising dollar and floating its currency, which would have allowed the market to determine the baht's proper level, the central bank tried to defend that value, spending its dollar reserves to buy baht on the foreign exchange markets. Meanwhile, the country's banks and financial institutions were in terrible shape, ridden with bad debts. And because of extensive lending to companies that had dollar debts but little or no dollar earnings, banks as well as their customers were vulnerable to any decline in the value of the baht.

As investors belatedly recognized the risks Thailand faced, capital that had flowed in too quickly flowed out even faster. As reserves diminished, the Thai government could no longer defend the exchange rate and went to the International Monetary Fund for help. Our Treasury team had been closely following the situation during the spring and summer. We discussed Thailand's difficulties at length and felt that the IMF could handle what we viewed at that point as a familiar kind of financial crisis that occurs when an exchange rate gets seriously out of line and a country is importing too much. Thailand's economy had been growing at an average rate of 9 percent per year for a decade. We thought that after the country dealt with this disruption, with some slowdown leading to fewer imports and increased exports, healthy growth would return. And although we were always cognizant of the risk of financial contagion, we didn't rate the probability as very high—in part because the Asian region was still so widely viewed as economically strong and attractive to investors.

Nevertheless, the dangers were great enough that we supported a larger-than-usual IMF package to address the financing needs opened up by a sudden rush of capital out of the country. In contemplating such a package, we did worry about the "moral hazard" problem that had gotten so much attention during the Mexican peso crisis. There were actually two separate moral-hazard issues. The first pertains to countries. Do large rescue packages encourage countries to borrow unwisely or adopt unsound policies? I didn't worry so much about that because, as this crisis itself would show, countries and their political leaders pay a high price for financial missteps. The possibility that a nation might be saved from devastation at the eleventh hour by international loans hardly constituted an incentive to mismanage the economy.

The other kind of moral hazard, the kind that affects creditors and investors, was a more serious concern: insulation from loss can sow the seeds of future crises. Part of the issue in Thailand had clearly been excessive and undisciplined investment from the developed world. "Rescuing" these investors, especially in a relatively small economy like Thailand's, could encourage lenders and investors to give insufficient weight to risk in pursuit of higher yield in other developing countries and undermine the discipline of the market-based system. In supporting an IMF rescue program, we would be interfering with the free play of market forces. As a result, investors would escape some of the burden of problems they had helped create.

This concern was outweighed by the importance of reestablishing stability and avoiding a dangerous worsening of the crisis. As negotiations between the IMF and Thailand came to a head, the question was not whether to help Thailand but how best to do so. The answer was official resources combined with a bold enough reform program to turn the economy and investor confidence around. Thailand, like the other so-called Asian tigers, had great cultural and economic strengths, including a strong work ethic and a high savings rate. But to restore the confidence of both domestic citizens and foreign creditors, the government needed to address both macroeconomic problems and structural flaws in the economy—not just its overvalued currency but its weak financial sector, which had contributed to a real estate and investment boom financed in foreign currency. Investors and lenders were now as single-mindedly focused on Thailand's economic flaws as they had been on its strengths. Only when sound policies were pursued would confidence—and investment capital—return and economic recovery take place.

While Treasury focused on a large IMF package allied with strong reform measures, officials from the State and Defense Departments as well as the National Security Council thought we should also contribute additional American resources, using the Exchange Stabilization Fund as we had done in Mexico. They argued that Thailand had been an important military ally of the United States since the Vietnam War and that failing to provide a specific American component to the support package, as many other countries were doing, sent a signal of abandoning the Thais in a time of need. And there was some feeling to that effect in the region. Even if the ESF didn't make much difference economically, they argued, the failure to offer direct bilateral support could have adverse political and strategic consequences.

On balance, the possible negative effects of trying to put up U.S. money seemed to me to outweigh the positives. We—and the IMF—thought that the money raised without a U.S. contribution was sufficient to address Thailand's problems. Another problem was that we did not have full use of the ESF as a result of the so-called D'Amato restrictions. These had been imposed by Congress after the Mexico crisis to curb future ESF lending to troubled economies and were due to expire in the fall. Attempting to use the ESF could easily result in a new, perhaps more stringent, version of the restrictions. I put great weight on preserving the ESF option going forward, both because unforeseen problems could arise and because loss of access to these funds could itself have damaging effects on confidence. In retrospect, I think protecting that option was the better decision on balance, but I probably did give too little weight to the symbolic benefits—economic and geopolitical—of a bilateral contribution to the Thai package.

This disagreement with the President's military and foreign policy advisers also raised a complicated question of who should perform what role. Thailand and the rest of the Asian crisis raised foreign policy and military issues that State and Defense were best equipped to handle, as well as international economic issues for which Treasury was best suited. The two chief levers for our financial intervention—control of the ESF and the U.S. government's relationship with the IMF and the World Bank—were at Treasury. I felt strongly about not trying to use the ESF and got a bit carried away in one meeting in the White House Situation Room. After I finished delivering a lecture on the subject, Sandy Berger asked me whether I was prepared to allow the President to have some input into the decision.

Sandy's point was right. In practice, Thailand was one of those cases where one agency, in this case Treasury, needed to have a clear lead role but within an interagency process. Handling a foreign financial crisis involves complex technical and economic questions, including effects on markets and confidence. Moreover, our military and foreign policy purposes would only be served over the long term if Thailand recovered economically. For this reason, the President tended to look to Treasury to take the lead throughout the Asian crisis, while the NEC, led by Gene Sperling, and the NSC, under Sandy Berger, made sure we did not act without a full airing in the interagency process. As we at Treasury became more and more caught up with the crisis, with discussions stretching into the night, others in the government were also drawn in more deeply. Later on, in the heat of the crisis, interagency process included a daily conference call among Treasury, NEC, NSC, State, Defense, and others. We also worked closely with our finance ministry counterparts in other countries and relied tremendously on the administration's foreign policy team, notably Dan Tarullo at the White House and Stu Eizenstat and Al Larson at the State Department, to lead the effort to reach out to leaders and governments around the world.

In the end, the IMF put together a $17 billion support package for Thailand—$4 billion from the IMF itself as well as bilateral contributions—that was huge relative to the size of Thailand's economy and to rescues prior to Mexico's. The August 1997 program specified economic reforms, including substantial restructuring of the financial sector and a more credible monetary policy regime to provide some stability to the still-falling exchange rate, as well as public disclosure of basic financial data. One controversial but technical issue Treasury had to deal with right at the start of the Thai program was whether or not to disclose how bad the government's financial position truly was. The IMF learned during the negotiations that the government had been hiding the extent of its currency intervention by selling dollars on the forward market. This meant that although the Thai central bank showed reserves on its books, almost none of those reserves were usable: the central bank had already promised to deliver them to someone else in the future, at a price that was by now highly disadvantageous to Thailand. When the program was announced, we insisted upon full disclosure about the unavailability of the Thai central bank's reserves. Our view was that this information was bound to leak out eventually and that Thailand's and the IMF's credibility would be harmed by keeping it secret. Moreover, without true transparency, no one would ever believe in the integrity of Thailand's finances. But this revelation spooked the nervous markets further.

Despite the size of the finance package, the IMF program failed to take hold in September and October, a reflection not just of the newly disclosed bad news about the reserves but, even more important, concern about the Thai government's commitment to reform. The Prime Minister closed insolvent finance companies that were undermining the health of the country's financial system but never fully followed through with the program. Policy drifted as the governing coalition fell apart. Only when the Prime Minister resigned several months later did the new Thai government begin to take real ownership of the reform conditions built into the IMF program. And only then did investor confidence slowly begin to return.

AFTER THAILAND BROKE the baht's link to the dollar in July 1997, financial crisis swept across the region. In the days and weeks that followed, it affected one country after another that had been widely viewed as on a strong footing. In the course of a few weeks, currencies came under attack in Malaysia, Singapore, the Philippines, and Hong Kong as investors scrambled to pull out their money. When the crisis began to affect Indonesia—a huge country with some 225 million people and a pro-Western anchor in Southeast Asia—it generated deep concern.

The markets were relatively calm into early October, but turmoil returned shortly thereafter. Investors' alarm showed in Hong Kong, where the Hang Seng index, the most important stock market gauge in the region, lost 23 percent of its value over four days, starting on October 20. South Korea, the third-largest economy in the region after Japan and China, was also coming under pressure. The region now clearly had serious problems that threatened to spread even more widely. On October 23, the stock markets in Brazil, Argentina, and Mexico dropped in concert with those of the Asian countries. Then our attention was forced back to the United States. On October 27, the Dow dropped 554 points, to 7,161, before the New York Stock Exchange suspended trading in advance of the closing bell. A meeting we'd convened to discuss Indonesia turned into the session where we drafted the public statement on the U.S. stock market that I read on the steps of the Treasury.

My focus wasn't on the level of markets per se, but I was concerned about the volatility in the markets and the ways the Asian crisis could affect us, in terms of both financial contagion and damage to our exports. The Asian countries were the biggest customers of the United States—at that time, 30 percent of our nation's exports went to Asia. For California, Oregon, and Washington, that figure was higher than 50 percent. If the Asian economies were seriously weakened, key sectors of our economy could suffer because consumers in Asia would be poorer and thus less able to buy our goods.

Within a few days, on October 31, the United States joined with others to add our bilateral money—money lent directly from one country to another—to an IMF package for Indonesia. This time there was less debate with the foreign policy team. The D'Amato restrictions had expired, and we were developing—with our G-7 and other partners—a framework whereby bilateral funds would be pledged as a "second line of defense," to be used only after the IMF money had been drawn and only in the context of a successful IMF program. Both made the risks of a congressional assault on our use of the ESF less likely. And in the context of a widening crisis, the balance of judgment shifted to using the ESF to build confidence and to demonstrate support for a crucial U.S. ally.

Despite these efforts, Indonesia's economy remained in turmoil and the broader crisis showed no signs of ebbing. By now there was immense focus around the world on what was happening in the financial markets and intense debate about what should be done. As additional countries in the region got into trouble, it drew more and more attention to the position of the region's two largest powers, Japan and China. The former had been America's chief Asian ally for fifty years and had become one of the world's richest countries. The latter had historically been part of the Communist world and was often a strategic antagonist. The irony was that Japan's policies and practices—by failing to reverse Japan's economic morass—were contributing to the crisis while, in important respects, China's policies promoted stability.

Our focus on Japan's economic weakness had begun long before the Asian crisis erupted. But as we became increasingly worried about the risk of contagion in the region during the fall of 1997, we became more troubled by the adverse impact Japan's failure to deal with its own economic problems was having on the region. Japan appeared to be experiencing not just a cyclical downturn but a serious, long-term economic quagmire that it lacked the political will to address. The country's monetary and fiscal policies were too tight, and more fundamentally, its economy had formal and informal rigidities that were a great impediment to growth. One critical problem was the deeply troubled Japanese banking sector. The government wouldn't move to close insolvent banks or require them to foreclose the nonperforming loans on their books. Dubious loans supported insolvent companies through the so-called *keiretsu* system of close cooperation between companies and banks. And with banks' assets tied up in these companies, the flow of credit to productive uses was severely hampered.

In our view, by far the most important action Japan could take on behalf of Asia was to get its own economic house in order. Japanese growth had slowed dramatically, and the Nikkei index, which had been as high as 39,000 yen at the end of the 1980s, was down to around 15,000 in November 1997. For the country responsible for what was, by some measures, two thirds of the region's GDP to be slumping so badly made the recovery elsewhere in Asia much harder and the risk of further contagion much greater. Japan was a major market for the other countries in the region, and the weakness of the yen, which mirrored the strength of the dollar, further undercut these export-dependent emerging-market countries. Japanese banks were also an important source of capital. But the Japanese banks were pulling their money out of Thailand, Indonesia, and South Korea.

The IMF can influence economic policy in emerging-market countries, at least when those countries need to borrow, by attaching conditions to its loans. But wealthy nations can influence each other in the direction of sound economic policy only through diplomacy and the kind of debate that takes place in the various international institutions and in such fora as the G-7 meetings. There is a great deal of formal and informal process around the G-7 that is useful in this regard. The finance ministers and central bank heads of the seven largest developed economies meet several times a year, aside from the better-known summit meetings of the heads of state. These meetings—and the need to agree on what to say to the press afterward—provide a vehicle for sharing advice and exerting some pressure. But the effect on any industrial country's policies is still very limited, at best.

Some in George H. W. Bush's administration had taken umbrage when Japan had chided us about the U.S. budget deficit in the late 1980s and early 1990s. My view had been that the Japanese had every right to raise the issue because of those deficits' effect on global economic conditions, just as we now had every right to point out the difficulty that Japan's problems were causing others. In 1997–98, the other G-7 countries often found themselves wishing they had more of a lever to get Japan to deal with its economic problems. It's the familiar conflict between national sovereignty and transnational issues in an interdependent international community. The United States would like to be able to pressure countries whose unsound policies have consequences beyond their borders. At the same time, we would not countenance outside intervention in our own policy decisions. And of course, the question of which policy choices make the most sense in any specific situation is often hotly debated.

We looked for ways to try to influence Japan by focusing attention on its economic problems, both publicly and privately. Privately, we stressed the need for action in our bilateral talks with Japan, coordinating our message at all levels of government, including, on occasion, presidential involvement. In multilateral sessions, especially of the G-7, other countries and the IMF could also weigh in. In the midst of the Asian crisis, I remember a G-7 meeting in London where Alan Greenspan was very effective in getting the highly respected German central bank president, Hans Tietmeyer, to join with us in expressing these concerns to Japan.

Publicly, I spoke rather bluntly about the problems in Japan. Such comments always raised touchy diplomatic issues. Japan was our close ally and tended to be acutely sensitive to criticism. But as time went on, I thought that the effort to make an impact through public comment was more and more appropriate because the country's political leadership seemed to be in a state of denial and Japan's economic recovery was increasingly important to the entire global economy. I recognized this kind of paralysis from my Goldman Sachs days. The attitude of much of Japan's political establishment seemed to be that of a trader praying over his weakening positions, when what he needed to do was to reevaluate them unsentimentally and make whatever changes made sense.

Inside the administration, we had many debates about what to do. Like almost everyone else on Clinton's team, I was something of a policy hawk on Japan, but Al Gore was even more so. We had one meeting in the Cabinet Room where we were talking about how to get through to the Japanese about fixing their economy. The Vice President, who was sitting across from Clinton, got very emphatic. He said to the President, "We've got to find some way to get their attention, to exert some pressure on them." Gore proposed a comprehensive strategy to influence broader attitudes in Japan that would involve flying American opinion leaders to Tokyo to speak publicly about the importance of the country getting back on track. Gore may have been trying to make more of a point than a serious suggestion, but it illustrated the frustration we felt when a First World ally's poor economic policies threatened to harm all of us.

One episode that remains vivid in my mind dates from April 1997, when Ryutaro Hashimoto came to Washington to meet with President Clinton for the first time as Prime Minister. Larry and I briefed the President for the meeting and reminded him how important it was for Japan to face its problems. I don't think Clinton particularly relished the prospect of hectoring the Japanese Prime Minister. But he understood the importance of pushing, and he pushed. Hashimoto had anticipated having to face this issue with Clinton. When the President brought up the economy, the Prime Minister took out charts he had brought with him that purportedly showed that Japan was on the verge of turning itself around. He said that it was going to start growing again. Hashimoto complained that "Rubin and Summers"—both of whom were sitting there in the meeting—were saying all these things publicly, but they were entirely wrong.

The world did eventually work its way through the global economic crisis without Japan recovering. But I still think we were correct that Japan's weakness made recovery more difficult and increased the risk of further instability in Asia. And Japan's weakness contrasted with China's role in contributing to stability. Had China made different choices at a moment when Japan's economy was so weak, the combined effect of the two on the region could have been very damaging. At that time, China was neither the leading export market nor a major lender to the rest of the region. It was, however, a competitor in exports, and some in the Chinese government seemed to feel that devaluing the renminbi would serve China's interests by making its exports cheaper. But doing so could have set off a new round of competitive devaluations throughout the region. Several times, in meetings with President Clinton, with others in the administration, or with me, President Jiang Zemin and Premier Zhu Rongji underscored the firmness of their commitment not to devalue the Chinese currency. And they never did.

Those meetings left me with some impressions about China that have continued to inform my view. Its leaders were tough, independent-minded, and unresponsive to pressure. Rightly or wrongly, I also had the sense that Chinese officials took a great deal of satisfaction in being seen by the United States and the world as playing a constructive role in contrast to Japan. But while China's nationalistic pride seems to me to have contributed to a constructive economic stance during the Asian financial crisis, I don't think international pressure would have been effective had the country's leaders been differently inclined. Early on in the administration, Clinton argued that instead of trying to pressure China by linking access to U.S. markets to its human rights progress, we should instead have a strategy of engaging China in the international economy through trade policy. The President supported his argument by citing the historic example of the Sino-Soviet split. China had refused Russia's demands when China was weak, Clinton said, and would be even less likely to respond to American pressure now that it was much stronger.

I saw that tough side of the Chinese government time and again in our discussions—for example, when we urged China to ease the Asian crisis by investing and importing more instead of increasing its large foreign currency reserves. I saw it again later, when we negotiated with China on lowering its trade barriers as a precondition to joining the World Trade Organization. As the increasing number of Americans attempting to do business in China are discovering, the Chinese may move, but not in direct response to demands or on someone else's timetable. In the twenty-first century, China will be a formidable and staunchly independent force. It is greatly to the benefit of both our countries to have an effective relationship. There undoubtedly will be frictions in our relationship—trade, for example, is likely to be contentious at times—but I think our common interest should motivate us to work through these.

WE HADN'T THOUGHT of South Korea as a country where trouble would develop. The South Korean economy was the eleventh largest in the world, the beneficiary of extraordinary growth during the previous several decades. It had graduated from being among the developing countries that borrow from the World Bank and, in 1996, had followed Mexico to become the second emerging-market nation to join the Organization for Economic Cooperation and Development (OECD).

But no sooner had agreement been reached on the loan package for Indonesia, on Halloween Day 1997, than market attention—and our concern—shifted to South Korea. At first, it was hard to believe that South Korea's finances could go the way that Indonesia's or Thailand's had. Even as the market pressures built, we did not expect the government to come for an IMF loan, especially since it faced presidential elections at the end of the year. What we did not realize—and neither did the IMF or South Korea's bank creditors—was that the country was already almost out of reserves. In late November, with an IMF team beginning to pore over the books, South Korean officials broke the news that what on paper were around $30 billion in government foreign reserves were basically gone. All but a few billion had been deposited in South Korean banks, which were now on the brink of insolvency. This sudden revelation ushered in a period of grave danger for the world economy.

Our concerns came to a head the day before Thanksgiving. Larry had called an emergency meeting of his G-7 colleagues in New York to talk about how to manage the deepening crisis. Alan Greenspan had been alerted to how desperate the situation was and how that also affected South Korean banks in the United States, and he came straight over to my office to tell me about it.

Our Asia team gathered in my office, with Larry coming in over the squawk box. As I looked around the room, I saw an extraordinarily capable group of public officials. Larry's presence had served as a prime draw for some extraordinarily well qualified figures in the field of international economics at just the time when the U.S. government had an immense need for them. Some called it a "dream team" of international economic crisis response. That was so not only because of the distinction of the individual résumés. It was the way we all worked together at both conceptual and operational levels. Our group would sit around for hours and intensely debate the merits of this or that policy option the way people might in an academic seminar—me with my shoes off, Larry with his tie loosened. Differences and disagreements were treated with a sense of mutual respect and collective good humor. But this easygoing group was also a formidable apparatus for making dauntingly complicated decisions with potentially vast real-world consequences.

In addition to Larry and Alan, the core group included remaining veterans of our Mexico team. Ted Truman, who had been at the Fed since before the Latin debt crisis of the early 1980s, was legendary in the field and a repository of the history of past rescue efforts. He once again became a de facto part of our team while still at the Fed—and later an official part when he moved over to Treasury. Dan Zelikow, who had done extensive work in Mexico, also remained. Dan was skeptical and hard-nosed about the terms of support in IMF or bilateral programs, always focused on the danger that the fine points of a loan agreement might undermine the larger effort. Another alumnus of the Mexico crisis was Tim Geithner, who had been a career official when Larry had spotted him and begun promoting him, all the way—eventually—to Larry's old job of undersecretary. Geithner knew a great deal about Asia. He had grown up in Thailand and India and in his Treasury career had worked in the Financial Section of the U.S. Embassy in Tokyo. Tim also had a natural talent for working with other people, terrific common sense, and instinctive political judgment.

Other familiar faces were playing new roles. There was Mike Froman, who prior to becoming my chief of staff had worked on economic reform issues in the Middle East and Eastern Europe, including a stint living in Albania. David Lipton, who had replaced Jeff Shafer as our top international official when Jeff had left for the private sector, had developed a considerable reputation among economists as a "country doctor." After getting his Ph.D. in economics from Harvard, where he had played tennis and argued a lot with Larry, David had spent eight years at the IMF, developing a specialty in dealing with countries in extreme financial distress. After that he had worked with Jeffrey Sachs, another Harvard colleague, as an adviser to countries with distressed economies, many of them in Eastern Europe. David had helped to engineer the transition to a free market in Poland, among other places, and had made an enormous contribution to the Bosnian peace settlement negotiated in Dayton, Ohio. (Warren Christopher had called me while still deeply embroiled in negotiating the agreement just to say that David was one of the most extraordinary people he'd ever worked with, which said a lot about both David and Christopher.) David's attitude was typical of our group. He was deeply committed to what he did and took it seriously—but he didn't take himself too seriously.

We were also joined by Caroline Atkinson, deputy assistant secretary for international monetary and financial policy—Tim's old job. Caroline, who had grown up in England, was a former official at the IMF and the Bank of England. She brought to the table a sharp mind and incisive analysis as well as experience in negotiating with troubled debtors. Where Larry and David were often intent on developing a plan, Caroline tended to join Dan Zelikow in reinforcing my own skepticism about what could work.

The group all felt great worry and concern that day. South Korea in crisis signaled something truly new, both geopolitically and economically. South Korea was a crucial military ally, with thirty-seven thousand U.S. troops stationed near the North Korean border. One fear was that instability would create an opportunity for North Korea to do something provocative. But what I think troubled us most was a different kind of unknown, namely the potential risk to the world's financial system. South Korea, much more than Thailand or Indonesia, was a mainstream economy with deep links to the rest of the world, both credit relationships and sizable Korean banks in the United States and Korean-owned factories in industrialized countries such as Great Britain.

The problem inside South Korea combined elements of what had happened in Mexico and Thailand. A fixed-exchange-rate regime had led gradually to a serious overvaluation of the South Korean won. At the same time, South Korea's banks had made a practice of borrowing money short term from foreign banks and lending it longer term to the domestic conglomerates known as *chaebols*. The *chaebols*, which became hugely indebted in foreign currency, had earnings mostly in local currency. With a sense of panic spreading, foreign banks were refusing to roll over their short-term loans, imperiling the survival of South Korea's banks, and capital now started to flee in earnest. The South Korean won plunged even as the government burned through billions in reserves trying to defend it.

Once again, the core issue was how to reestablish confidence and stop the flood of capital out of the country. For an economy as large as South Korea's, this clearly would take a huge amount of money, as well as a serious policy commitment. The stakes were high, not just for South Korea but for the rest of the world. Many creditors and investors thought as follows: if mighty South Korea is going to default, how secure are loans and investments in other emerging-market countries? Banks, mutual funds, and hedge funds in the United States, Europe, and Japan that hadn't thought much about risk when times were good were already pulling back from developing countries without distinguishing among the circumstances. And there was no reason why this pullback would be limited to Asia. Latin America, Eastern Europe, and Russia were all in jeopardy. And if crisis spread throughout the developing world, the developed world could easily be pulled in as well.

This sort of contagion can involve a ripple effect, as the failure of one financial institution works its way through the system, causing an expanding number of other institutions to fail as a result. Financial linkages, though less broadly recognized than trade connections, are highly complex and diverse. Say, for instance, that Japanese banks were heavily exposed to South Korea. And say that U.S. commercial and investment banks had heavy exposure to Japanese banks. South Korea's troubles could feed back in unexpected ways to U.S. banks that had not considered themselves unduly exposed to South Korea.

In an extreme situation, the entire financial system could be threatened, with the health of the world's largest banking institutions at risk.

But even without conditions growing that severe, major international lenders could become less willing or able to extend credit. If that happened, capital could quickly dry up, not only for the developing world but within developed countries as well. The potential existed for the whole international credit system to freeze, with untold consequences. In our discussions, we focused intently on the question of whether a failure in South Korea could trigger that kind of domino effect.

Over Thanksgiving, I was up at my house in Westchester County, where I was supposed to be spending a quiet holiday with Judy and my family. Instead, I spent much of the day and evening on a series of urgent conference calls with Treasury and Fed officials, the President, the national security advisor, and the Secretary of State. Madeleine Albright said she was basting a turkey while we talked about whether South Korea's financial problems could encourage a more aggressive military posture across the demilitarized zone to the North. At some point, we all took a break to eat dinner with our families before getting back on the phone.

For understandable reasons, we at Treasury and the foreign policy people in the administration looked at the issue from somewhat different perspectives. Madeleine and the other foreign policy advisers on the phone were mainly worried about our relationship with a crucially important military ally, as well as national security issues. They thought any instability in South Korea might encourage a reaction from the North, where troops had reportedly gone to some heightened state of alert. Their view was that we economic types were insufficiently focused on geopolitical concerns and that the United States needed to move quickly to show support for South Korea through the IMF and a backup loan from the ESF, as we had just done for Indonesia—what we were now calling a "second line of defense." I felt strongly that if economic stability wasn't reestablished, our geopolitical goals wouldn't be accomplished either. Substantial money—from the United States and the IMF—had been a significant help in Mexico, but only in the context of the government adopting sensible policies. So far, the money we had pledged for Indonesia had not done much to mitigate the crisis there. Committing the IMF and ourselves to a show of financial support for South Korea without an adequate commitment to reform might even make it less likely that South Korea would get back on track, because providing money without strong conditions would reduce our leverage in getting the country to adopt a program that would work.

Late in the evening, I was still on the phone with the President and Sandy Berger. After speaking to South Korean President Kim Young Sam to strongly urge reform, Clinton, who was at Camp David, was waiting to be connected to the Japanese Prime Minister. President Clinton was supposed to urge Hashimoto to address Japan's problems and to discuss the South Korean problem more generally. But Hashimoto was on an airplane and couldn't be reached right away. As we waited and waited, some wondered if the Prime Minister didn't want to take this call. While we were standing by, Clinton was doing the *New York Times* crossword puzzle, which he reputedly could dispatch in a matter of minutes. He asked me about a clue—a three-letter word starting with some letter or other. I had no idea, so I asked my son Jamie.

"Who's so stupid that they don't know that?" Jamie retorted in a voice that could be heard at the other end of the phone.

"The President of the United States," I said.

IMF Managing Director Michel Camdessus had already gone to South Korea once to begin negotiations. That trip had been made in secret to prevent spreading additional alarm. Now Camdessus was headed back to South Korea officially to negotiate the terms of an IMF program. Facing the prospect of a huge U.S. commitment to South Korea, we decided to send David Lipton to Seoul right away. We wanted to get an independent assessment of the situation as well as to reinforce the importance of strong reform measures.

Our view was increasingly that nothing short of a major reform program in South Korea would bring back market confidence. And more than in Mexico, the necessary policy changes needed to go beyond macroeconomic issues such as interest rates and exchange rates to encompass a range of structural issues that went to the heart of the South Korean economic system. One troubling practice was "directed lending," whereby government officials could tell banks to whom to extend credit. That kind of arrangement was the lifeblood of what was being called "crony capitalism." Korea also limited foreign investment and competition. The result of all this was that banks that had little discipline and that favored businesses were protected from failure and had virtually no financial constraints. South Korea would have to tackle fundamental issues for the economy to recover. But in negotiations with the IMF staff and direct discussions with David, officials of the Ministry of Finance and Economy offered inadequate proposals on key structural issues.

Our discussions within Treasury—about what South Korea needed to do to stop the crisis—continued almost around the clock. For many of these meetings, we relied on the Treasury telephone operators to connect us from disparate spots on the globe. During an intense phase of this discussion, I was in Chile at a meeting of Latin American finance ministers, David was in Seoul, in a completely different time zone, and Larry and others were in Washington. I remember placing a call from Chile to Michel Camdessus, who was under heavy pressure in Seoul to reach an agreement. The South Koreans kept announcing that they were about to sign a deal, perhaps trying to force the IMF's hand. We hoped that the South Korean intelligence service would be listening in, so my discussion with Michel—about the extreme importance of a strong program—was meant for the South Koreans as well.

As we continued to hold out, the South Koreans began to take the IMF conditions more seriously. They agreed that interest rates would be set at levels sufficient to restore a willingness to hold won-denominated assets. Directed lending would be abolished. Failed financial institutions would be closed or else restructured and sold. And South Korea's financial sector would open to competition, including from foreign companies. With these concessions in hand, Camdessus announced a $55 billion assistance package on December 3. This was the largest support program the IMF had ever assembled, although smaller relative to the size of the South Korean economy than the Mexican program had been.

Signing a deal didn't make us think South Korea's problems were solved—far from it. The big question was whether the commitments the government had made on paper would be implemented in practice and whether the markets would respond. The immediate reaction of the financial markets was positive, giving us initial cause for optimism. The South Korean won moved up a bit, and the South Korean stock market rose a good deal. But after two good days, the situation began to darken again. Beginning on Monday, December 8, the won plunged 10 percent a day for four days in a row—as much as it was allowed to move under the existing currency regime. That decline triggered a further downward spiral in other world markets, especially those in Asia.

What went wrong? One problem was that South Korea did not really want to let interest rates rise to the levels necessary to induce investors and creditors to stay. The government faced a kind of Catch-22: higher interest rates threatened to hurt the over-indebted *chaebol*s and weaken the South Korean banks still further. But companies and banks would also be damaged if the won fell more against the dollar, pushing up the won value of their dollar debts. And that was likely to happen if interest rates were kept too low.

As the situation deteriorated, foreign banks became more desperate to pull out their money. None of them wanted to be the last ones in when there were no reserves left to pay them. We kept daily tabs on what we called "the drain," or the rate of hard currency outflows from South Korea. We now knew that the South Korean central bank was depositing its hard-currency reserves in South Korean banks. These banks promptly used the dollars to repay foreign bank loans, so the central bank could not feasibly get the dollars back. In early December, even after drawing $5.5 billion from the IMF, South Korea's foreign currency reserves were down to around $9 billion, with a "drain rate" of $1 billion a day.

We also had a problem, as with Thailand, of belated disclosure. The revelation that South Korea's buffer of reserves was almost gone spooked the markets. Rumors began flying about the size of South Korea's foreign debt. One estimate put the total foreign debt coming due in the next year at $116 billion. That meant that even the huge IMF program couldn't save South Korea if confidence didn't return. Around that time, Barton Biggs, a well-respected Wall Street analyst, estimated that South Korea could run out of reserves by the end of the month.

An additional problem was that the South Korean elections were rapidly approaching. With the country's political leadership in flux, the markets were skeptical that the government would be able to take ownership of the IMF program. Although the IMF had gotten the three leading candidates for the South Korean presidency to sign on, none of them evinced much enthusiasm for the reform measures that President Kim Young Sam had agreed to. The front-runner in the campaign was Kim Dae-jung, a heroic former dissident and eventual winner of the Nobel Peace Prize, who had spent time on death row under the military dictatorship that fell in 1987. Kim was a trade-union populist who, despite an election manifesto that in some respects echoed the IMF program, said in one interview that if elected, he wanted to renegotiate the terms of South Korea's deal with the IMF.

On December 18, the day of the election, top Treasury and Federal Reserve officials met to address what we all viewed as the threat of an imminent collapse of the South Korean economy. Of the many, many discussions we had about the deepening financial storm in Asia, the dinner we had that night at the Jefferson Hotel stands out in my mind as a critical moment. During the evening, there were several calls from the White House to work on the wording of the message President Clinton would deliver in a congratulatory call to the apparently victorious Kim Dae-jung that night. The basic point we wanted Clinton to convey was that President Kim had a real opportunity to change the way his country did business—and that the consequences of not doing so could be very bleak indeed.

Over dinner, we all discussed the situation. Our first attempt at an intervention—the biggest package ever negotiated by the IMF, backed up with additional support from the United States and other nations—hadn't restored the confidence of foreign investors in the South Korean economy. South Korea was significantly larger than Thailand and Indonesia put together. If the South Korean government or banking sector failed to make its scheduled loan payments, contagion could spread quickly through other emerging markets in Asia, Eastern Europe, and Latin America. We were very focused on the risk to the global financial system and the possible consequences for the industrial countries, including the United States. Some people at the table tried to convey their sense of this with a somewhat hyperbolic reference to a "1930s scenario."

Most of the discussion that night was about our remaining options, none of which was very promising. One alternative was to "let South Korea go" and somehow try to build a firebreak around it by supporting other countries. But no one thought this was likely to work. So we focused much of our effort on other ways to shore up confidence: accelerating the disbursement of IMF funds and putting together a stronger international aid package—with more upfront money from the United States and Europe—as backing for stronger reforms in South Korea. Larry Summers said that the IMF money should be disbursed aggressively to avoid a "Vietnam" situation—that is, a gradual escalation that didn't work. Because the problem was confidence, he felt that we needed, as we had in Mexico, something more akin to the famous Colin Powell Doctrine—a massive show of financial force.

But even the more robust support package we were considering seemed insufficient to restore confidence by itself. Dinner ended with a better understanding of various unpromising options, but without any clear decision about which way to go. At the end of the evening, Tim Geithner's pager transmitted the news that concern about the effects of Kim Dae-jung's election victory was driving the won down further. Markets had opened in Seoul, where it was already morning.

In this case, not choosing immediately turned out for the best. Over the next few days, Treasury and Federal Reserve officials turned attention to another idea that we hadn't thought wise or feasible when it was first floated in the IMF a few weeks earlier. The proposal was a voluntary version of what's known as a "standstill," whereby banks would agree to roll over their loans, extending their due dates and converting short-term obligations to longer-term ones. I don't think the banks would have considered doing this earlier because they hadn't yet realized how dire the situation was. But now was the eleventh hour, and the banks were staring default in the face. Still, they would not act on their own; we would need to provide a catalyst. The plan had two other elements: a stronger reform package on the part of South Korea and accelerated money from the IMF and creditor governments, including the United States.

As well as being more likely to work, this three-pronged plan could also reduce the moral-hazard problem by involving private creditors in the resolution of the crisis. The banks were reluctant to roll over South Korea's loans and would not have chosen to take the continued exposure on their own. Under this plan, they shared the continuing risk of non-payment with one another and to some extent with the multilateral institutions. I never liked calling our rescue efforts "bailouts"—rescuing investors was an unavoidable side effect of restoring stability—but you could reasonably describe this approach as a private-sector "bail-in." My view of the extent to which creditors and investors had lost their sense of the risks involved in emerging markets was borne out when we began to explore the idea. We asked the commercial and investment banks how much exposure they had to South Korea by way of financial derivatives, apart from their direct loans. Most had a very imprecise idea, and some took a full week to find out.

Among the risks of the plan was the considerable difficulty of successful execution. Every bank had an interest in being a free rider, in not participating while others did. But if a preponderance of the major financial institutions didn't agree to participate on equal terms, the deal would fall apart. We had little practical leverage to induce their cooperation. We could only try to affect the outcome by making phone calls, asking bank CEOs to do what was in their collective self-interest, and, in the case of some reluctant parties, suggesting that the world might know who was responsible for failure and its consequences, should they occur.

Meanwhile, David Lipton was on his way back to Seoul again, in part to try to gauge Kim Dae-jung's commitment to reform. Some people at the State Department at first objected to the President-elect of South Korea meeting with a Treasury Department official before a more ceremonial visit from someone at State. But the new ambassador to South Korea, Stephen Bosworth, overruled the objection, saying the situation was so pressing that we couldn't stand on ceremony. Bosworth, a distinguished former ambassador to the Philippines who had previously also worked at the State Department's Economic Desk, was not only very sensible and effective but also an example of the kind of diplomat we're going to need more of in the future—one who combines foreign policy expertise and skill with a good understanding of economic issues. Bosworth said that Lipton should see Kim Dae-jung as soon as possible, and Lipton's first stop in Seoul was the union headquarters that had served as the former labor leader's campaign office.

I left that day for Virgin Gorda in the British Virgin Islands on a family vacation that we'd taken annually for fifteen years. As usual, I had hired Garfield Faulkner, a local guide, to take me fly fishing for bonefish off the neighboring sleepy island of Anegada—where arriving pilots used to have to be on the lookout for cattle blocking the airstrip. You fish from a boat or wade in the ocean flats and try to spot the silvery bonefish, which never stop moving in the clear water. The fish are fast, finicky, and immensely powerful. One weighing only a few pounds will run out several hundred feet of fishing line in an instant. But this time I had to cancel Garfield while I spent the day talking on the phone with Alan and Larry in Washington and David in Seoul.

As I stared longingly at the water, David reported back that his meeting with Kim Dae-jung had been highly encouraging. Kim, despite having been elected on a populist platform, told him that the South Koreans would never be able to deal with their problems if they kept blaming them on America and the IMF. The new President also said the burden would have to be shared three ways: the government would have to be reorganized to take power away from the Ministry of Finance. The *chaebols* would have to restructure. But, perhaps most important given his background, Kim told David that unions would have to accept layoffs and wage reductions if South Korean companies were to become profitable again. Only then would investment and growth recover. At the end of the meeting, David described Kim as becoming more philosophical. "For thirty years, they arrested me, drove me into exile, and tried to kill me," he said. "Now I come back and get elected President, just in time to face the collapse of my country."

That Kim was committing himself to reform meant we were going to move ahead with the bail-in proposal. South Korea owed money to banks in Japan, Germany, and many other countries, as well as the United States. To be successful, we needed our G-7 partners and other key countries on board. Many of them had favored trying some form of bail-in, but we also needed their support for the stepped-up financing from the IMF as well as their individual contributions. I flew back to Washington as Larry juggled phone calls with the top management of the IMF and his G-7 colleagues in Japan, Europe, and Canada while briefing the White House and the foreign policy team on our progress.

We must have set some kind of record that holiday for disturbing the slumber of finance ministers and central bankers all over the world. But the calls we made paid off. With twelve other countries on board, we released a statement on Christmas Eve saying that the IMF would speed up the disbursement of funds in the context of voluntary rollovers that we would seek from banks throughout the developed world. The statement listed all the countries willing to put bilateral funds on the table, provided the private banks and the South Koreans did their part.

A massive, synchronized international effort to encourage the banks to act together was also put into effect by the Federal Reserve, acting primarily through the Federal Reserve Bank of New York and the Treasury Department. Compounding the intrinsic difficulty of the situation was that the bankers we needed to convene had all dispersed for their Christmas vacations. I made calls to U.S. banks and investment banks from the conference table in Larry's office. William McDonough, the president of the New York Fed, made calls to his international counterparts, who made similar calls to banks in Europe and Japan.

These calls required great tact. I had to be persuasive about the banks' collective self-interest—and even on a few occasions suggest that a poor citizen would probably become known in the event of failure—without overstepping an uncertain line. And for Bill McDonough, the balance was even more difficult. The Federal Reserve is the nation's chief financial regulator and could apply pressure just by convening a meeting. If such pressure went beyond a strong sense of "moral suasion," that could be an improper use of the Fed's regulatory position and could also prove counterproductive by scaring the banks further. As a former commercial banker himself, Bill knew how to frame the issue. When the heads of the leading U.S. banks came together at his office, he suggested that they act collectively, not for the sake of South Korea but in their self-interest and that of their shareholders. Otherwise, the vast South Korean debt they held could become uncollectible. Some bankers grumbled, but nearly everyone agreed to participate. Critical to the effort was Bill Rhodes, a banker who was central in the world of international finance and whose "golden Rolodex" and tireless cajoling had brought renown in global financial circles during the 1980s debt crisis. Meetings like ours took place in financial capitals around the world. In London, where there are probably more foreign banks than anywhere else, Bank of England governor Eddie George summoned key bankers back from vacation to a meeting on Boxing Day, when The City, London's financial district, was usually shuttered for the holidays.

In combination with President Kim's public commitment to economic and financial sector reform and the international community's financial support, our coordinated effort showed signs of having the desired effect. South Korea's currency and stock markets soon stabilized, although they did not rise appreciably for some time. Contagion seemed to abate and our fears about the global financial system eased for the moment. In the end, the banks did not suffer from their participation. They were paid back in full and ended up receiving a higher rate of interest in the interim. And in the end we did not disburse any U.S. funds. Treasury's discussions on the loan agreement with South Korea—initially quite heated—petered out after a few months. The money turned out not to be needed.

That wasn't the end of the South Korean stage of the crisis. At several points in 1998, there were dicey moments when we feared that the plan wasn't working, or when political developments elsewhere threatened to plunge the country back into economic gloom. But basically, the South Korean economy was on the mend. And what had mattered most wasn't anything the IMF or U.S. Treasury had done but South Korea's own response. President Kim Dae-jung and his colleagues, the heroes of the South Korean recovery in my view, showed how sound, courageous political leaders can make a great difference—in fact, the key difference—in overcoming economic duress.

CHAPTER NINE

A Crisis Considered

W HEN THE ASIAN FINANCIAL crisis swept through a country, it often changed not just the economy but the political landscape as well. By early 1998, new governments were in place in Thailand and South Korea, and their commitment to economic reform was essential to calming financial markets. But in Indonesia, the prospect of political change only threatened to make financial difficulties worse. For me, Indonesia's escalating crisis highlighted how difficult overcoming financial turmoil can be when political, economic, and foreign policy concerns are interwoven.

Indonesia, the fourth most populous nation in the world, was a key strategic U.S. ally in Southeast Asia. It had been under military rule for more than thirty years, dominated by one man, seventy-six-year-old President Suharto (who, like many Indonesians, has no other name). Suharto's autocratic regime had delivered both stability and a dramatic rise in living standards to what had been a largely rural and very poor country when he took control in 1965. A mix of economic openness and tight political control had allowed the economy to develop rapidly. Domestic and foreign-owned businesses flourished, while ethnic tensions were kept at bay. Ethnic Chinese entrepreneurs, who had suffered persecution in the past, prospered in relative safety, while Indonesians mainly of Javanese descent controlled the military and the powerful state sector. Foreign investment was encouraged, foreign banks poured money into Indonesian companies, and jobs were plentiful.

But as financial turmoil moved across the region, the pervasive corruption and crony capitalism that helped to shore up Suharto's support came under closer scrutiny. Political and family connections were all-important in business. Indonesia's legal system was corrupt and slow-moving. Public money was siphoned from the budget for projects that enriched family and friends. Officially sanctioned monopolies in plywood, cars, and cloves—used in cigarettes and a mainstay of Indonesia's economy—channeled money into corrupt hands. Foreign investors and creditors who were now fleeing the country called for fundamental reform to put the economy on a sounder footing. But the reforms they wanted risked undermining a regime already under pressure from the spreading economic chaos.

Unlike Thailand and South Korea, Indonesia had no early prospect of a democratic shift of power. As Suharto's government wrestled with the worsening economy, the danger that the society could explode into violence made the task of recovery vastly more difficult. The confidence of domestic businessmen and savers, many of whom were ethnic Chinese, was closely bound up with Suharto's survival. They—and we—were afraid of a replay of the civil unrest that had marked the previous change in power in 1965, when half a million people, including many Chinese, had been murdered. Domestic capital was now also flooding out of the country, from local entrepreneurs who feared a change in the regime that had served their economic and political interests.

This made reestablishing market confidence particularly difficult, because reforms that would reassure foreign investors might alarm domestic investors. Certain Indonesian officials themselves had identified a wide array of reforms to combat corruption, from restructuring banks to curbing key monopolies and opening up the government's books to scrutiny. Foreign confidence now hinged to a significant degree on these reforms being implemented. But such reforms could further weaken Suharto and thereby worsen domestic capital flight.

There was no easy way to deal with the inherent political and economic conflicts, and the handling of the Indonesian situation sparked widespread criticism of Treasury and of the IMF, including from Capitol Hill. We at Treasury and officials at the Fund may well have underestimated how damaging certain reforms would be to Suharto and how destabilizing the growing threat of his departure was in itself. But these issues were on investors' and creditors' minds and couldn't be ignored. Whether triggered by foreign or local money leaving the country, the escalating crisis threatened an economic unraveling that could quickly spiral as investors became frightened.

An initial IMF program for Indonesia in the fall of 1997 underscored this problem. In that episode, Suharto's government had failed to follow through on commitments that hit at entrenched interests close to the President. Though the government closed some debt-ridden banks, doing so only helped to create a run on the others left open—including banks that were also insolvent but politically connected, and that were, in some cases, owned by Suharto's friends and family. Many people believed that the IMF should have foreseen this. To show how complicated crisis response is, many criticized the IMF for pressing for bank closures at all (at least without putting into place full deposit insurance to reassure depositors at those banks left open), while others thought that the IMF should have insisted on closing more banks. One case in particular was highly publicized and became a symbol of the concerns about whether Suharto would ever truly reform. A bank owned by Suharto's son Bambang was closed but reopened three weeks later under a different name. News reports described workers pulling up to Bambang's skyscraper in downtown Jakarta, pulling down a blue Bank Andromeda sign in the lobby, and putting up a blue Bank Alfa sign in its place.

At the same time, rather than keeping monetary policy tight, Indonesia's central bank supplied whatever loans were needed to prop up those banks facing massive withdrawals. The rupiah plunged and inflation soared. We had significant evidence by now that adhering to a tight monetary policy, even if this meant sharply higher interest rates, was an essential element in stopping a financial market panic. But that would mean cutting off government credit to failing banks and companies, many of which had close ties to Suharto.

As it became clear in early 1998 that the first IMF program had failed and the crisis was deepening, we at Treasury felt keenly the need to understand Indonesia's political situation better. In addition to internal discussions with the foreign policy experts in the administration, we reached out to others. Larry and I both knew Henry Kissinger, and he paid a quiet visit to us at Treasury. In addition, Paul Wolfowitz, former U.S. ambassador to Indonesia and later number two at the Pentagon in the second Bush administration, also came to Treasury for a lengthy discussion. And Larry and I both spoke to Lee Kuan Yew, the strongman who had built Singapore. Lee is deeply knowledgeable about geopolitical and cultural matters and had done much thinking about Southeast Asia from a realpolitik point of view. Although he had earlier been supportive of Suharto, he had become doubtful that Suharto would take needed steps on the economy. As a consequence, Lee was highly pessimistic about Indonesia's future. He worried that ethnic conflict and political unrest generated by Indonesia's sinking economy could have a spillover effect, leading to clashes between ethnic Chinese and non-Chinese elsewhere in the region.

We made a series of attempts to get through to Suharto about the need to take ownership of reform, including a phone call from President Clinton on January 8. The response from Suharto, who felt that he had run his economy successfully for a quarter century, was not promising. When Clinton encouraged him to continue dealing with the IMF, Suharto blamed foreign "speculators" for driving down his country's currency. When Clinton pressed Suharto on corruption and mentioned specifically the reopening of his son's bank, the Indonesian leader buried him in legal technicalities. This mighty autocrat said he had no power in the matter— it was all up to the courts.

Our next move was to send Larry to Jakarta to meet with Suharto in person. The two of them sat down in the presidential palace for an hour-long session, but Larry, who was seldom reticent, hardly got a word in. As he described it to me, he got only one turn at bat, while Suharto played nine innings. Next to arrive in Jakarta was Michel Camdessus, who succeeded in securing Suharto's signature on a second, strengthened IMF program on January 15, 1998. There's a notorious photograph of Camdessus standing with his arms folded, looking over Suharto's shoulder as Suharto signs the document, an image that seemed to many critics to typify the heavy hand of IMF conditionality.

Ironically, we saw in the coming days how much countries themselves determine their own fate and how little the IMF or anyone else can do in the absence of a genuine commitment to reform. Suharto had agreed to stringent conditions on a broad array of issues—from the government clove monopoly to aircraft manufacturing. He also promised to keep tight control of monetary policy. I was skeptical about whether this program would work any better than the first. Suharto hadn't done anything to suggest that his basic attitude toward reform had changed. But the situation was sufficiently worrisome that even an uncertain IMF program—designed, as was usual, so that the government wouldn't be able to draw down much of the money if Suharto didn't follow through on reforms—seemed better than none.

This program was hugely controversial. Some outside critics thought the West was simply taking the opportunity to force our own free-market policy preferences on Indonesia via IMF conditionality, and ignoring the government's views about what would be best. Others argued that in focusing on confidence in this way, the IMF and we at Treasury were following the whims of the financial markets—which might be irrelevant or even counterproductive—rather than focusing on fundamental problems. If the markets wanted Indonesians to wear blue shirts, would blue shirts become essential to the restoration of confidence?

My view was that by and large the markets tend to shine a spotlight on real economic problems, although they may exaggerate the importance of those problems at times (as well as ignoring them at other times). In a situation like Indonesia's, foreign investors and creditors might become preoccupied with a symbol, such as the ending of a specific monopoly or the removal of a single corrupt official. But those symbols weren't just blue shirts; in most cases they related to significant underlying issues: monopolies, corruption, mismanagement, and weak financial systems.

In Indonesia, many of the changes that the IMF pushed were outside its usual realm of expertise on exchange rates, interest rates, and government finances. And in hindsight, many people involved agree that there were too many conditions spread across too many different areas. Expecting the government to fix so many problems at once just wasn't realistic and probably blurred focus on the most urgent ones. The most controversial structural measures, however, were not dreamed up by the IMF, the U.S. Treasury, or other outsiders. The IMF had often been criticized for following a "cookie cutter" approach that ignored the distinctive features of different countries. In this case, the Fund's policy conditions were informed by the views of a number of Indonesian officials, such as the respected economist Widjoyo Nitisastro, whom Suharto had put in charge of negotiations, as well as by the World Bank.

But as happened with the first program, financial markets seemed to have no faith that Suharto would do what he said. At the same time, spreading violence and fears of a political breakdown worsened capital flight. Many merchants closed their businesses and factories and fled. The rupiah dropped from 7,300/dollar the day before the announcement to 15,450 on January 23. Indonesia stood on the brink of hyperinflation.

Rather than implement reforms, Suharto continued to look for another way out. One idea he turned to was a "currency board," a mechanism to stop the fall of the Indonesian rupiah by tying it to the U.S. dollar and putting Indonesia's monetary policy on autopilot. But this kind of regime is difficult to maintain even for countries with the economic requisites: ample foreign currency reserves, a real commitment to sound monetary and fiscal policies, and a strong banking system, which is needed because the central bank would no longer be able to provide finance to prop up ailing banks. We feared that trying to fix the exchange rate in this way might merely be an opportunity for Suharto's cronies to get their money out of the country before the arrangement collapsed and the rupiah fell still further.

Eventually, the IMF persuaded Suharto to drop the idea. But that got us no closer to solving the problem, which was how to structure something Suharto would credibly agree to that would also reassure international markets and persuade Indonesians to keep their money at home. In wrestling with these issues, Treasury worked closely with other countries that had a huge stake in the region, such as Australia, Japan, and Germany, which had particularly close ties to Indonesia.

The immense difficulty of dealing with Suharto—who reportedly promised his cabinet that he would fight a "guerrilla war" against his own economic program—was brought home to us in February, when he formally nominated B. J. Habibie as Vice President. A loyal crony with little independent standing, Habibie now looked like the obvious successor should the President leave. Some saw the move as a way to show critics that Suharto's ouster would only make things worse. Jim Steinberg of the NSC said in one of our meetings that perhaps we should be reaching out to the reform forces in Indonesia, so that if Suharto did fall, they wouldn't feel we'd been their opponents. The argument on the other side was that doing so could hurt our relations and effectiveness with Suharto and might destabilize the situation even further if it became known.

I remember sitting in Erskine Bowles's office one day in early February and saying, "We've got to find some way to get our message across to this guy." We needed someone Suharto would take seriously. Out of that discussion, we decided to ask Walter Mondale to go to Indonesia. The question of what Mondale would say to Suharto showed yet again the difficulty of balancing financial market and other concerns. Our view at Treasury was that Mondale should be as direct as possible with Suharto and tell him his government didn't have much of a future if it didn't become serious about economic reform. The State Department worried about the danger of appearing to withdraw our support from a crucial ally. Suharto was seen as the only glue holding a fragile country together; Indonesia falling again into chaos or civil war was a real danger. The foreign policy team also felt that we risked turning Suharto hostile to the United States by insisting he meet strong conditions. This is the kind of complexity that arises in dealing with the wide range of issues relating to crisis response. Persuading countries to adopt good policies and improve governance is a vast challenge in itself. But when doing so touches foreign policy and national security goals, that difficulty greatly increases.

We negotiated vigorously over Mondale's script. On the one hand, we had to respect Suharto's sensitivities, but on the other, the IMF program wasn't going to work unless his policies changed. David Lipton, our liaison with the foreign policy team on the Mondale trip, worked on the plane on the economic message before Mondale himself took it over, impressing

David with his adroit way of getting the sensitive points across. Essentially, Mondale told Suharto that Clinton was not attempting to displace him, but was just trying to help his country do well. If he adopted sensible reforms, he would find us to be extremely supportive. Beyond the touchy structural issues, Mondale stressed that the solution to the crisis required Suharto's commitment to fighting inflation and restoring financial stability, as he had done when he had become President thirty years earlier. But Mondale felt that he was no more successful than the President and Larry had been at getting Suharto to change his attitude on the fundamental issues of corruption and transparency.

Shortly afterward, Suharto appointed a "crony cabinet," which included his daughter and various other friends who had accumulated great fortunes with his assistance. To many, this was just one more reason to doubt Suharto's commitment to reform. Others felt that he chose this group of trusted allies to make one last stab at stabilizing the economy. And in fact the government did begin to get serious about monetary control, markets began to recover, and the IMF and World Bank structured new programs around this effort. Multilateral pressure had been critical in getting Indonesia to pay attention to the message about monetary control to stop the dangerous spiral of a weakening exchange rate and accelerating inflation. In this case, Japan and Germany—the second- and third-largest economies in the world—also weighed in with us directly. A high-level team was sent from our three countries to work with the Indonesians, including Ginandjar Kartasasmita, now the coordinating minister for economics and finance, whom I called ahead of time to ask him to receive the team.

In the succeeding weeks, however, the political situation became more precarious and riots spread throughout the country. Scenes of violence on the news each evening were another reminder of the human toll involved in these crises. There were acrimonious discussions between Indonesia and the IMF about what Indonesia had to do to qualify for each disbursement of the loan. One battle concerned fuel prices, which had a costly subsidy that was politically highly sensitive. In May, Suharto raised fuel prices dramatically, which led to violent protests that left several hundred people dead. There remains a question as to whether Suharto had to act so drastically, raising prices all at once, to meet the IMF conditions. An IMF study by an internal review board released in July 2003, though critical of the IMF program in other respects, reviewed internal documents and stated that the decision to accelerate the fuel price increase was Suharto's.

As the fuel crisis spiraled out of control, the Indonesian Parliament demanded Suharto's resignation. Suharto asked the Indonesian people "for forgiveness" for his mistakes and shortcomings and, on May 21, 1998, handed off his presidency to Vice President Habibie.

The IMF's efforts in Indonesia were widely viewed as a failure. However you apportion the blame, whether it was more Indonesia's fault or that of the IMF working with the U.S. Treasury and others, one central issue is that Indonesia never took ownership of reform. The economy did not begin to recover quickly, as had happened in Thailand and Korea. The severe hardships caused by the crisis continued, with high unemployment and increased poverty. Political and financial uncertainty held back growth and investment, companies remained mired in debt, and the corrupt, slow-moving legal system slowed efforts to rebuild the banks and renegotiate foreign debts. But that is only a part of the story. At the height of the crisis, Indonesia faced a real risk of hyperinflation, economic chaos, and, possibly, a bloody civil war. Instead, the government continued to work on financial stability and on overcoming inflationary pressures. The exchange rate that had depreciated as low as 16,000 in June 1998 steadily strengthened and was around 8,500 in mid-2003. And Indonesia has now had two democratic elections, with peaceful transfers of power, while over the four years from 1998 to 2002 the economy recorded 13.4 percent growth. The international community's efforts did not accomplish what any of us had hoped, but, by catalyzing some stabilizing policy actions and stemming possible collapse at critical moments, they did help to prevent the dire circumstances that many people had feared.

AS EVENTS UNFOLDED, I became more and more convinced that we were facing not just a serious regional problem but one with dangerous global dimensions. The immediate challenge was to deal with whatever country was in trouble and to try to prevent the contagion from spreading. But by early 1998, we were also giving more thought to the related questions of what was causing the crisis, how best to prevent similar events in the future, and how to improve our crisis response.

I think my overall approach to dealing with the unfolding crisis was well characterized by a list of principles that Tim Geithner and two of his colleagues in the international section of the Treasury, Stephanie Flanders and Brad Setser, assembled and presented to me in a framed copy when I retired as Secretary under the half-serious rubric of "The Rubin Doctrine of International Finance." I had brought some of these principles with me to Treasury. Others developed out of dealing with Mexico and Asia and the other international policy issues faced by Treasury.

1. The only certainty in life is that nothing is ever certain.
2. Markets are good, but they are not the solution to all problems.
3. The credibility and the quality of a nation's policies matter more for its prospects than anything the United States, the G-7, or the international financial institutions can do.
4. Money is no substitute for strong policy, but there are times when it is more costly to provide too little money than to provide too much.
5. Borrowers must bear the consequences of the debts they incur—and creditors of the lending they provide.
6. The United States must be willing to be defined by what it is against, as well as what it is for.
7. The dollar is too important to be used as an instrument of trade policy.
8. Optionality is good in itself.
9. Never let your rhetoric commit you to something you cannot deliver.
10. Gimmicks are no substitute for serious analysis and care in decision making.

Today, I would add a number 11: *The self-interest of the United States requires us to engage and work closely with other nations on issues of the global economy.* But while these principles provided a general framework for our response to the crisis, they don't offer a view of what caused it or specific answers to critics of our approach.

Perhaps unsurprisingly, criticism of the IMF and the United States became much sharper as the financial contagion spread—apparently unstoppably—around the world in late 1997 and 1998, creating severe economic hardship for many people. Some of the most vocal critics rejected outright the premise that underlay our thinking—that globalization and open markets were on balance greatly beneficial, both to the United States and to the rest of the world, and that what was needed was to make them work better. Some saw what was happening in Asia as a crisis of global capitalism, which they disliked and believed was harmful to poor people. Others objected to any help for other nations as long as there were unmet needs at home and believed that open markets were detrimental to American workers. These perspectives echoed through the rhetoric of much of the antiglobalization movement that first attracted worldwide attention with the protests at the meeting, or attempted meeting, of the World Trade Organization in Seattle in 1999.

But the vast majority of those who took issue with us on some aspect of policy or another shared our broad view in favor of globalization and saw market-based economics and economic integration as the most promising approach to raising living standards around the world. Their criticism can be broken into three broad strands. Of course, brief analysis can't do justice to all the nuances and overlapping views in what became an intense international debate. And I would not claim to be giving a complete account of the views even of those critics that I cite, but rather a description of how the debate played out.

The first set of critiques revolved around the idea that the West, especially the IMF and the U.S. Treasury, had contributed to causing the financial instability. The second strand was that we were mishandling the crisis in various ways. The third was that we were failing to take steps to prevent such problems in the future or, worse, that our actions were actually making future crises more likely.

Some who said the West was to blame for the crisis attributed the whole problem to First World "speculators." Mahathir Mohamad, the Prime Minister of Malaysia, was the most prominent proponent of this view. Mahathir is a capitalist who wouldn't have much in common with the protesters outside McDonald's. But he argued that speculators had created the Asian crisis for the purpose of exploiting the developing world and buying its assets cheaply. At the IMF annual meeting in Hong Kong in September 1997, Mahathir called currency trading "immoral," having previously singled out currency trader George Soros as part of a Wall Street conspiracy to bet against Malaysia's currency and then drive it down to make the bets come good. Although Mahathir's denunciation was extreme, many others felt that financial market players had deliberately disrupted currencies and economies for their own gain.

Another set of objections in this first category came from people who were largely advocates of a market-based system but who saw danger in unleashing market forces too rapidly. They argued that the United States had helped to create the problems in Asia by pushing countries to open up their economies to global flows of trade, and especially capital, before those markets were ready. Richer, more developed economies could better absorb large inflows of capital and withstand big shifts in capital flows and exchange rates as market sentiment changed. In less developed nations with weaker financial institutions and without well-established safety nets for those hurt by economic change, these flows were more likely to be used poorly and the swings from inflows to outflows proved devastating.

Many who blamed the West for causing the crisis also agreed with the second broad strand of criticism, that the response of the international community—the IMF, the United States and other governments, the World Bank, and so on—had worsened the problems in Asia. In the view of some, Asian countries that had careened from rapid growth to negative growth hadn't done much wrong in either their macroeconomic or structural policies, and the IMF calls for higher interest rates and budget cuts had only exacerbated their problems. One vocal critic who took this view, despite his position as the chief economist at the World Bank, was Joseph Stiglitz. In addition to attacking the IMF's macroeconomic prescription, he said that the IMF shouldn't be getting involved in structural economic issues, which were irrelevant to the crisis and none of its business. More broadly, he charged that the IMF's approach in developing countries was sometimes reminiscent of colonialism.

Some other academic economists also took issue with aspects of the international community's response to crisis. Paul Krugman, then at MIT, and Jeffrey Sachs, then at Harvard, argued that South Korea and other countries were facing liquidity difficulties rather than deep-rooted problems. Far from helping to calm the crisis, the IMF-supported policy reforms risked making it worse by scaring investors more and setting back economic growth. With markets in a self-fulfilling panic, the response should focus on providing liquidity, aided perhaps, Krugman argued, by temporary controls on capital outflows. In a widely read article, Harvard's Martin Feldstein targeted for criticism the structural conditionality in the Asia programs.

Finally, there was a third category of critiques that called for sweeping changes to the global economic system to help avoid crises in the future. Some conservatives wanted an end to large-scale lending by the IMF, or even in some cases an end to the IMF itself. They emphasized the dangers of moral hazard and argued that insulating investors and creditors from their losses sowed the seeds of future crises. In the view of these critics, the United States had helped set the stage for the crisis in Asia by "bailing out" investors in Mexico. They argued that our actions in Asia were likely to create a cycle of overlending and retreat elsewhere. In the future, the United States should let mismanaged emerging-market economies fail, in order to teach both creditors and borrowers a lesson. Others in this camp took precisely the opposite approach, suggesting grand new institutions from a new world regulator to an international lender of last resort.

While many of these criticisms raised real and valid issues, none of them seemed to provide a realistic alternative approach to dealing with the spreading financial crisis or to reforming the international system of financial markets. The immediate imperative was to overcome the crises in the various countries. In our view that needed to be done in the context of market-based economics and globalization, which had served developing countries well, and meant reestablishing the confidence of domestic and foreign creditors and investors. To me, no simple, single solution was responsive to what was a very complex set of issues. As time went on, the international community's approach to the immediate crises evolved in reaction to changing circumstances—both the contagion that increased the danger and the experience from earlier cases.

What caused the crisis? Development economists have grappled for decades with the question of why some developing countries have done better than others. But now, in 1997 and 1998, the question was why even some of the apparently most successful were having severe difficulties. In general, the Asian and Latin American countries that were the brightest success stories had embraced political and economic change of various kinds, seeking to export and opening up in varying degrees to foreign trade and investment, privatizing state-run industries in some cases, reducing regulation and injecting market forces—again, in varying degrees—and constructing legal frameworks for financial markets.

In certain respects, however, the Asian "miracle" economies remained less than free markets, afflicted by too-close relationships between banks and corporate borrowers and various kinds of self-dealing and protectionism. In some countries, corruption was a serious problem. And most of them lacked financial transparency at the corporate, banking, and government levels, which meant that creditors and investors could be suddenly surprised by the revelation of concealed problems.

In addition to structural weaknesses, in 1997–98 the crisis countries had made themselves considerably more vulnerable to market pressures by locking into fixed-exchange-rate systems, whether formal or informal. They were hesitant to depart from these currency regimes, most importantly because of fear of instability, but also because the promise of relative safety from exchange risk had helped to bring in foreign capital. The trouble was that a currency can stay pegged to the dollar only if economic policies are appropriate and if the markets believe that domestic concerns will be sacrificed to keep the peg intact. Over time, strains almost inevitably build up, as happened in one Asian country after another and later in both Russia and Brazil. And once the market starts to bet that a currency peg will break, it can take enormous commitment and powerful policy measures to convince it otherwise. But letting the exchange rate go is also damaging. All of a sudden, the debts of companies and governments that have borrowed in dollars or other hard currencies became much more burdensome. This "balance sheet" effect, as it came to be called, had a devastating impact on production and jobs in the afflicted countries. And, compounding the difficulties, several of the countries that got into trouble were also undergoing significant political transitions, which diffused the sense of responsibility for dealing with the crisis.

However, the global financial crisis was far from solely the fault of the countries that got into trouble. Many faulted the United States for pressing emerging markets to open up to external capital too fast. It is legitimate to ask whether some of the crisis countries deregulated their capital markets too rapidly and, if they did, how much responsibility the industrialized countries should bear. At the Treasury Department, in particular after the Mexican crisis, we emphasized the need for an adequate institutional framework and appropriate policy regimes in emerging markets. However, in hindsight, that emphasis should have been more intense. Better regulatory infrastructure and stronger financial institutions alongside more open capital markets would have reduced the potential for instability. A great difficulty in doing all of this is developing the credit culture, the trained people, and the internal practices requisite for strong financial institutions.

Absent a crisis, however, I'm not sure a greater emphasis by the United States and IMF on financial market infrastructure would have had much effect on borrowing-country behavior. In practice, most of the countries that suffered from overborrowing had gone out and sought that capital. They had also, in many cases, resisted the entry of foreign banks—which could have provided immediate aggregations of trained personnel and management, technology, and capital to their banking sectors (a view I held while I was still at Treasury, before I joined such a bank myself). And some countries restricted the longer-term investment that could have been a stabilizing force, while encouraging short-term borrowing.

Moreover, there's a danger that arguments for opening financial markets slowly, or in stages, can become excuses for not opening them at all—since tight controls on capital flows are an easier political solution than fundamental financial system reform. I think history demonstrates that freer capital markets are conducive to a well-functioning modern economy, but they do need to be combined with appropriate regulatory systems and sufficiently strong financial institutions.

Although that is my basic orientation, I have some sympathy for those who argue that controls on the inflow, as opposed to the outflow, of short-term investments might sometimes make sense as a transitional device. Chile had some apparent success in reducing reliance on volatile funds through restrictions on the inflow of short-term capital, but it did not use controls to avoid reform. The central reasons for Chile's success were sound policies and a floating exchange rate.

I do believe that a significant share of blame for the crisis should go to private investors and creditors. They systematically underweighted the risks of investing in and lending to underdeveloped markets over a number of years, and consequently supplied capital greatly in excess of what would have been sound and sensible. And that excess capital, in time, fueled the extremes—overvalued exchange rates, unsound lending by domestic banks, and the rest—that led to the crisis. I remember one conversation I had with Anwar Ibrahim, the finance minister of Malaysia, who had a keen analytical mind and was highly regarded in international financial circles. Anwar ultimately had a falling-out with Prime Minister Mahathir and languishes in prison today. But just before that, Anwar said to me, "For every bad borrower, there's a bad lender." That comment crystallized the issue for me. In New York and Washington, the tendency was often to put all the blame on the policy mistakes of the borrowing countries. In Malaysia and elsewhere in Asia, the tendency was often to put all of it on First World lenders and investors. Anwar understood that the fault belonged on both sides—with economic management in developing countries and with creditors and investors who had poured money in while ignoring problems.

My own experience with financial markets gave Anwar's comment a special resonance. On Wall Street, I had often seen how excesses of optimism undermined sensible approaches to valuation and risk. I remember, at the time of the South Korea crisis, being struck in discussion with a prominent New York banker by how little he and his company knew about a country to which they had extended a considerable amount of credit. That conversation reinforced for me the notion that in extended good times, even major financial institutions can become less sound in their lending practices, making the same kind of mistake that traders and individual investors do. Though the basic hazard of investing in countries with major economic and political problems should have been obvious, the prevailing mentality was to downplay or ignore those risks in the "reach for yield."

Did the response make the crisis worse? Many people who shared the view that First World investors bore a significant share of the responsibility for what had happened in Asia were antagonistic toward the IMF for forcing "austerity" programs on developing countries. I think this criticism misses the point. The IMF—and we at Treasury in working with them—sometimes did make mistakes in the technical design and implementation of its programs. In the face of rapidly changing and in many ways unprecedented circumstances, it would be amazing if we hadn't. But by and large, the IMF got it right. What triggers an economic crisis is a loss of confidence. This results from underlying macroeconomic and structural problems as well as an often sudden reevaluation by domestic and foreign investors of the attractiveness of a country as a place to put savings. The cause of the hardship in crisis countries was not the IMF-backed programs but the crisis itself—the fact that capital was fleeing.

A common complaint was that the IMF's programs forced countries to tighten their fiscal and monetary policies, which sent their economies into a tailspin, when they should in fact have followed a Keynesian policy and tried to stimulate growth. A developed country might have sufficient credibility with credit markets to take stimulative measures to fight off recession. Unfortunately, a developing country gripped by financial panic and fleeing capital does not have the luxury of borrowing more or of cutting interest rates without worsening the panic.

In general, a restrained fiscal regime is required because investors dumping a country's bonds are likely to be further spooked by additional debt. The IMF believed that fiscal policy should be tighter to make room for more exports, without inflation, and to counteract the huge costs that would be incurred in cleaning up banking failures. But fiscal adjustment can be overdone, and in a subsequent reexamination the IMF has concluded that, in the Asian crisis, the initial recommended fiscal or budgetary policies were often more stringent than necessary. Officials at the Fund, and many other people, underestimated how much the crisis itself would cause these economies to contract. However, the Fund moved promptly to correct the excessive requirements and evidence is that this did not contribute significantly to the hardship. The economic impact of the fiscal tightening was dwarfed by the effect of capital outflows.

As to high interest rates, I don't think there was any ambiguity, although others disagree. Savers and investors would regain confidence and be willing to leave their money only in a country that would provide a reward for the risks involved and that was committed to fighting inflation. In the short term, higher interest rates did hurt indebted companies and banks. But they were essential for restoring financial stability, which in turn was required for recovery. Moreover, rates could be—and were— quickly brought down once confidence was reestablished. On the other hand, failing to tighten monetary policy during a crisis risked provoking more of a run. Deeper currency declines could, in turn, lead—in a worsening spiral—to higher inflation, more capital flight, and still further exchange rate decline. Either solution—higher interest rates or a weaker currency—can put a strain on indebted companies and banks. But with higher interest rates, the strain would be temporary if a government succeeded in reestablishing confidence. Treasury kept track throughout the crisis of how interest rates compared with pre-crisis levels. Surprisingly soon, the governments in South Korea and Thailand, which addressed their problems convincingly, were able to bring rates back down, even to below pre-crisis levels, and begin the process of recovery.

Critics who argued that "structural" reforms were intrusive and unwarranted said that passing financial market fashions were being treated as imperatives. But attending to the question of what factors were affecting confidence was not just a matter of following the whims of fickle investors. Markets may worry too much, but their worries generally tend to focus on serious issues. It was always difficult to determine which measures were truly needed to restore confidence and put the economy on a stronger path. If we sometimes erred on the side of excessive pressure for reform, that may have been wiser than erring on the other side and being ineffective. As Mexican President Ernesto Zedillo said, "Markets overshoot, so sometimes policies have to overshoot as well."

Finally, some people who argued against the IMF programs believed that a market panic fed on itself and the problem in many cases was primarily a lack of liquidity. I felt then—and feel even more firmly today—that this was an oversimplification. Experience showed that market confidence, and capital flows from foreign and domestic investors, tended to turn around only when governments implemented reform. Without that, continued and deepening outward flows could swamp whatever money the IMF and others might provide. On the other hand, the combination of official backing and strong reform embedded in the IMF-led approach was able to stem the crisis and eventually spur recovery.

Did the IMF-led "rescues" make future crises more likely? In Mexico, and again in the Asia-crisis countries, the IMF lent far greater amounts than was its usual practice. In a number of cases, the United States, other governments, and the World Bank lent additional funds on top of that. In capital account crises, where market psychology was often of critical importance, the firepower had to be sufficient to restore confidence. To some of our critics, these large loans only encouraged private creditors and investors to take more risks in emerging-market economies. While I had a lot of sympathy for moral-hazard concerns, I thought they were overplayed. I had never heard anyone say that they had been more inclined to invest in emerging-market economies because of the Mexican support program. Moreover, the surge of money into these markets was matched by a surge of money into a broad range of higher-yielding, riskier assets. In addition, those who argued for smaller IMF packages and greater "private-sector burden sharing"—which I agreed with to the extent feasible—were ignoring the enormous practical difficulties in managing a debt restructuring and the costs of allowing crises to widen.

Have we fixed the system for the future? At the same time as the IMF, we at Treasury, the Fed, and other governments were dealing with the crisis on a day-to-day basis, we became very focused on a longer-run effort to improve the workings of the global economy—what came to be called the "international financial architecture." We had begun the reform effort after the Mexico crisis at the 1995 G-7 summit in Halifax, Nova Scotia. But now this took on a new sense of urgency, and in 1998 it developed into a broad effort involving many countries, both industrialized countries and emerging markets. My view of what had caused the Asian crisis carried implications for both response and prevention. If borrowers and lenders are both at fault, why should the borrowing countries, and their much poorer people, bear the entire cost of repairing the damage? My view was that the burden should be shared to the greatest extent possible. This is an issue of fairness but, even leaving that aside, goes to the essential logic of capitalism. To allocate resources efficiently, a free-market system must allow people who take risks and lose to suffer accordingly, so that future decisions will have the best likelihood of being made with due concern for risk. Unfortunately, this theoretical framework did not provide an effective answer to many of the problems we faced in the muddled reality of the actual crisis.

Too often, well-meaning but simple and sweeping proposals for dramatic change in the system weren't congruent with the complex realities we faced. They often ignored market behavior and unintended consequences and tended to focus on only one aspect of crisis. Looked at most broadly, the system needed change that would work practically to strengthen emerging-market economies and make them less vulnerable, to promote better risk management among banks and financial institutions, whose poor judgment had first masked and then exaggerated the underlying weaknesses in many countries, and to improve the international community response to financial crises.

The first key to prevention is to reduce countries' vulnerability to crisis. There is no simple way to promote this, although a number of ideas were put forward. Some focused on tying future IMF and World Bank money to the adoption of good policies in advance. Others looked at new systems that would send an official signal about countries' policies—for example, some kind of red flag that the IMF should wave when it was concerned about a country. Neither type of scheme was practical. In a time of crisis, the IMF and its shareholder governments will always need flexibility, if only because of the risk of contagion. I thought that an IMF warning system simply wasn't sensible. Predicting what will happen to a country's financial circumstances is highly uncertain at best, and IMF warnings could precipitate crises that might otherwise not occur.

One decision we did make was to focus attention on the dangers of a fixed-exchange-rate system. Attempts to hold a currency fixed when economic fundamentals were not in line had led to trouble time and again. These situations were inherently unstable and provided a kind of one-way bet for market speculators, as a central bank would first defend a particular rate but then had to let the currency move sharply when its foreign exchange reserves were exhausted. Exchange rates that are allowed to fluctuate with market movements are less subject to such bets. More important, they allow countries' currencies and economies to adjust to outside shocks more gradually. In this case, we did call for the Fund to adopt a policy that prohibited lending to countries that maintain fixed exchange rates except under very unusual circumstances. Though that policy was not officially adopted at the IMF, the practical effect of the crisis, and of the general change in thinking that was taking place, was to eliminate almost all fixed-exchange-rate systems. By now, there are only a few economies left, such as those of China and Hong Kong, with the reserves and the policy determination to hold the pegs. And in the case of China, at least, this peg has become quite controversial, though for trade reasons, not financial stability reasons. My own view is that in time China will move to a more flexible exchange rate regime in its own interest. China has a large trade imbalance with the United States, but that's because so much of non-Japan Asia's exports to the United States pass through China. China's global trade surplus is relatively small and has been declining.

Another idea for improving country policies was to develop a catalogue of best practices in such areas as debt management, bankruptcy, public statistics including disclosure of levels of international reserves, deposit insurance, and bank supervision. U.K. chancellor of the exchequer Gordon Brown pressed particularly hard for codes and standards in these areas and some progress has been made. The question going forward is how to encourage countries to adopt these policies, with due allowance for differences in cultural, economic, and historical circumstances.

The crisis also showed how much countries need adequate social safety nets, such as unemployment insurance and programs for the poor, to mitigate the hardship of financial turmoil and to protect the most vulnerable from economic downturns. The World Bank has greatly stepped up its work in this area, both to develop understanding of the policies that are needed and to provide financing for countries to implement better social programs.

Since poor lending and investment decisions helped cause the crisis, it is important to search for ways to improve risk assessment and management by industrial-country creditors and lenders. Again, this is very hard to effect with official policy. But greater transparency—involving both information on the IMF's views and analysis of a country and data about that country's economic situation—could be helpful, and progress has been made. For example, today any country that hopes to attract foreign investment feels obligated to disclose data about its currency reserves and forward obligations. It would be close to impossible for a country to do what Thailand or South Korea or, earlier, Mexico did and hide its true reserve position. The IMF also now publishes information that countries provide about their adherence to the various codes and standards of best practice that have been developed, reinforcing the pressure to put such standards into place. Greater disclosure should reduce capital flows into riskier situations. This in turn should encourage countries to reform before a crisis occurs. At the same time, transparency on its own will not prevent Asian-type crises. The United States is generally regarded as having the most advanced transparency regime in the world, and it still experiences speculative excesses.

Perhaps the greatest challenge in improving financial architecture is finding more effective ways to induce investors and creditors to exercise discipline and focus appropriately on risk during good times. One key here is for creditors and investors to bear the consequences of their decisions to the greatest extent practical. Some pointed to the big losses that many lenders and investors had suffered on their emerging-market positions in the Asian crisis and argued that the lesson about risk had been learned. But I felt strongly—based on all of my own market experience—that the moral-hazard argument had not been adequately addressed, and I fully supported private-sector burden sharing conceptually. But it was no easy matter to allocate more of the burden to private-sector foreign lenders and less to the poor of the affected countries, without making the situation worse for the poor by scaring creditors off from the country in crisis or from other emerging-market countries. Also, there were often legal problems in doing this.

In South Korea, where most of the foreign debt was held by banks, private-sector involvement was feasible because banks could be involved in an organized fashion and came to see that their interest was to restructure the debt. But in Mexico, and later Russia and Brazil, where foreign debt was in the form of securities widely dispersed among individual investors and institutions, there was no practical mechanism to create a "bail-in." And the risk of provoking a wider pullback was much greater. This leads to another important rule of mine that Tim and his colleagues neglected to put on their list: number 12: *Reality is always more complex than concepts and models.*

In domestic markets, bankruptcy procedures serve the purpose of sorting out the allocation of losses in an orderly fashion and giving those who fail financially a chance to start over. The Federal Reserve and Treasury had explored this idea after the Mexico crisis in concert with the G-10 group of industrialized countries but had eventually concluded that it wasn't practical for a host of reasons, and that idea seems to have fallen by the wayside at least for now.

We also looked at the possibility of a "collective action" clause in bonds that would authorize some party to negotiate for bondholders in the event of default. This kind of binding arbitration would promote more cohesive action among creditors and could provide for private-sector burden sharing when there are thousands of bondholders. I always believed such clauses would be introduced when there was sufficient market pressure for them, and a number of emerging-market countries have issued new bonds with these clauses. Most important to me was that IMF programs should have the maximum practicable focus on private-sector burden sharing, and we pursued this where feasible, as in South Korea. Finally, I supported a new framework for IMF decisions that stressed burden sharing and laid out considerations to guide the Fund on a case-by-case basis, given the practical difficulties that made a rigid mandate infeasible.

The greater focus on private-sector burden sharing is just one of the changes that has taken place since the Asia crisis. In addition, as we had hoped, most countries have shifted to floating exchange rates and have become much more transparent, as have the IMF and the World Bank. The enormous leverage in the system that contributed to the Asia crisis spreading so rapidly has also been reduced, at least for now. This does not, however, warrant any degree of complacency. Financial crises have continued to rock emerging markets and are likely to remain a factor in the decades ahead. The international community must continue to try to improve its means of prevention and response.

FROM EARLY 1998, we faced the intensification of a long-simmering issue in Congress over support for the IMF. Even as the criticism of IMF actions in Asia increased, we had to go to Congress to ask for more funding for it. I had signed on to a routine replenishment of the IMF's resources in September 1997, at the annual meeting in Hong Kong, but fulfilling that agreement required congressional action. And now this money was urgently needed, in case still more countries fell victim to the spreading financial market contagion and had to borrow from an IMF that was beginning to face the possibility of running short of funds. The President's January budget asked Congress for an $18 billion contribution, our share of a $90 billion increase in the IMF's resources. Although the amount seemed large, it did not come at the expense of other programs. Our contribution to the Fund is more like a deposit at a credit union. We get an asset in exchange—a claim against the IMF—and we have never suffered a loss. But niceties of this kind were hard to explain in the heated atmosphere of the budget debate that year.

The debate over IMF funding was overwhelmed by another story that broke that January, the one concerning Monica Lewinsky. The Lewinsky revelations became the subject of a media firestorm that lasted through 1998 and resulted in far less attention being paid to events overseas. This disproportionate focus on the Lewinsky matter didn't make any difference to what we did in responding to the crisis. In another sense, though, it did real damage by crowding out media coverage of what was happening in

Asia. As a consequence, the American people didn't learn what they might have learned about the critically important issues raised by the crisis. The distraction kept the public from recognizing the threat from crisis abroad to the stability of the U.S. economy. Thus, when we most needed support from a well-informed public, that public was nowhere to be found.

The struggle over IMF funding was just one more example of how complicated the issues regarding our interdependence with the rest of the global economy are, how little they are understood by the American people, and how difficult dealing with international economic issues in our political system often is. I saw the IMF as a vital and necessary institution, in the front line of the fight to contain the spreading financial crisis. Although the international financial architecture needed to be modernized, I believed strongly that the IMF was critically important and should be strengthened through reform. Some of our critics thought we'd be better off having no IMF at all.

Talking about the need for these funds put us in a delicate situation of a familiar sort. We didn't want to say that the world would collapse if Congress didn't act—which might have helped to secure congressional support—because doing so might increase the level of distress in the global financial markets. On the other hand, there was a pressing problem, because in our view the IMF was in danger of running out of ammunition. Even if it had enough money to deal with the immediate problems, the Fund needed to have—and to be seen as having—the power to deal with new problems that might arise. By calling this into question, Congress's failure to act could itself contribute to the loss of confidence afflicting the markets. The IMF's other major shareholders, who viewed the increase in funding as a routine manner, had all already acted. By holding up the new funding, Congress was diminishing our leverage within the IMF, diminishing confidence in American leadership in Asia and elsewhere, harming our ability to exercise leadership in the crisis, and, most important, risking extending or deepening that crisis.

Some of the hostility we encountered in Congress recapitulated the opposition's arguments at the time of the Mexican rescue. But once again, the underlying substantive issues didn't quite explain the intensity of the opposition. This time it seemed to me that the reaction of many in Congress was exacerbated by irritation at their lack of input into our previous decisions about Thailand, South Korea, and Indonesia. With the IMF funding issue, members of Congress now had an outlet for doing something about their objections.

Politically, we confronted objections from both sides of the aisle. Some Democrats took the position that IMF programs were too hard on people in developing countries, who were already suffering from collapsing economies. Others complained that IMF programs didn't require nations to take steps to protect the environment, uphold labor standards, or respect human rights. A focal point for many of these issues was Indonesia. A number of liberal Democrats, such as Barney Frank of Massachusetts and David Bonior of Michigan, told us they wouldn't support IMF funding unless Suharto released an Indonesian labor leader named Muchtar Pakpahan, who was being held in prison. Bonior, the tough-minded House Democratic whip, who represented a district outside Detroit that is heavy with unionized autoworkers, argued that respecting the right to organize unions should be a condition of any country receiving IMF money.

My answer to Bonior—whose intellectual integrity and concern for the least well off was unquestionable—was that the test for getting IMF support should be doing what is needed to reestablish the fundamentals for economic growth and market confidence. Reestablishing stability was imperative for the very people Bonior was most concerned about, and trying to use the IMF to serve purposes other than effectively promoting economic recovery could impede those efforts. But for me personally, there was another point as well—one I didn't make to Bonior. Civil and political rights are at the core of America's identity and beliefs, and I think we should promote our values abroad through moral suasion, advocacy, and public exposure. But it seems to me there are complex conceptual and practical questions about *imposing* our values—however strongly we believe in them—on other people.

But I seldom said anything to question whether human rights should play a central role in our foreign policy. Once or twice I tried to raise the philosophical issue. For example, why are freedom of speech and due process universal values, but not the right to food and health care? And why is the United States in a morally superior position because of our adherence to human rights when we use only around 0.1 percent of our enormous prosperity to aid desperately poor people around the world? But if you did that, people would categorize you as someone who just didn't care about human rights. In fact, I care greatly about them and agreed with the administration's view that human rights goals could be better accomplished through engagement than imposition. That was our position in moving to replace the annual process of renewing China's trade status with what we called "permanent normal trade relations." China, in our view, would be more likely to change as part of the global community than if it were isolated, and that seems to me clearly right.

The practical complexity of the issue came out in my discussions with Bonior over Indonesia. David would say, "I don't think we should support corrupt governments that jail labor leaders."

And I would respond, "David, I agree in principle. If you had no other considerations, that would be the right issue to focus on. But the principled position you're taking is enormously detrimental to the interests of the Indonesian people."

Indonesian workers, I told him, would be far better off if their country got an IMF program, which would minimize the severity and duration of the financial crisis. If we took the position Bonior supported, by contrast, we'd be punishing the Indonesian people for the misdeeds of their leaders. What's more, the return of financial stability and growth to Indonesia would be conducive to the progress of labor rights and other issues that we as a nation cared about. Certainly, there were places where the United States could never support an IMF program because the regime's practices were so abhorrent to our values—Saddam Hussein's Iraq, apartheid-era South Africa, or Afghanistan under the Taliban, for example. Even in those cases, I find troubling the idea of punishing people who are already in dire straits because of government actions over which they have no control. But Suharto's Indonesia didn't fall into this extreme category.

There was another problem involved in making such stipulations. Once you tasked the IMF with worrying about issues that weren't directly related to reestablishing confidence, where would you stop? Bonior was focused on labor rights. Phil Gramm, the Republican senator from Texas, insisted that recipients of IMF programs should have no trade restrictions against the United States. We didn't disagree with Gramm's substantive view any more than we did with Bonior's. But putting conditions of this kind on the IMF would make working out programs with crisis countries more difficult and would make the IMF more intrusive. We also faced a political problem in having to deal with such issues simultaneously. Many measures proposed to satisfy Democrats would be opposed by Republicans—and vice versa. As one aide to House Majority Leader Dick Armey said at the time, Republicans weren't "going to vote for a bill that turns the IMF into a union-organizing institution." But Republicans wanted to attach conditions of their own. Some had to do with internal IMF reforms. Others, which had almost nothing to do with the IMF, drove Democrats crazy. Some conservatives wanted to use the legislation as a vehicle for what was known as the "Mexico City" language—a ban on funding for family-planning programs abroad that made mention of abortion.

This issue had derailed IMF funding in 1997, and even after we'd resolved most of these other issues just before the 1998 midterm elections, Newt Gingrich threatened to hold up the IMF bill if the antiabortion language wasn't included. Larry, Linda Robertson, our extraordinarily effective congressional liaison, and I all visited Gingrich in his office to argue that the two issues had nothing to do with one another. Newt responded that unconnected matters were often tied together in legislation. It was like the debt ceiling battle all over again; we argued that the IMF funding was too important to be drawn into a political battle over abortion. If IMF funding is so important, Newt said, you should give in on the Mexico City language. He was very friendly and completely unyielding.

In response to the opposition of the conservatives, many of whom saw the IMF as a kind of foreign aid, I made the same arguments over and over again. Our contribution to the IMF didn't cost us anything. Since we received a liquid, interest-bearing claim in exchange for our contribution, it wasn't a budgetary expense and didn't increase the deficit or divert resources from other areas. And, most important, it was enormously in our self-interest as a country to support the IMF. Even if one had no concern about what happened to people in the rest of the world—which clearly was not our view—one should still be in favor of IMF funding for the protection and benefit of the American people, since what happened else-where could so strongly affect our economic and national security inter-ests. Throughout the fifty-plus years that the IMF and World Bank have been in existence, successive administrations have concluded that the United States benefits from these institutions. Both Republican and Demo-cratic Presidents have fought for additional funding. But it is always an uphill battle.

In the end, we reached agreement on the multitrack negotiations with various members and constituencies. We asked all our G-7 partners to sign a letter that laid out their support for internal IMF reforms—including the greater transparency and openness that were being put in place—so that Congress could rightly say it was funding a new, improved IMF. We compromised on the Mexico City language, putting in a very lim-ited provision. Through quiet diplomacy, the IMF managed to secure Muchtar Pakpahan's release from prison, and we met some of the other Democrats' concerns as well.

But the larger factor that helped us was that, over time, the attitude of many legislators toward the crisis began to change. Some, such as Sena-tors Chuck Hagel of Nebraska, Paul Sarbanes of Maryland, and Chris Dodd of Connecticut, all serious internationalists in a difficult environ-ment, recognized early on that the United States had a powerful interest in combating the global crisis and that doing so would require a strong IMF. And as the financial turmoil continued, more and more members of Con-gress realized that the problem was serious and the danger to our own economy was real. No one wanted to be blamed for an economic derail-ment in the United States.

Another useful development was that a number of legislators came to recognize that specific interests in their districts—manufacturing, agri-culture, and other export-related industries—were suffering from the de-cline in Asia and might suffer a great deal more without the IMF. Most striking to me was the way the agricultural committees in the House and Senate turned into supporters, as the farm lobby drove home the effect of the crisis on farmers' exports.

An example of this phenomenon was what happened with Represen-tative Sonny Callahan of Alabama, a likable and powerful Republican on the House Appropriations Committee who had been on the other side of the issue for many months. At some point, Sonny decided to support IMF funding. It turned out that his constituency in southern Alabama included a big pulp mill. All of a sudden, this company was laying people off because its exports were being affected by the Asian crisis; one of its primary customers was a paper manufacturer in Indonesia. That drove home to Sonny more clearly than anything we could say that we now lived in a global economy where what happened to an institution like the IMF could matter to businesses and workers in Monroe County, Alabama.

CHAPTER TEN

Hitting Bottom

O N   T H E   S A M E   D A Y   in August 1998 that Russia became the first of the crisis countries to default on its foreign debt, the President testified before a grand jury and made a televised speech apologizing to the nation about Monica Lewinsky. On September 10, he convened a meeting of the cabinet in the White House residence to apologize for misleading us. After Clinton apologized and explained himself, others got a chance to speak.

I wasn't planning to say anything. But I thought to myself: *We're all human, and we all make mistakes—sometimes very large ones. And Clinton's mistakes should be seen in the context of his accomplishments.* I also thought that the whole issue—though certainly serious—had been disproportionately covered by the news media, with the result that other issues of great significance, including the momentous events in Indonesia and Russia, hadn't gotten enough attention.

After a while I finally raised my hand. "You know, Mr. President, there's no question you screwed up," I said. "But we all make mistakes, even big ones. In my opinion, the bigger issue is the disproportion of the media coverage and the hypocrisy of some of your critics."

I truly admired the way Clinton had dealt with the crisis—even though the crisis was of his own making. He was remarkably focused and intent, doing his work while the storm raged around him. Talking to the

President about Russia, you wouldn't have known he had anything else to worry about. He came to work every day and did his job as President. I remember one afternoon when he invited about fifty members of Congress—split evenly between Republicans and Democrats—to discuss Social Security reform. This was at a moment when the Lewinsky problems were at their height and Republicans were aggressively calling for impeachment. We all sat around the table at Blair House, and he led the discussion as if nothing else were going on in the world. It was a remarkable seminar on the many aspects of this issue. Even Clinton's demeanor was relaxed, engaged, and engaging—as much with Republicans trying to impeach him as with the Democrats who were supporting him.

Like everyone else, I wondered how the President could do this. Sometime later, we had an interesting conversation. We'd been discussing the Vice President's campaigning difficulties during the primaries, and Clinton told me that he had used "mental devices" to help him through the Lewinsky period. I didn't ask him specifically what those were, but he thought Gore might use similar techniques to overcome his difficulties and campaign more effectively.

Whether or not it might have helped Gore on the campaign trail, the notion of consciously adopting the right frame of mind did help my tennis game by reducing my tendency to hesitate and to be too tentative, something that impedes most amateur players. While playing, I kept in mind the thought that even a very good basketball player misses 55 percent of his shots. Even a fine tennis player makes a lot of errors; the object is to focus on hitting the shot as well as possible and not to worry about either the likelihood of messing up or the outcome of the point. When I told Steve Friedman that the Lewinsky matter had improved my tennis game, he waited with bated breath for what I had to say. He may have been somewhat disappointed by my explanation.

Did the Lewinsky scandal harm Clinton's second term on a substantive level? Some people argue that the administration missed opportunities as a result, particularly with regard to reform of the Social Security system. But my instinct is that Clinton could not have gotten more done, at least in this area, even if the scandal had never struck. We had begun to explore Social Security reform in 1997. When we floated one relatively modest change—revising the annual cost-of-living adjustment to better reflect inflation—we basically had our heads handed to us by Democrats in Congress and interest groups. Projections of a budget surplus had just materialized, and while they didn't at all solve Social Security's very serious long-term problems, they provided politicians with an easy way out. First, instead of reforms, they'd use the new surpluses to fund the Social Security deficits, and second, they'd put part of the Social Security trust fund into equities in the hope of earning greater returns.

Some might argue that Clinton should have gone to war with his own supporters on this issue or that he could have done so if he hadn't needed their support in the impeachment fight. But well before the scandal, we already felt stuck. If we put a proposal out that was dead on arrival, the reaction would not only require us to retreat but would also make ultimate progress on the issue more difficult. No one will ever know whether the politics might have worked out differently in a more normal environment, but my sense is that meaningful changes weren't viable independent of the impeachment issue. What is certain, however, is that the hangover from the Lewinsky matter did make Gore's job as a presidential candidate more difficult.

BY AUGUST 1998, we had been fighting to contain the Asian crisis for close to a year. But no sooner did one country's problems seem to be under control than pressures would erupt somewhere else. The most dramatic and final stage began in August 1998, when the Russian government defaulted on its debt, triggering what we'd feared all along and had come close to in December 1997 in South Korea. Markets around the world, including in the United States, were severely disrupted, and the world felt the threat of a truly global financial crisis.

Large IMF loans had been a key part of the crisis response. But those loans were provided only when matched by adequate policy reforms. The crisis countries had eventually put reforms in place, even though it took a while in Indonesia, enabling the IMF money to continue to flow. But in the case of Russia, the point came when the IMF had to say no.

Our concerns about Russia had been intensifying during the spring of 1998. The growing turmoil there reflected elements of most of the previous crises. The ruble exchange rate was linked to the dollar's. The government had a significant budget shortfall financed by issuing large amounts of short-term ruble-denominated bonds known as GKOs. Attracted by the promise of high yields and a boom mentality, foreign investors had bought these bonds aggressively. Though the post-Soviet economy clearly had enormous problems, investors had assumed that the IMF would step in to help during any emergency. Russia was, as the saying went in markets, "too nuclear to fail."

But as the psychology that had tripled the price level of the Russian stock market in a single year shifted, Russia found itself in terrible difficulty. Yields on Russia's debt skyrocketed, hitting 60 percent in May 1998. It became doubtful whether Russia could continue to roll over the GKOs, which were coming due at the rate of $1 billion per week, or meet the payments on other Russian bonds. Yet the country's political system seemed paralyzed, lacking the will or desire to take the kind of steps—such as collecting taxes, cutting government spending, and letting the ruble float—that would have helped to restore confidence. For us, Russia raised a new version of a by now familiar problem: What to do about a country that isn't prepared to participate adequately in its own rescue? And what if that country happens to be an unstable former superpower with thousands of nuclear warheads still pointed at you?

Larry and David Lipton had been deeply involved in trying to help Russia since 1993. Their hopes for an economic transformation had waxed and waned with the coming and going of reform-minded politicians within Boris Yeltsin's government. As Russia's economic situation deteriorated in the spring of 1998, such optimism as remained was closely tied to the figure of Anatoly Chubais, a deputy prime minister who had handled a series of major privatizations. Chubais, who spoke not only good English but the more arcane jargon of Western finance officials, visited Washington in May 1998 to push for a large new IMF support package. Larry and David felt that Chubais was an honest figure fighting to do the right thing in a corrupt environment. My only real sense from meeting him was that he was a shrewd operator with a considerable degree of Russian pride.

My view of Russia was considerably more pessimistic than David and Larry's—and the President's. Bill Clinton spoke to his friend Boris Yeltsin regularly and was very focused on trying to be helpful to Russia in whatever way possible. I fully recognized the importance of helping Russia but also felt that the country had poor economic policies and enormous problems. I didn't know a great deal about the subject, but my view had been colored by a few experiences I'd had before joining the government. In 1992, I had traveled to Moscow with Judy. The impression I formed on that trip was of pervasive corruption and economic disarray. I remembered some of the stories related by my friend Robert Strauss, who was then serving as the American ambassador. One in particular stuck in my mind, about a high Russian official who had been demanding enormous payments from American businessmen to allow routine transactions to go forward. Bob had solved the problem in a quiet meeting where he threatened public disclosure of this extortion.

I supported the $23 billion program for Russia that was announced by the IMF in July on strict probabilistic grounds. Larry and David agreed with me that the odds were against the program being successful, but the risks to the United States from destabilization in Russia seemed so enormous—from both economic and security standpoints—that going ahead made sense despite the relatively limited chance of success. I also accepted a point that Strobe Talbott, the State Department's chief Russia specialist, often made about the danger of further alienating the Russian public. Even if the chances of success were remote, just trying to be helpful to Russia's government could be valuable in this way. Supporting the reformers was also important, because failure to do so could strengthen the hand of reactionary political forces and endanger the prospects for change in Russia, a particular concern given its nuclear stockpile. (The issue wasn't so much whether the arsenal would be used but whether Russia would sell nuclear materials to Iran and other nations and whether Russian nuclear scientists would sell their expertise to countries hostile to the United States.) At that point, Boris Yeltsin was desperate for assistance, and all the emphasis within the Clinton administration was on trying to find a way to respond affirmatively. A small chance of success was worth a high risk of failure. And as usual with IMF programs, the money would not be disbursed all at once, leaving the option of withholding later drawings if policies went off track.

Something less than $5 billion of the total IMF loan was disbursed at the outset. But within a very short time, it became apparent that releasing additional money would be highly unlikely to confer an additional chance of success. The clearest sign was the Russian Duma's refusal, later in July, to support Yeltsin and Chubais on the issue of tax collection and other reform measures that were conditions of the IMF loans. Even though Yeltsin overrode the Duma unilaterally, I didn't think more money would raise the odds of Russia getting on the right track without a broader commitment from the Russian government.

At that point, both continuing the flow of IMF money and not continuing it had potentially very damaging effects, and those effects had to be weighed against each other. If Russia's economic deterioration led to the wrong people coming into power in Russia and blame was put on the IMF, the decision to cut off aid might later appear disastrously wrong. On the other hand, sending more money in the face of the Duma's defiance, in addition to almost surely being futile in terms of promoting recovery, would have undermined the credibility of the IMF in its efforts to apply conditionality elsewhere in the world and created an immense moral-hazard problem with respect to creditors. Investors were buying Russian bonds at tremendous yields in the expectation of being bailed out. Providing more money to Russia without imposing appropriate conditions could do serious harm by giving foreign investors and domestic oligarchs just enough breathing space to get their money out before a collapse. All of this raised the moral-hazard problem we'd been dealing with to a new dimension. An additional dimension of the debate was whether to also put up money from the Exchange Stabilization Fund. My own judgment was that, weighing these competing considerations, the better choice was to discontinue the IMF program and do nothing with the ESF.

One problem in this episode was that the people in the geopolitical sphere tended not to relate fully to the issues in the economic sphere, and vice versa. Even after the Duma vote, members of the Clinton foreign policy team were still very focused on trying to find a way to help Russia. Sandy Berger called a meeting in the White House Situation Room to persuade Treasury to agree to more support. Many people were on his side of the issue, including Secretary of Defense Bill Cohen, Madeleine Albright, and General Henry "Hugh" Shelton, chairman of the Joint Chiefs of Staff. They all argued for doing everything we could to help the Russian people and avoid the national security nightmare that could ensue if Russia disintegrated. After these officials made their comments, they turned to me and asked what I thought.

I said that in one sense they were right. We all wanted to support the forces of reform in Russia and avoid further alienation of the Russian people. But I also thought that the Duma's unwillingness to act meant that the odds of more money helping were close to nil, especially given the immense role of organized crime and corruption in the Russian economy. Then I turned to Steve Sestanovich, a Russia expert at the State Department who was sitting in back of me, and asked him if he disagreed. He said that some parts of Russia were more corrupt than others—which seemed to be a reluctant assent.

I also argued that providing money under these conditions would create an immense moral-hazard problem. I had lived in the markets, and I could feel people taking advantage of the situation. I knew that if I were running a trading operation, I'd be trying to make sure my firm profited from it. During all my time at Treasury, I was very conscious of market sensitivity and avoided discussing Treasury matters with friends in New York, many of whom still worked in the financial markets. Even by asking a question, a Secretary of the Treasury can indicate what's on his mind. But Treasury and Fed officials do need to understand what market participants are thinking, which requires listening carefully to what people are saying as well as monitoring what the markets are doing. In the midst of the Russia debate, a friend of mine on Wall Street told me that investors were assuming the United States wouldn't allow a Russian default. At the same time, David Lipton mentioned that earlier in the year he had heard investors refer to people buying Russian government bonds at 80 percent yields as a "moral-hazard play."

On the whole, the foreign policy and economic teams worked together well on Russia as on other issues. But at this meeting, there was a lot of pressure on us to proceed with less conditionality. I recognized the validity of the argument about the need to appear helpful even if additional support was exceedingly unlikely to do any good. But I believed very strongly that the risks on the other side were greater—so strongly that I felt that if they wanted to get another Treasury Secretary who would use the ESF, or who would try to force the IMF to act, that was fine with me.

But declining to provide more liquidity didn't mean giving up on encouraging Russia to take the steps that would allow the IMF to disburse more money. The IMF was in Russia, working very hard to persuade the Russians to implement the needed measures, and had warned the government in late July that if it did not act it would likely face the prospect of being forced into a default and devaluation as it ran out of reserves. On August 10, David Lipton flew to Moscow to try to give us at Treasury a direct sense of what was happening on the ground. He also conveyed to Russian officials the message that their country faced very dire consequences by not confronting the rapidly deteriorating situation, and that there would be no further disbursement of IMF funds unless its conditions were met. Russia's reserves were falling faster than most politicians knew, and the "burn" rate could accelerate dramatically if the government failed to take the necessary steps to reform and IMF talks failed. But David's sense was that no one in the government seemed to understand how precarious the situation was or to be too concerned about the loss of reserves. Many in the government simply opposed reforms without having any idea how dangerous the failure to take action could be.

On August 17, Russia announced that it was devaluing the ruble and defaulting on its foreign-held debt. The default triggered immediate consequences, not just for the Russian people but for financial markets around the globe, which became increasingly volatile. The moral-hazard problem that had preoccupied us, of course, diminished. A lot of investors paid a high price for their faulty assumptions about our willingness to provide support without Russia's meeting the appropriate conditions.

Several days after the default, I left for a vacation in a place that used to be Russia—Alaska, where I aspired to catch some fish. There I was, fly casting for silver salmon at a lodge a short plane ride away from Anchorage, with a Secret Service agent standing a few feet away. Silver salmon are much smaller than Atlantic salmon—they weigh eight or twelve pounds—but they're strong. You wade into the river or fish from the bank, wearing polarized lenses to reduce glare so you can spot the salmon under the water and cast to the fish you see.

Right at noon on my first day of fishing, the Secret Service agent, an enormous man named Kevin Gimblett, told me that Betty Currie, the President's secretary, was on the cell phone for me. He relayed the message that the President wanted to talk to me about Russia in an hour. Clinton, who was on vacation on Martha's Vineyard, was terribly concerned about the situation, and I'd been briefing him regularly. I assumed the President wanted to discuss the latest bad news, which was that the default had led to a suspension of ruble-dollar transactions and a run on the Russian banks.

"Kevin, I'll bet you that at five to one I get a fish on the line," I said. And sure enough, at 12:55, I hooked a big silver salmon. While I was wrestling with it, Kevin's phone rang.

So I said to Kevin, "Just tell the President that I'm someplace else and you'll have to go get me."

"I can't do that Mr. Secretary," Kevin said. "I'm a Secret Service agent." He had a point—it wouldn't look so great if he said he'd lost track of me someplace where I could be eaten by bears.

So I said, "Okay, just ask Betty if I can call the President back in a few minutes." And he did. I finished catching my fish, released it, and phoned the President to talk about Russia again.

RUSSIA'S DEFAULT USHERED in a period of grave danger for the global economy—and for the second time in less than a year (the first was when South Korea had stood on the brink of default), I was very worried about the threat to our own economy and financial markets. So was President Clinton. He had been deeply engaged in the Asian crisis from its beginnings in 1997, holding private discussions with leaders from the region as well as the heads of the other major economies. For some months, he'd been content for Treasury to take the lead on our public response.

But as the situation worsened in 1998, the President felt more and more strongly that he should speak out. In times of crisis, he said, leaders should be engaged with the public. Larry and I disagreed with this idea. We worried that we did not have a strong enough policy message for the President to communicate and that a presidential speech without concrete measures could be counterproductive for confidence. Clinton countered that engagement itself, even in the absence of definitive answers, could engender confidence—by showing a thoughtful understanding of the issues and providing a sensible discussion of possible approaches. As the crisis wore on, other world leaders began to take a similar view. They wanted to hold a joint meeting to emphasize their commitment to resolving the crisis. We all agreed that financial market disruptions tended to feed on themselves and that providing reassurance before the turmoil spread further was important, but the question was how and when to do so. The President felt strongly about his view and brought it up several times. Initially, he acceded—though reluctantly and somewhat irritably—to our suggestion to wait.

To the American public, the most visible spillover effect from Russia was a period of worrying instability and decline in the stock market. One day in late August, the Dow dropped 357 points, and by early September, the index was down nearly 20 percent from its summer peak. Our concerns went beyond what was happening in the stock market. The U.S. economy had stayed remarkably strong throughout the crisis, but we were unsure how long that could last. On September 4, Alan Greenspan captured our fears in a speech in Berkeley, California, when he warned that the United States could not remain an "oasis of prosperity" if the rest of the global economy continued to weaken. Financial markets, attuned to every nuance in the Fed chairman's carefully chosen words, understood the signal: short-term interest rates in the United States might be heading down.

The Fed had last moved the federal funds rate—which is the overnight lending rate between banks and the key rate the Fed directly controls—in

March 1997, tightening it a notch to fight inflation against the backdrop of a strong economy. In the eighteen months since, the official interest rates had been on hold and the market rates for government and corporate borrowing had broadly followed the Fed's lead. But developments in the bond markets now became extremely troubling. Bond traders like to talk about the "spread" between the yield on Treasury bonds, which are considered as close as you can come to absolutely safe investments, and the yields of various other bonds, from high-grade corporate debt to lower-grade, higher-yielding "junk" bonds and emerging-market debt. When the spread between Treasuries and other bonds widens, investors are demanding more of a "risk premium," i.e., a higher return for investments that aren't as secure. In the fall of 1998, investors were fleeing from risk. This was now affecting not just emerging-market debt but countries and companies around the world, including in the United States. As a result, companies had to pay more to borrow from the capital markets. At the beginning of the year, lower-grade corporate debt had been yielding only around 2.75 percent more than Treasury bonds with similar maturities. Now, eight months later, the spread over Treasuries was 6 percent.

If it lasted, this increase in the cost of longer-term credit would dampen the economy and undermine investment and jobs just as surely as a deliberate tightening by the Fed of the short-term interest rates it controlled. Moreover, credit wasn't just becoming more expensive. It was also getting harder and harder to obtain as both creditors and investors became less willing to take risks. Fed and Treasury officials focused on how to relieve these strains before a severe credit crunch took hold.

The easing signal from Greenspan helped somewhat. But a cut in U.S. interest rates alone seemed unlikely to quell the sense of a world in crisis. Now Larry and I agreed with President Clinton: we should try to elicit as powerful a statement as possible from the world community, and the President himself should deliver a message to the American people. Views had been crystallizing around steps to bolster the international response to the crisis. With the IMF quota increase still languishing in Congress, these included a new mechanism to speed provision of money from a group of individual countries, if needed, alongside that from the IMF. In the tight-knit circle of central bankers, the Fed was trying to convince colleagues in other countries of the need for an infusion of liquidity, with lower interest rates across the industrialized world. I remember Alan Greenspan saying, first privately, then publicly, that in watching markets for fifty years, he had never seen a set of circumstances like this.

At first, we had considerable difficulty convincing some of our major partners in Japan and Europe of the need to act. On the eve of his Berkeley speech, Alan Greenspan and I flew to the West Coast to meet the Japanese finance minister, Kiichi Miyazawa, whom Alan had known for many years, and Japan's central bank governor. We were troubled at how little Japan was doing to address its deepening malaise; one major bank had collapsed, and the situation seemed very fragile. Miyazawa, a very sensible man with a keen appreciation of Japan's problems, nevertheless seemed to view the meeting more as a negotiation about how we would refer publicly to Japan's economy than as a substantive exchange between the two major economic powers about a situation that was extremely threatening to both.

In Europe, officials had been focusing on preparation for the run-up to European monetary union and for the introduction of a new currency, the euro, to replace the national currencies of the union's member countries. Many also had qualms about the IMF's big financing packages and the effects of moral hazard on financial markets. It took days of intense discussions and negotiations to convince them that global recession was now a bigger threat than inflation or the moral hazard from IMF lending. Finally we were able to reach agreement on a carefully worded joint communiqué by the G-7 central bank governors and finance ministers. At the last minute, one central bank governor got cold feet and tried to back off the statement, but Alan Greenspan talked him into coming back on board. The communiqué said that the "balance of risks has shifted" on monetary policy, away from solely fighting inflation and toward the need to promote growth. Those five words—probably anodyne-sounding to most people—were a big deal in the global financial world and had a significant impact. Every war has its weapons, and when you're dealing with volatile financial markets and jittery investors, the subtleties of a carefully crafted communiqué—signed by the top financial authorities in the world's seven largest industrialized nations—can make a crucial differ-ence.

In the United States, President Clinton delivered a major address at the Council on Foreign Relations in New York. He made a broader case for U.S. leadership in resolving the crisis, and outlined a series of new proposals for doing so. As Clinton put it, continued turmoil in the emerging world could create a real risk to democracy, reducing support for democratic lib-erties as well as for free and open markets. Looking back, I think Clinton was right about the value of making a statement like this. In a period of high anxiety, leaders need to communicate with the public. If they convey a sensible understanding of the complexity of issues and discuss alterna-tive approaches thoughtfully, that in itself can have an impact on the psy-chology around a crisis. Gordon Brown, Britain's chancellor of the exchequer, strongly supported that view and skillfully orchestrated subse-quent joint public statements by heads of state as well as by finance min-isters and central bank governors. Though the sense of gloom persisted for several months, in retrospect I think this public engagement of and focus by major leaders on the global problems was an important step in eventually turning around the crisis.

ANOTHER BLOW to an already strained system came only days later. Russia's default had triggered a chain of events in financial markets that now threatened the solvency of a huge hedge fund in the United States, Long-Term Capital Management, whose failure many feared could signifi-cantly exacerbate the stresses on the U.S. markets. The weekend after the President's speech, I was at home in New York when Gary Gensler, then our assistant secretary for financial markets and a former partner at Goldman Sachs, called me. Gary said that LTCM, which had made enor-mous profits trading on the basis of mathematical models, was on the verge of collapse. Gary wanted to go out to the firm's headquarters in Connecticut with Peter Fisher, an official from the Federal Reserve Bank of New York, to investigate the situation. I told him to go ahead.

Gary called again on Sunday evening, September 20, to tell me what he had learned. LTCM had taken vast positions financed by billions of dollars in loans from major financial institutions—positions that would work out only if the financial markets calmed down and the spreads reverted to more normal relationships. Now LTCM was facing massive losses, and its imminent bankruptcy portended uncertain effects on the financial markets. My first reaction was to say to Gary, "I don't understand how someone like John Meriwether—who was thought of as such a sophisticated and experienced guy when he worked at Salomon Brothers—could get into this kind of trouble." Before founding LTCM, Meriwether had run a massive trading operation at Salomon and had done very well over a long period. He had some of the top minds in finance—Nobel Prize winners Robert Merton and Myron Scholes—working with him at LTCM. I was amazed that they had done what it seemed they had, betting the ranch on the basis of mathematical models, even ones built by such sophisticated people.

Models can be a useful way of looking at markets and can provide useful input to making decisions. But ultimately traders have to make judgments because reality is always far messier and more complicated than even the most sophisticated models can capture. In fact, LTCM's models may have been valid, over a long enough time frame. As a theoretical proposition, yield spreads probably would have returned to the mean, and I gather that many of LTCM's positions would have worked out in time. But LTCM was essentially betting that a return to normal would come without some prior highly aberrational move. The unusually high degree of leverage LTCM employed meant that the firm lacked the staying power to weather severe temporary aberrations. Creditors would require additional margin as spreads moved against LTCM. LTCM's forecasts might be vindicated long after it had gone broke.

I remembered this kind of situation well from 1986, when Steve Friedman and I had taken over responsibility for the fixed-income division at Goldman Sachs. As in the LTCM case, the problem then wasn't just that one company had a set of bad positions. Traders at other firms had similar kinds of positions, because they all used similar models and similar historical data. When positions began to move against them, they all wanted out at the same time, exacerbating the movement. And since the major players already had these positions, there were no buyers. That meant that traders and investors had to unload other, better investments to obtain cash. This selling skewed the ordinary relationships and patterns that traders expected. Bond spreads that according to historical norms should have contracted instead got wider, and spreads that should have widened got narrower.

Everyone who had similar positions lost money. But LTCM was faced with massive losses that threatened to become much larger than the remaining capital the firm held. The immediate public policy question this raised was what kind of harm a forced liquidation of LTCM's assets could do. In normal circumstances, governments shouldn't worry about the tribulations of any particular firm or corporation. But if a situation threatens the financial system, some kind of government action might be the best among bad choices. No one wanted to rescue LTCM's partners or investors. But there was a concern that liquidating such large positions could lead to a general unraveling of the markets. With the hedge fund's creditors—Chase, Citigroup, Goldman Sachs, Bear Stearns, Morgan Stanley, Merrill Lynch, and many others—all selling into the same decline, the entire financial system could freeze up, with a spillover into the real economy as confidence was damaged and businesses and consumers found credit less available and more expensive.

The ideal solution would have been for LTCM's creditors to agree to extend their loans on terms that might be somewhat harmful to each of them but less harmful to all than a default—as in South Korea. But doing anything to promote this kind of agreement raised tricky problems. The Fed regulates financial institutions and wouldn't want to be seen as coercing the lenders to act. Yet without some outside pressure, LTCM's creditors would almost surely not come together in their own self-interest. The banks collectively would benefit from working out an agreement that would prevent LTCM from going into default. But each of the banks stood to benefit even more by free riding on whatever agreement was reached—that is, by pulling out at full value while the others made some sacrifice to keep LTCM intact.

New York Federal Reserve president Bill McDonough convened the heads of the big investment and commercial banks at the Fed's New York headquarters. He walked a fine line, calling the CEOs of the country's biggest banks in but then leaving the room so they could work out the details on their own. After a lot of jockeying, fourteen different institutions agreed to provide a total of nearly $4 billion in additional credit to LTCM, with strict terms attached. This capital infusion gave the hedge fund breathing room to liquidate its positions in a more orderly fashion. Although I did not share the view that a collapse of LTCM was likely to lead to systemic disruptions, I thought the concerns—and Bill's actions—were sensible and appropriate, given the general market and economic duress at the time.

The broader public policy question arising out of the LTCM mess was whether anything could be done to reduce the probability and severity of this kind of event in the future. This was a frequent topic of discussion among Larry, Alan, and me, with some of the discussion taking place in meetings of the Financial Markets Working Group, which also included Bill McDonough; SEC chairman Arthur Levitt; Brooksley Born, the chair of the Commodity Futures Trading Commission; the heads of the other principal financial market regulatory bodies; and Gene Sperling from the NEC. Some members of this group thought that derivatives—instruments such as options, futures, and forwards whose value depends on the performance of an underlying security, currency, or commodity and whose value can change in complicated ways that is hard for even experienced traders to anticipate—by their nature could pose a systemic risk. Others thought the unrestricted leverage available to hedge funds such as LTCM was a problem. Some thought neither was a problem.

I thought both derivatives and leverage could pose problems. I had been involved with derivatives from the pioneering days of the founding of the Chicago Board Options Exchange. Derivatives serve a useful purpose by providing a means to manage risk more effectively and precisely, but they can create additional problems when the system is stressed. One way to contain those risks is by limiting the permissible leverage of buyers and sellers of derivatives. If you think periodic market excesses are inevitable because human nature is likely to lead to excess, you should try at least to limit the damage to the system. Capital requirements and margin requirements—both leverage limits—help to do that, both by decreasing the size of positions and by increasing the amount of money backing each position.

Larry thought I was overly concerned with the risks of derivatives. His argument was characteristic of many students of markets, who argue that derivatives serve an important purpose in allocating risk by letting each person take as much of whatever kind of risk he wants. That is right in principle, but it is not the whole story. Throughout my career, I had seen situations where derivatives put additional pressure on volatile markets (for example, through the additional selling in the stock market that can occur when portfolio managers sell calls to arbitrageurs, who in turn hedge by shorting stock against the calls for protection as the market falls). I also thought that many people who used derivatives didn't fully understand the risks they were taking—the situation we had found ourselves in at Goldman in 1986. Larry's position held together under normal circumstances but seemed to me not to take into account what might happen under extraordinary circumstances. Of course, Larry thought I just wanted to keep markets the way they were when I'd learned the arbitrage business in the 1960s—his point about "playing tennis with wooden racquets" again.

THE ASIA CONTAGION finally hit Latin America in late summer 1998, adding to the sense of gloom during the darkest period of the crisis. In September, people began to talk about Brazil, the world's eighth-largest economy, the way they'd been speaking about Russia a few months earlier. Brazil had a fixed currency, large current account and budget deficits, a great deal of short-term debt coming due, and an impending presidential election. The turmoil in the bond market, exacerbated by Russia and LTCM, was making it difficult and expensive for Brazil to roll over its debt. Underlying worries about debt sustainability and fiscal control in the country's provinces—problems that had been present for some time— now came to the fore. Foreign banks started to reduce their lines of credit, and foreign investment slowed to a trickle. The central bank's once very large foreign currency reserves were being depleted rapidly as the government clung to an exchange rate fixed against the dollar. Market rumors began to fly that Brazil was on the verge of defaulting on its debts, devaluing, or both.

With financial markets under great strain worldwide, we were fearful that either event could have severe consequences for the global economy. The IMF, U.S. Treasury, and Federal Reserve and other major countries began to work intensively on putting together a convincing rescue package. The stakes were high enough to warrant putting U.S. government money at risk alongside that of the IMF, provided the IMF could reach agreement with Brazil on a workable reform program.

Unlike in Russia, we had considerable confidence in Brazil's commitment to reform. Under the leadership of President Fernando Cardoso, Brazil's historic hyperinflation problem—the subject of my senior thesis in college—seemed finally to have been solved. The nation, which accounted for around 45 percent of South America's GDP, had taken important steps toward implementing sound macroeconomic policies since recovering from the debt crisis of the 1980s and had a political leader prepared to call upon his people to support measures that, while difficult in the short term, were necessary for stability and growth. Cardoso's highly capable and experienced economic team—headed by Finance Minister Pedro Malan—recognized that the alternative would have been even worse.

But there was one enormous issue in dispute: the country's exchange rate policy. President Cardoso adopted some significant reforms that made sense in light of Brazil's fiscal deficit, such as cutting spending and raising taxes. But the Brazilians were unwilling to devalue the real. Cardoso had been elected in 1994 largely on the promise of his Plan Real, which had fixed Brazil's currency to the U.S. dollar and, by so doing, had succeeded in taming a 2,700 percent annual inflation rate. Brazilian policy makers had a deep-seated and understandable fear of their economy's historical demon and felt that going to a float risked reviving inflation. But we thought floating the real—which was significantly overvalued—could prove essential to making an IMF program work. This left us with the unhappy choice between proceeding with a huge IMF program in a situation where the odds seemed unfavorable or trying to force a devaluation by refusing to lend unless Brazil agreed to a floating exchange rate. I thought there was only a fifty-fifty chance, at best, of an IMF support program working with a fixed, overvalued currency. But we were hesitant to push the issue too hard, because the inflation problem was genuine and Cardoso and his team could be right that letting the real decline would tip Brazil back into an inflationary spiral.

As with Russia, Indonesia, and South Korea, some in the U.S. administration thought a robust IMF program, backed by money from the ESF, should settle the problem. If Brazil had X billion in reserves and Y billion in loans coming due, a Z billion program should cover it. But there's one other number that is incalculable and can swamp all those other numbers in the calculation: the size of potential domestic capital flight. For some reason, most discussions of the subject ignore what can be the largest issue in crisis recovery. If Brazilians started losing confidence in the country's currency and converted their reals to dollars, then the potential would exist for vast additional outflows.

But proceeding with a loan to Brazil that fall was nonetheless compelling, even without the devaluation and despite the unfavorable odds. In Russia, concerns about politics and nuclear weapons had been the key. In the case of Brazil, the external environment tipped the balance. The fragility of the global economy was so great that I believed that a program was worth trying. Even buying only a few months of breathing room could be enough to get through a dangerous period of financial market strain. And demanding that Brazil float the real in the fall of 1998 in the face of the continuing instability in world markets could be very risky. A disorderly currency devaluation in Brazil could lead to additional currency disruption and contagion elsewhere, and Brazil could go into a deeper crisis. After Asia, Russia, and LTCM, and in an already fragile environment, another such shock to the system could lead to a true global meltdown.

To me, there was never a real question about whether or not to help Brazil, although the decision to go ahead without floating the exchange rate was a hard one. I remember sitting at a meeting in Larry's office and thinking to myself that this was another choice among bad options: *The odds aren't in our favor. But even if it fails, it could still be the right decision. While the chances of success are small, the risks of inaction are enormous. And even if we fail to save Brazil, we can probably defer the impact of the collapse for six or eight months, and that will more than justify the effort.* I did not believe these arguments would forestall criticism. If the Brazilian program failed, nobody was going to look at the quality of the decision or the benefit of deferral. They were just going say: you took a whole bunch of the American people's money and threw it down the drain.

I remember this as another case where Clinton's understanding and intuition were rather extraordinary. Larry and I had gone to the Oval Office and laid out our case for supporting an IMF program and putting U.S. money on the line alongside the IMF funds, not just as a backup option. We had persuaded other major governments to do the same. Clinton agreed that we should go ahead. But then he said, "You know, I felt very good about the Mexico program. I had a feeling it was going to work. I don't feel as good about this one working. It just seems chancier to me."

The large IMF program did help Brazil for a while, during November and December. But then the instability returned with a vengeance in January 1999, when Brazil did not follow through on some of its planned fiscal actions, monetary policy was loosened prematurely, and Brazil's second-largest state refused to make debt payments that were due to the central government. Brazil's deteriorating fiscal position sent investors running for the exits once again, further diminishing the government's foreign reserves. With the coffers emptying, the central bank governor resigned. Brazil tried, as Mexico had, to modify its exchange rate policy in a staged way that didn't work. A controlled devaluation seldom, if ever, works once trouble has begun—and didn't in this situation, collapsing after only two days. The real plunged dramatically, losing 10 percent of its value in a day and more than 30 percent by the end of January. In less than three weeks, the new central bank governor was also out.

But by then the global environment was much better and the financial markets took the renewed problems in Brazil in stride. In that important sense, our bet paid off; by that point, the Fed had cut interest rates three times and the monetary easing had contributed greatly to calming financial markets. Finally letting the exchange rate go also proved a turning point for the Brazilian economy. The Brazilians' fear that a floating exchange rate would bring back inflation turned out not to be realized. This had a lot to do with Cardoso and Malan's choice of Arminio Fraga, a respected economist and experienced market trader, who arrived as central bank governor at the beginning of February. Fraga moved quickly to raise interest rates and make the central bank more credible.

In line with a growing international focus on involving the private sector—a particular concern for our European colleagues who had put their own government money forward for Brazil—the IMF and G-7 had been searching for ways to "bail in" foreign banks. By this time, global capital markets had calmed sufficiently that we weren't as concerned about prompting creditors to pull back from risk, whether in the United States or in other emerging markets. In a meeting in the New York Fed's office, Brazil's major U.S. bank creditors agreed to extend Brazil's credit while the IMF agreed to release additional support funds. A short time later, the worst of the crisis seemed to be over in Latin America and there were reassuring signs of a healthier economy around the globe.

BY APRIL, conditions really seemed to be getting better. In the United States, financial markets were operating normally again and the sense of fear had abated. This owed much to the Fed's swift action to provide liquidity and cut interest rates. Brazil was able to borrow in private capital markets again. Its economy actually grew in 1999, and inflation was in check. South Korea was making early repayments on its IMF loans and was also able to borrow privately. Other Asian countries were returning to a growth path.

The pattern of recovery, though different in every country, seemed to me to validate the international community's response to the crisis. Across the board, the switch to floating exchange rates, although initially painful, was now providing a basis for recovery as a surge in exports led the crisis countries back to growth. In Thailand, South Korea, and Brazil—countries that had taken ownership of the broader array of reforms—confidence was returning and substantial foreign reserves were building up. The combination of international loans and policy reform had been effective. For others, notably Indonesia and Russia, the picture was more mixed. Exchange rate declines were helping them to become more competitive and less reliant on foreign capital. But continued confusion about the direction of policy and how their debt difficulties would be worked out cast a shadow. Investors, both domestic and foreign, would be reluctant to put their money at risk until these uncertainties were resolved.

Looking back, I feel even more strongly that our approach to combating the crisis made sense. Cooperation and engagement between the IMF and World Bank with the United States and other governments helped to reverse the financial turmoil in countries that took appropriate actions. These efforts led to great improvements in economic fundamentals and growth prospects in developing countries and helped avoid a more severe global crisis that could have greatly affected the industrial countries.

That doesn't mean that even the "success stories" came out of the crisis with their problems resolved. As the sense of crisis abated, the politics of economic reform in many of those countries once again became more difficult. And the closer one looked, the clearer it became that no economy in the world had perfect policies. There was something too neat about the way many people tried to explain the faults of those countries that ran into serious trouble. No matter how sound economic policy and practices may appear, every economy falls far short of perfection—including our own.

I remember something Caroline Atkinson said about this in one of our team's many meetings. We had the whole crowd around a conference table during the Brazilian phase of the crisis. Someone was saying that Brazil had all of these strong policies and that ought to make it easier for an IMF program to work. In economic terms, it was a "good" country.

And Caroline jumped in and said, "Yeah. And if they go into default, then we'll say they were hopeless all along and look at all their horrible mistakes and bad policies." That was an insightful comment. Every country has various unsound policies and structural problems, as well as various advantages. If the United States faced some kind of economic crisis, people would point to a whole host of problems as the reasons—our low savings rate, our large trade deficit, our high levels of consumer and corporate debt, and today I would add the deeply troubled long-term fiscal situation.

While many—particularly in the financial community—seemed to believe that financial crises were solely a function of the structural and policy problems of developing countries, I believed that the excesses of credit and investment in good times were also to blame. As Anwar noted, every bad loan had a creditor as well as a borrower. The tendency to go to financial excess seems to stem from something inherent in human nature, as does the remarkable failure to draw lessons from past experience. The collapse of the southwest real estate bubble in the United States didn't prevent investors from overinvesting in Asia. The Asian crisis didn't prevent the NASDAQ bubble from developing. The proclivity to go to excess is a phenomenon of collective psychology that seems to repeat itself again and again.

I was surprised, nonetheless, by how rapidly the crisis mentality vanished. People can forget the lessons of a painful experience very quickly, and that can lead to poor decisions. An illustration is what happened when South Korea was first able to borrow again in private markets. This was a massive step forward for the country. Borrowing privately at a reasonable rate of interest would create confidence in South Korea's postcrisis economy, underscore the credibility of the policy direction the country was pursuing under Kim Dae-jung, and promote growth.

A new South Korean finance minister was stopping in Washington on his way to New York to sign a new loan agreement. But before he came to visit us at the Treasury, our people told me that the minister wasn't going to go ahead with the loan after all because their investment bankers told him it was going to cost 25 basis points—or one quarter of 1 percent—more than he had expected.

"You've got to be kidding," I said. Here was a country that a year earlier had been on the verge of a default that could have had vast, even calamitous consequences. And now the government wasn't going to raise money when it could because of 25 basis points? Perhaps he was under political pressure from home not to pay more than someone's idea of the right price—but I still almost didn't believe it. The chance for South Korea to reestablish itself with global financial markets through this bond issue was worth vastly more than 25 basis points.

The finance minister came in with his interpreters, and they all sat down at the table in my conference room. We started talking, and I said,

"I understand you're going to raise this money and there's a little problem because you think it's twenty-five basis points too high. What difference are twenty-five basis points, or one hundred basis points, when reestablishing yourself is so important?"

The finance minister said, well, 25 basis points are 25 basis points. We shouldn't have to pay so much. I told him I'd been around markets a long time and my advice was to take the money while they could get it—circumstances can change very quickly in markets. If the issue went well, South Korea could borrow more and probably would see some rate improvement. But pulling out could raise doubts again in investors' minds. But our debate continued, and after a while I began to lose my patience a bit. "You know something?" I said. "I don't really care what you do. It's your country, not mine." Everyone in the meeting looked at me as if I'd taken leave of my senses. And perhaps I had, momentarily. South Korea's government and the South Korean people had done a remarkable job. But I was reacting to the spectacle of intelligent people behaving shortsightedly with respect to financial markets. I'd seen this kind of behavior many times at Goldman Sachs, on the part of both traders and clients. Someone who has gotten into trouble is offered what might be a brief opportunity to escape. And often the person's response is to forget the mess of a few days earlier and resume quibbling over a quarter point.

By the summer of 1999, I'd been in Washington for six and a half years, and I was ready to leave. Sandy Berger once said about working in government that as time goes on, the positives provide less reinforcement and the negatives feel more onerous. For me, the lines had clearly crossed. I felt I wanted to be free of the weight I'd been carrying. And now, with the impeachment battle finished and the Asian crisis ebbing, there was a moment when I could go. I wasn't abandoning a President under fire. And should new economic problems develop, the administration would have strong leadership with Larry at Treasury and Gene in the White House. I wasn't going to press my luck holding out for another quarter point.

As for the Asian crisis, critics argued that a categorical position of one kind or another would have worked better than our pragmatic approach to restoring confidence and addressing policy problems. But these conceptual views, which often came with important insights, didn't take into account all the complexities of responding to an actual crisis. Dealing with crises was messy because the reality was messy. At one point, aiding Russia made sense. At a later stage, it didn't. As much as one might have wished for one, there was no categorical response or absolutist position that could definitively solve these problems. In hindsight, there were some elements of the programs that could have been done better. But, having said that, the people of these countries were far better off as a result of our engagement than they would have been otherwise. Dwelling on the mistakes tends to obscure the larger point, which is that a market-based approach—of IMF loans combined with essential reforms—led to relatively rapid recovery in countries that took a reasonable degree of ownership of reform and avoided the real risk of much more severe global disruption. Perhaps the best testimonial to the market-based approach—as opposed to trying to solve these problems through additional regulation, capital market controls, and trade restrictions—comes from decisions taken by emerging-market governments themselves, including some with an electoral mandate from the disadvantaged in their societies. Both Kim Dae-jung in South Korea and, more recently, President Luiz Inácio Lula da Silva in Brazil had come to power on populist platforms. Both chose to embrace global integration and policy regimes designed to engender market confidence as a part of fulfilling their mandates to reduce poverty and raise living standards.

At the same time, the entire Asia experience left me with the view that future financial crises are almost surely inevitable and could be even more severe. The markets are getting bigger, information is moving faster, flows are larger, and trade and capital markets have continued to integrate. So it's imperative to focus on how to minimize the frequency and severity of such crises and how best to respond if and when they do occur. It's also important to point out that no one can predict in what area—real estate, emerging markets, or wherever else—the next crisis will occur. I remember something John Whitehead said to me at Goldman Sachs at the time of the Penn Central bankruptcy. "Now we'll put in all sorts of new processes to deal with commercial paper," he said. "But the next crisis will come from a direction nobody is focused on now."

The global economic crisis also left me deeply concerned about the politics of globalization. For many people, the Asia crisis highlighted the potential hazards and shortcomings of globalization for the first time. These problems appear against the backdrop of benefits that on balance are far greater but are often inadequately recognized. In the midst of the Asia crisis, Congress failed to renew President Clinton's fast-track authority to negotiate international trade agreements. As I prepared to leave Washington—some months before protestors took to the streets in Seattle to demonstrate against the World Trade Organization—I could already see that maintaining support for market-based policies and trade liberalization was becoming a far greater political problem around the world.

Sometime later, sitting at my breakfast table in New York, I read some comments in the paper by President Bush's newly appointed Treasury Secretary, Paul O'Neill. O'Neill was highly critical of the way we'd handled the Asia crisis. He called me the "chief of the fire department" and said that our theory of interconnected markets was a passing fashion that needed to be retired like the "hula hoop." O'Neill's view of crisis response was that the new administration could avoid the moral-hazard problem simply by letting poorly managed emerging-market economies fail.

I liked Paul. I didn't even mind him calling me the chief of the fire department. But as I read the story, I said to myself: *They say they won't intervene. But they will.*

And they did. When Turkey erupted in early 2001, the Bush administration got involved because of the country's strategic importance. When Argentina got into trouble that same year, the administration supported another large IMF program, before refusing to do so again at the end of 2001. The following year, it provided direct U.S. money through the Exchange Stabilization Fund to Uruguay and supported a very large IMF program in Brazil. Whether the administration was philosophically in favor of support programs or against them, it was bound to end up doing them, because U.S. self-interest was so much involved, geopolitically and economically. A lot of people begin their analysis with a priori constructs. But the orderly view from one's armchair is not the perspective you have when you're facing the messy reality of a global financial crisis.

CHAPTER ELEVEN

Politics and Business

STEPPING DOWN AS Treasury Secretary was a process that needed to be managed. Though the global economic crisis was on the wane by the spring of 1999 and the impeachment battle was over, there was still much to be concerned about—both in relation to the world I was leaving behind and the one I was thinking of going back to.

Having Larry Summers as my designated successor took care of the biggest problem. More than any other single person, Larry had driven the substance of the U.S. policy response to the Asia crisis. Many people both inside and outside the administration recognized the intellectual leadership he had provided. But Larry wasn't just a rigorous and insightful thinker. As a manager, he had come a long way. I was comfortable with his readiness for the job and his capacity to deal with others in the administration, Congress, the business community, and the financial markets.

I remember once being in the chief of staff's office and being handed a sheet of budget numbers. Larry and I both went to work on them, circling some, scribbling question marks next to others, making rough calculations in the margins. Larry said to me afterward that people react to sheets of figures in two ways. Some people look at them, take them as a given, and go on from there. Others look at numbers and start to question them, looking for inconsistencies, asking what they mean and what stories they tell, wondering about the relationships between them. Larry and

I shared that kind of disposition, not just toward numbers but toward all sorts of supposed certainties. As different as we were in many ways, we shared a cast of mind that made us highly compatible as colleagues.

I was confident about the rest of the economic team I'd be leaving behind as well. Gene Sperling was now in my old job at the NEC. Gene had developed over the years a great seriousness of purpose around the issues we faced: fiscal discipline, trade liberalization, engaging with economic crises internationally, and the whole set of issues concerning education and the inner cities. In the second term, Gene put together highly substantive, effective processes around such issues as Social Security reform and the emerging budget surplus.

And that was emblematic of a larger point. First under the strong leadership of Laura Tyson—who was insightful and always told the President what she thought—and then of Gene, the NEC had remained at the center of economic policy making for six and a half years, providing an honest-broker process for almost all economic issues, which augured well for the future. Responses to international financial crises were handled differently, with Treasury in the lead, but even there the NEC and NSC brought the relevant cabinet agencies and White House staff together to consider the large policy choices. A simple vignette illustrates how well this vision of President-elect Bill Clinton had worked out. At one point in the second term, there was some internal disagreement over how to respond to strong pressure for increased barriers to steel imports. Madeleine Albright and I were so strongly opposed to increasing barriers that we wanted to send a joint memo to the President. On the other hand, Gene and I agreed that could undermine the NEC process and would give the President only one point of view. So, instead, Gene ran an expedited NEC process, submitted a memo to the President with the arguments on both sides, and attached memos from the cabinet members who wished to express their views themselves. By taking good process seriously, the President was given the material to make a fully informed decision, in the context of a fair process that best promoted buy-in.

As to my departure, my most immediate concern was how to handle it. I was leaving because I felt ready to go after six and a half years and I didn't want anyone to think it was because of differences of opinion inside the administration or problems of some other sort. Market participants needed to be comfortable with my successor and the economic team. A particular concern was one Gene had raised with me: some people might interpret my departure as meaning that Clinton was essentially done with economic policy—either because there were no major issues still facing us or because the President couldn't do anything politically with a Republican Congress during his last year and a half in office. I was also anxious to avoid becoming a lame duck during the period between my announcement and my departure—which I'd seen happen repeatedly in corporate settings, when a CEO announces his resignation in advance of actually stepping down. Part of the challenge was to figure out ways to talk publicly about my departure that met these various needs.

In a high-level business job, stepping down can create many problems that have to be managed, but a cabinet-level departure in Washington is even more complicated, with possible ramifications one wouldn't face in the private sector. I thought about my departure as yet another process that needed to be managed thoughtfully. To create a seamless transition, I needed a savvy adviser. So I asked Tom Donilon, a former assistant secretary of state and a political pro I'd known since the Mondale campaign, to come over to talk to me in confidence about my announcement and how to manage what was likely to be a five- or six-week period between it and Larry's Senate confirmation. Talking to Tom, I made pages and pages of notes about what I was going to say internally, what I was going to say externally, whom I was going to speak to, when I was going to speak to them, what the hard questions would be, and so forth. I tried to anticipate every difficulty.

The first thing Tom told me was to quit worrying about the lame-duck issue. "This kind of departure is different," he told me. "Until you leave, you are Secretary of the Treasury. You won't be a lame duck, because the outside world will continue to view you as having the authority of that position until the day you step down." In fact, I was more concerned about my informal role sitting around the NEC table or the chief of staff's table, where your influence doesn't depend merely on the authority vested in your office. But here, too, Tom felt I wasn't going to have a problem, possibly because I had been in the administration since the beginning, had a well-established role in fact as well as in title, and retained the authority of my cabinet position until I left. And Donilon was right. In this and all other respects, my departure and Larry's assumption of the job went as smoothly as I could have hoped.

The other major issue I faced was what to do next. To help myself think through the issues, I took a yellow pad and began to write down questions for myself: What do I want to be doing with my time after I leave? Do I care about being in the financial world again? About remaining involved in public policy? About being involved in Democratic politics? About making money?

During my six and a half years in Washington, I had remained focused on markets, but from the outside. I was concerned that despite the many years I'd spent on Wall Street, I might have lost some of the feel for markets that comes from working in New York. To answer the question of what to do next, I needed to wander around Wall Street a bit and speak to people more candidly than was possible as Treasury Secretary. The financial environment had clearly changed since 1992 and, before I could make an informed decision about my own future, I needed to have a better sense of what was going on. I also had to decide where to put my personal assets. During my time in Washington, my assets had been in a blind trust. A friend who served in the Nixon administration told me that he had lost half of his net worth under such an arrangement. Not wanting to lose what I had and not being able to play any role in choosing investments or even in protecting myself if I became uneasy about the market, I had directed my trustee to invest very conservatively. But now that I could be personally involved in the markets again, I faced the question of whether I should invest more aggressively. In many ways, my career and personal financial issues were linked. Only by reimmersing myself in the financial world in New York and fleshing out my view of markets could I determine whether I wanted to participate in them at any level.

Back in New York during the summer of 1999, I set up shop at the Council on Foreign Relations, which had offered to take me in during my transition out of government. I spent the next several months in a garret-like office with a view over the backs of East Side town houses. Using that pleasant attic space as my temporary base, I visited with all sorts of people I'd known over the years—from hedge fund managers, private equity fund investors, and investment and commercial bankers to Henry Kissinger and Warren Buffett. I took copious notes about people's views on the economic outlook, the geopolitical outlook, the state of markets, the changing structure of the financial sector, and my own job options and personal financial issues.

The first decision I made was to become chairman of a national not-for-profit organization called the Local Initiatives Support Corporation, whose work I had developed tremendous respect for when I was at Treasury. I knew I wanted to stay involved with issues relating to the inner cities, and LISC, which provides funding and technical assistance for urban and rural community development, seemed a great opportunity for doing that. I also returned to the boards of Mt. Sinai Hospital Medical Center, which I'd had to resign from in late 1992 when I had first joined the Clinton administration.

Beyond that, I knew I wanted to stay active in public policy issues, but I didn't quite know how. Now that I'd left Washington, how could I continue to be sufficiently well informed as to remain relevant? Would anybody care what I had to say now that I was an ex–government official with no power? When I put that question to him just before I left Washington, Bob Strauss answered me with characteristic candor:

"You're a grape now, and you're going to become a raisin," he said. "The only question is how long it takes." It struck me that grapes can also become fine wines, but I had the feeling that Bob would quickly have ridiculed that notion.

MY FORMER GOLDMAN SACHS colleague Steve Friedman told me there were two basic career models for someone in my position: I could put together a menu of different involvements I wanted to have. Or I could have one central job, as I had at Goldman Sachs, with various additional involvements on the outside.

As I continued talking to people and making notes, the second model seemed to suit me better. I decided that I wanted to go back into the financial world. At some level, perhaps I was just returning to familiar ground. I liked that world and could apply what I knew best most effectively there. But working in the financial sector would also give me an opportunity to stay current, to have the knowledge and insight that come from being engaged. That would help provide a basis for my involvement with the public policy issues I cared about and make my efforts to contribute to them more valuable. I wasn't pressed financially, but I am also a reasonably commercial person, and I felt that I wanted something that would be financially rewarding. And finally, for whatever reason, I actually find the management issues of large organizations interesting. (Most of my friends view this as a personality problem that I should try to work out in some other way.)

But some of my other job criteria complicated the picture. I was extremely cognizant of the difference between being the deputy and being the Secretary, of having great responsibility within an organization as opposed to having the ultimate responsibility. I'd had the ultimate responsibility both at Goldman Sachs and at Treasury, and I didn't want that again. I was at a stage in my life where I wanted to try to live a little differently, with more time and focus for my family, fishing, reading, and whatever I might care about or find interesting. So I wasn't going to be a CEO.

But I did want to be part of the central management structure wherever I went. A colleague who had left the Clinton administration and taken a very attractive, highly paid position at a financial firm had a big influence on my thinking. He visited me at Treasury and said, "I've got a terrific job, but I'm never going to be in the inner management. And if you're not in the inner management, it lacks something. You don't feel like you're a central part of the place." When he said that, something clicked with me. People with outsized résumés are often viewed from outside as being importantly involved in a company, when in fact they have no real role in management. From that point on, I added that criterion to my job search.

Having a former Treasury Secretary as a kind of elder statesman— though I didn't think of myself as either elder or a statesman—to provide advice and deal with clients, as Henry Fowler had been hired to do at

Goldman Sachs, would probably appeal to almost any financial institution. But creating a role in central management was more of a challenge. Fitting someone like that into the top level of an organization can be awkward. He's not going to be CEO or COO or CFO or have decision-making authority with respect to any of the company's activities. So what does he do and where does he fit in?

What I was really trying to create for myself was some type of *consigliere* position, or to become a minister without portfolio who lends a hand in many areas. At one point, I had been interested in finding an adviser to play this role for me at Treasury—someone who was deeply experienced but had no agenda of his own, who could serve as a sounding board for me and for other people around the department. Now I was looking for that kind of role for myself in a private-sector context. This is a good management idea in theory. Many CEOs would probably benefit greatly from the advice of someone loyal to the institution but without a personal stake in major decisions. But for various reasons, this is almost unheard of in practice. Most executives probably don't want a figure with independent standing within their own organization. And coming in from the outside, such a figure could easily seem threatening to others within a company. There also aren't many people who have had the requisite responsibilities and experiences who would be satisfied simply to provide advice—advice that might well be ignored.

I wasn't sure anyone would be amenable to creating the kind of role I was looking for. But almost every organization I talked seriously with did develop a solution, each in a slightly different way. Their answers were all unconventional, because the situation was unconventional. Most of the possibilities involved variations on being a nonexecutive chairman of the board or part of a chairman's office. One company proposed that I run a kind of internal think tank. Another suggested that I focus on guiding a generational transition among senior management. Each represented a potentially attractive opportunity, but they all raised some level of doubt about their workability.

I was close to deciding where to go when Judy threw a "Welcome Back to New York" party for me at the Metropolitan Museum of Art (this may have been her clever way of trying to ensure that I didn't take another job in Washington). Sandy Weill, the co-CEO of Citigroup, was there, and while we were chatting, he invited me to come by his office for a talk.

I said, "I'm happy to talk to you, if you'd like. But I can tell you I am fairly close to accepting something else and I just don't think working at Citigroup is what I want to do." I didn't want to meet with Sandy under false pretenses. But Sandy still wanted to talk, so I went to see him at his office.

Sandy is known for being a good salesman. He made Citigroup sound like a fascinating place. He told me it operated in 102 countries and had a huge diversity of activities: investment banking, insurance, retail and commercial banking, credit cards, asset management, a private bank, and a whole range of emerging-market involvements. We ended up talking for a couple of hours. Citigroup had joint CEOs: Sandy and John Reed, who had been brought together as a result of the Citicorp-Travelers merger. This was an unconventional structure, and press accounts indicated that there were some issues between them. What I didn't understand until sometime after I got there was that, while Sandy and John's personal relationship was very good and both were extremely able, their working relationship was not commensurately effective.

After meeting with Sandy, I met with John. Then I met with Sandy again. It seemed as though he called me almost every day for a month. I started to develop a sense that despite his reputation as a large, dominating personality, Sandy was someone I could work with. And after about my fourth visit, I said to Judy, "You know, I'm not going to do it, but this place is really remarkably interesting."

And she said to me, "You know, this is the first thing you really seem excited about. Shouldn't you do it?"

And I did. Shortly after the announcement, Al Hunt wrote a column in *The Wall Street Journal* criticizing my decision to take a high-paying job in the private sector. He was disappointed that I was going back into commerce and said I could do more good elsewhere. I have great respect for Al, but I didn't see why I shouldn't do what I wanted to do or why I had to become a monk just because I'd spent time in public service. Also, I did intend to stay involved in public policy and social endeavors—in fact, my contract with Citi specifically recognized that part of my time would be spent that way and that I would be expressing my own, independent views on issues. If Al's position became the standard, I thought to myself, people in the business world would be discouraged from going into government—to the detriment of both sides. You'd have something more like the European system, where civil servants and politicians rarely have any experience in the private sector and the private sector has relatively few people who understand how government works.

I also think Al missed an important point about my ability to be useful on the very issues he cared about. My contribution could be far greater if informed not only by my understanding of issues based on the experience I'd had in government but also by a current engagement with financial matters and markets around the world. In Bob Strauss's terms, I'd shrivel into raisinhood much more quickly if I didn't immerse myself in the business and financial world again.

FOR THE REASONS I've discussed, working in government was more preoccupying than anything else I'd ever done. It's always with you. You're in the public eye. Your role is never entirely clear. You can have the rug pulled out from you at any moment. You can have similar experiences in the private sector, especially when an issue blows up unexpectedly, but, except at extraordinary moments, the degree and constancy of the pressure are not the same. In my new capacity at Citigroup, I was hoping to have much more control over my own time—both to be freer to do whatever I felt like doing and also to have a greater feeling of freedom.

I remember talking about this with Sam Nunn, who had retired from the Senate a few years before I left Treasury. Sam told me to be careful, because I'd find myself overcommitted very quickly. He said that's what had happened to him since leaving the Senate. I said, "Sam, I understand you may have that problem, and that's a shame. But I actually understand myself pretty well, and I know I can handle this." Though I tend to invest myself very deeply in whatever I do and find almost everything interesting, I thought I had the self-knowledge and discipline to develop a reasonably balanced life, to manage a little bit differently this time.

But I quickly found myself in precisely the situation Sam Nunn had described. Partly I misjudged myself, but I also underestimated the influx of opportunities outside Citigroup as well as the sheer size and range of Citigroup, the largest financial company in the world, which does everything from conducting the industry's biggest emerging-market trading operation to running the world's largest credit card business. From the outside, it's very difficult to have any sense of what this kind of scale and scope in businesses of this complexity mean. Goldman Sachs had 6,000 people when I left, and that had seemed immense to me. We had made one acquisition in all the years I was there, when we took over the commodity-trading firm J. Aron. Citigroup had 180,000 employees when I joined and typically made several acquisitions every year—one or more of them major.

I tried to get a handle on Citigroup's activities in my usual way: I took out my yellow pad and went around talking to various people about their businesses. Michael Froman, who had been my chief of staff at Treasury and was also moving to Citi, went around with me. What we found was nothing like what I had expected. For example, I assumed that the credit card business was an office filled with clerks who kept track of payments. In fact, it's an actuarial business that uses highly sophisticated statistical models developed and constantly experimented with by a large team of people with graduate degrees, including twenty-seven with Ph.D.s in areas related to "decision management." They use computer simulations to test credit decisions and model how minor adjustments in credit card terms or marketing may affect consumer behavior and thus the business's rate of return.

I was soon learning about other areas of finance I'd never had much direct involvement in: commercial lending, consumer banking, asset management, private banking, subprime lending, and a range of emerging-market activities. I took the better part of a year just to gain a rudimentary understanding of Citigroup and its various businesses. In the course of that year, I began to feel much more personally invested in the company than I ever thought I would be.

Shortly after I arrived, I was drawn into issues related to Salomon Smith Barney, the investment bank that had come into being when Travelers had merged its subsidiary, Smith Barney, with Salomon in 1997. Before I arrived, a major New York financial figure told me that Salomon, which had always been a major force in fixed-income trading, was no longer a first-tier firm. I quickly realized that this comment wasn't correct. Despite having weathered a series of setbacks in the late 1980s and early 1990s, Salomon was still a force and seemed very focused on moving forward. Having both the capabilities of the old Salomon Brothers firm, especially its place as the world's premier fixed-income house, and credit extension abilities gave Citigroup multiple ways to meet a client's needs. But the firm did face a number of substantial strategic challenges, one of which was establishing itself more effectively in Europe. Toward that end, Citigroup had been negotiating to acquire an established British firm, Schroders PLC, as a platform for European expansion. The merger ran into trouble over the Schroders people's concerns that Salomon might still resemble the Salomon Brothers of the era of *Liar's Poker*, the book by Michael Lewis that famously described the Salomon of an earlier time as rather rough-and-tumble. The Schroders people asked me to fly to London for a Saturday night dinner to discuss the Salomon culture with them and to satisfy themselves that Salomon now functioned in a more civilized, client-focused manner—all of which I was comfortable doing.

Perhaps the most difficult issue at Citi was its management structure. I assumed that Sandy's desire to hire me was driven in part by the feeling that I might be able to help him and John reach decisions more readily. The complexities and potential of the co-CEO structure interested me, based on the very good experience Steve and I had had as co-COOs and co-CEOs at Goldman Sachs. I thought that I might be able to draw on that experience to help the two of them develop processes that would work more effectively.

Since I was now the third member of the office of chairman, though not a co-CEO, I suggested that we have a meeting once a week, called the "Office of the Chairman Meeting," with the three of us as well as Chuck Prince, Citigroup's general counsel, acting as secretary. I would function as a facilitator to try to help John and Sandy work through decisions. John was fine with the process, but it was Sandy who really used these meetings, arriving with a prepared agenda. He would say, "I've got these five things I want to talk about today." And we would go through them one by one.

These meetings helped John and Sandy somewhat, but making decisions and setting direction continued to be very difficult. One of the big issues in that initial period was something called e-Citi, an effort John had begun before the merger to take advantage of the Internet. John took the view that was common among Internet-savvy people at that time—and that may well have been right—that big, traditional companies weren't prepared to make the cultural changes necessary to employ the Internet effectively. Lest it be smothered, John thought the only way to get an Internet business started at Citi was to go outside traditional channels. Sandy, on the other hand, thought we were spending a great deal of money on the initiative relative to what we were getting. He thought Internet activities should be run within Citi's established structure and subjected to the familiar forms of budgetary discipline. My own view was that the problem of culture-shaking innovation at big companies was real and that John's way of getting the project off the ground was better initially. It did lead the company energetically into the Internet age. On the other hand, I felt that by the time of this discussion, awareness of the technology's significance had developed enough that transferring Internet activities into the various business units made sense.

That was just one of several unsettled issues outstanding in February 2000 when Citigroup's management committee, which consisted of the top twenty or so executives in the company, flew to Boulder, Colorado, for a three-day retreat. On the first day, we had a discussion about managing the company in relation to future growth. Deryck Maughan, former CEO of Salomon Brothers and a highly respected senior officer of the company, made a presentation that to me is still thought-provoking. At that point, we had around 180,000 people. Leaving aside Deryck's actual numbers, if, hypothetically, earnings grow at 10 to 12 percent a year, which with compounding means doubling in six or seven years, we would probably have around 400,000 people—allowing for increased productivity— within a decade. Deryck posed a major conceptual and practical question: What processes would we need to manage a staff that large and still growing? Coming up with an answer meant, among many other issues, finding

the right balance between central control of fundamental strategic decisions, budgets, risk limits, and major legal affairs on the one hand and
delegation of the more specific strategies and operations of the individual
businesses on the other. And there are other challenges: treating customers as if it were a small company, giving employees the feeling that
the strength of a great organization can help them best realize their own
potential rather than being a bureaucratic anchor, making expeditious
decisions where issues cross business, product, or geographic lines, and
creating mutual cooperation across those lines to realize efficiencies in
terms of revenues and expenses. I believe that these challenges are being
met, but, like any successful organization, Citigroup is a work in progress,
guided not only by its leaders but in its case also by an entrepreneurial,
numbers-focused approach to business.

On the second day of the meeting, the discussion got around to how
well we were functioning as an organization. People started talking about
the co-CEO structure, and most said it wasn't working well, principally
because of the difficulty in making major decisions and setting strategic
direction. The discussion was remarkably candid. One longtime Citibank
person made the point in a memorable phrase, saying, "We need one
North Star." I later got the impression that Sandy and John had both come
away from the Boulder meeting thinking to themselves that the co-CEO
structure couldn't continue. As a result, the two of them agreed to bring
the issue to the corporation's board of directors at a special Sunday meeting a month later. Since so much has been written and reported about
that meeting, I feel comfortable in speaking a little about my views.

When asked, I said that I thought Sandy and John were both extremely capable people, and my first choice was for both to stay and work
together effectively. But if that couldn't happen, with most of the people in
the company's top management coming from the old Travelers and Citigroup revolving mostly around Sandy, I didn't think the board really had
a choice. I left the room, and their discussion went on for several hours. I
was waiting in an office, watching a Knicks game on TV, while the board
tried to resolve the issue. Sandy and John were sitting with each other in a
different office, kidding around and trying to appear relaxed. Then the

board came out and announced to the three of us that Sandy would be the sole CEO.

That experience caused me to revise my views about the issue of joint CEOs. Steve Friedman and I had worked together effectively in running Goldman Sachs a decade before because our fundamental views were compatible, because we were both relatively analytical and fell easily into a process for working out differences, and because we didn't have ego conflicts over decision making. But very rarely will the kind of people who are likely to become CEOs be able to function in this way. The experience of John and Sandy, and other similar situations I've seen, left me with the feeling that the odds of co-CEOs working together effectively in a corporate setting are actually very low. In most cases, corporations are best off with a single North Star, though I still feel, contrary to virtually all established opinion, that in the rare circumstances where the co-CEO structure will work, the benefits can be substantial.

IN EARLIER CHAPTERS, I discussed how my previous experience in business served me when I went into government—and considered some of the differences between the corporate and government worlds. There's a widespread view that the public sector has more to learn from the private sector than the other way around. But the traffic seems to me to go in both directions. The private-sector prejudice against the public sector is such that people are often surprised when I say that for-profit enterprises have much to learn from the way government works.

One area where I think business can gain from government is in interagency process—getting people from separate units and with different points of view together around a table to reach common ground on issues that cut across unit boundaries. Two others that can be closely related are managing in the kinds of crises that are becoming more common and often thrust companies into the public eye in unexpected ways, and dealing with the political and "message" dimensions of high-profile issues. Yet another is dealing directly with government itself.

After returning to New York in 1999, the area where I was most keenly aware that the private sector could gain from the experience of government was in managing the decision-making processes around complex issues with multiple internal stakeholders. In government, a chief of staff or a cabinet-level official spends a great deal of time trying to get groups of people from different units to work together in an effective way. This is an inherent need, because most major issues cross organizational lines and require coordination among different agencies, constituencies, and centers of authority to be resolved most effectively (though the history of our government is rife with examples of breakdowns of this needed coordination, often with untoward effects on policy decisions). For example, a major new initiative for inner-city problems probably wouldn't be properly developed unless officials from, at the very least, HUD, OMB, HHS, Treasury, and the White House got together in a room and hashed out a recommendation for the President.

At big corporations with many different business units, the same kind of need exists. These units maximize their collective profits over time by working together effectively—and the private sector has the advantage of being able to use accounting and compensation to encourage people to work together, which the public sector for the most part cannot do. But the separate business units of a big company usually aren't as used to working through their differences and problems with one another to enhance the well-being of the whole as government is of necessity. They're more used to operating in separate "silos" and being held accountable for their own individual bottom lines. That issue often comes to the fore when companies seek to cross-sell—that is, to use the sales force of one unit to sell related products from other units—or to make product/geography matrices work. (Who runs a credit card business in South Korea—the person in charge of credit cards or the person in charge of South Korea?) People who have learned how to manage interagency processes in Washington have a crucial set of skills that are not likely to have been as well developed in business and can add much to a company if they are properly supported by the CEO.

Another area where corporations clearly have much to learn from Washington is in understanding political considerations, both in dealing directly with governments, domestic and foreign, and in handling business issues that are political by their nature. In December 2001, Sandy and I traveled to the People's Republic of China and met with Premier Zhu Rongji to discuss a strategic alliance with a Chinese bank to issue credit cards. In putting together our proposal, we focused only on solving complicated substantive problems and failed to consider an even more intricate set of issues related to the distribution of political power within the Chinese government. What political interests would the Premier have to think about if he wanted to support our plan? Who, within that political structure, would view our proposal as threatening, and who as beneficial? A robust credit card business in China would promote consumption, which was clearly an economic goal of the government. But it might also threaten elements of the banking sector or of the bureaucracy that maintained control over the banking sector. Zhu was supportive of the project, but it foundered, seemingly because of internal political opposition. Perhaps if we had recognized these problems in advance, we might have devised a plan that would have helped to satisfy those other constituencies.

Political experience can also be valuable in the private sector when companies find themselves involved in issues with a significant political dimension. A good illustration of the corporate world's difficulties in dealing with political-style controversy that I experienced firsthand was the conflict that erupted over Ford Motor Company's potential liability for accidents involving SUVs that rolled over after tire failures. In 2000, the press reported that a number of people had been killed or injured in car accidents that had occurred when the tread on tires manufactured by Bridgestone/Firestone had separated. Firestone was Ford's main tire supplier, and many of the accidents involved Explorer sport-utility vehicles, which were outfitted primarily with Firestone tires. Ford blamed the defective tires; Firestone claimed that the design of the Explorer made it more likely to roll over than other cars, and that Ford hadn't warned buyers about the need to keep their tires properly inflated. Ultimately, the National Highway Traffic Safety Administration found that Firestone, not Ford, was at fault for the failures. The reputation of Ford and the Explorer emerged intact, but in the interim, Ford suffered reputational and political damage that might have been avoided or lessened.

Other than Citigroup's, Ford's was the only corporate board I'd agreed to sit on after leaving Treasury. For me, joining Ford's board was an opportunity to learn something about how big industrial companies are run. Ford also had a significant family influence, which made it more interesting at a personal level and seemed to me likely to result in more of a long-term focus. Also, Ford had been Goldman Sachs's flagship client in my early years there, and the idea of now being on Ford's board carried a special meaning for me.

After becoming a board member, I began having conversations from time to time about issues facing the company with Bill Ford, who was then the nonexecutive chairman. (In more recent conversations, Bill and Jacques Nasser, the CEO of Ford when I joined the board, agreed to let me relate the discussions about Ford that appear in this chapter.) Bill has a disarming manner and a modest style that belies his having grown up in Detroit with the Ford surname. He also knows and cares a great deal about environmental issues.

When the Ford/Firestone story broke, Bill and I discussed how to deal with its political dimensions. Substantively, the company seemed to be handling this serious matter wisely, immediately offering to replace the relevant Firestone tires free of charge. That decision cost Ford some $3 billion but reflected Jacques Nasser's immediate decision that the highest priority was to avoid further injuries or loss of life. But in dealing with the media and political aspects of the problem, the company's natural instinct was to have its own legal and public relations officials handle the situation. I thought that these corporate people, who as far as I knew didn't have extensive political experience, would be unlikely to deal with this kind of firestorm effectively. I said, "Bill, you're not in a corporate situation anymore. You're at the nexus of corporate issues, politics, the media, congressional investigation, and possibly even criminal prosecution. And you need people who are experienced working at that intersection."

Bill said: "I think you're right. Call Jac." I'd gotten to know Nasser at Ford board meetings a bit and liked him a great deal. Born in Lebanon and raised in Australia, where he had begun working for Ford in 1968, Nasser had deep knowledge of and many interesting ideas about the automobile business. I called him and repeated the points I'd made to Bill Ford. Then I told Nasser that I'd like to make a few suggestions, which basically involved putting company officials in touch with people I knew who were savvy about Washington and the media.

I think that Nasser, never having lived through an event of this type before, understood my points more intellectually than viscerally. Like most senior executives in businesses, he was not experienced in this kind of crisis. As a result, even though Ford did hire some experienced Washington people, the company, for the most part, dealt with the problem with regular corporate programs and personnel. Firestone, meanwhile, shrewdly retained Akin Gump—my friend Bob Strauss's politically connected and savvy law firm. And Firestone seemed to outmaneuver Ford on the media and message dimensions of the issue for some time. In the longer run, that didn't matter, but in the shorter run, Ford's reputational damage might have been more limited had the company adopted a more effective political and communications strategy.

While this matter was unfolding, I found myself being drawn into issues over Ford's management that were unrelated to the Firestone problem. Bill Ford, unlike most nonexecutive chairmen, was involved in the company on a daily basis and had his office there. Moreover, the Ford family controlled 40 percent of the shareholder vote, which meant that he held considerable influence over the company in some ultimate sense. But Bill wasn't the boss at Ford. Nasser, who had become CEO in 1999, ran the business. Though Bill liked and respected Nasser, over time he developed ever-deeper concerns about the condition of the company. Every so often, he would call me to discuss them.

That situation was difficult to interpret from the outside. Nasser was clearly at Ford as an agent of change, which Bill and everyone else agreed the company needed. But Jacques had run into significant difficulties in transforming the company. Like a number of executives in those days, he was trying to apply techniques that had been popularized by Jack Welch, who had made dramatic changes in the culture of General Electric. For instance, Nasser was trying to implement more rigorous personnel reviews, and he especially insisted that managers identify the bottom 10 percent of their people and develop tough-minded requirements for improvement. But what some of these CEOs overlooked was that Welch had had two decades to gain people's confidence. Welch also had the personality of a coach—a natural ability to motivate people and breed enthusiasm.

Bill Ford's view—as reported in the press at the time—was that Nasser's efforts were hurting morale at the company. He thought that Nasser's manner in pushing for change at Ford meant that the desired transformation was less likely to be accomplished. To remake a corporate culture successfully means not only being willing to incur some opposition but also winning the support of the preponderance of a corporation's people. You can't just impose change by fiat. Nasser pointed out that Ford was a hundred-year-old company with a large number of lifetime employees and a deeply entrenched culture, and that antagonism and resistance to change were inevitable—which was also true. That's typically the conundrum around significant change in a corporate—or any other—setting: it won't happen unless you're willing to break some eggs and incur sharp opposition. But change also won't take hold without broad buy-in. It is usually very difficult—if not impossible—for an outsider to judge whether an effort at change is meeting both these tests or is either too aggressive or not aggressive enough.

In the case of Ford Motor, I suspect both perspectives may have reflected an element of the truth. For example, focusing on the bottom 10 percent of executives every year ought to have had the benefit of forcing managers at Ford to face the difficult realities of improving the company's workforce. But what had worked for Welch at GE might not fit at Ford, where long-term job security had always been the norm. At the same time, other difficulties were surfacing. Bill began to report to me and others on the board that even though corporate profits were strong, people who worked at the company were increasingly dissatisfied. The company's relations with its dealers were worsening. And new surveys coming out indicated that Ford's quality and productivity were declining relative to other automakers'.

Nasser, who is very smart, had been very focused on repositioning Ford as a consumer-products, services, and financing company. But too little attention had been paid to manufacturing and design, with the result that there were too few new models in development and meaningful cost disadvantages. Bill said he did not want to be CEO himself. He wanted

Nasser to be successful. But he felt Jac was excluding him. Bill said that if he was going to help with the company's problems, he needed to be in on decisions.

The difficulties at Ford brought home to me how little you can know as an outside board member of a company, even if you are very conscientious about your duties. At Ford board meetings, the issues that ultimately led to Nasser's departure were often raised. My immediate reaction to hearing them would be: *My God, we really do have a problem here and we have to deal with it.* Then Nasser would respond. He'd either say that some issue sounded like a problem but really wasn't for the following reasons. Or he'd say, "Yes, there is a problem, but here's our plan for dealing with it." *That's a good answer,* I'd think, listening to him. *There's really not a problem.* Or: *There's a problem here, but he really does have a plan for dealing with it.* An outside board member has an obligation to learn as much as possible about the issues facing the company. But in truth, it's very hard to know enough to disagree confidently with management about a problem until matters have reached a relatively serious state.

This thought was very much on my mind when issues about corporate governance came to the fore with the scandals at Enron, WorldCom, and elsewhere. Our system of corporate governance is based on oversight by directors. But if a board meets several times a year for a full day of substantive discussion, even a board member who also sits on a couple of committees and prepares diligently for meetings is unlikely to spend more than two or three hours a week immersed in a company's issues. Some insist that this limitation is an argument for the kind of system that exists in Europe, where directors are much more active and constitute a second layer of management. More active directors may be able to ferret out problems more readily, though Europe has had its share of corporate governance problems over time. In any case, the European system also has real drawbacks, the biggest being that what is in some measure management by committee leaves companies less agile and adaptable, less willing to experiment and take risks, and less decisive.

On balance I much prefer our system of corporate governance—a strong CEO and outside directors with a more limited involvement. There are many who feel that under our system, especially as strengthened by the Sarbanes-Oxley Act of 2002, there is a flow of information to the board that is as effective as under the European model. But even if that is not so, and the potential for undetected mismanagement and corporate disasters is somewhat greater, I still think the benefits of our system greatly outweigh the costs, in terms of overall economic performance over the long run.

The decisive factor in Nasser's eventual departure was the mounting evidence that major problems at Ford did not seem to be improving. A year went by and Nasser still had strong answers, but the cumulative negative evidence seemed weightier. Given more time, Nasser might have turned Ford around and accomplished the much-needed changes, but the risk was that more time would pass without his doing so. Weighing the risks on both sides, the board decided to change direction and make Bill the CEO.

When Bill had said he was prepared to take over the chief executive job himself to get the company back on the right track, I told him I thought the board would be fully supportive. But then I asked him, "Have you thought about how you're going to frame what you're doing in the press?" I warned Bill that the media might depict this change in all kinds of negative ways. "And you won't have two months to get the story right," I said. "You'll have one day."

Bill had to walk a fine line on his message. On the one hand, he was stepping in because he was concerned about the company—this wasn't some kind of power grab. On the other hand, he didn't want to focus attention on the company's problems or make them sound worse than they really were. That was another illustration of the principle that providing the prism through which the issue is seen is critical, whether the issue is deficit spending versus tax increases or strengthening Ford versus Ford in trouble or a boardroom coup.

My advice to Bill was to focus very carefully on crafting his message and on a strategy for getting it across in the media. He had to present a constructive view of the future under new leadership and not focus unduly on problems or on past conflict that might make Ford look like a troubled company. I told Bill about my having asked Tom Donilon to help me plan this kind of communications strategy when I had left Treasury, and I suggested that he do something similar. It wasn't that Bill lacked sensitivity to these issues, just that people in corporate life don't tend to develop that kind of political awareness, despite its relevance to their jobs. As it turned out, Bill handled the transition well—both in the media and inside the company—very much helped by Jac's constructive and gracious attitude. And Bill has clearly taken hold as CEO.

AFTER I'D BEEN back in New York for some time, Judy and I spent a week traveling around Sicily by boat with six old friends, including Diana and Leon Brittan, who after our days together at Yale Law School had gone on to serve as home secretary under Margaret Thatcher. One day when we were hiking onshore, Diana observed that some British politicians she knew were unable to let go when their time was over and sought to hang on in one way or another, always hoping to re-create what they once had had.

I said I had the same impression about some American political figures. In a similar vein, Richard Holbrooke, who served with great distinction in a variety of high-level foreign policy posts in the Carter and Clinton administrations, once said to me that some people have a sense of self that is so dependent on what they were in Washington that they forever define themselves by that earlier position. Others, Dick added, look back at their time in government as a very special experience, but remain focused on what they're going to do in the future.

The point both Diana and Dick made was an extension of something I'd often observed. People who are heavily dependent on a job for their sense of self become hostage to the job and to those who have power over them. Someone whose identity is not job-dependent, on the other hand, has the ability to walk away, which creates a sense of psychological independence.

In my own case, I can remember back to my early days at Goldman Sachs, when I certainly didn't have the financial freedom I had when I entered government but nonetheless had that same feeling of being able to leave and lead a whole other kind of life. That made it easier both to be independent and candid in my views and to function in a high-pressure environment.

In that same conversation, Diana Brittan also mentioned a friend who held a distinguished British title and had been very successful in business. He had so much, but he had never succeeded in fulfilling his lifelong ambition of becoming a member of the House of Commons. Rather than reflecting proudly on all he had accomplished, he always looked back with great regret on the one distinction he didn't have. That reminded me of a story about Robert Jackson, a distinguished Supreme Court justice who, despite the enormous respect in which he was held, was always consumed by his desire to be chief justice, an ambition that was never fulfilled. Even extremely successful people always seem to want something beyond what they have. Inner needs drive external accomplishments but can never be satisfied by those external accomplishments. Which is merely to say that, for some people, the inability to be satisfied is a chronic condition.

MY OWN TIME back in the private sector has been a mix of positives and negatives. First of all, it's been nice to be home again. And in many ways, my arrangement with Citigroup has worked out considerably better than I hoped. I've immersed myself in a set of fascinating substantive and management issues, and I've been at the center of a remarkable institution without having to shoulder operating responsibility. Outside Citi, I've had the good fortune to be deeply involved in public policy issues I care about and institutions that matter to me, including the Harvard Corporation, LISC, the Council on Foreign Relations, and Mount Sinai Medical Center. I don't miss the activities or the perquisites of government, though I do miss the people I worked with and disagree with the direction our country has taken on many fronts.

On the other hand, I've not owned my own time as I thought I would. To some extent, I simply misread myself. Some people seem to be good at moderating their level of engagement, but I've never functioned that way. My post-government experience has reinforced something I've long believed: you take yourself with you wherever you go, so you had better know who you are.

CHAPTER TWELVE

Greed, Fear, and Complacency

W HEN I RETURNED TO NEW YORK in July 1999 and reimmersed myself in the world of markets and finance, I realized in a more palpable way how much had changed in the six and a half years since I'd left. My son Jamie, who was at that time working at the investment firm of Allen & Co., told me that even though I felt I'd kept current, the changes were greater than I thought—partly because of the Internet and technology. Once I began to focus more deeply on what was happening, I realized what Jamie meant.

I started to understand the technological aspect of the change more fully when Arthur Levitt, who was nearing the end of his tenure as chairman of the Securities and Exchange Commission, asked me to sit on an informal task force he had set up to discuss market structure. Arthur and others felt the new technology should enable better, more efficient ways of doing business, and in fact, some market participants were already beginning to do business differently. This study group afforded some insight into the battles waged by the New York Stock Exchange to preserve its traditional advantages and the changes major firms and innovative newcomers were advocating in their own self-interest. The Levitt group wasn't intended to develop firm conclusions, but the debate did help me to understand the technological and other factors that were transforming the financial marketplace—and that continue to do so.

One element was the new scale of activity. I knew that daily trading volumes on the major exchanges had increased by a factor of five—for example, from 211 million shares traded on NASDAQ on my last day at Goldman to 1.1 billion the week I returned to New York. But you had to be around the financial services industry to get a feel for what that increase really meant. The business of private equity, for instance, had mushroomed with the growth of the market, as had hedge funds. In 1992, a hedge fund that managed $100 million in assets would have been considered large. In 1999, many funds exceeded $1 billion, a few ran more than $5 billion, and the number of funds had doubled.

In New York, the social consequences of the boom mentality were everywhere. People had made a ton of money in the market and had increased their spending just as sharply. I heard about couples who instead of getting married in New York City would fly their entire wedding party to Europe. People were building immense houses—often second or third residences. Real estate prices were crazy. Judy and I were thinking of moving out of the co-op we'd lived in since the early 1970s, and we saw an apartment we liked. So we made a bid, well below what seemed to us a bloated asking price, but in our broker's judgment a reasonable offer. Then someone made an offer above the asking price. We gave up looking for a new apartment. What was happening just seemed bizarre.

Several years into the stock market boom, many people seemed to think we'd reached a kind of economic Nirvana. In late 1999, dot-com and telecom stock prices were still increasing rapidly. That summer when I arrived back in New York, the NASDAQ was trading at a little over 2,500—it would hit 4,000 before the end of the year and a high of 5,049 on March 10, 2000. The comments one heard called to mind the fate of Irving Fisher, an eminent economist at Yale in the 1920s. A week before the Crash of 1929, Fisher famously said stock prices had reached a "permanently high plateau." It was always possible that the world really had changed in the way the market imagined—but a better bet was that the market had gone a bit crazy. I remember a chart I saw in a financial magazine that depicted the historical relationship of the market capitalization of all publicly held stocks to the U.S. gross domestic product. Until 1996, the value of the stock market had never risen above our GDP, which is, after all, the value of all goods and services produced in the United States. In fact, the average since 1925 is a little over 50 percent; at the market's 1929 peak, the ratio was 81 percent. But by March 2000, it had hit 181 percent. The price-earnings ratio of the NASDAQ had risen even more drastically. During the 1980s, it averaged 18.5. In March 2000, it peaked at 82.3. At that point, information technology stocks provided around 16 percent of the earnings of the S&P 500 but represented over twice as much—around 36 percent—of its market capitalization.

Some people I greatly respect do not share my skepticism about many of the widely accepted views about the stock market. One is Steve Einhorn, whom I had worked with at Goldman Sachs, where he had been head of our investment policy and stock selection committees, and later head of global research. For several years, Steve, a top-ranked equity strategist for more than a decade by *Institutional Investor* magazine, has been vice chairman of a large hedge fund in New York. When I sent him a draft of this chapter for comment, Steve reminded me of our first encounter. In his third week at Goldman, he had gotten into a big dispute with me over an arbitrage question about a merger. After being advised by the partner he worked for that this was perhaps not a smart way to start his career at the firm, he came to my office to apologize. He says I told him not to apologize—and to please keep disagreeing with me in the future. A bracing clash of opinions has characterized our relationship ever since. Steve thinks that long-term investors should usually have most of their assets in equities, which have historically outperformed other kinds of investments. He did not think the market levels of the late 1990s reflected collective insanity. Given the strong underlying economic conditions and the low-interest-rate environment, Steve argued that stock prices in the late 1990s, while very high by historical standards, were not demonstrably irrational outside of the tech sector—and therefore subject to normal correction.

My view is that the late 1990s were but one example of the periodic episodes of financial excess that have occurred all through the history of markets. I remember well several of the more recent: the euphoria about conglomerates, whose stock prices went to vast multiples of their earnings in the 1960s; the so-called nifty fifty in the early 1970s—growth stocks such as Polaroid and Avon Products that had innovative products or marketing and were thought to have a limitless future of high growth; the "energy darlings" of the late 1970s; and the southwest real-estate bubble in the early 1980s. The early 1990s saw a biotech boom that fore-shadowed another biotech boom at the end of the decade. Excess flows of credit produced by a similar kind of mind-set were at the heart of the Asian financial crisis.

But people involved in markets don't seem to learn from past episodes. They always think, *This time it's different, and here are the reasons why.* Often those reasons are based on genuinely constructive developments, but investors extrapolate too much from the developments and provoke a market overreaction. And that overreaction can endanger the strength of the underlying economy. You might think people would learn from the collective financial experience of mankind. For some reason, they don't.

I expressed something of my view about the seeming inevitability of periodic excesses at the London School of Economics in February 2000, at what turned out to be the eleventh hour of the stock market boom. I said that what had struck me after returning to New York was the pervasive assumption that everything would always be well and that any interruptions in the advance of prosperity would be temporary and mild—solvable, in any case, by the Federal Reserve Board. I was surprised that relatively few others were concerned about historically extreme stock market valuations and other imbalances in the U.S. economy. But even though I was no longer Treasury Secretary, I still had to be careful, on the chance that a comment of mine might affect markets and because I'm mindful of the fact that nobody is very good at predicting the markets' short-term behavior. So I didn't say I thought stocks were overvalued. I said that risk premiums were at historic lows and that discipline tends to get lost in good times.

A number of the people I went to seeking career and financial advice shared my opinion that the market had gone to excess, perhaps badly so. But few were prepared to act in the face of the upward momentum of stocks and the experience of the previous eighteen years. One of the very few who both agreed and acted on that view was Warren Buffett, whom I had known since the 1960s. When we met for breakfast at The Mark hotel in Manhattan, he defended his skepticism about the market.

"Assume today's stock prices are right," Warren said. "What kind of earnings growth would companies need to warrant those prices?"

The number, extended out to the future and calculated as a share of GDP, was implausibly large. At that point, Buffett's Berkshire Hathaway fund, which had avoided high-priced technology companies, was substantially underperforming the market for the first time in thirty years. People had started to write that Buffett had enjoyed a great career as an investor but hadn't kept current. They said he just didn't understand the fundamental changes taking place.

Others I met with had an interesting duality of view. One of the first people I went to see in New York was Michael Steinhardt, whom I'd known since I'd first gone to work at Goldman Sachs in the late 1960s. Michael had been an extremely successful hedge fund manager for more than thirty years with a reputation as a shrewd and energetic investor.

"I'm a former public servant, coming to seek your assistance," I said with mock seriousness. "How would you advise this public servant about how to invest his savings?"

Michael laughed. He had disbanded his hedge fund but still actively managed his own not inconsiderable fortune. Karen Cook, whom I had known from the Goldman Sachs trading room, worked with him, reviewing hedge funds as possible investment vehicles. Michael generously offered me full access to Karen's research. He told me he was investing in various stocks and hedge funds.

"But Michael, I don't understand," I said. "You agree that the market may well be overvalued. And yet you say that you're invested in the market."

"People like you keep telling me the market is overvalued," he answered. "But tell me what you think will precipitate a correction."

"I don't really know exactly what will cause it," I said. "Won't it just fall of its own weight?"

"But something has to precipitate it," Michael responded. "And the problem with people like you who keep talking about how overvalued the market is, you can't point to anything that's going to precipitate a fall."

"Well, it's true," I said. "I don't have any idea what it will be. But if it's overvalued, it's going to correct. Whatever the proximate precipitator is doesn't matter. It could be anything."

By 1999, many shrewd investors were in Michael's position. In an analytic sense, they thought the market was overvalued but stayed invested anyway, perhaps on the "greater fool" theory that they could profit from an irrational rise and then sell their positions before it was too late. In any case, the relatively few nonbelievers were irrelevant after an eighteen-year bull market that simply fed on itself. The skeptics among market analysts and forecasters had lost their credibility. Nobody—including me—is particularly good at predicting shorter-term market movement, and if I had been invested in stocks during the later half of the 1990s, I would have sold or lightened up much too early. But it does seem to me that investors should at the least have recognized that many conditions had gone to excess by any historical standards and have given that serious consideration in their decision making.

It was striking during that period not just that financial markets went to extremes but that, when they did, people developed convincing intellectual rationales for those extremes. Those rationales seemed plausible both because they reflected real and positive economic developments and because the ongoing behavior of the market appeared to confirm them. By 1999, after an eight-year boom, many commentators were asserting that productivity growth was going to continue at much higher levels indefinitely and that business cycles were history. Two other widely held views were that the Fed was omnipotent and that the market had misunderstood equities all along, with the result that historical risk premiums—the additional return investors demand to hold stocks rather than "risk free" Treasury bonds—were much too high. While Steve Einhorn is correct that equities have outperformed bonds over any extended period of time historically, some digested this view into the shorthand that stocks simply weren't risky over the long term, or even that short-term declines would always be temporary and that stocks would quickly bounce back.

As an aside, these views provided support for a movement to convert part of the Social Security system into private accounts that could be invested in equities—a political cause that largely faded away after the dramatic market rise of the 1990s came to an end. If this proposal is going to be seriously revived in the political arena at some future time, the very substantial risks attendant to stock ownership should be fully included in the analysis. But it concerns me that the outcome of the debate may be unduly influenced by an ebullient market environment—the only context in which such a proposal is likely to have political viability. Another problem is that there could be irresistible political pressure to make up for shortfalls in accounts for people who retire when market conditions are adverse. This could create additional fiscal problems and skew investment incentives for private account holders. My own view is that we should preserve the guarantee of Social Security, but consider establishing tax credits for savings accounts on top of that, when this is fiscally feasible. If the Social Security guarantee itself needs reform because the system is underfunded, then that is a separate matter that should be dealt with directly.

Each claim about what had changed in the economy reflected some underlying reality. But in most cases, the conclusions for markets were greatly overdrawn. Take the theory that technological advance had led to a structural increase in productivity growth. The issue may not be fully settled, but assume for the sake of argument that the theory's proponents were right. Surely that would be good news for the economy and for stocks. But it was an immense and illogical leap, as some proponents argued, from technological development to permanent and uninterrupted prosperity, with at most brief and mild interruptions. Or consider the view that business cycles had become a thing of the past. It is true that cyclical recessions have tended to become progressively less severe since the end of the Second World War, in part because of various social safety net programs, such as unemployment insurance and welfare, which increase government spending when the economy is weaker, and because monetary policy has become more effective. However, business cycles remain, because the constants of human nature, such as greed, fear, and complacency, have not changed. As for the Fed, it has indeed become a far more important factor in the economy in recent decades, but it is not powerful enough to prevent all slowdowns. Perhaps risk premiums were once too high, but that didn't mean that stocks weren't still significantly riskier than Treasury bonds.

In that kind of environment, the highly charged atmosphere, not evidence and logic, tends to carry the day. Even Sir Isaac Newton, the great English mathematician and physicist of the seventeenth century, was a major investor in the most extreme financial excess of his day, which became known as the South Sea Bubble. The South Sea Bubble grew out of a scheme to convert British government obligations into common stock in a company with a theoretical monopoly on British trade with South America. Practical obstacles abounded: the company's "officers" had never been to South America; they had scant ships or supplies; and there was no reason to believe the King of Spain would allow Britain to trade with his colonies. Thousands who invested were destroyed financially.

That episode typifies the psychology of market excess. You're sitting on the sidelines, telling the people around you all the reasons why you think the market may be badly overvalued. And they're all looking at you, saying, "There's a new reality, and you don't get it. You don't understand how much the world has changed—which is why people like you always fall by the wayside." That was my experience from the mid-1990s on. Though the underlying strength of the economy was very real, I thought the stock market was probably overreacting.

My concern about market excesses, as I mentioned earlier, inevitably raises a question of great importance to future policy makers: Could Treasury or the Fed have done something to moderate the stock market excesses that seemed to be developing and that could endanger the economy? Alan, Larry, and I discussed this frequently. Though I felt strongly that the markets had gone to excess, I couldn't be sure I was right and the market wrong. (And in fact, had I chosen to give a warning, I would have done so years before what turned out to be the peak.) Secondly, it was not clear that what we said would have had any real effect. Finally, if our comments did have an effect, they could precipitate a sudden unraveling rather than an orderly decline. And issuing market forecasts that turn out to be wrong can quickly undermine the more general credibility of the prognosticating public official.

But, in speeches and TV interviews, I did the most I thought was sensible for a public official to do: I urged investors to focus seriously on risk and on valuation and said that discipline seemed to have flagged. I don't think many people paid much attention. Some commentators have since said that tightening margin requirements on common stocks to limit leverage could have helped—either through the limit itself or as a symbol of concern. My own view is that doing so probably would not have had any effect, or at least not enough to make a real difference. Some have also argued that Greenspan should have managed interest rates for the express purpose of dampening the market. I strongly share Alan's view that monetary policy should be directed toward the economy, not the stock market, both because the Fed is no more able to judge whether markets are too high, too low, or just right than anyone else, and because Fed actions driven by markets might be at variance with the best policy for the economy. But as Alan has explained in testimony to Congress, this issue can become extremely complicated, in part because the stock market affects the economy in many different ways. In any event, critics who argue for using interest rates to influence the stock market might quickly change their minds if the Federal Reserve Board actually did that.

BY THE TIME the long bull market finally came to an end, a sense of unreality permeated the entire business world. Many in Silicon Valley were of the opinion that nothing that took place outside the Valley was relevant to them. You would meet twenty-five-year-olds who thought that nothing that had happened before the Internet mattered. We were in a new world, free of business cycles and traditional notions of valuation. Those who didn't understand these new realities were hopelessly outmoded in their thinking.

My sense of the delusions of that era is encapsulated in a story from January 2000, just before the technology bubble began to deflate. The CEO of a dot-com company came to see me at Citigroup. Just what his company did was unclear to me, but at the time it was seen as possessing new technology of immense potential. At its peak stock price, the company, which had no earnings to speak of, had a market capitalization that exceeded $20 billion—far more than that of many very large, historically profitable industrial concerns—and the CEO was a multibillionaire.

Not given to modest claims, the CEO told me that the company had developed technologies that were going to "obliterate" the financial services industry in its current form. Citigroup's only hope for survival was to partner with him.

"You may well be right, but I'm not qualified to judge your technology, so how can I evaluate that statement?" I responded. I suggested he meet with our technology people.

He was nonplussed. "I don't meet with technology people," he said. "I just told you how you can save your bank. Don't you want to save your bank?"

It was an amazing meeting. The CEO did eventually meet with people in our technology division, but nothing came of that. The company's stock later fell dramatically.

The S&P 500 dropped from 1,527 in early 2000 to 777 in the fall of 2002. The NASDAQ went from 5,049 to less than 1,114—a drop of almost 80 percent. And the Dow Jones Industrial Average fell from a high of 11,723 to a low of 7,286. All in all, from peak to trough some $8.5 trillion in paper wealth, of what had been a total market capitalization of almost $18 trillion, was lost. More than one thousand publicly traded companies either went bankrupt or were delisted from the major exchanges.

Steve Einhorn argues that the market reversed course for specific reasons. And I agree that there were real changes in that period that certainly would have been expected to affect stock prices: the fear of terrorism after the World Trade Center attack, the economic slowdown, and the whole host of corporate governance and Wall Street issues, to name three. But, in my view, the change in market prices and market psychology was far greater than the change in the underlying economic realities. I still think that the most fundamental explanation is that the market fell of its own weight. A substantially overvalued market has to come down—and better sooner than later. Everyone would have been better off if stocks had regained a semblance of sanity sooner. But it's good that it didn't happen even later, with an even steeper fall from even higher levels. The market drop also caused at least some people to begin discussing valuation more realistically.

Even after the decline, however, many of the old assumptions about the long-term behavior of stocks persisted. The belated effects of the eighteen-year bull market—the only kind of market people younger than forty had ever known—continued to support unrealistic views about equities. Complacency about stocks and the view that they would regularly provide returns of 15 to 20 percent, with interruptions being brief and quickly repaired, had become so powerful that they partially survived the sharp decline and the large losses incurred.

In the search for the villains who had caused the market excesses, people tended to disregard the most obvious one of all: the widespread notion that the stock market was a path to easy riches. For many years, the securities industry has emphasized the benefits of everyone owning stocks and "investing in America." In one sense this may be right, but my view is more complicated. The great broadening of stock ownership over the past couple of decades has been a positive force, both for individual investors and for society, by sharing the benefits of ownership more broadly and by giving more people the feeling of having a greater stake in our system. And allocating a portion of one's assets to stocks probably does make sense for most people. But any investment should be accompanied by a realistic focus on the risks of equity ownership and a rigorous approach to valuation. Some who invest understand the risks, but too many do not. And too often, the industry—and the media—have not done a good job of explaining these risks to the investing public.

MANY OF THE FACTORS that contributed to the market excesses remain issues even after the collapse. One that continues to trouble me is the prevalence of short-term thinking and an excessive focus on quarterly earnings, rather than on long-term results. Indeed, the disproportionate attention paid to the short term, which preceded the market boom of the 1990s, seems to have survived the decline largely intact.

How did this attitude develop? There have always been people trying to get rich quickly in the stock market, of course. But my sense is that the mentality of the market changed significantly around the time I joined Goldman Sachs in the mid-1960s. During my early years on Wall Street, investing in stocks was still viewed by many as a long-term proposition, primarily for institutions and wealthy individuals, though all that was already changing rapidly. I remember Bob Danforth, the head of our research department, telling a story about the 1950s. Bob said he had sent out a research report recommending Chesebrough-Pond's, the cosmetics company that made Pond's Cold Cream and Vaseline. A year later, he got a big order. The client called and said, "We've read your report, we've studied it and thought about it. And now we're ready to buy the stock." Bob was very pleased.

In those days, markets were slower, transaction costs were higher, and middle-income people were far less focused on the stock market in general. When I graduated from law school, 6 million shares would trade on a busy day on the New York Stock Exchange, compared to an average volume today of more than a billion shares. Contrary to the common view on Wall Street, I would say that this was better in some ways. The markets were less efficient, to be sure, but there was also less emphasis on short-term trading, more emphasis on long-term prospects and the fundamentals of companies, and a more balanced sense of the risks in owning stocks.

I don't want to draw too rosy a picture of what markets were like before the '90s boom. Greed, fear, and complacency are constants of human nature. Speculative excesses have always occurred. The mid- to late 1960s, in particular, were marked by a lot of volatility and excess; a well-known book about that period was titled *The Go-Go Years.* But even at the height of the 1960s excesses, many people remained affected, at least to some extent, by the 1930s. Memories of the Great Depression influenced thinking about markets for the older generation working on Wall Street, in the media, and for much of the American public. Many people still retained a sense that stocks were inherently risky. They knew in their bones that the worst could happen in markets.

By the 1990s, most of the people of Gus Levy's generation, who had experienced the Depression personally, were gone, and attitudes had continued to shift more broadly. The change in mentality coincided with enormous changes in the market, driven in part by the increasing clout of institutional investors: pension funds, charitable endowments, and mutual funds. You might think that these funds, which were professionally run, would have been long-term investors, so-called patient capital. After all, pension funds fund long-term liabilities—retirement savings. But that wasn't what happened. Pension funds became a driving force for short-term thinking in corporate America.

Consider how it worked for a big industrial company such as General Motors in the 1960s. The company's pension fund was required to have sufficient resources to fully meet future expected pension costs. So, every year, General Motors had to make a contribution of more than $40 million to its pension fund. That contribution is a charge against earnings. But the better the performance of the stocks in the fund's portfolio, the smaller the company's annual contribution would have to be—or perhaps no contribution would be needed at all. Earnings would thus be higher, which would help raise the company's stock price. So, as companies were being evaluated more and more on their quarterly earnings, those companies began to focus more on the short-term performance of their own pension-fund portfolios. The very CEOs who complained about quarterly pressure were putting quarterly pressure on their own money managers, who would in turn put pressure on the companies in whose stocks they were invested. The result was a cycle that was, depending on one's perspective, either virtuous or vicious. And as mutual funds turned into popular investment vehicles and a competitive industry, the same phenomenon occurred there.

Other changes fueled this increased focus on quarterly earnings as well. Fixed commissions on the New York Stock Exchange were abolished on "May Day," May 1, 1975, and firms started to give discounts on large trades. This meant that wealthy individuals and institutional investors were able to trade much less expensively, which intensified their short-term focus on the market and increased portfolio turnover. Transaction costs for middle-class investors remained relatively high until the early 1990s, which discouraged individuals from trading small quantities of stock frequently. But with the rise of discount brokerage houses such as Charles Schwab, and the advent of on-line trading, people of modest means could buy and sell a few hundred shares for a commission of $20 or less at the touch of a button. The bull market that began in 1982 and the advent of easier and cheaper trading encouraged less sophisticated investors to trade more and more. Again, the conventional view is that reduced costs and greater ease were a uniformly positive development. In my view, they were a mixed blessing.

By the end of the long bull market, America was living through an explosion of amateur investing unlike any the world has ever known, except perhaps in the late 1920s. Twenty-four-hour business news channels such as CNBC and CNNfn began providing the background hum in airports, restaurants, and gyms. Securities analysts, once the least glamorous toilers on Wall Street, became well-paid celebrities. People with no background or training were quitting their jobs and setting up shop as day traders. All of this tremendously accelerated the emphasis on the short term.

Of course, the focus on quarterly earnings is not purely a pernicious development, but has both positive and negative consequences. In the mid-1980s, I talked about this with Mark Winkelman, my partner at Goldman, who ran our foreign exchange and commodities activities. "You know, the terrible weakness of our system is that it's so short-term focused," I said.

Mark didn't agree with me, because he felt that a short-term focus forced companies to face problems. With ideal corporate managers, a focus only on the long term would be optimal. But human nature being what it is, managers can use the long term as an excuse for not addressing problems. "Look at Japan," Mark said. "They have patient capital and a long-term focus. And the result is they don't face their problems." At that point, many people thought Japan had developed an economic model superior to our own. I've come to appreciate that Mark was at least partly right. People who aren't held accountable in the short term often won't make tough decisions and use the long term as their excuse. They say, "We're investing in the future."

But as time went on, the short-term focus became greater and the balance got out of proportion. Focus on the short term caused corporate decision makers not only to face problems—which was good—but also to give too little weight to the long term. When I left Washington in 1999, I was astonished at how much greater the short-term focus had become during the bull market. Commentators on the business news channels virtually never spoke about the five-year prospects of companies or had serious discussions of valuation. They talked instead about the short-term direction of the stock and quarterly earnings—or, with dot-coms, revenue growth, "eyeballs," and visions of days to come. Today, an analyst who forecasts the five-year prospects for Ford Motor Company will probably never make a living. His customers want to know what the next quarter's going to be like. Virtually every time a company misses expectations about quarterly earnings, by even a penny or so, the stock goes down in knee-jerk reaction, rather than the "missed quarter" being analyzed to see whether that miss had any ramifications for the longer term. As an illustration of how distorted the system has become, any technology purchasing manager for a big company will tell you that the best time to buy a high-tech service is in the last week before the end of the quarter, when technology companies are desperate to find income they can recognize in time to boost their quarterly earnings.

I remember one lunchtime conversation I had with the CEO of a well-known industrial company. He said, with great frustration, that the market's short-term focus made it impossible for him to adequately implement an exciting long-term strategy his company had developed. To make the point, he described how he had just met with a major institutional investor and had set forth his company's long-term strategy. "To accomplish this long-term purpose, we need to invest now," he had said, "and we'll have these wonderful benefits down the road." And the institution's response had been: "We don't want you investing for the future. Not because we disagree with you about the long-term benefits, but because we're not going to be there for the long-term. What we care about is your next quarter."

When I got to Citigroup and began working at a public company for the first time in my life, the realities of this problem were driven home to me. My initial reaction was that Sandy Weill was focused on quarterly results in a way that might not maximize our income over time. But I've come to recognize that Sandy's near-term drive exemplified what's sensible about the Mark Winkelman point—and is one of Sandy's great strengths as a manager. Sandy's view is that you have to keep on top of people ferociously with respect to the current quarter for two reasons. The first is that people are forced to face issues they might otherwise defer. The second is that the short-term stock price does matter. A quarterly numbers disappointment generally drives a stock down. And the lower stock price hurts morale, reduces your ability to make acquisitions, and makes it harder to retain key employees who have been given stock options or shares that become theirs only after they've been with the company for a specified period. In fact, stock options themselves have been greatly criticized for exacerbating the problem of excessive short-term focus. But properly used, they can serve a useful purpose in giving employees a long-term ownership stake in the company.

But to the extent that companies place undue weight on short-term performance, corporate earnings may be suboptimal over the long term and our economy as a whole may fail to realize its full potential. Given the realities of life, companies may rightly feel that the right balance is more toward the short term than is needed to accomplish the purposes Mark Winkelman identified. The thus far unanswered policy challenge is what, if anything, can be done to create an environment where investors— and, by extension, companies—shift their focus more toward the longer term.

ONE FACTOR IN the changing public attitudes toward the stock market was the wave of corporate scandal that overtook markets beginning in late 2001. After companies including Enron, WorldCom, and Tyco, once touted as models of the new economy, collapsed in recriminations, investigations, and prosecutions, the idealization of corporate America gave way to a sense of mistrust. Citigroup was enmeshed in this because it was involved in lending, structured finance, or other transactions with many of these companies, which were among the largest in the country. In addition, Citigroup owned Salomon Smith Barney, one of Wall Street's major investment banking firms. And while the specific circumstances differed from place to place, all of the major firms were engaged in activities that, while clearly troubling in retrospect, were common to the whole industry. Practices such as allocating desirable IPO shares to favored customers and not clearly separating stock research from investment banking were well known to the regulators and the media, but they had seldom been seen as problematic until the great bull market came apart.

Once people focused on these practices, it was obvious that they, as well as issues around accounting and corporate governance, needed to be addressed. Citigroup did that by making some fundamental changes in the way it did business, and it settled with its regulators on Wall Street research issues as well as Enron-structured finance transactions, though private civil litigation relating to these matters is likely to continue for some time. The other major Wall Street firms went through a similar process and all adopted roughly the same new standards and practices. There were also important and useful legislative responses, such as the Sarbanes-Oxley Act of 2002, as well as new regulations from the federal agencies—though all of this is not without cost in terms of increased process and paperwork.

But a broader question remains—one that, if understood, may help to minimize the incidence of future problems. Why didn't regulators, legislators, and industry participants—myself included—recognize and act upon these issues much sooner? Why didn't more members of the media, who in writing about some of the accomplishments of star research analysts sometimes cited their success in developing investment banking business, focus on the issue of conflict of interest? How was it that the gatekeepers—the accountants and lawyers—did not recognize and act on these matters? Perhaps the answer is that the great bull market masked many sins, or created powerful incentives not to dwell on problems when all seemed to be going so well—a natural human inclination. Also, I do think most people assumed that, even with the conflicts, research analysts—and, in the context of another set of issues, accountants—wouldn't intentionally mislead investors, and I think that was true in the great preponderance of cases.

The key to successful reform—with both corporate governance issues and Wall Street practices—was to make sure legislative and regulatory responses effectively addressed the problems without undermining the efficiency of our capital market system or the many strengths of our corporate government system. One cautionary note is that many worry that what has been done has had unintended effects on corporate decision making. Jack Welch put it well at a small dinner we attended together in 2003. He said that the only topic CEOs used to want to talk about was growth. Now all they wanted to talk about was corporate governance. In a climate where in hindsight honest mistakes or risk-taking decisions that turn out badly are confused with dishonesty, managers can become far less willing to take a chance of failure. While clearly there was a need for additional protections, the key going forward is to make sure reforms are implemented in a way that preserves the strengths of our system.

THE ENRON STORY also had an unexpected side effect for me. In November 2001, when Enron was already in very serious financial trouble, the company was seeking to merge with Dynegy, another energy-trading firm. Citigroup was a creditor of Enron and would ultimately recognize losses on that position. Enron's well-being also raised a substantial public policy issue for the country—a concern, widely reported in the press, that the company's possible bankruptcy could seriously disrupt energy markets in the United States because Enron was the central trading hub in a number of those markets. Although those feared consequences ultimately didn't materialize, at the time they resembled the concerns about the collapse of Long-Term Capital Management, which had led to intervention by the New York Fed in 1998.

In Enron's case, creditors were concerned that if the credit rating agencies downgraded Enron's debt, counterparties would no longer be willing to engage in trades or long-term contracts with Enron. That would almost surely doom a Dynegy merger and lead to Enron's collapse since, at this point, without the financial support of Dynegy, Enron could no longer remain a viable trading company. Enron's creditors would certainly suffer if it went bankrupt, but many feared that the economy as a whole could take a significant hit as well.

Several banks that were Enron creditors agreed that they might be willing to put up more money to support Enron in order to maintain its credit ratings and the strength necessary to keep trading, thus allowing the Dynegy merger to go through. There was, however, a substantial concern that the ratings agencies would downgrade Enron before the rescue package could be put in place, and a corresponding view that with just a few more days, a package might well be assembled. In that context, I placed a call to Peter Fisher, a senior official at the Treasury Department, whom I had known when he was at the Federal Reserve Bank of New York. I asked Peter whether he thought it would make sense for him or someone else at Treasury to place a call to the rating agencies and suggest briefly holding off on any downgrade of Enron's debt while the banks considered putting in more money. I prefaced our conversation by saying that my suggestion was "probably a bad idea," but that I wanted to see what he thought. As it happened, Peter thought it would be a mistake for Treasury to intervene in this manner, and that was the end of it.

I was, however, subjected to a good deal of subsequent scrutiny about my call to Peter. Of course, in the wake of Enron's implosion and the stunning revelations of fraud and misconduct that followed, it became obvious that the company couldn't have been salvaged. I can see why that call might be questioned, but I would make it again, under those circumstances and knowing what I knew at the time. There was an important public policy concern about the energy markets—not just a parochial concern about Citigroup's exposure—and I felt that if a modest intervention by Treasury could potentially make the difference in avoiding a significant economic shock for the country it was worth raising the idea with an official there.

I was guided in this thinking by the knowledge that I would have wanted to hear suggestions of that kind when I was at Treasury, and knowing that I would have been entirely comfortable rejecting them if I thought they didn't make sense for the country. I believed that Peter Fisher would have a similar mind-set—interested in hearing ideas that might conceivably be helpful, but unabashed about turning such ideas down if he thought that was the right course. And that is exactly what Peter did.

A subsequent bipartisan congressional staff review of my call to Peter concluded that nothing improper had transpired. By that time, however, the call had become fodder for a personal attack against me, not because of anything related to the call itself, but because of my role in the ongoing debate about economic policy and because I'd come to personify the policies of the Clinton era. At that time, the economy was still very weak and commentators were increasingly comparing President Bush's economic stewardship unfavorably to President Clinton's. I wrote a lengthy op-ed piece in the Sunday *Washington Post* about how to rebuild economic confidence, which expressed great concern about tax cuts that undermined long-term fiscal discipline. My engagement in the economic debate seemed to infuriate some tax-cut proponents, who then seized upon the Peter Fisher call and everything else they could think of to attack me. ("You're a mouse and they think you're a gorilla," Bob Strauss pointed out.) The nature of the attack became clear when the Republican National Committee e-mailed hundreds of journalists an inflammatory "opposition research" memo that dredged up long-discredited accusations that I misled Congress during the debt-limit crisis in 1995 and made various unwarranted assertions about Enron. A Republican congressman went on CNN and made the connection explicit: he said my call to Peter Fisher was fair game for attack because I had chosen to criticize the administration's economic policies.

After my years in government, I suppose I shouldn't have been surprised about being the object of ad hominem attacks when I challenged the opposition on policy issues. But I still think that this approach to policy differences and to politics does a deep disservice to the vigorous exchange of views so essential to our democratic political system.

ANYONE WHO PARTICIPATES in financial markets—whether as an individual investor, a Wall Street bond trader, or a company CEO—has to make fundamental decisions about risk. At an individual level, such choices affect one's financial well-being and peace of mind. At the corporate level, they affect profitability levels. And at the broadest collective level, decisions about risk have potentially enormous economic consequences. In a world of immense global trading markets, the success of institutions, the liquidity and efficiency of markets, and the safety of our financial system depend to a great extent on how well the complex process of risk determination is carried out by the vast numbers of participants—individuals and businesses—involved in the financial markets.

Many people arrive at accepting some level of market or trading risk through instinct, aversion, or feel. My approach, by contrast, has always been to try to make risk decisions on an analytic basis—even if they involve judgments about such intangibles as how much one can handle emotionally and the less-than-rational actions of others in the markets.

In making any decision about risk, the logical first step is to try to determine at what point additional risk no longer carries potential rewards that exceed the potential losses, given the respective probabilities of the good and the bad. The actual measurement of these probabilities, of course, is immensely complicated. But this calculation, which can be organized on an expected-value table, remains the most fundamental basis for decisions about risk.

However, the problem quickly grows more complicated. As an illustration, consider the choice a major financial institution such as Citigroup faces in choosing an optimal level of trading risk—that is, the level of risk incurred by the firm's own traders trying to maximize return on some portion of the firm's own capital. That is a far more complex question than it might seem to be at first, with many dimensions that can't be quantified on an expected-value table.

To begin with, a public company such as Citigroup is very different from the private firm Goldman Sachs was when I was there. A public company's stock price is a function of its earnings and the multiple the market decides to put on those earnings. And financial markets value stable earnings growth more highly than a volatile earnings path, even if the total profits at some projected end point are the same. So a public company has to determine both what will maximize its earnings over time—adjusting that calculation for risk—and also the effect of greater volatility on the multiple. Only after making these judgments can one make an educated guess about what level of risk will maximize a company's share price over time.

At a large financial company today, none of this is easy. In part, the difficulty arises because of the immense size and complexity of a firm's positions, which typically include stocks, bonds, derivatives, and currencies. In part, it arises because of the intrinsic difficulty of deciding which risks correlate with one another and which are likely to offset one another. And in part, it is due to the inherent uncertainty in trying to estimate rewards, risks, and probabilities. It is also extremely difficult to get managers to be ruthlessly analytic and to put their emotions and opinions aside.

Nor is that the end of the road with respect to risk management. Maximizing the expected value of results over time is a critical but not sufficient guide to decision making. Even when the expected value for additional risk is positive, every trader or investor—from the smallest individual to the largest commercial or investment bank—must decide, as a separate matter, how much loss he or it can tolerate, financially and psychologically. As an additional complication, there is one type of financial risk, the risk of remote contingencies—which, if they occur, can be devastating—that market participants of all kinds almost always systematically underestimate. The list of firms and individuals who have gone broke by failing to focus on remote risks is a long one. Even people who think probabilistically, and are highly analytical and systematic, often dismiss remote contingencies as irrelevant.

In this regard, I often think of an example from Goldman Sachs when Jon Corzine, then the firm's exceedingly successful head of fixed-income activities, wanted to take a large position in farm credit bonds. The expectation was of a high return, and because the bonds were backed by the "moral obligation" of the U.S. government through a new agency known as Farmer Mac, the probability of their defaulting seemed close to zero. But what Steve Friedman and I asked Jon was "What if a problem develops in farm credit and as extremely unlikely as it might be, the government declines to stand by its so-called moral obligation?"

"That's silly," Corzine replied. It was inconceivable to him that the government would not honor its moral obligation, and in a sense he was right.

But Steve and I didn't want Goldman Sachs to cease to exist after 130 years because something that we agreed was virtually inconceivable actually happened. In theory, you don't ever want to be in a position where even a remote risk can hurt you beyond a certain point—and you have to decide what that point is. Too often, risks that seem remote are treated as essentially nonexistent. In this case, the remote contingency never occurred, but the decision to limit the risk was right.

As a practical matter, if you want to be in the business of trading or want to invest, all sorts of remote contingencies have to be set aside, from systemic financial collapse to catastrophic meteorites to nuclear war. We once explored this idea at Goldman and concluded that if we really wanted to take into account every catastrophic contingency, we couldn't be in business. But even if you can't avoid all distant risks in practice, it's sensible to think explicitly about which ones you're choosing to take and which should be diminished or avoided.

WHEN I ARRIVED at Citigroup, it had of course done much risk analysis, and Sandy Weill and his team had reached judgments suited to the institution. But from time to time, senior executives revisited the issue. After becoming Citigroup's president in 2002, Bob Willumstad raised a risk-related question not just about trading but about our allocation of capital overall. We had more than $80 billion in equity capital employed in our various businesses. Were our assets allocated in the most effective way possible? Perhaps a bit more should be in Brazil and a bit less in credit cards, or vice versa. Willumstad pointed out that at Citi, as at any company, all kinds of operating assumptions had built up over time, none of which was necessarily right. Some additional analytical work on risks and returns could challenge a lot of the conventional thinking, perhaps causing us to reduce some activities and increase others.

This kicked off an even broader discussion of how to evaluate conventional wisdom inside a company. I remember one meeting in my office that included Hamid Biglari, an Iranian-born Ph.D. in nuclear physics who was then our head of corporate strategy; Chuck Prince, then Citi's chief administrative officer; Kim Schoenholtz, our chief economist; and

Lewis Alexander, our chief emerging-market economist. My response to Willumstad was that any institution will always have immense resistance to conclusions that differ from the conventional wisdom. Any conclusion that pointed toward significant change would inevitably be attacked. People with a vested interest in the status quo would find flaws in the study's methodology, in the way risks were calculated, in indirect effects and factors that hadn't been considered. Under that kind of attack, a program for change can easily dissolve into an endless, irresolvable debate.

Moreover, the people who raised these objections to analytic conclusions pointing to change wouldn't necessarily be wrong. Analytic rigor was a critical starting point for the discussion. But financial analysis could never encompass all of the relevant considerations. There were factors in some of our businesses that couldn't be quantified but that could have great economic impact, including synergies between the businesses, impact on our image, and so on.

Not long after I became a partner at Goldman in the early 1970s, the late Hyman Weinberg, our capable CFO, did a business-by-business profit and loss statement. That would now seem rudimentary, but we'd never done one because some people felt it might cause discord in the partnership. Hy found that investment banking—the business Goldman was best known for—wasn't actually profitable for the period he was looking at. John Whitehead, the highly respected head of investment banking at the time, responded that he knew that investment banking was profitable. If Hy's methodology didn't show that result, the methodology must be flawed.

Oddly enough, both Hy and John may have been correct. Investment banking is people-intensive, and the people tend to be extremely well paid. Thus at times good profit margins can be hard to achieve, although, as in Goldman Sachs's case, the business can be highly profitable over long periods, when conditions are at least moderately favorable. But even if Hy was right about investment banking not being profitable for the period he was looking at, John may also have been right in the sense that investment banking probably made a substantial nonquantifiable contribution to profitability by enhancing the prestige and standing of the firm, thereby attracting clients in other areas.

The right conclusion, I think, is that ongoing change is critical to success, and even to survival, but that ultimately challenging conventional wisdom is a matter of judgment. For example, measuring risk-adjusted returns on capital, as Bob Willumstad originally suggested, can be very useful as a tool to inform judgments. But a great danger for any institution is that such tools can take on a bureaucratic life of their own—especially as they come to be viewed as more sophisticated and "scientific"—and begin to drive decisions formulaically rather than contributing as inputs to broader judgments.

EVEN AFTER THE MARKET had started to fall, the tendency of otherwise intelligent and thoughtful people not to think clearly about stocks and investing continued to strike me. I remember when a shrewd venture capitalist came to my office and gave me a book. "These people have a system that works," he said.

"Well, you know, I'm pretty skeptical about systems," I responded.

And my friend said, "You read this, and you'll see. These people have done it."

The book covered a period from about 1995 to 1999, during which the stock market had essentially gone straight up except for a severe downdraft in 1998. Once I saw the four-year track record, I didn't bother reading to see what the theory was. During those years, all you had to do was buy stocks to do extremely well. I threw the book out because I was afraid someone might see it on my desk.

During the strong market of the 1990s, most investors who rode the wave ignored traditional ideas about valuation. Some money managers remained invested on the basis of a practical calculation: "If the market continues to rise and I'm not participating, I'll lose my job. But if it falls dramatically, I'll be in the same situation as everyone else." Others were conscious market cynics who thought they could successfully exploit the foolishness of others. Momentum investors didn't need an opinion about valuation. They were consciously saying, "The market may be overvalued—we don't know and we don't care. All we know is, it's been going up, and we're going to invest as long as it does—and get off the train before everyone else." The problem lies in executing the greater-fool theory. If you get off every time the market ticks down and then reestablish your position when the market starts to go up again, you're going to get killed, because even rising markets fluctuate on the way up. And if you wait, you risk going down with everyone else.

With the stock market decline after 2000, many of the new-paradigm theories lost credibility. That should have brought renewed attention to the failure of most "active" fund managers—people who pick individual stocks rather than passively investing in an index—to outperform the market over the long run. Over long periods, the S&P 500 index has done better than the preponderance of active managers. Few mutual funds, hedge funds, or money managers consistently beat the indexes over a decade, let alone several decades.

When I express these kinds of views in speeches or interviews, I am often asked, "How should people with limited resources think about investing?" I'm not in the business of giving financial advice, but I have learned something about how to think about these matters. My guidance is fairly conventional and hardly exciting. But however commonplace it may seem, people tend not to follow it, especially when the adrenaline starts rushing.

The most important part of my answer is that investors should recognize the risks they're taking. Stocks outperformed bonds for every decade of the twentieth century, except for the 1930s and a roughly equal performance in the 1970s. But there is no guarantee that the future will replicate the past or, at the least, that there won't be long periods of poor or mediocre stock market performance. And even if stocks as a whole continue to outperform bonds over the long run, many individual stocks will still perform badly. You might simply pick the wrong stocks and as a result significantly underperform the market—just as many professional money managers do.

And even if the historical outperformance of equities holds true and you do not pick the wrong stock or group of stocks, there may still be extended periods of adverse market performance. You, as an investor, simply may not be able to stand a wait of five to ten years or even longer, either financially or psychologically. Stocks that outperform bonds in the long run may also underperform them badly for lengthy periods within that "long run." Over the seventeen-year stretch from the last day of 1964 to the last day of 1981, the Dow closed at the same level—874 in 1964 versus 875 in 1981. While the S&P 500 did rise by 45 percent during the same period, that is still only roughly 2½ percent per annum (plus the average dividend yield of roughly 4 percent). And after several years of difficulty, you have no way of knowing if the markets will improve or continue to deteriorate. Investors who want to retire or send their children to college may discover that they can't continue to wait for the hoped-for benefits of the long term, while other investors may simply not be able to live with the stress of large loans and the uncertainty of what might happen next. In reality, people often can't tolerate an extended downturn, so they get out and take their losses, only to reinvest when the market rises. When it falls again, they get whipsawed.

Even with all those qualifications, most investors who are in a position to have a long-term perspective should probably have some portion—and in appropriate cases even a fairly substantial portion—of their savings in stocks. The threshold questions are: How much? And should decisions about asset allocation be subject to short-term market views? There are all kinds of models that recommend the proportion of investible assets to put into stocks, based on performance data in stocks over some long prior period of time and the circumstances of the individual investor. An alternative is for an investor to start with a full understanding of the risks and then to decide how much he could live with losing if his investments fell substantially. That would set the outer limit of the equity allocation. The amount to actually invest in equities within that limit would be affected by a whole host of factors, including the investor's time horizon and income needs, and a disciplined approach to calculating likely risks and rewards over whatever the time horizon may be. In my own case, I have also made the judgment that I should avoid what I thought were times of market excess, while recognizing the uncertainty of those judgments. I certainly would not put all of my money into stocks, or put too much into a single stock or small number of individual stocks, or into any one sector of the economy. And I would buy stocks based only on the long-term prospects of a company, with a view toward holding any investment for a very long time unless those prospects change or valuation rises to irrational levels.

Warren Buffett is famous for this "value investing" approach—buying companies only when their prices are low relative to their long-term earnings prospects, with a view to being a very-long-term holder of the stock. I think that approach, carefully and consistently executed, provides the best opportunity to outperform the market indexes over time. Those who aren't particularly well positioned to make judgments about individual stocks can choose a mutual fund that has executed this approach successfully for a long time or a financial advisor who seems well equipped to do so. Another approach is simply to invest in an index fund, whose performance will track the market's. For those with sufficient resources, a wider range of possibilities has become available: so-called alternative investments, such as a private equity fund or various kinds of hedge funds. Conceptually, these alternatives can make good sense, but they are now becoming popular and faddish and may quickly become a new set of excesses, with unhappy results for many investors. For example, one post-boom fashion has been "long-short" funds that attempt to be at least somewhat market-neutral by having long and short portfolios that are close to equal in size. The idea is to get the benefit of your selections whether stocks as a whole go up or down. Most active managers have made money over the last twenty years not because of their active management but because the market as a whole went up so much. With a market-neutral approach, you take away the one factor that has allowed most active managers to reap gains over the last twenty years—namely, the rise in stock prices—and keep the factor that history has shown most don't succeed at—namely, active management. I do believe that some investors have the judgment, skills, and patience to outperform the market indexes over time and, consequently, some long-short funds will almost surely do well, but I would guess that the great majority probably will not.

Finally, there is the challenge of evaluating results. For stretches of time, a stock picker may outperform the market for reasons that have nothing to do with skill. He may simply be in sync with the biases of the

market—favoring telecommunications stocks, for example, during a period when the market as a whole favors them. Or he may be lucky. The
"random walk" theory posits that if a large number of monkeys pick
stocks by throwing darts at stock tables, half will do better than the average stock picker and half will do worse. If the winning monkeys then repeat the exercise once each year for ten years in a row, one out of 1,024
will beat the average every year, merely on the basis of probabilities. A
stock picker who beats the S&P 500 ten years running will almost surely
be lionized as having a special genius—and some may—but others will do
so merely as a matter of chance.

THINKING BACK ON my own financial behavior, I'm reminded how
commonly markets fail to behave the way you expect, feel, and hope. I've
always had a cautious view toward stocks and have never invested a lot,
partly because for most of my career I had significant exposure to the behavior of markets through my stake in Goldman Sachs. But in 1973,
when the market slumped badly, a few companies whose fundamentals I
knew well had come way down and seemed very cheap relative to their
long-term value. Yet from the time I bought them to the time the market
bottomed out in 1974, my investments fell in price by 50 percent.

The point of that story is that even a careful and highly disciplined investor can't see a market bottom any more easily than he can see the top.
The broader point is that no one is very good at predicting the direction of
the market in the relatively near term, and investors should allocate their
assets based on long-term judgments about risks, rewards, and personal
risk tolerance. However, as I said, that's a bit of advice I've never taken
myself, tending instead to inject my own shorter-term market views. If I
remember only the times I was right, for example 1998 to 2000, I have a
terrific track record. If I'm more honest and remember all my judgments,
I'm probably not much better than fifty-fifty on shorter-term market
judgments—and I don't think anyone else is either. My experience in
1973 is probably also a warning that one should never be an absolutist
about anything—including being a contrarian. If you see a long trend in

one direction, question its soundness. But if you decide to bet against the herd, as I did in 1973, recognize that the stampede may go on for a very long time—and the herd may even be right. As my Goldman partner Bob Mnuchin used to say, people who sell at the bottom aren't stupid. The problems are real and the outcome is uncertain. Only in retrospect can you tell when the worst is over.

CHAPTER THIRTEEN

They Called It Rubinomics

I HAD FELT FOR SOME TIME that Al Gore would be a good presidential candidate and a good president. During the height of the focus on the Vice President in connection with a controversy around fund-raising practices in 1997, I had said to Gore's chief of staff, Ron Klain—a former Supreme Court clerk who combines enormous intelligence with great political savvy—that if I were to leave Treasury before the end of the Clinton presidency, I would very much like to help the Vice President in his quest for the presidency. This was a period when Gore was under a lot of pressure, and I felt that perhaps even a small gesture of encouragement would be useful. Later that same day, we were all in the Oval Office in preparation for a meeting with a foreign leader, and the Vice President came over to where I was standing and elaborately helped me into my chair.

Gore can be awkward in interpersonal interactions—an unusual and unfortunate characteristic for someone in political life. But that awkwardness can be misleading. Gore is very bright, vigorous in his thinking, and possessed of a sharp and often self-deprecating wit that I very much enjoy. I remember when the Prime Minister of Poland was visiting Washington and had the usual meeting in the Oval Office with the President, the Vice President, and a few senior officials from each side. It was a busy time at the White House, with electoral politics very much on people's minds, and I thought the meeting was probably a less than optimal use of the President's time—though, in fairness, Poland was the poster child for economic reform in Eastern Europe. At the end of the meeting, the Prime Minister noted that there were many people of Polish extraction living in the United States. The Vice President looked at him with mock astonishment and said, "We had heard something about that." I told the Vice President afterward that I had practically broken up, because in his own ironic way, Gore was making the point to the earnest Prime Minister that this was exactly why the meeting was taking place.

I tended to agree with Gore on most of his policy positions. He strongly opposed George W. Bush's campaign proposals for a massive tax cut and for the partial privatization of Social Security. Gore had been a strong force for deficit reduction from the beginning of the administration, had worked hard on the Hill to pass the Mexican support program, and had very publicly supported trade liberalization, especially during the struggle to pass NAFTA—even though that had been politically difficult at times within the Democratic Party. He also had a strong focus on inner-city problems.

Gore's greatest passion, of course, was the environment. I had entered the administration with great skepticism about what seemed to me absolutism on the part of at least some environmentalists. But Gore persuaded me that the threats to the environment were a serious danger and that environmental protection and economic growth were not necessarily a trade-off; that, indeed, long-term economic growth would depend on sensible environmental policy. I came to believe that measures of the gross domestic product would more accurately reflect economic output if environmental costs and benefits could be included—though that is not yet feasible, either politically or technically. I remember a long conversation we had in the Vice President's West Wing office about global warming. Gore said that even if science didn't provide certainty, the evidence was considerable that global warming was occurring, and measures to repair it would take a long time to have substantial effect. If we waited too long and the evidence turned out to be correct, the result could be an unpreventable catastrophe. And with risk of catastrophe, you cannot afford to be wrong. This was in a way analogous to the problem a trader faces when he has a position that is almost certain to produce a positive return but is so large that failure could put him out of business. That is a chance he can't afford to take. And of course, with global warming, most experts believe that the risk of a catastrophe is real. Any sensible analysis of global warming seems to me to lead to the conclusion that putting effective preventive measures in place is imperative—though that still leaves questions about which ones make the most sense.

Unfortunately, rather than running primarily on the economic record of the Clinton-Gore administration, the Gore campaign took something of a populist tone. Income distribution is a critically important economic issue for any society; the question is the language you choose and the sense you convey with your words. At any time, but especially at a moment when people were broadly benefiting economically, language tinged with class resentment seemed to me politically and substantively counterproductive. If Gore were to win, his populist rhetoric in the campaign could hurt business confidence and investment, which was not the way to start a new administration.

All of this, of course, is a long-standing debate within the Democratic Party, which has its philosophical schisms just as the Republican Party does. I am not a political analyst, but I've been around this debate for many years, listening to the vigorous policy and political arguments on both sides. My view remained what I remember Hillary Clinton telling Bob Reich after the 1994 midterm election debacle: that the key in the general election is the 20 percent of swing voters in the middle of the electorate, and that class conflict is not an effective approach with those people. In response to this kind of criticism, Gore's campaign strategists are quick to point out that Gore got more popular votes than Bush. But whatever one's view of the outcome, I think the Gore campaign should have done better, given that he was running as an incumbent Vice President amid the best economic conditions in many decades.

AFTER BEING SOMEWHAT involved in the 2000 election, I didn't give much thought to what role, if any, I would have in the policy debate going forward. But three events quickly got me reinvolved: the new administration's tax cut proposals in early 2001, which I considered fiscally unsound; the Democrats' need for economic policy advice from people they were comfortable working with; and the September 11 attacks. All of these factors pulled me back into the policy-making process. It's useful to separate the history of the Great Fiscal Debate from current arguments around the question of whether deficits matter. After analyzing the issue, I'll relate the story of how I reengaged with the debate.

The Great Fiscal Debate: More than anything else, it was my deeply troubled reaction to the administration's tax cut proposals that led me to reengage. The tax bill, debated and passed in the first half of 2001, began a period in which tax cut advocates dismissed mainstream views about the direct and indirect effects of large tax cuts on the government's fiscal position, the value of sound fiscal policy, and the harm caused by large, long-term structural deficits.

Conservatives often framed the debate over Bush's proposals as a question of lower taxes versus more spending. (Here and throughout the chapter, my reference to conservatives is to those who, through the 1980s and 1990s, coalesced around fervent advocacy of the tax cuts as an overriding priority, rather than more traditional conservatives, who, whatever their social and other views, were strong advocates of sound fiscal policy.) The Concord Coalition, an organization dedicated to fiscal discipline, and led successively by two Republicans, former Commerce Secretary Pete Peterson and former Senator Warren Rudman, was advocating policies that once were at the core of the conservative movement and the Republican Party (and eschewed by most Democrats). One of the ironies of this period is that today those policies are opposed by many leading conservatives and supported by many Democrats.

If government didn't give back the surpluses to the public in the form of a tax cut, leading conservatives argued, "Washington" would find a way to spend the money. Another version was that the surpluses were the people's money and should be returned to them. These formulations are as politically shrewd as they are simplistic and in many ways misleading. Nobody likes what government does when it's described as "spending." Yet the major programs that make up the vast preponderance of government spending—from Social Security and Medicare to defense, law enforcement, education, and environmental protection—command widespread public support. In practice, even conservative supporters of tax cuts are reluctant to scale back these popular programs, and they even vote for increases at the same time as they inveigh against "spending." These programs are the people's programs, just as tax dollars are the people's money. If tax cuts are not matched by spending reductions, they increase the size of the federal debt—a debt that is the people's debt.

The Bush administration's approach to tax cuts framed a new stage in the Great Fiscal Debate, an ongoing clash about the effects of fiscal discipline and of tax cuts on economic growth. This argument first affected policy in a significant way during the 1980 presidential campaign, when a group of conservative "supply-siders" attained prominence. The core of the supply-side theory was that lower marginal tax rates would cause people to "supply" more labor, working more and harder, which would increase growth—and the positive effect on growth would be so large that government tax revenue would actually increase rather than decrease in response to the tax cut.

George H. W. Bush, Ronald Reagan's opponent for the Republican nomination in the 1980 election, referred to this as "voodoo economics." And not all of Reagan's advisers believed this theory. Some committed conservatives understood that reducing the size of government is difficult because of the popularity of most spending programs of significant size. Tax cuts seemed to offer a way around this political problem. If government's revenues were squeezed, this line of reasoning went, spending could no longer grow and might even be forced to shrink. Despite that theory, spending throughout the 1980s, agreed to by both the Reagan administration and Congress, consistently and significantly exceeded levels necessary to offset the tax cuts. The result was the large deficits of the 1980s, deficits that kept increasing during the early 1990s and were projected by the outgoing administration in 1992 to grow even more in the years ahead.

For a government to run a cyclical deficit—a short-term and temporary deficit in conjunction with a recession or an economic slowdown—isn't necessarily bad and at times may be entirely sensible. Keynesian economics explicitly advocates cyclical deficits produced by temporarily higher spending or temporarily lower taxes as a way of dealing with recessions. In the 1960s and '70s, some liberal Democrats who accepted that theory also found in Keynesian economics a convenient argument for advocating permanent increases in programs. But the Reagan tax cuts, combined with the Reagan-era defense spending increases, created something different: large and intractable long-term structural deficits, which persisted even when economic conditions were good. The Walter Mondale campaign of 1984 and the Michael Dukakis campaign of 1988 both argued that the existence of this structural deficit was a significant, long-term threat to the American economy. Essentially, they didn't get any response, because so few people understood the problem. Mondale told me some years later about his frustration at not being able to talk about the deficit in a way people could relate to.

By 1989, the deficit had begun to seriously affect the economy. People began to understand that deficits were contributing in some way to the difficult economic conditions of the very late 1980s and early 1990s, which changed the political dynamics of the issue. By 1992, the deficit was 4.7 percent of GDP—nearly $300 billion. Dealing with the deficit was a centerpiece of Clinton's 1992 campaign. One of the reasons Clinton focused so intently on the deficit is that it not only was causing harm to the economy but was also undermining confidence in government, limiting its ability to deal with problems and issues that people cared about. Though he supported reductions in many areas, Clinton wanted government to be more active in others.

After Clinton took office, the Great Fiscal Debate mutated. In 1993, the debate was between supporters of Clinton's economic plan—which included revenue increases, principally an income tax increase on the top 1.2 percent of taxpayers and a small gas tax—and opponents who argued that tax increases of any kind would harm the economy. Loyal supply-siders such as Jack Kemp and Paul Gigot of *The Wall Street Journal* argued that our economic program would harm the economy and lead to higher unemployment. Some were even more specific in their predictions. "I believe this will lead to a recession next year," Newt Gingrich said at the time. "This is the Democrat machine's recession and each one of them will be held personally accountable."

The 1993 deficit reduction program was a test case for supply-side theory. Instead of the job losses, increased deficits, and recession the supply-siders predicted, the economy had a remarkable eight years—the longest period of continuous economic expansion yet recorded. Unemployment fell from more than 7 percent to 4 percent, accompanied by the creation of more than 20 million new private-sector jobs. Inflation remained low while GDP growth averaged 3.5 percent per annum. Productivity growth averaged 2.5 percent a year between 1995 and 2000, a level not seen since the early 1970s. Poverty rates went down significantly, including among Blacks and Hispanics, and incomes rose for both higher and lower earners. For the first time in nearly thirty years, the budget balanced in 1998.

President Clinton's economic plan contributed greatly to these conditions. That success created an immense anger on the part of some conservatives, who saw a policy they decried lead to conditions they said wouldn't occur. Ever since, they've been trying to find other ways to explain what happened to the economy and to denigrate Clinton's accomplishment. During the 1990s, some moved to the position that the economy was booming for reasons they said had nothing to do with declining deficits and balanced budgets, and pointed instead to technological progress and trade liberalization (both of which were, indeed, also important, and promoted strongly by President Clinton). A number of supply-siders advanced the theory that the boom of the 1990s was a delayed reaction to Reagan's 1981 tax cut.

My response was that you might as well give the credit to Herbert Hoover, though I do think in other respects, such as trade and some aspects of deregulation, the Reagan administration made meaningful contributions. George H. W. Bush's administration also had important, constructive initiatives, in trade and—though not often cited by supply-side conservatives—the tax increases and new budget rules he put in place in 1990. These measures were a useful step toward reestablishing fiscal discipline, although far short of what was needed to stem the tide, with the result that actual and projected deficits were at very high levels—and growing—by the end of his administration.

By 2002, conservatives had a different argument: the collapse in stock prices that had followed the eighteen-year bull market showed that the

1990s hadn't really been that healthy an economic period after all. In fact, the 1990s were years of extraordinarily favorable and sound economic conditions, but extended good times almost always produce imbalances that lead to a period of adjustment. Of course, the view that some adjustment was probably inevitable still left an important debate about what policies would best serve to minimize the duration and severity of that adjustment and best position us for the long term. I felt that our policy choices during this difficult period of adjustment did neither.

In 1994, the Democrats lost control of Congress. After the election, conservatives took the political offensive, pushing for big new tax cuts to be paid for with deep reductions in Medicare and other programs. These proposed spending cuts, which were highly unpopular, faded away after the government shutdowns in 1995. However, the tax cut proposals remained—which showed how unwilling the proponents of tax cuts usually are to take the political heat for actually cutting specific programs in a way commensurate with the reduction in tax revenues. Because specific proposals to cut the budget step on toes, conservatives often advocated ameliorating the effects of their tax cuts through "dynamic scoring"—revising the projected cost of a tax cut downward on the basis of the supply-side theory that tax cuts would create enough additional growth to pay for themselves, partially or entirely.

In the 1996 campaign, Bob Dole argued for an across-the-board reduction in rates that would have cost $548 billion over six years; President Clinton responded with the position that any tax cut should be much more modest. In earlier decades, demands for balanced budgets tended to come from Republicans, while Democratic Keynesians argued that deficits should be disregarded. The Reagan administration began to change this traditional alignment, with its supply-side approach to tax cuts. And during the Clinton presidency these roles were reversed: it was Democrats who wanted to hew to the path of fiscal responsibility and many Republicans who seemed relatively indifferent to fiscal effects, so long as the money went to reducing taxes.

As the deficits diminished and a surplus emerged during Clinton's second term, the debate evolved again. Conservatives now argued for "giving back" the large projected surpluses to taxpayers in the form of a tax cut. It seemed that other uses of the surplus better reflected the preferences of the American people and we felt that continued fiscal discipline—in this case, beginning to pay down the debt of the federal government—would best promote economic growth. What's more, Social Security and Medicare were facing huge deficits once the baby-boom generation began to retire in significant numbers. We couldn't literally prepay these future obligations out of general revenues, but if the government had paid off its debt and was in a sound fiscal condition when those enormous bills began coming due, the country would be much better positioned to deal with them.

All of this argued against massive tax cuts. But dealing with the surplus left the Democrats in a tricky situation politically. Most voters don't even understand the difference between the government's annual deficit and its accumulated debt. So it was almost impossible to explain, in a way that people would relate to, why entitlement obligations we faced decades down the road meant that a government that was running a surplus should use the money to pay down its long-term debt instead of refunding it to taxpayers. Preserving the surplus as savings and using that to pay down debt would contribute to lower interest rates, greater job creation, and higher standards of living. But the reasons this was true were complicated. To better bring home to people the advantages of saving the surplus, the administration in 1998 reframed the issue as "Saving Social Security First." The idea was to offset the political appeal of giving back the surplus in the form of a tax cut and remind the public that if the surplus was their money, the debt was their debt as well, and to connect saving the surplus with a purpose that was easy to explain. That argument worked to hold the line against massive tax cuts for a couple of years more.

In January 2001, the nonpartisan Congressional Budget Office projected a ten-year federal government surplus of $5.6 trillion. Because of certain long-established methodological practices that are widely viewed as unrealistic—for example, assuming that expiring tax credits, such as the research and development tax credit, won't be renewed—that number was probably overstated. By September 2003, after two rounds of tax cuts, Goldman Sachs, using more realistic assumptions, estimated a ten-year *deficit* of $5.5 trillion. That's a swing of $11.1 trillion, but adjusting for certain methodological inconsistencies, the better number to use is a

$9 trillion deterioration from surplus to deficit. (Obviously, ten-year projections are extremely unreliable, but the risk of actual results being worse than these projections seems, if anything, to be greater than the chance of them being better—these projections all assume healthy growth rates, which might be undermined by these very deficits.)

Though many factors contributed, the tax cuts of June 2001 and May 2003 were central to this reversal. The CBO estimated that the first tax cut would cost $1.7 trillion, including debt service (the interest that the federal government will have to pay on debt that would have been retired absent the tax cut), but those figures assumed that the tax cuts will actually "sunset," or expire, when scheduled to do so. Independent analysts suggested the cost would be higher, exceeding $2 trillion with debt service, if the tax cuts were instead made permanent. The second tax cut was officially estimated to cost $550 billion with debt service, again assuming the tax cuts would expire. If, instead, the tax cuts are made permanent, as proponents argued they should be, the cost would exceed $1 trillion over a ten-year period, with debt service. The combined tax cuts, then, represented roughly a third of the total deterioration of $9 trillion, and roughly two thirds of the $5.5 trillion deficit estimated by Goldman Sachs.

The tax cuts also helped to undermine the fragile political consensus around fiscal discipline that came out of the 1990s. The natural inertial tendency in Washington is toward passing more immediately gratifying tax cuts or spending increases, rather than what is best for the long term. A large tax cut, especially one that benefited higher-income taxpayers so much, made it hard to argue for discipline in other areas and thereby worked to unravel the reluctant sense of obligation to maintain sound fiscal policy. The federal debt, which would have fallen from one third of GDP to zero well within ten years under earlier fiscal estimates, instead was estimated two years later in that Goldman Sachs study to increase to more than 50 percent of GDP by the end of the ten years. Moreover, the numbers of baby boomers retiring will increase rapidly in the years ahead, raising Medicare and Social Security costs and making prospects as the years go on even worse.

Do Deficits Matter? With this as a background, the Great Fiscal Debate now moved to the question of whether these projected deficits mattered. This is clearly the heart of the issue. The proponents of tax cuts had to argue that they didn't matter—or at least didn't matter much—because large tax cuts and a sound fiscal position could not be reconciled. And tax cut advocates, including President George W. Bush's CEA chairman, Glenn Hubbard, pointed to me as the symbol of the position that deficits have a significant effect on interest rates and therefore on economic activity, job creation, and growth. The *Wall Street Journal* editorial page dismissed the theory that deficits affect interest rates as "Rubinomics."

Flattered as I was, at first I didn't think this position could possibly get traction. But it was loudly trumpeted, and the countervailing view wasn't. As a result, what seemed to me arrant nonsense came to be treated as a serious point of view. One tax cut proponent testifying beside me at a congressional hearing went so far as to say that nothing in the literature supported the concern about fiscal conditions affecting interest rates.

Nothing in the literature? The first thing you learn in Introductory Economics is that supply and demand determine price. It's curious to me that people whose basic credo is that markets explain everything don't think that an important factor in the supply and demand for debt financing—the federal government's fiscal position—has any effect on interest rates. Put another way, it's an even more obvious point: when the government borrows, the pool of savings available for private purposes shrinks and the price of capital—expressed as the interest rate—rises. If the Treasury ceases borrowing and instead begins paying down some of its outstanding $3.8 trillion debt, the savings pool available to the private sector increases and interest rates go down. A study by Robert Cumby at Georgetown University and two of his colleagues, completed sometime after that hearing, found a strong correlation between bond market interest rates and expectations about future fiscal conditions. The Cumby paper overcame a serious problem with previous papers that had examined only the relationship between interest rates and current fiscal conditions. Focusing instead on the relationship between interest rates and expected future conditions makes sense: a buyer of a five- or ten-year bond should logically be influenced primarily by expectations about inter-est rates and bond prices over the life of the asset.

But Cumby's paper didn't get much public visibility. Then Bill Gale and Peter Orszag of the Brookings Institution prepared a fifty-five-page paper with analysis and conclusions similar to Cumby's. It cited other well-established economists in support of the impact of projected fiscal condi-tions on interest rates—including Martin Feldstein of Harvard, who has also long been a major voice supporting a moderate version of supply-side tax theory. Gale and Orszag went one critical step further and actively briefed the media and members of Congress and their staffs. As a result, their work received widespread attention and contributed meaningfully to the growing concern about our fiscal mess. This exemplifies an impor-tant point often deeply frustrating to serious policy analysts outside gov-ernment, whose work seldom has any significant effect on the policy process. Having a significant influence ordinarily requires not only an im-portant piece of work but also a savvy sense of how to get attention in the media, Congress, and elsewhere in official Washington.

Interest rates are affected by many factors, which makes isolating the impact of fiscal conditions more difficult. Also, though fundamentals win out over time, at any given moment the psychology of the market may be at variance with the fundamentals. For example, when the economy and private demand for capital are sluggish, markets may focus very little on unsound long-term fiscal conditions and interest rates may remain low, as happened in 2002 and the first half of 2003. (Although even during this weak period the historically large spread between higher long-term interest rates and the lower short-term rates the Fed controls suggests that the deficits might have been having some effect.)

But whatever the effects may be when the economy is weak, once economic conditions are again healthy, the private demand for capital will increase. Then markets will at some point focus on long-term fiscal condi-tions, and that increase in private demand will then collide with the gov-ernment demand for financing to fund its budget deficits. Virtually all mainstream economists agree that there is no fiscal free lunch. Though no one can predict when, interest rates will react strongly to expectations of substantial long-term deficits and the effect of those deficits on the demand to borrow.

Let me put numbers on these concepts, to show how powerfully adverse the effects on our economy could be. When used to look at the effects of tax cuts, the Federal Reserve Board model projects that for each increase in the deficit of 1 percent of GDP, long-term interest rates will increase by 0.5 percent to 0.7 percent. Some analysts use lower estimates of that relationship, so, for purposes of this calculation, I assume that if the deficit increases by 1 percent of GDP, long-term interest rates will increase by 0.4 percent.

The $9 trillion deterioration in the Federal government's fiscal position over ten years that I mentioned previously is an average annual deterioration of 7 percent of GDP per year. That is, the swing from the previously projected surplus to the now projected deficit averages 7 percent of GDP per annum. Since each 1 percent of GDP will increase interest rates by 0.4 percent, a change of 7 percent of GDP per year will increase interest rates by 2.8 percent (0.4 percent × 7).

With ten-year long-term bonds at roughly 4½ percent, that is an increase in interest rates of more than 60 percent. However, the situation is actually substantially worse. A key interest rate for most economists is the market rate of the ten-year bond adjusted for inflation, which is called the "real" interest rate. With today's ten-year rate of 4½ percent and an inflation rate of 1½ percent, that means real interest rates are 3 percent (that is to say, the interest rate is 3 percent over and above the inflation rate). Using that figure, the 2.8 percent increase in interest rates that I've just described amounts to over 90 percent of real interest rates.

The deterioration from a surplus to a deficit is the most accurate way to look at the effect of current fiscal policy. However, analysts often refer to just the projected deficit. So, let me apply the same analysis to the projected deficit of $5.5 trillion over ten years, which averages roughly 4 percent of GDP per annum. This translates into higher long-term interest rates of 1.6 percent (4 percent of GDP × 0.4 percent). With an inflation-adjusted interest rate on the ten-year bond of 3 percent, that's an increase in real interest rates of over 50 percent.

These are serious numbers. But the effects could be far more severe.

If fiscal imprudence continues, at some point markets may become concerned, not just about the projected future demand of the federal government on the available savings pool, but also about the risk of even greater fiscal disarray—with the possibility that the government will rely on inflation rather than fiscal discipline to work out its long-term fiscal problems. Then, the markets may pile on top of the already higher interest rates an unpredictable additional "deficit premium" reflecting those risks. Economists describe this as the risk that deficits could have a "nonlinear" effect on rates. And that could be hugely consequential, and could be even further exacerbated by the impact that an unsound fiscal policy can have on the interest rates foreign creditors require to lend to the United States.

Moreover, interest rate effects are only part of the picture. An unsound long-term fiscal situation can also badly damage business and consumer confidence—as was evident in the few years before the 1992 election. Large structural deficits can also diminish confidence in our economy and currency abroad, impair the ability of the federal government to serve the purposes the American people wish it to serve (including Social Security and Medicare), and undermine our resilience in dealing with future recessions or emergencies. In fact, our ability in 2001 to increase national security spending, and to put into place a stimulus to fight recession without running a serious risk of producing a large increase in interest rates, was the product of a sound inherited fiscal position.

In addition to the proposition that deficits don't affect interest rates, some tax cut proponents also assert that tax cuts will increase private savings, work, and investment activity. This, in a nutshell, was Reagan's theory in the 1980 Republican primary—that is, that tax cuts would pay for themselves through supply-side effects. But the deficit grew instead of diminishing, and by 1992 the federal debt had quadrupled. By the very end of the 1980s, this fiscal morass led to higher interest rates and diminished confidence, which fed the economic difficulties of the late 1980s and early 1990s. Moreover, the evidence that tax rates have significant effects on private savings or work is very thin. Most of the mainstream academic literature suggests that private savings is affected very little, if at all, by interest rates. Thus, reducing taxes would seem unlikely to affect private savings much, despite increasing the after-tax rate of interest. The academic literature also predominantly holds that decisions about how much to work are not significantly affected by marginal tax rates, at least within the ranges of the tax rate debate of the last two decades, with the possible exception of some effect on secondary earners in a family—and that effect on the economy is relatively modest. In fact, the effect of tax cuts on the incentive to work can even be negative, since lower average tax rates enable someone to work less for the same after-tax income. Tax cuts may also affect choices between nontaxable perks (e.g., a larger corner office) and taxable income, but such choices don't significantly affect economic growth. My own experience in setting corporate compensation is that the effect of tax rates on work effort is nonexistent—at least with top tax rates in their current range, as opposed to the rates of 70 percent or higher that we once had.

Tax cut proponents often argue that "dynamic scoring"—that is, budget rules that assume supply-side effects—show that tax cuts pay for themselves. In 2003, the Congressional Budget Office and the Joint Committee on Taxation—both with leadership appointed by the Republican majority—each produced dynamic estimates that refuted these claims. The JCT, examining a version of the 2003 tax cut, concluded that the supply-side effect of the cuts themselves on growth would be slight, and that the overall effect of the cuts plus the deficits they create on growth over the long run would, if anything, be negative. Similarly, the CBO examined the administration budget proposal as a whole and found little effect—and possibly a negative—effect on long-term growth.

Some tax cut proponents argue that the real market for capital is global and that increased demand for capital in the United States can be met by increased inflows from abroad, with relatively little impact on interest rates. It is true that global capital markets will satisfy demand for financing that is not met by U.S. savings, including the demand created by increased deficits. But it is not true that the capital flows into the United States at the same interest rates as would have existed in the United States if we didn't need that capital. And, in fact, the effect long-term fiscal deficits can have on the cost of flows of capital from abroad is one of the great dangers of these deficits. Funding some or all of our large fiscal deficits from abroad means attracting a greater inflow of foreign capital, and that will require paying a higher rate of interest. Moreover, studies clearly show that capital has a substantial home-country bias, making the interest rate increase needed all the greater. Secondly, the United States is such a large factor in capital markets that our excess demand—unlike that of smaller countries—can affect global interest rates. And, most troubling, if foreign capital markets become concerned about our fiscal policy and the soundness of our currency, suppliers of capital are likely to greatly increase the price demanded for use of their capital. This is exactly what happened to many countries during the second half of the twentieth century. And this potential consequence of fiscal ill-discipline could be especially dangerous to the United States under current circumstances, when we are dependent on large inflows of foreign capital to sustain a trade deficit and substantial savings shortfall. Finally, the empirical studies showing that deficits affect interest rates are based on data that reflect all factors, including whatever impact foreign inflows might have.

Because public understanding of these issues is so limited, serious discussion about and proposals to deal with the problem of deficits can easily be misrepresented. For example, in January 2002, Tom Daschle gave a speech arguing that our long-term fiscal situation posed grave dangers and needed to be repaired, without making any specific proposals for doing so. He went on to agree that short-term deficits might make sense when dealing with the currently weak economic conditions. But he was sharply attacked the next day for advocating tax increases during a recession. Daschle had actually done nothing of the sort, but the attack—which was widely and pretty much uncritically reported—took hold. And that deterred others from advancing the arguments Daschle had made.

One major impediment to serious discussion of our fiscal morass in the political arena is that it immediately raises the question of whether the country now needs to raise taxes to deal with the deficit. My view is that dealing with the fiscal deterioration that current policy has led to will inevitably mean shared sacrifice, as it did in 1993, and will involve both spending and tax measures. But whatever the components of the eventual solution, the President and congressional leaders of both parties should get together—sooner rather than later—to deal with what has become a serious threat to our future well-being.

Despite the difficulties Daschle and others encountered in trying to raise the deficit issue, the prevailing tone of the debate began to shift in 2003. The media perspectives shifted, influenced in part by the Gale-Orszag paper as well as more frequent comments by other prominent economic analysts, by the ballooning current deficits, and by the sharply increased long-term deficit projections. In this changing climate, the administration moved to acknowledge that long-term deficits do, in fact, affect interest rates. Under new leadership, President Bush's Council of Economic Advisers accepted this point in an on-line *Wall Street Journal* article. But the tax cut proponents then argued that even if deficits did matter, the projected amounts were "manageable." In making this case, however, they used estimates much lower than those used by mainstream analysts, and they did not acknowledge the potential for severe nonlinear effects, the immense entitlement costs on the horizon, or the potentially powerful adverse non-interest-rate effects of deficits on growth.

Robert Reischauer, a former head of the CBO and one of the wisest and most practical budget experts I know, thinks that those who run our political system may well be unwilling to repair our long-term fiscal mess until we reach what he considers an inevitable day of reckoning. When that crisis arrives, we will either have to make the decision to increase revenues substantially—at what may well be an inopportune time—or face severe and prolonged economic tribulations. Then the American people will look back with dismay at what happened. Unfortunately, no one who is now concerned about deficits has yet found a way to explain these future costs in a way that has political resonance in the shorter term, while these most serious problems are being created and can still be prevented. Leaving aside debates about whether deficits matter and about whether the supply-side effects are real, tax cuts and spending increases often seem attractive in the short term to politicians—and voters—who either don't focus on the long term or perhaps, in some cases, recognize the potential problems but feel that they will fall on somebody else's watch.

AS THIS DEBATE WAS evolving, my role in it evolved as well. I was still in touch with a number of Democrat senators and House members and, just as important, their staffs. In Washington, businesspeople tend to congregate around the elected official. But very often, if you want to be effective—either in knowing what's going on or in actually getting something done—you're well advised to develop a relationship with the right staff people as well. A good example is Mark Patterson, at that time staff director for Tom Daschle's Democratic Leadership Committee, whom I got to know when he worked for Pat Moynihan. Mark is the kind of staff member who understands substantive issues, can read the politics of the Senate, and has a lot of good-humored insight into what's likely to happen on the floor and in the various committees. It was through Mark and other congressional staff members that I started to get a sense of how I might be useful again in the debate over Bush's 2001 tax cut proposal. When the Democrats controlled the White House, the administration had a series of policy positions that were a regular part of the public debate. Democrats in Congress could decide where they wanted to be on economic issues in relation to where the administration was. Most often, the Democrats on Capitol Hill, whether accepting or critical of our positions, used us as a resource for both policy and politics.

Now, all of a sudden, the Democrats didn't have any of the support structure of a Democratic administration—the fixed star from which to navigate, if they chose, along with the resources, data, and expertise of the cabinet departments and the White House. For example, on tax issues, legislators from the party that controls the White House have at their disposal both the substantive analysis of professional economists at Treasury and the talking points that communications people at Treasury and the White House tailor to different constituencies and different states. They have people they can call on who are deeply involved in economic issues and are thinking about them from the same general perspective. If you're a U.S. senator, there are always plenty of professional economists at your disposal. What you may lack are people who not only understand economic issues but have also lived in your world and have faced the same kinds of policy choices and political realities you have to face every day.

Once the Republicans retook the White House, the Democrats on Capitol Hill began to realize that the Clinton people had been a useful resource, and they seemed to miss having us. Alan Greenspan was seen by most as supporting Republicans on the tax cut issue when he testified before the Senate Budget Committee on January 25, 2001—though in that same testimony, he stated his concerns about not encroaching upon the Social Security surpluses and warned that a tax cut should not be so large as to plunge the government back into deficit. The Democrats needed people with significant economic policy-making credentials and political experience to support them in developing their positions and to validate those positions.

I remember one Democratic congressman saying to me, "Our members are ready to go out and fight on the tax cut. But many of them don't fully understand this substantively. They want to have a comfort level with the issues." It's an important point: if you're a member, you're constantly being asked what you think about a vast range of complicated subjects. Even legislators who are very diligent and dedicated can't be experts on more than a few issues. The leadership and other members who are deeply involved may give you material to help you understand an issue or answer questions from the press. But legislators don't want to take a position and realize six weeks or six months later that they were wrong. The bipartisan Concord Coalition played an important role in meeting these needs on fiscal matters, providing analysis of fiscal conditions and the dangers of large long-term deficits, as well as the reassurance that comes from the support of well-respected figures. Among those associated with the organization who opposed fiscally unsound tax cuts were former Senators Bob Kerrey, Sam Nunn, and Warren Rudman, former Federal Reserve chairman Paul Volcker, and former Commerce Secretary Pete Peterson. They held press conferences and their work was widely circulated on the Hill during hotly contested struggles over tax cuts.

In early February 2001, at Tom Daschle's invitation, I went, along with Laura Tyson, to an issues conference at the Library of Congress that the Senate Democrats were holding to prepare for the budget process. The

following day I joined Leon Panetta at the House Democratic Caucus retreat in Farmington, Pennsylvania. I went to the House caucus meeting
thinking that I would say what I thought and the members would be
pleased that I agreed with them in opposing the size and distribution of
the Bush tax cut—more or less what had happened at the Senate discussion. Instead, I was actually attacked. Members responded to my comments by castigating me for not speaking out and providing more of a
public voice on their side of the issue. I remember Barney Frank saying,
"What you're doing is terrible." He was really angry about it.

"First of all, you're the politicians—I'm not," I responded. That was
true. It seemed appropriate to comment about policy issues I cared about,
but I didn't think I should have to be a public spokesman. Nevertheless,
the complaint bothered me, and in the days afterward I thought about
what more I could do. Traveling to a Ford board meeting in Detroit, I
sketched out a long op-ed article laying out my reasons for opposing the
administration's tax cut. I began by saying that I had not intended to get
involved in the public debate on fiscal policy at that point, but I felt
strongly that a tax cut of the magnitude Bush had proposed was a serious
error in economic policy. The piece appeared in the Sunday *New York
Times* on February 11, 2001. Afterward, there was about a two-week
stretch during which eight or ten senators called me. I had never had a period at the Treasury Department when that many senators had called on
their own initiative to discuss a policy issue.

Of course, the majority of Democrats who opposed the tax cut
didn't win their fight. The tax cut was highly inefficient as a short-term
stimulus—too much went to high-income groups who would spend less
of what they received, and most of the cut occurred in later years, which
helps little if at all in the short term and damages our long-term fiscal position. The tax cut also undermined our cushion for the unexpected.
Within a year, the tragedy of 9/11, the enormous drop in the stock market, and the generally deteriorating economic conditions showed how
dramatically unexpected events can affect the country's fiscal condition.

The debate about what policies would have most effectively dealt with
the slowdown will persist for years. The remarkable economic conditions

of the 1990s inevitably led to excesses and imbalances—including high levels of consumer and corporate debt, a large current account deficit, and a stock market that was high by any conventional standard—that pointed toward a more difficult period in both financial markets and the economy. However, great strengths—such as low unemployment, high productivity growth, low inflation, and, initially, a strong fiscal position— also persisted. During the slowdown, monetary policy as well as tax cuts and increased spending on both military and homeland security provided strong stimulus to the weak economy. (These tax cuts in 2001 and 2003 could have provided this stimulus in a much less expensive, more effective way—and without long-term damage—had they been better targeted and temporary.) All of that stimulus was likely to lead to a cyclical upsurge. But the overriding questions remain: How well suited were the policy choices made in that period to minimizing the severity and duration of the downturn? And how did those choices affect our economy's position for the long term? My own view is that on both scores the policy decisions during this time were far from optimal, and that on the second question they have created a serious threat to our future.

I WAS IN my office at Citigroup on the morning of September 11, 2001, when Sandy Weill came into my office and told me a plane had hit the World Trade Center. My first thought was that it must have been a small propeller plane and some kind of freak accident. Then, twenty minutes later, Sandy came in again to say that another plane had hit—and that they were big planes. At that point, it became clear what had happened.

Our first thought was for the several thousand Citigroup employees who worked in the complex, though not in the twin towers themselves. We leased twenty-five floors in 7 World Trade Center, which fell about eight hours later, though thankfully without killing anyone. We also occupied two large buildings several blocks north of the World Trade Center on Greenwich Street, which housed the trading rooms of Salomon Smith Barney, and owned or leased three smaller buildings in the Wall Street area. All of them had to be evacuated. Tragically, we later learned that six

Citigroup people who were in the towers on sales calls were killed, and that brought home to all of us in a more personal way the horror of what had occurred.

Sandy quickly organized what turned into a running meeting in one of the conference rooms to manage our crisis response. Our primary focus, after accounting for all of our people, was to continue functioning. As the nation's largest financial institution, that mattered not just to us but to the entire financial system. We weren't able to use our Salomon trading rooms on Greenwich Street or any of our other downtown offices. Moving to a backup facility in East Rutherford, New Jersey, kept us operational, but parts of our business still weren't functioning on September 12. The New York Stock Exchange was closed, initially for an undefined period. The clearing systems at the Bank of New York, an important clearing bank, went down. We were able to make payments, but it wasn't clear that other financial institutions would be able to make payments to us. We were concerned about the possibility of cascading defaults.

In this instance, the fundamental payment systems and financial systems on which our economy depends continued to function. The Federal Reserve Board acted promptly to make liquidity available to banks until payments could start to flow again. But the warning about how little it would take to create immense financial and economic disruption in this country was clear. Measures have since been taken to reduce this vulnerability, but a complex, modern society is inherently at risk.

IN THE IMMEDIATE aftermath of September 11, there was a great deal of fear about what the attacks might do to the national economy and a great deal of uncertainty on the part of most people about how they should respond. The stock market was closed for several days after the attacks, and no one had any idea how dramatically stocks might fall when it reopened. Many people I spoke to were worried that the shock might have major consequences for asset prices and liquidity.

My own initial reaction was that the attacks could have an immense impact on economic confidence. Consumers, investors, and businesses make their decisions in the context of some framework, whether conscious or unconscious. People go to excesses within that framework, then conditions revert to the mean, and so forth. But the attacks injected new variables that were far outside almost everybody's previous experience. People needed to develop new parameters—and hadn't yet. A fundamental change of that kind is very rare and can temporarily stifle economic activity by putting everybody on hold until they can figure out how to relate to the new realities. And given that I had thought the economy—both here and internationally—was in more difficulty before the attacks than most people had, my personal view was that conditions could be even worse than many feared.

In those initial days, I received many calls to go on television and discuss the economic implications. For a week, I declined all invitations. In the first place, I wasn't sure how to think about this, and I didn't want to say anything publicly until I was clearer about my views. I also didn't think that articulating my initial impressions would be helpful. People were looking for some kind of reassurance about the economy. And I didn't have much that was reassuring to say. However I phrased my views, they could have had the effect of unsettling people further.

But day by day, I kept working through the question of how to think and talk about the economic consequences of September 11, making notes on a legal pad as usual. Given my concerns, the basic problem was how to speak publicly in a way that was truthful but also calming and reassuring. This was an issue I'd faced before. After speaking several times with Gene Sperling, I arrived at the framework of "competing considerations." On the one hand, the attacks were likely to harm confidence, as well as having a negative impact on various economic sectors, including airlines, hotels, and tourism. The ease and cost of trade would also suffer due to security requirements—and security costs throughout the economy would increase. On the other hand, government spending on the military and security would increase, providing an economic stimulus. The net effect of September 11 on an already troubled economy would be the balance of all such positives and negatives. My notion was to combine that approach for the short term with some kind of affirmative statement about the long-term economic potential of the country—but always noting that realizing this potential would require meeting many challenges. This enabled me to focus again on such issues as long-term fiscal conditions, trade liberalization, education, and the inner cities.

Ad-libbing at a speech I'd been scheduled to give at the Japan Society in New York, I suggested two scenarios. The positive scenario was that even if the United States continued to face a significant terrorist threat in the months and years ahead, any attacks would be of a magnitude that our society could adapt to. Over the course of the following year, the imbalances that had existed prior to 9/11 would work themselves out and the impact of the attack on economic confidence would abate. At the same time, we would have a powerful dose of economic stimulus coming through the system. The result of all this would be that by the third quarter of 2002, confidence would return and the country would be back to a healthy rate of growth. The negative scenario was that terrorist events might continue in some significant way, unsettling economic confidence for a lengthier period of time, and that, combined with the problems that had already existed prior to September 11, would bring about a much more extended period of difficulty.

I had no idea what probability to put on those scenarios. And despite the many predictions people were making about the prospects for the economy, no one else, no matter how well informed, had any real ability to judge the relative probabilities. What I avoided saying that evening was that my private instinct was to give more weight to the negative scenario than the positive one.

Toward the end of that first week, I got a call from Jack Welch, the former CEO of General Electric, who said that Lesley Stahl at CBS had asked him to be on 60 Minutes. The program wanted to have a discussion that would air on Sunday night, before the New York Stock Exchange and other financial markets reopened the next morning. Warren Buffett had agreed to go on, and Jack said he would, too, if I would appear on the program as well.

At first I was inclined not to, because what I had to say, even in the competing-considerations formulation, just didn't seem constructive. But I did think that the three of us calmly discussing the economy on television might conceivably provide some reassurance, even with my mixed views of the outlook. So I told Jack I'd do it. Then I had a conference call with Ron Klain, Gene Sperling, and David Dreyer. The three of them tried to help me anticipate the kinds of questions I might be asked. Would you buy stock when the market opens, or would you sell? What do you think the market is going to do tomorrow? What do you think people should do with their investments?

My view, as always, was that investments should be made with a long-term view. But that didn't get me out of answering the questions I was likely to face about my short-term view of economic conditions and of the stock market. I spent a fair bit of time thinking about how to talk about all this. By the time the interview was taped that weekend, I had decided to express my analysis in two conclusions. I thought the odds of a substantial period of difficulty had increased because of the attacks. But I also continued to believe that the long-term potential of the American economy was strong. This seemed both nonalarmist and true to my views.

We had a preparatory conference call before the taping, and Lesley Stahl said, "One question I might ask is, 'What do you think the market's going to do on Monday? Would you buy or sell?' " Warren gave his answer—he wouldn't be selling anything when the market opened and might even buy some stocks if they got cheap enough. Then Jack answered, saying that he'd probably hold his stocks, because the United States remained the best place in the world to invest.

Then Lesley said, "What about you, Bob?"

"Well, I don't want to talk about the market," I said. I felt that a former Treasury Secretary, whose voice some people might listen to, should exercise care in what he said—especially about stock market levels and the Fed—even after leaving office.

"You've got to talk about the market," she said.

"No, I'm not going to talk about the market."

"Okay, then I'll ask you about the Fed and whether they should lower rates," she said.

"You can do that," I said. "But I'm not going to talk about the Fed, either."

"Aren't you going to talk about anything?" she asked. She was getting very worried. "I want you to be part of the show."

"Don't worry, I'll find things to say."

So we did the taping, and I did find things to say, though most of what I said was lost in the editing.

THERE WAS BROAD-BASED support across the political spectrum for the President's military response to terrorism, but the issue of how to deal with the economic impact was much more complicated both substantively and politically. A variety of issues arose. Should the government support the airline industry, the insurance industry, or others affected by September 11? Should the government act to stimulate the economy in some way? If so, with what kind of stimulus—emergency spending, tax cuts, or both? And if tax cuts, what kind of tax cuts? I quickly began getting calls from members of Congress who were grappling with all this.

On the issue of helping specific industries, I thought the general principle was that we shouldn't have government support for any industry except in extraordinary circumstances. We have a market-based economy and ought to let the market adjust to the new conditions, except for considering intervention if some sector systemically important to our economy may be severely affected. The airlines are systemically important to the economy and were in danger of ceasing to operate because of their mounting losses stemming from a shutdown of several days and weak passenger demand thereafter on top of already weak industry conditions. So I was in favor of doing something that would enable the major air carriers to continue functioning. But the $15 billion package that Congress very quickly passed to help the airline industry seemed excessive and an attempt to make up for poor market conditions that the airlines had been experiencing well before September 11.

The insurance question was complicated. Though the insurers, including Citigroup's Travelers subsidiary, faced significant losses, the biggest casualty companies were not facing bankruptcy or a major disruption in their business and in my view shouldn't receive public money to compensate for losses resulting from the attacks. But the industry faced a problem going forward that government did need to address: because of the attacks, insurers were no longer willing to provide coverage for terrorism or war—the losses could simply be too great.

As businesses rethought the probabilities not only of terrorism but also of other geopolitical events, risks were recognized that should have been but hadn't been before September 11. This is another illustration of the broader issue of dealing with extremely-low-probability events that can have catastrophic consequences if they occur. In this case, the belated recognition of such risks created a serious economic problem. Without the availability of insurance that would cover the risk of another September 11–type attack, construction of new office buildings, shopping centers, and other major structures could be severely impeded. So in one way or another, the government had to become the insurer of last resort for these risks going forward.

This problem—and the need for a public-sector solution to it—is part of a larger principle that I have already discussed. Even in a market-based economy, there are many needs that markets by their nature cannot fulfill. One set of such needs is the risks we socialize because the private sector can't handle them effectively—whether because the potential losses are too large to be treated actuarially or because a voluntary insurance program won't work. For example, the Social Security system is designed to provide a safety net both for people too poor to save enough for retirement and for people who might be able to save enough but don't. Like certain kinds of natural disasters, retirement security for the elderly falls into the category of risks our society has decided to protect against through government. After September 11, the risk of terrorism, which had always been present, was added to that list.

On top of these industry-specific issues, there was also a lot of discussion of moving very quickly on some kind of economic stimulus. September 11 was an extraordinary event that demanded action targeted to the circumstances. But the economic debate that ensued was too often a return to familiar issues. What can happen in such a situation is that people who hold strong positions take any change in circumstances as a new argument for their preexisting point of view. In the first days after the attacks, some long-standing advocates of tax cuts quickly seized the initiative to argue for their usual proposals. The circumstances were changed, but their proposals remained the same. Three specific ideas came to the fore: accelerating the phase-in of the rate reductions included in the Bush tax cut, passing a new reduction in the capital gains rate, and cutting the corporate rate. All of these measures would further undermine the country's rapidly deteriorating long-term fiscal position. This was precisely the type of situation in which bad policy can easily be made—a sense of emergency, a set of superficially appealing policy proposals, and an eagerness on the part of politicians to act quickly. My view was basically pragmatic: I thought that additional tax cuts intended for stimulus should be temporary and, for reasons not just of fairness but of efficiency, should go to lower- and middle-income people, who had the highest propensity to spend rather than save. I would also have included temporary unemployment benefits and medical coverage for the unemployed, as well as some assistance to cities and states to help with their increased cost—all funds that also would have been spent right away. All of this would provide a more effective stimulus without an adverse long-term fiscal effect.

On September 17, the day after the *60 Minutes* broadcast, the New York Stock Exchange reopened and the Dow fell by 7 percent. After the close, I sat for an interview with Tom Brokaw on the *NBC Nightly News*. Brokaw asked me a series of very straightforward questions. He said something about the capital gains tax cut, and I offered my arguments against it. I didn't think a capital gains tax cut would add to our economic well-being under ordinary circumstances. Mainstream academic work strongly suggests that the savings rate is relatively indifferent to the tax rate on the return on savings (whether interest, dividends, or capital gains) and thus that reducing the capital gains rate is not likely to increase savings. Similarly, there is little mainstream evidence to suggest that investment rises with lower capital gains tax rates—investment in the stock market increased enormously in the years *prior* to the reduction in capital gains rates in 1997. My own decades of experience with investors and markets support this. And on the other side of the ledger, a capital gains tax cut does cost the Treasury over time and can create tax-driven distortions in the allocation of investment capital. Perhaps all this analysis would be different if extremely high tax rates were involved, but that was not the case here.

And under the circumstances that existed after September 11, a capital gains cut could have been outright counterproductive, since it might have encouraged people to sell stocks into a falling market. After the program, Gene Sperling said, "Bob, after all the years we were in the White House, that was the first time we've ever been able to systematically take on the arguments in favor of a capital gains tax cut in prime time."

The next day I got a call from Janice Mays, the chief staff person for the House Ways and Means Democrats. The Democrats were trying to figure out what response they should make to the Republican tax cut agenda. Janice said that they'd distributed the transcript of the Brokaw interview to all their members, to help in their arguments against the capital gains tax cut.

The Democrats on the Ways and Means Committee subsequently invited me to Washington to meet with them about these issues. Then House Speaker Dennis Hastert and the bipartisan congressional leadership held a very unusual, formal, closed-door meeting on September 19—inviting the President's chief economic adviser, Larry Lindsey, Alan Greenspan, and me—to explore possible economic responses to the attacks. That meeting was followed by a closed-door session with the Senate Finance Committee and various other meetings. For a few weeks, I was going back and forth between New York and BWI airport outside Baltimore, since Reagan National Airport remained closed for security reasons.

Moving forward the personal tax rate reductions that were supposed to be phased in under the Bush plan and passing a new reduction in corporate rates were, in my view, like the capital gains cut, immensely flawed ideas. Both would cause further damage to the country's long-term fiscal position and would be highly inefficient in terms of their short-term stimulative effect relative to their cost. But in the prevailing climate, such proposals clearly had the potential to pass—especially after the Business Roundtable, an influential organization of large corporations, supported the idea of a corporate rate reduction. Democrats in the House and Senate, by contrast, had developed a program that in my view was much better tailored to the problem at hand.

I WOULDN'T HAVE guessed that the stock market would bounce back so quickly in the fall of 2001. The decline in the immediate aftermath of September 11 was never worse than 14 percent. For the month, less than 1 percent of the assets of stock mutual funds flowed out—versus more than 3 percent during the month after the day in 1987 that the market fell 22 percent. On October 11, a month after the attacks, the S&P 500 passed its level of September 10. Soon assets were flowing back into the market again. There was a certain wariness, and later in 2002 and in the first quarter of 2003 the market declined sharply, only to recover strongly in the second quarter. Throughout these ups and downs—exacerbated on the downside by corporate scandals and Wall Street regulatory and governance issues—the market still seemed to me to inadequately reflect economic and geopolitical risks. The imbalances that had grown out of the 1990s also remained largely intact. A major terrorist act had brought to the fore a whole host of destructive possibilities. In this context, stock valuations seemed high by many historical measures.

Indeed, quite a number of advisers and investors, such as Warren Buffett, were saying that equities were likely to provide lower than historical returns for an extended period. Also, bullish forecasts were usually based on projections of strong earnings growth and relatively low interest rates. But the strong economic conditions necessary for strong sustained earnings growth would likely lead to substantially higher interest rates—especially given our long-term fiscal morass. Yet this dynamic seemed not to be on forecasters' minds.

My interpretation of the market's behavior was that the psychological forces that had developed over an eighteen-year period persisted despite the significant decline of the market and the substantial losses incurred. In some ways, there was a strange sense of unreality to financial markets in the post-9/11 world. On the one hand, there was a widespread recognition that the world had changed—or, more accurately, a widespread recognition that the world had not been quite what it had seemed to be before the twin towers fell. On the other hand, this newly recognized reality seemed to have less effect than I would have thought on how most people thought about valuation and risk in relation to financial markets—the post-1930s phenomenon in reverse. This may have reflected a tendency of markets both to manifest the expectations of an excessive period long after the conditions that gave rise to the excess were over and not to take into account broader factors that don't fit within the framework that analysts use in evaluating stocks.

The people with national security backgrounds whom I spoke to were deeply concerned about what the country now faced. I shared a plane ride with Sandy Berger, President Clinton's pragmatic and insightful national security advisor, who talked at length about the seriousness of the terrorist threat that people were only beginning to recognize. The fanaticism that was developing in segments of the Islamic world could affect our country and our economy very substantially for a long time to come. Terrorism could affect the economy in a whole host of ways—by raising security costs, by making trade more expensive, by increasing oil prices, and by creating political instability in key countries abroad. Beyond the obvious potential for catastrophic events and disruptions is the effect of increased fear and uncertainty on confidence—which is always central to business and consumer behavior, economic conditions, and risk premiums.

Why, after a couple of months, did professional economic forecasters continue to be nearly as positive about the near-term outlook as they had been since the economic slowdown had begun in early 2000? Throughout 2001, most had been predicting that strong action by the Federal Reserve Board to lower interest rates would work relatively quickly to restore healthy growth for the country. Before September 11, I had felt that forecasters were overstating the potential effectiveness of action by the Fed—it is powerful and did ameliorate the slowdown, but it is not omnipotent—and greatly underweighting the impact of continuing economic excesses and imbalances. In the aftermath of September 11, Wall Street economic forecasters acknowledged the potential for future terrorist acts and political conflict abroad. But all of this had relatively little impact on their analysis and predictions, perhaps because they had no way to quantify these risks and because of an inertial tendency to stick with a familiar framework.

Somewhat later, Citigroup hosted a dinner at a Manhattan restaurant for a group of very senior professional money managers. The long and interesting discussion of the outlook for the global economy focused mostly on terrorism and geopolitical matters. But at the end of the evening, when the participants offered their predictions, those predictions reflected frameworks that made no reference to most of what we'd been talking about throughout the dinner. Apparently, their models couldn't accommodate such risks, so they weren't included.

What struck me after September 11 was that not only did the forecasts from the leading Wall Street firms tend to be predominantly positive in the face of grave new uncertainties and continued imbalances, but they continued to be the same kind of single-point forecasts that gave a growth rate for the next year as a single number instead of a range. It has always seemed to me that such single-point forecasts imply an unrealistic degree of precision, since the outlook for the future is always a probabilistic array across a broad spectrum. Forecasters presumably recognize the limits on their forecasts, but consumers may be less sophisticated and, in any case, have no basis for judging the odds on a predicted outcome. Life is uncertain. Forecasters who try to predict how much the economy is going to grow next year often fail to take into account not only specific uncertainties, but uncertainty as a guide to life.

CHAPTER FOURTEEN

A Declaration of Interdependence

WHEN I BEGAN WORKING on Wall Street, what happened to the global economy outside the United States had little impact on me and my colleagues. At that time, Goldman Sachs, one of the top investment banking firms in New York, did not have a single overseas office. We had some limited business links with the industrialized countries in Europe and with Japan, but we could not even have imagined doing significant business in the developing world.

That seems hard to believe today. One of the most fundamentally important changes I have seen over the course of my career is the vast increase in the links between our country and the rest of the world, including the developing countries. Decades ago, when Treasury Secretaries traveled abroad, they visited London, Paris, Bonn, and Tokyo. In my tenure as Treasury Secretary, among the countries I traveled to were Argentina, Brazil, China, Côte d'Ivoire, India, Indonesia, Mozambique, the Philippines, Ukraine, and Vietnam. As we saw during the Asian crisis, our economic health is more and more affected by what happens in the rest of the globe. Developing economies, which now buy 40 percent of American exports, have become an important part of our world.

In my career, I have been concerned mostly with the economic and financial links that tie our interests to those of other nations. These are still, for the most part, insufficiently appreciated by the American public. Our people badly need a better understanding of the complex phenomena of trade liberalization, the spread of market-based economics, and financial market openness—which are often lumped together under the rubric of globalization. And economic ties are only one aspect of a broader interdependence that is even less well recognized by most people and equally needs better public understanding. All of this should lead, I think, to a deeper realization of how important the economic and social conditions of people around the world are to our own national well-being.

On a business trip to Asia during the summer of 2002, I had a two-hour conversation with Lee Kuan Yew, the Senior Minister of Singapore. I'd gotten to know the Senior Minister somewhat during the Asian financial crisis, when he had demonstrated the enormous depth of his geopolitical understanding and grasp of regional issues. He said that there was as yet no paradigm, of the kind that existed during the Cold War, for understanding militant Islamic fanaticism as a factor in world affairs, and that much of the thinking about the issue was simplistic. I agreed with him that most people didn't know how to think about terrorism and other geopolitical risks. From my point of view, the question of fanatical religious violence in general and anti-Western terrorism specifically remains bound up with issues of poverty, inequality, and the fact that, even with the dramatic increases in living standards in many parts of the world in recent decades, there remain huge areas of terrible poverty and isolation from the benefits of the modern economy.

To be sure, the relationship between poverty and terrorism is hotly debated and complex. The terrorists behind September 11 came primarily from middle-class families, and experts point to a wide array of factors that have led to the deep anger underlying terrorism. Still, poverty breeds resentment, alienation, and hopelessness, which can foster an environment hospitable to terrorists, such as Afghanistan in the period leading up to the World Trade Center attacks.

In fact, terrorism is only one of the risks we face that have a connection to global poverty. Early in his administration, President Clinton passed around an article by Robert Kaplan entitled "The Coming Anarchy," which argued that the terrible problems most visible in West Africa—environmental destruction, disease, poverty, and political conflict—were likely to spill across borders, undermining the security of wealthy nations. That led me to read Kaplan's book *The Ends of the Earth: A Journey at the Dawn of the 21st Century,* which elaborated the case that the "gated-community approach" to life that I had seen in some developing countries, and even to some extent in New York, was less and less effective in insulating industrial countries from problems in other parts of the world.

Kaplan's book crystallized a set of thoughts for me that had been developing for a long time about the threat global poverty poses not just to developing countries, but to developed ones. Today, public health hazards have spread rapidly from countries that simply cannot afford even modest medical care for most of their people. Cross-border environmental dangers—such as the loss of biodiversity and contamination of the atmosphere—reach us from countries where most people's daily struggle for existence precludes any real focus on the environment. In some industrial countries, an influx of immigrants trying to escape from poverty is creating social and political problems. And when states collapse, or dissolve into conflict, the international community tends to become responsible for the massive humanitarian problems that result. There are strong reasons for trying to deal with poverty in poorer countries for the sake of those who live there. But success in bettering conditions in the developing world is also critical to our national self-interest.

Many of those who care deeply about global poverty have expressed great skepticism about globalization and open markets. I believe that what is sometimes framed as a divide between those who care about poverty and supporters of globalization is a false debate. President Clinton's comment that a strong economy is the best social program also applies to developing countries, where rapid economic growth is critical to raising living standards and lifting people out of poverty. Globalization and market-based economics are central to growth and have contributed greatly to huge increases in living standards for many nations and vast numbers of people.

But as President Clinton also used to say, growth and markets on their own are not enough. Government also needs to put in place policies to promote the broad-based sharing of growth, and to address many important needs that markets by themselves will not deal with adequately.

And those measures will, in turn, increase growth by improving the productivity of the workforce. The same is true in the global arena, where poverty and inequality and their attendant social ills remain huge problems—and powerful impediments to productivity and growth. In poor countries, some of the most basic prerequisites for a functioning market economy, such as the rule of law and effective and noncorrupt governments, as well as adequate education, health care, and the like, are too often lacking.

Every time I've visited a developing country, I've come away with a renewed appreciation of how difficult the problems in such countries can be. Mexico, for instance, had a succession of Presidents and finance ministers, starting in the mid-1980s, who implemented broad-based reform. Largely because of intelligent policy choices, many economic fundamentals in Mexico are sound and the country's prospects are good. Nevertheless, growth rates have been modest. Too much of the population still has little access to reasonable health care and adequate public education, and public resources to address these problems are insufficient. Beyond that, Mexico faces the challenges of establishing the clear rule of law needed for an effective market-based system, including fighting corruption more effectively. It also needs to encourage a higher savings rate. All of these changes are difficult, not only substantively, but politically.

It was in the context of thinking about inner cities and poverty here in the United States that I first came to focus on the idea of a "parallel agenda." What this means is that market-based economics and integration with the wider economy, the fundamental policies for growth, should be allied with a "parallel" set of policies to help fulfill the needs that markets will not adequately meet, such as a reasonable social safety net and retraining programs for those workers dislocated by change. Later, as a result of the Mexican and Asian crises, I focused on these issues as they relate to emerging markets. Effective implementation of a parallel agenda in developing nations would promote a broader sharing of the benefits of globalization, which in turn would increase productivity and so advance growth as well as enhance political support for globalization in the developing world.

Despite the gains in living standards of recent decades, the World

Bank and most experts estimate that roughly half the world's population still lives on less than $2 a day, and 20 percent lives on less than $1 a day. Some analysts contend that these numbers overstate the problem, perhaps by as much as half. But even using the more conservative estimates, an enormous and unacceptable number of people are still living in poverty, often without adequate access to clean water, basic health services, and so on—and the greatest benefits of globalization and growth have too often accrued to relatively few. However much progress there has been, it clearly has not been nearly enough.

For many years, it seemed to me that the well-off in developing countries too often viewed these terrible disparities as acceptable. But on trips to a number of developing countries in more recent years, I've noted a growing and by now substantial recognition on the part of many business people that they're not going to have the kinds of economies or societies they want unless they become more effective at dealing with poverty.

There remain enormous uncertainties about how best to come to grips with these problems. In the fall of 2002, some members of my old Treasury team—Larry Summers, David Lipton, Tim Geithner, and Caroline Atkinson—got together at Larry's house in Cambridge to discuss some of these issues in relation to this book. During a spirited four-hour discussion, it was striking that even as well-versed as all of these people were on the subject, their views sometimes conflicted and they recognized large areas of uncertainty. Most serious-minded experts acknowledge that there's simply a great deal they don't yet know about poverty and growth in the developing world. We all agreed that certain factors—such as global integration and market-based economics, at least reasonably effective government, some level of social cohesion, a decent and broad-based education system, basic health care, sound fiscal policy, and a high savings rate—tend to figure prominently in rapid economic progress. What is much less certain is how to encourage countries to pursue the kinds of policies and conditions most strongly correlated with success.

It is also unclear why apparently similar reforms have produced such widely varying results across different countries. And perhaps the most challenging questions involve how to address the needs of the millions of poor people who live in countries with governments that, due to corruption or ineffectiveness, are unlikely to deliver reform. While emerging-market countries—and, for that matter, developed nations—all have less than perfectly effective government and at least some corruption, government that is fundamentally ineffective seems to preclude successful development.

BUT WHY DO MANY COUNTRIES that seem to choose sound policies not enjoy the same kind of progress as others? The "success stories" do seem to offer some guidance. One lesson that seems clear is that despite the problems associated with global integration, no economy has managed to grow in a sustained fashion without pursuing integration with the rest of the world, at the very least by promoting exports. In addition, increasing reliance on market forces has been central to improving economic performance. Even in Africa, where economic conditions have been so difficult for the most part, some countries that have embraced market reforms—such as Uganda and Mozambique—have achieved impressive levels of growth and significant improvements in health care and other social indicators.

In Asia, standards of living have grown steadily and in some cases dramatically over the past three or four decades, improving the lives of hundreds of millions of people. South Korea stands as a particularly vivid example: between 1960 and 2000, the country went from around $100 in per capita annual income to around $10,000, due in great measure to some degree of market-based economics, limited liberalization, and a strong export orientation. There were many other factors in the "Asian miracle" beyond freer trade and the integration of global markets. But the kind of growth that countries such as South Korea, Thailand, Malaysia, and Singapore have experienced simply wouldn't have been possible without elements of globalization.

A counterpoint to this is Latin America, which has had generally disappointing results, growing at relatively slow rates. Even during the reform era of the late 1980s and the 1990s, when most Latin American countries liberalized trade, promoted exports, and relied increasingly on private markets, these nations continued to have low growth rates—with the notable exception of Chile. As Larry said at our Cambridge meeting, Latin America remains something of an enigma for advocates of our approach. Our understanding of the difference between Asian and Latin American growth needs to be vastly improved in order to provide better judgments about development strategies and policies going forward.

Some have suggested cultural explanations for Asia's relative prosperity. Although this interpretation is in some ways hard to apply to a region that has such heterogeneous cultures, the strongest Asian economies generally have in common such traits as a strong work ethic, a dedication to education, and high savings rates. The success stories in Asia also tend to have less skewed wealth, land, and income distribution than much of Latin America, and many have implemented growth- and productivity-oriented policies and reasonably sound fiscal management over a long period of time. In addition, the foreign minister of one of Latin America's largest countries once told me that he thought that the difference between these two regions lay largely in the effectiveness of governmental structures and processes in Asia as compared to Latin America, and the comparative political inability in Latin America—despite great strides in recent years—to do enough of what was needed and at the same time maintain sound fiscal conditions.

China is sometimes offered as an example of a thriving closed economic system. In fact, it is the opposite. China's economic boom began when Deng Xiaoping began moving the country toward exports and market incentives, albeit in the context of state-owned enterprises and a carefully controlled opening to capital flows. This mind-set has taken hold to a remarkable degree—though much still remains to be done to convert China to a true market economy. Every time I've visited with people running banks and industrial companies in China, I've found that they sound much like their American counterparts when they talk about their businesses—discussing prices, competition, growth, and economic issues. Our view at Treasury was that China could do even better if it opened its markets more quickly to imports as well as promoting exports. And while China did not do that, as it pursued a policy of export-led growth it also slowly opened its own markets to both imports and capital flows, and then took the dramatic step of joining the WTO. India, which is also in the process of transforming itself from a state-dominated to a market-based economy, albeit at a slower rate than China, also grew rapidly during the 1990s.

Sub-Saharan Africa doesn't fit into any neat category. The problems in most of these countries are momentous. But my trip to Africa as Treasury Secretary left me with the impression that there were also great opportunities. For example, the Finance Minister of Mozambique, where strong economic policies have led to high growth from a low base, explained to me how much could be done with even small amounts of capital. To move forward, Africa needs to develop more effective governments and stronger institutions. The industrial world also needs to focus much more of its attention—and provide adequate resources—to deal with Africa's special problems.

ADDRESSING GLOBAL POVERTY and the dislocations sometimes caused by globalization is an immense moral issue, but is also enormously in America's national self-interest. Unfortunately, the importance of this endeavor is not reflected in American politics. The American public does not understand the stakes involved, nor do people generally appreciate how little we currently spend relative to the magnitude of the problem.

While at Treasury I was deeply involved in seeking the annual congressional appropriations for certain programs of the World Bank, which uses those contributions from the industrialized countries to fund a wide variety of programs to combat poverty and improve living conditions in the developing countries. This was always an uphill struggle in Congress. After leaving government, I had the opportunity to revisit these issues in a systematic fashion in the context of a United Nations commission on foreign assistance on which I served in 2001. The commission, chaired by former Mexican President Ernesto Zedillo and including representatives from the developed and developing worlds, was intended to draw attention to these issues in connection with a conference held in March 2002 in Monterrey, Mexico, to support increased financial assistance for developing countries.

The Zedillo commission advocated the same basic approach of integrating with the global economy, market-based economics, "parallel agenda" policies to deal with needs markets won't fulfill, and effective government. But it also focused heavily on what the industrial nations can do to support developing-country growth, the large shortfalls in these areas, and the difficult politics around these issues in the industrialized countries.

The developing countries are heavily dependent on industrial countries' markets for exports, and those markets are dependent on industrial countries' growth. Both Japan and, to a lesser extent, Europe have had relatively weak economic performance in recent years, in large measure because structural rigidities—in labor laws, social safety nets, regulation, and so on—have deterred investment and private-sector growth. The United States grew strongly in the 1990s but is now positioning itself for long-term fiscal deficits that could undermine that growth over the longer term. And as we urged Japan in connection with the Asian financial crisis, the industrial countries should feel a responsibility for sound growth policies, not only for their own people, but for the rest of the world.

In addition to managing our own economic policies so as to contribute to strong global growth and better markets for developing countries, there are two primary ways in which the industrial countries can support developing-country growth: trade and aid. Trade—improving access for developing countries' goods to our markets—is almost certainly the single most important measure industrial nations could take to help developing ones. President Zedillo made this point in our commission discussions as he expressed, in his understated way, enormous frustration with how advanced countries such as ours advocate free trade while impeding imports from the poorest countries. Virtually all developing countries have a strong comparative advantage in cheaper low-skilled labor. In many of the poorest countries, the most important export industries are agricultural products and textiles, which are produced by labor-intensive means. But agriculture and textiles are among the most politically powerful and economically protected sectors in developed countries, and developing nations often find themselves very limited in their access to export markets in Europe, Japan, and the United States. Barriers to trade can be direct—such as tariffs or trade restrictions—or indirect, through subsidies to goods produced in the industrialized world that make it harder for imports to compete. Lowering such import barriers—primarily on textiles and agricultural products, but also on steel, an important product to some emerging markets—would be of enormous benefit to the developing world, especially the poorest countries.

I remember the negotiations around an African trade bill that the Clinton administration supported. We wanted to remove textile duties but were opposed by unions and some manufacturers in this country. Because of their influence, the best compromise we could negotiate was reducing tariffs on African textiles that were made from fiber originating in the United States. The bill that passed has already produced significant gains for the products and nations that were included and is projected to raise the level of nonoil exports from Africa by roughly 10 percent. But the benefit would have been nearly five times greater without adding restrictive conditions on the terms of market access, according to an IMF estimate. And the bill did not apply to developing countries outside Africa, such as Bangladesh, which has more than one million women working in the textile industry and could increase export revenues from such products by an estimated 45 percent, if granted this kind of duty-free access to markets in industrialized countries such as the United States and Japan.

Trade barriers are estimated to cost the developing world at least $100 billion of lost opportunity a year, or by some estimates much more, a multiple of foreign aid spending by all governments. For example, one study estimates that if Africa's share of world exports increased by 1 percent, its trade revenues could grow by $70 billion a year—five times what it receives in aid and debt relief. *The New York Times* ran a series of valuable editorials on this issue, pointing out that subsidies to the major cotton farmers in the United States were a critical factor in keeping the two million cotton farmers of the small African nation of Burkina Faso from competing on a level playing field in the global marketplace. The United States took a step backward by passing a ten-year, $180 billion agricultural subsidy bill in 2002, which increased the subsidies that American farmers receive by almost 80 percent. The United States also moved its trade policy in the wrong direction in 2002 when we increased restrictions on steel imports. These measures were damaging to the developing world and make it harder for us to argue for more open trade in the international arena.

In political terms, protecting industries is usually appealing, because the negative consequences of free trade are so visible while the benefits—though much greater—are diffuse. In a discussion with President Clinton about a Japanese trade agreement, I mentioned that one sector where we needed to push for reduced trade barriers was fish. Clinton remembered being in Japan and seeing some poor fishermen casting their lines off the rocks. He said quite determinedly that he wasn't going to do anything to hurt those vulnerable people. "But Mr. President," I said, "to help those poor fishermen, you're going to prevent the vastly greater benefit that would come to the poor throughout Japan from being able to buy cheaper fish." The damage of trade liberalization to the fisherman was the most palpable. But the preponderant effect would be to benefit a much larger number of other, invisible poor and consumers more generally.

Developing countries benefit from trade and openness, but so do industrialized countries such as our own. Trade and economic ties are sometimes discussed in terms of winners and losers. But while nations are in some sense economic "competitors," in a more important sense trade is a mutually beneficial dynamic. Success in one country can raise living standards in another, rather than coming at the other's expense. The United States is already a huge market for the rest of the world and our growth creates opportunities elsewhere. Conversely, growth in Europe and Japan, and successful development in emerging economies, provides better markets for us.

Politicians don't like to say this, but imports also contribute greatly to our economic well-being, by reducing prices paid by American consumers and producers, by shifting our allocation of resources to areas where we have a comparative advantage in the global economy, and, very importantly, by creating competitive pressure on American companies to be more efficient and productive. This latter factor was central to the revival of American competitiveness in the late 1980s. In contrast, the more restricted trade regimes in Europe and Japan have sheltered protected industries, contributing significantly to lagging productivity growth.

Between 1996 and 1999, U.S. imports of goods and services increased by almost $400 billion. Virtually every household in America has a better and cheaper TV, or toaster, or computer, or T-shirt, than would be possible without imports. According to a calculation by a former Federal Reserve economist, if those additional goods and services had not been available to American consumers, U.S. inflation could have been as much as 1 percentage point higher and interest rates could have been more than 2 percentage points higher. When I was at Treasury, I made this case for imports in testimony before congressional committees. Once, Phil Crane, a conservative Republican from Illinois, said I was the only government official he'd ever heard defend imports in public testimony. In speeches and testimony, I joined this case for imports with a strong statement saying that all change—whether from technology or trade—even if predominantly beneficial, will inevitably and unavoidably be harmful to some. Consequently, trade must be accompanied by effective programs to help dislocated workers find new places in our economy. This is not only fair, but will contribute both to productivity and to political acceptance of trade liberalization.

Dramatic changes in the world economy, including technology that links us easily with people working thousands of miles away, mean that low-wage workers elsewhere can provide goods and services in ways that were scarcely imaginable before. India and China in particular have very large numbers of lower-wage workers who are also skilled. Almost all mainstream economists believe that this change will provide great opportunities for both developing and industrial countries, as have past innovations. But all of this will almost surely increase the already sharp debate over trade in the political arena.

That makes efforts to improve the American people's understanding of trade all the more important. Protectionism may seem tempting in the face of competition from large pools of well-educated workers in low-wage countries. But policies that restrict trade—likely to be matched by similar policies in other countries—would be damaging to our economy and to our consumers, workers, and businesses. However, this new competition does call for the United States to act aggressively to safeguard the drivers of our own growth in productivity by increasing public investments in areas such as education, health care, the inner cities, and effective assistance for those dislocated by trade. Restoring a sound fiscal position will also serve this purpose by promoting lower interest rates, greater confidence, and higher levels of private investment.

While not as central as trade, the emergence of well-functioning capital markets and banking systems is also essential to the advancement of developing countries. Financial institutions are necessary to intermediate between savers and users of capital, and to allocate that capital efficiently. In the Mexican and Asian financial crises, the weak banking systems in almost every case either were part of the cause of the crisis or exacerbated the crisis. Industrial country expertise—from both the public sector and the private sector—can help developing countries create effective legal and regulatory infrastructures and strong banking and capital market institutions. Lack of access to capital in developing countries is a particular problem for smaller and medium-sized companies, which are key to growth. Providing access to capital for these companies has become a strong focus of public policy in many developing countries.

When I traveled to China as Treasury Secretary in 1997, I visited a jewelry manufacturer and exporter in central China that had been state-owned but was now a private corporation that had successfully raised the capital necessary to expand its operations by selling shares on the Shanghai Stock Exchange. If the expansion went well, that would mean more jobs, and, it was hoped, a better quality of life for women such as those I saw making jewelry that day—a direct result of better-functioning domestic capital markets, and a development that would have been unthinkable just a decade earlier in China.

On other trips to developing countries, I also saw several much smaller-scale microfinance projects. These projects provide small loans, with relatively low interest rates, to entrepreneurs who would not be able to get the capital to start a business otherwise. They promote better use of domestic savings by intermediating between small-scale savers and users of capital, and by providing technical assistance and advice to borrowers. In Brazil, Judy and I went to São Paulo's terrible *favelas*, or slums, where we saw a small business supported by microlending in which workers were sewing designs onto T-shirts. I toured a child-care facility in Soweto,

South Africa, a microenterprise that not only creates jobs but also enables parents to go to work more readily. These projects were examples of ways to make capital markets work better for the benefit of the poorest. Though their capital was provided by domestic savings, most had originally been established by the World Bank, which under the deeply committed leadership of James Wolfensohn has focused far more effectively on issues of poverty and on how to spread the benefits of the global economy more widely.

On the other hand, some countries may be simply too small in terms of population or GDP to have deep and liquid capital markets of their own, or to have domestic banking systems of a size, depth, and sophistication capable of withstanding the vicissitudes of global markets. Many people I worked with disagree, and point out that Singapore and Hong Kong were successful in building up international financial centers from small city-states. But I do not think that's a realistic model for many others. I remember a poignant conversation I had with Cassim Chilumpha, the finance minister of Malawi, at a meeting in Namibia of the Southern African Development Community in 1998. Mr. Chilumpha told me that his country had tried to do everything right in the eyes of the IMF—it welcomed foreign investment, allowed its currency to float, and so forth. But as a tiny, landlocked, and desperately poor nation lacking in significant natural resources, Malawi had little to export and nothing to attract foreign capital. Policy in Malawi at that point may or may not have been as sound as the finance minister asserted, but the issues he raised seem valid to me. How could tiny and impoverished Malawi develop the institutions or bring in the capital necessary for sustained growth?

One alternative to national financial systems for small countries is to develop regional markets to pool the costs of strong private-sector and regulatory institutions and provide broader and deeper markets. There are often major political obstacles to such multinational cooperation, but the possible benefit is worth the effort if that collaboration is sustainable over time. Another approach is for these countries to be more open to foreign banks and investment banks so as to benefit from their expertise, home-based regulation, global reach, and capital. Although I now work for a private financial institution that operates in many developing countries, I thought this long before I found myself involved in that business. Alan Greenspan once said to me that the biggest problem for many countries in building an effective financial sector is the shortage of skilled personnel for both the private sector and the public sector. This scarcity can be overcome by utilizing the expertise of large global firms.

Finally, foreign aid—carefully designed and well used—is essential to enable developing countries to implement policies to reduce poverty, improve basic living standards, and make a market economy work. On this the United States has done far too little. We now contribute just over one tenth of 1 percent of GDP to foreign aid—directly and through multilateral organizations such as the World Bank—as compared to the long-standing U.N. goal for the industrial countries of spending seven-tenths of 1 percent of their GDP to overcome developing-country poverty. There are serious issues around the effectiveness of foreign aid. But while the problems are real, so are the achievements. There have been great gains in life expectancy and literacy over recent decades and, while there were many factors involved, aid clearly played an important part. Improvements in health care—including the eradication of smallpox, the near-eradication of river blindness in Africa, and much more widespread vaccination programs for children—stand as an extraordinary accomplishment. And in successful Asian countries like South Korea, high levels of foreign aid in the early stages of development combined with a focus on appropriate policies to foster robust growth. Much needs to be done to improve understanding of how to make aid more effective, and industrial countries can do much to help devise and promote sound practices in developing countries and provide technical assistance to support those policies. But based on everything I saw while I was at Treasury, I have no doubt that enough is known to warrant a far more robust program.

In conjunction with the United Nations Monterrey conference, President Bush proposed an ambitious new plan to provide foreign aid to developing countries, called the Millennium Challenge Account. The proposal, which involves spending an additional $5 billion a year, would increase U.S. foreign aid by 50 percent. The program is intended to focus aid on economic growth and development and, importantly, to maximize its effectiveness by giving the money only to countries with sound policies in place. That is a big step forward—assuming the administration vigorously pursues this initiative and Congress fully appropriates the funds—but much more needs to be done.

We in the Clinton administration always argued that foreign aid designed to promote economic growth—as opposed to emergency relief—was truly effective only when joined with real and sustained economic reform, and that aid should therefore be conditioned on reform. This approach to foreign aid is consistent with the crisis response programs I talked about in the context of Mexico, Asia, Russia, and Brazil: assistance will work only if it is conditioned on strong economic policies developed and owned by the countries themselves. Moreover, if financial support is not linked to reform and as a result fails to be effective, this further undermines political support for such financing when it can be useful. That said, there are hundreds of millions of people in countries where the governments are too corrupt or too ineffective to meet conditions attached to aid. And we can't simply ignore these people until their governments someday change. The international financial institutions, the United Nations, and individual nations need to be far more effectively focused on finding better means to address the needs of the populations of such countries, including affordable medicines, access to clean water, food assistance, and strategies for raising living standards—both because of the enormous humanitarian issue and because it is in our interests.

In any endeavor, however, it is important to make rigorous judgments about the effectiveness—and the risk of unintended consequences—of even the best-intentioned ideas. One proposal that provides assistance for the poorest—broad debt relief—has won support thanks to the involvement of Pope John Paul II and the Irish rock star Bono. I met with Bono after I left the Treasury and before I joined Citigroup, at the suggestion of former Fed chairman Paul Volcker. Despite wearing sunglasses indoors and having only one name, Bono is a thoughtful and serious person with a range of ideas on how to support the developing world. I strongly agree with his separate efforts to get Europe, Japan, and the United States to open their textile and agriculture markets to imports from Africa. But on debt relief I told Bono that while I supported the concept up to a point, his proposal for far-reaching and broad-based relief struck me as potentially counterproductive.

When a borrower is clearly overextended and unable to pay its debts, limited debt relief from the official creditors—governments and multilateral agencies—makes sense. Such a program was put in place during the Clinton years. Perhaps that program should be somewhat improved or expanded. But if debt forgiveness became a broad policy, instead of an infrequent exception, it could undermine private creditor confidence that the principle of debt repayment will be rigorously applied in developing countries—or perhaps even more broadly. Credit markets only work effectively on the basis of this principle. Undermining it could thereby reduce flows of credit, and increase interest costs for the developing world, especially for the poorest countries. Since debt relief is treated as a form of foreign aid in the U.S. federal government budget, my strong preference would be to devote the same resources to alleviating the debt burden of the poorest and most heavily indebted countries through foreign assistance.

Beyond what the United States can do as a country, private citizens can address the problem of global poverty through their businesses, through philanthropy, and through political involvement. Corporations can contribute not just money but also business and technical expertise, as Cisco has done recently in Afghanistan by setting up academies to train people in computer networking. Focused philanthropic efforts, such as the Bill & Melinda Gates Foundation's emphasis on AIDS and global health or George Soros's activities in Eastern Europe and West Africa, have made an enormous difference in recent years and have arguably been more cost-effective than governmental efforts aimed at the same problems. People with less money than Bill Gates or George Soros can contribute as well, not just by giving to charities that focus on poorer countries but by becoming informed, engaged, and politically active on behalf of trade and aid.

Most fundamentally, a dramatic change in public attitudes is needed. At one point when I was at Treasury, I thought of going to President Clinton and suggesting that he set up an interagency process to work through the whole set of substantive and political issues surrounding global poverty. Amid the distracting rush of events, I never did. Given President Clinton's deep interest and involvement in these issues, I now see that as a real lost opportunity. Such an effort could have addressed the difficult issues around growth in developing countries, including questions about what mechanisms would best encourage governments to adopt better policies. We might also have looked at how to overcome the political obstacles to winning support for substantially increasing foreign assistance at home and opening our markets more fully to developing countries. I hope that some future administration will set up such a process, and give it a high priority.

The political challenge, in any case, is immense. My many discussions with senators, House members, and others as I sought to develop support for foreign assistance have led me to believe that what is needed is a large-scale, multi-year public relations and education campaign in support of both foreign assistance and trade liberalization for developing-country exports—something more honest than, but just as effective as, the "Harry and Louise" ads that helped defeat our administration's health care plan in 1994. Other, more positive examples include highly successful campaigns against smoking and drunk driving. Such a public education effort focused on trade and aid should stress both moral issues and our self-interest imperative in combating global poverty. It should also highlight success stories, such as the eradication of river blindness in Africa. I've argued to a number of individuals and foundations that the considerable financial resources this would take could have an immensely leveraged impact if the project changed the political dynamic around these issues. So far, my arguments have been without effect.

LET ME CLOSE with a story from an earlier stage of life. I remember once sitting at a lunch counter in Brooklyn, just after finishing law school in 1964. I had a few spare weeks before starting work at a firm in New York and was spending the time auditing trials at the county courthouse. My waitress, a middle-aged Black woman, asked me—out of the blue—

whether I thought the day would ever come when all people would be treated with respect and dignity.

I don't remember very clearly what my answer was, but her question has stayed with me all these years. The desire for dignity and respect is as real for a waitress in Brooklyn as it is for a member of the President's cabinet, or a student in Pakistan, or a bond trader at Citigroup. People strive to accommodate their physical needs and desires. But once the basics for life are met, their psychological needs—some might say needs of the soul—are key. If the latter are satisfied, life can work well. On the other hand, if the soul isn't satisfied, possessions won't fill the void. Among the most basic needs is what I took to be that waitress's point: the need to have one's dignity and humanity acknowledged, to be listened to, to have what you say and what you believe taken seriously.

This, to me, should be central to the focus on poverty in the developing world. Our fundamental goal is to satisfy the nutritional, basic health care, educational, and other essential requirements of all of the world's population. But material sustenance isn't the sole objective. People suffering in desperate poverty in remote places have the same needs and desires as each of us in the wealthiest nation in the world does—not just for food, medicine, and clean drinking water, but also to be respected as human beings.

In an era when the threat from people who don't feel respected can lead to dire consequences, treating other nations and their people with dignity may be a simple matter of self-protection. But to me, listening respectfully even to critics and opponents makes even more fundamental sense, as an acknowledgment of the uncertainty and complexity that I believe to be inherent in virtually all issues of import. I think we've learned a great deal about how to foster better economic conditions, both in this country and in the developing world—though whether we as a society will choose policies that reflect that understanding is another matter. But in an uncertain world there is no finality about any of these questions. Even thoughtful people who eschew ideology, recognize complexity, and try to work with great analytic rigor will continue to disagree about them.

But while we cannot overcome the uncertainty around economic and other public policy choices, I do think it's possible to sharpen our sense of the probabilities and thereby improve our decision making. We are living in a time of great geopolitical and economic change, when the choices we make can have huge consequences. Since leaving Washington, I have remained deeply involved in public policy not only because I find it engrossing but because it matters so much. Working on this book over the past few years has furthered my own thinking about these issues while reminding me of what I've felt for most of my adult life—that the quest for the best possible answers is never-ending.

ACKNOWLEDGMENTS

T HIS BOOK wouldn't have been possible without the generous contributions of many friends, family members, and colleagues. Caroline Atkinson, Stanley Fischer, Michael Froman, Ron Klain, Sylvia Mathews, Linda Robertson, Judith Rubin, Gene Sperling, and Fareed Zakaria all read the entire manuscript or a substantial portion of it, sometimes in various drafts, and offered innumerable improvements and suggestions.

A number of others read chapters and sections of the manuscript, saving us from countless mistakes of fact and judgment and deepening my own appreciation of many of the complex and controversial issues examined here: Lew Alexander, Robert Boorstin, Lisa Caputo, Steve Einhorn, Steve Friedman, Tim Geithner, Michael Helfer, Elli Kaplan, Jennifer Klein, Ed Knight, David Lipton, Mark Malloch Brown, Michael Masin, Peter Orszag, Larry Pedowitz, Jeff Shafer, Jane Sherburne, Peter Sherry, Todd Stern, Susan Tanaka, Ted Truman, and Dan Zelikow.

I am grateful as well to a number of people who helped me reconstruct bits of history from earlier stages of my life: in chapter 2, I drew extensively on the recollections of my parents, Alexander and Sylvia Rubin, and my sister, Jane Zirin. I also relied on the memories of my old friends Leon Brittan, David Scott, George Lefcoe, and Charles Toder. Steve Hyman, the provost of Harvard University, served as a philosophical consultant of sorts, and Marne Levine, Michael O'Mary, and Jung Hye Paik also helped with Harvard matters. Jan Conroy at Yale Law School provided class history.

Former colleagues at Goldman Sachs contributed similarly to chapters 2 and 3. In particular, I owe gratitude to Ken Brody, Jon Cohen, Jon Corzine, George Doty, Steve Einhorn, Bob Freeman, Steve Friedman, Jacob Goldfield, Bob Katz, Howard Katz, Richard Menschel, Norma Ranieri, John Rogers, L. Jay Tenenbaum, Peter Thompson, John Whitehead, and Mark Winkelman.

Clinton-era colleagues were generous in helping to reconstruct and reexamine key events discussed in chapters 4 through 10. Among them are Erskine Bowles, Warren Christopher, President Bill Clinton, Hillary Clinton, Neal Comstock, Bo Cutter, David Dreyer, Vice President Al Gore, Alan Greenspan, Cheryl Matera, Mack McLarty, Linda McLaughlin, Annabella Mejia, Leon Panetta, John Podesta, Howard Schloss, Jim Steinberg, Michael Waldman, and Neal Wolin.

At Citigroup, I received generous help from Steve Bernstein, Judy Carbone, Yvette Damiani, Meyrick DeCoteau, Robert DiFazio, Evrard Fraise, Connie Garone, Sheryl Harden, Margaret Jenkins, Tobias Levkovich, Ann-Marie Lyew-Vizzini, Peter Mangano, Paul Masco, Karen McGruder, Robert Moore, Chuck Prince, Johnny Sabater, Michael Schlein, Kim Schoenholtz, Ellen Thompson, Dotti Ward, Sandy Weill, and David Weisberger.

My wife, Judy, helped in countless ways. Most important, she served as an additional and very thoughtful editor of our manuscript, a monumental task that led to many improvements. She combed through our vast collection of family photographs to help put together the photo section. And she also offered sensible counsel on some of our larger decisions and provided much-needed support at difficult moments.

Meeghan Prunty Edelstein, a veteran of the 1992 Clinton campaign and the Clinton White House and a graduate of Columbia Business School, began as our researcher and rapidly evolved into the indispensable manager of what became a very complicated project. Meeghan wove together Jacob's and my work in the text, helped with drafting, and offered elegant solutions to any number of difficult problems. She kept everything, and everyone, on track with good grace and a sense of humor that at times was much needed.

Caroline Atkinson, my former colleague from Treasury, took on the additional role of consultant and became invaluable—an overused word, but in this case accurate—on our chapters dealing with Mexico, the Asian financial crisis, and international matters more generally.

Stan Fischer, who gained renown at MIT and then as deputy managing director of the IMF, and who is now my colleague at Citigroup, provided thoughtful commentary on multiple drafts until he probably could have recited some sections from memory.

Peter Orszag worked for Gene Sperling in the White House but now, as a scholar at the Brookings Institution, has emerged as a strong voice in his own right on fiscal matters. His advice and counsel indispensably informed the discussion of fiscal matters.

Michael Froman, my former chief of staff at the Treasury Department and now my colleague at Citigroup, like Stan, read and commented on successive drafts with patience and insight and probably also could recite sections from memory.

We also relied on a daily basis on my remarkable executive assistant, Joann McGrath at Citigroup, who always solved our problems, large and small, as well as Kaminie Bharat, who helped us unfailingly at every stage of this process. Eugene Corey at Brave New Words meticulously transcribed hours of taped interviews.

Every author should have a Michael O'Loughlin, fact-checker extraordinaire, to verify the things no one else would have even thought to check. In addition, Susan Cumiskey, Duncan King, and Jason Solomon worked overtime on research and fact-checking in the frantic weeks before our deadline. Earlier research help was provided by Sushan Demirjian and Jeremy Cleaver. Thanks to my former Treasury colleague Les Samuels, the Cleary, Gottlieb, Steen & Hamilton word-processing department—and the hard work of Michelle Zulli, in particular—helped us make that final deadline.

The photographs used in this book reflect the work of many talented photographers; I thank them for granting us permission to use their work. Special thanks to Frances Jane Mabe for her persistent efforts to track all the photographs down. In addition, I owe thanks to Karen Butler, Phyllis Collazo at *The New York Times*, Tony Cretaro at Citigroup, Diana El-Azar at Reuters, John Fox, Russell James at *The Washington Post*, Gloria Knudsen, Mario Lussich, Vera Murray, Robert Penney, Luis and Vivian Schuchinski, and Mittpheap You at the World Bank. And I'm grateful to John Keller and Marlene Ware at the Clinton Presidential Materials Project for their help.

I also want to thank all of the people who generously agreed to let me discuss private conversations we've had, whether they were giving me advice, I was giving them advice, or we were trying to figure something out together.

Most books have but one editor. We were lucky enough to work with two of the best: Ann Godoff, who signed the book up and offered valuable insights and criticism of our early drafts, and Bob Loomis, who took over from Ann in midstream and is a legend in the business for good reason. Others at Random House assisted us in many ways: Lynn Anderson, Rachel Bernstein, Liz Fogarty, Libby McGuire, Steve Messina, Tom Perry, Casey Reivich, Carol Schneider, and Katherine Trager. Timely and sensible legal advice was provided by Mary DeRosa, Beth Nolan, and Heather Wingate. Our agents, Mort Janklow and Tina Bennett, have offered sage counsel throughout, as has our foreign rights agent, Andrew Wylie.

Finally, for their patience and support through a lengthy project that cut deeply into family time, Jacob, Meeghan, and I wish to thank our spouses: Jacob's wife, Deborah Needleman; Meeghan's husband, Steve Edelstein; and my wife, Judy. I'd also like to thank my sons, Philip and Jamie, and my daughter-in-law, Gretchen.

Robert E. Rubin

Index